Oracle® PL/SQL

FOR

DUMMIES®

by Michael Rosenblum and Dr. Paul Dorsey

WILEY

Wiley Publishing, Inc.

Oracle® PL/SQL For Dummies®

Published by
Wiley Publishing, Inc.
111 River Street
Hoboken, NJ 07030-5774
www.wiley.com

WILEY

About the Authors

Michael Rosenblum is originally from Kremenchuk, Ukraine. In 2000, he moved to the United States, where he lives with his family in Edison, New Jersey. He works as a Development DBA at Dulcian, Inc. Michael is responsible for system tuning and application architecture. He also supports Dulcian developers by writing complex PL/SQL routines and researching new features. He is a frequent presenter at various regional and national Oracle user group conferences. In his native Ukraine, he received the scholarship of the President of Ukraine, a Masters Degree in Information Systems, and a Diploma with Honors from the Kiev National University of Economics, Ukraine.

Dr. Paul Dorsey is the founder and President of Dulcian, Inc. (www.dulcian. com), an Oracle consulting firm that specializes in business rules-based Oracle Client-Server and Web custom application development. He is the chief architect of Dulcian's Business Rules Information Manager (BRIM®) tool. Paul is the co author of seven Oracle Press books that have been translated into nine languages: *Oracle JDeveloper 10g Handbook*, *Oracle9i JDeveloper Handbook*, *Oracle JDeveloper 3 Handbook*, *Oracle Designer Handbook* (2 editions), *Oracle Developer Forms and Reports: Advanced Techniques and Development Standards*, *Oracle8 Design Using UML Object Modeling*. In 2003, he was honored by ODTUG as volunteer of the year, in 2001 by IOUG as volunteer of the year and by Oracle as one of the six initial honorary Oracle 9i Certified Masters. Paul is an Oracle Fusion Middleware Regional Director. He is the President of the New York Oracle Users' Group and a Contributing Editor of the International Oracle User Group's SELECT Journal. He is also the founder and chairperson of the ODTUG Business Rules Symposium (now called Best Practices Symposium), currently in its sixth year, and the J2EE SIG.

Dedications

Dedicated to the memory of my grandfather, Vladimir Zaguskin, who was always able to give me a simple explanation of not-so-simple things.

— Michael Rosenblum, Edison, NJ, 2006

Dedicated to Dr. Robert Stafford Sterling (my mentor in graduate school and no dummy) and to his namesake Robert Stefan Dorsey (born December 2005, who I hope will also not be a dummy).

— Dr. Paul Dorsey, Colonia, NJ, 2006

Authors' Acknowledgments

Michael Rosenblum: I would like to thank my co-author, Dr. Paul Dorsey (a well-known guru in the Oracle world), for inviting me to take part in writing this book and for all his patience working with me for the last five years. Also, I would like to acknowledge the efforts of our project manager, Caryl Lee Fisher. She not only kept the lazy authors on track, but even managed to convert my not-exactly-native English into something people could read. Of course, the book in the form you are reading it would not have been possible without our wonderful technical editor Leslie Tierstein (you can't imagine the number of small "bugs" she discovered in the original drafts). And, last but not least, love and special thanks to my wife Dora for withstanding the added pressure on her while I was writing this book.

Dr. Paul Dorsey: I would first like to acknowledge my co-author Michael ("Misha") Rosenblum. It is a joy to work with someone possessing such drive and intellect. His unwillingness to be sloppy in his code and thinking have given not only this book, but all his work, an aspect of excellence all too unusual in this industry. I would also like to thank Caryl Lee Fisher (our unacknowledged "co-author"). Caryl Lee kept Misha and me on track and helped wordsmith the entire manuscript. This is my eighth such collaboration involving Caryl Lee, and I can safely say that I am not sure whether I ever would have published even my first book without her assistance. She acted as the intermediary between the excellent editors at Wiley and the authors, thereby averting virtually certain bloodshed. She helped to foster the illusion that we are very easy authors to work with. Leslie Tierstein provided her always impeccable technical edits. I have worked with her on a number of projects, and she provides many valuable contributions to the finished product. A special thank you goes to my lovely wife Ileana. She not only endured all my time away from home (for the 3 months preceding and following my son's birth) working on this book, but she also provided serious technical assistance, since she is a first-rate developer in her own right.

Both authors would like to thank their colleagues Mark Hernandez, Marc Bacchus, John Rydzy, and Stephen Germany for their help in reviewing the code samples and text for accuracy.

The authors would also like to thank the Wiley team of Rebecca Huehls, Virginia Sanders, Tiffany Ma, and Terri Varveris for their help with this project.

Publisher's Acknowledgments

We're proud of this book; please send us your comments through our online registration form located at www.dummies.com/register/.

Some of the people who helped bring this book to market include the following:

Acquisitions, Editorial, and Media Development

Project Editor: Rebecca Huehls

Acquisitions Editors: Tiffany Ma, Terri Varveris

Copy Editor: Virginia Sanders

Technical Editor: Leslie Tierstein

Editorial Manager: Leah P. Cameron

Media Development Manager: Laura VanWinkle

Editorial Assistant: Amanda Foxworth

Cartoons: Rich Tennant (www.the5thwave.com)

Composition Services

Project Coordinator: Patrick Redmond

Layout and Graphics: Claudia Bell, Carl Byers, Denny Hager, Alicia B. South

Proofreaders: Dwight Ramsey, Techbooks

Indexer: Techbooks

Publishing and Editorial for Technology Dummies

    Richard Swadley, Vice President and Executive Group Publisher

    Andy Cummings, Vice President and Publisher

    Mary Bednarek, Executive Acquisitions Director

    Mary C. Corder, Editorial Director

Publishing for Consumer Dummies

    Diane Graves Steele, Vice President and Publisher

    Joyce Pepple, Acquisitions Director

Composition Services

    Gerry Fahey, Vice President of Production Services

    Debbie Stailey, Director of Composition Services

Contents at a Glance

Table of Contents

Introduction

*P*L/SQL (pronounced P-L-S-Q-L or P-L-*see-quel*) is a programming language that was created by Oracle as a procedural language fully integrated with SQL, to be used in working with Oracle databases. Anyone contemplating working in the Oracle environment needs to know PL/SQL.

In many ways, PL/SQL is a standard procedural programming language. It has functions, procedures, variable declarations, loops, recursion, and so on. If you're familiar with the programming language Ada, you'll find it's similar to PL/SQL. If you've used any standard programming language, such as C or Pascal, you'll find yourself quite at home with PL/SQL. If you're an object-oriented (OO) programmer who is used to languages like C++ or Java, you can't use your OO techniques as easily in PL/SQL, but all your procedural experience will transfer quite easily.

What makes PL/SQL special is that it is fully integrated with SQL. This makes it a wonderful language to use when programming applications that need to interact with an Oracle database.

About This Book

This book doesn't include everything you need to know about PL/SQL. However, it does provide many examples of good coding practice, and it warns you about what to avoid when writing code. We are experienced Oracle professionals who have designed and built many working systems and have written many thousands of lines of PL/SQL code. The information we provide in this book should whet your appetite for discovering many of the ways in which you can use PL/SQL to communicate with a relational database. We also point you to numerous other handy resources that can help you consolidate and expand your knowledge of this programming language.

This book gives you the core information that every PL/SQL developer should know. When we started writing this book, we asked many of our friends and colleagues in the industry what they thought PL/SQL developers should know. If you practice everything we show you in this book, you'll be on your way to becoming an excellent developer.

To help you practice, we've posted the code examples that appear in this book on our Web site, www.dulcian.com (click the publications link), or at www.dummies.com/go/oracle_pl_sql.

Foolish Assumptions

This book is written for people just getting started with the PL/SQL language but does assume that you have some programming language experience. You should understand the basics of computer programming and be familiar with SQL in order to benefit from the information contained in this book.

If you have some basic computer programming experience and are planning to work in the Oracle environment as an application developer, this book is for you. If your goal is to become a database administrator (DBA), it might be a good additional reference, but you should see *Oracle 9i For Dummies* (latest version as of this writing), by Carol McCullough-Dieter, published by Wiley, or other books about Oracle 10g for information relevant for DBAs.

When an author writes a book, he or she must try to imagine who the readers might be. For this book, we imagine that you might be an individual who recently graduated from college and who is working at a job where you'll be creating programs in an Oracle environment. This book will also be useful as part of a database course if you are still in college. You might be an experienced Java developer who wants an easy way to get to know some of the basics of PL/SQL. This book includes the information that we would want to tell any new colleagues who came to work with us.

How This Book Is Organized

You might not need to read the chapters of this book in sequence. However, Parts I and II present the basic concepts you'll need to understand later parts. If you're already an experienced programmer, the basic concepts might be familiar, but you'll need to see how to specifically apply them in PL/SQL.

Part I: Basic PL/SQL Concepts

This part provides an introduction to the Oracle environment as a whole and explains how PL/SQL fits into it. It includes an overview of how relational databases work as well as a review of some basic database concepts and terminology that you need to understand for later chapters. We tell you about the hardware and software needed to set up a simple Oracle database and some useful Integrated Development Environments (IDEs) available to help you practice using PL/SQL.

Part II: Getting Started with PL/SQL

In this part, you discover the different structures and ways to create code to accomplish common programming tasks. Chapter 3 includes descriptions of the datatypes and variables that you'll need to work with, and extras to enhance your coding expertise. Chapter 4 delves into control structures and provides examples of how to use conditions and loops correctly. In Chapter 5, you find out how to structure code and handle errors and exceptions. And you can't be a good PL/SQL programmer without understanding a bit about SQL, so Chapter 6 discusses how SQL and PL/SQL can work together and introduces cursors. (If you don't know any SQL, this isn't the book for you quite yet. First read *SQL For Dummies,* 5th Edition, by Allan G. Taylor.)

Part III: Standards and Structures

In this part, we discuss standards and guidelines for writing good code — some of the most important material in the book. Chapter 7 presents the various options for where to place PL/SQL code in a system project. In Chapters 8 and 9, you find out about the importance of creating and enforcing both naming and coding standards. The sample standards shown are based on our experiences in building large production systems.

Part IV: PL/SQL Data Manipulations

This part goes into more detail about different datatypes and how to use them. We cover basic datatypes in Chapter 10 and discuss more advanced constructs (using large objects, collections, and bulk operations) in Chapter 11.

Part V: Taking PL/SQL to the Next Level

For those who have some basic experience with PL/SQL, Part V discusses more complex concepts, including database interaction and transaction control in Chapter 12 and using dynamic SQL and PL/SQL in Chapter 13. Chapter 14 lists some PL/SQL coding best practices to follow based on our wide experiences in building working systems.

Part VI: The Part of Tens

This part summarizes some critical do's and don'ts to keep in mind as you create PL/SQL programs. Our advice provides useful tips to assist your first programming attempts as well as describes pitfalls to avoid.

Icons Used in This Book

These tips provide shortcuts or easier and better ways of doing things.

This icon notes information that's important to keep in mind when writing code, or that we've found very useful in our work building real systems.

This icon appears when we discuss advanced concepts or additional information that isn't essential to your understanding of PL/SQL but might be useful for doing additional reading or investigation.

This icon warns you about things in your code that can cause problems or even stop a system from working properly.

Where to Go from Here

There are many sources of information about computer programming and PL/SQL. This is merely a starting point for you to use as a list of additional helpful information about PL/SQL to expand your knowledge. You can't program successfully in isolation. It is very important to be plugged into the broader Oracle community through local user groups, conferences, the Internet, and other PL/SQL programmers.

Many useful sources of information about PL/SQL and the Oracle Environment are on the Internet. Keep in mind that not all information and code samples on the Internet are accurate and bug free. Always be aware of the source of the information and test any code carefully before deploying it. The following are two particularly useful Web sites for obtaining the latest information about PL/SQL:

✔ Oracle Technology Network (OTN) (`www.otn.oracle.com`) is Oracle's online resource for all its database and application products. See especially the special technology section devoted to PL/SQL (`www.oracle.com/technology/tech/pl_sql/index.html`). Chapter 2 has more details.

✔ Steven Feuerstein writes often about PL/SQL. His Web site (`www.stevenfeuerstein.com`) is a great resource.

The many Oracle User Groups can provide lots of helpful information and events for Oracle professionals. By attending a user group conference, you can discover more about the Oracle environment.

✔ **Oracle Development Tools User Group (ODTUG) (`www.odtug.com`)** is the leading Oracle user group for developers. It focuses on the tools that developers use to build Oracle systems (not just tools sold by Oracle).

✔ **Independent Oracle Users Group (IOUG) (`www.ioug.org`)** is a worldwide organization that encompasses many regional user groups in the United States and abroad. To find a regional group in your area, do an online search for "Oracle User Groups".

Be sure to join the user group nearest you and go to meetings, talk to other PL/SQL developers, and connect with other Oracle professionals. That is the best way to keep up with the rapidly changing Oracle environment.

Part I
Basic PL/SQL Concepts

The 5th Wave   By Rich Tennant

"I need someone to find that function declaration, someone to locate the exceptions, and someone to find my office."

In this part . . .

Part I includes two chapters to get you started with PL/SQL. Because you need to understand something about relational databases to be a good PL/SQL programmer, Chapter 1 provides a quick overview of the most important concepts. It also reviews some database terminology and explains some of the differences between SQL and PL/SQL. For those with very little programming experience, Chapter 1 includes a very brief explanation of the basic structure and syntax of PL/SQL and explains where it is most useful.

Chapter 2 describes the total PL/SQL environment and explains how to set up this environment so you can begin writing code. You discover how to set up a database, connect to it, and access the Oracle sample schemas that you can use to practice.

Chapter 1

PL/SQL and Your Database

- -

- -

*P*L/SQL is an extension to the industry-standard SQL language. Oracle Corporation developed PL/SQL and released the first version in 1991. PL/SQL is an easy-to-use procedural language that interacts seamlessly with the Oracle database. Server-side PL/SQL is part of the Oracle database and needs no explicit installation or licensing.

This chapter introduces you to PL/SQL and provides some basics about relational databases.

Knowing Just Enough about Relational Databases

Building a system in Oracle or some other relational database product does not automatically make it a relational database. Similarly, you can design a perfectly good relational database and implement it in something other than a relational database product. We discuss two important areas:

↙ What do people mean by *relational database?*

↙ What is the Oracle relational database product?

What makes a database "relational"?

When a database is described as *relational,* it has been designed to conform (at least mostly) to a set of practices called the *rules of normalization.* A normalized database is one that follows the rules of normalization.

For example, in an organization, you have employees who work in specific departments. Each employee and department has a number and a name. You could organize this information as shown in Table 1-1.

Table 1-1	Sample Employee Information		
EmpNo	*Ename*	*DeptNo*	*DeptName*
101	Abigail	10	Marketing
102	Bob	20	Purchasing
103	Carolyn	10	Marketing
104	Doug	20	Purchasing
105	Evelyn	10	Marketing

If you structure your data this way and make certain changes to it, you'll have problems. For example, deleting all the employees in the Purchasing department will eliminate the department itself. If you change the name of the Marketing department to "Advertising," you would need to change the record of each employee in that department.

Using the principles of relational databases, the Employee and Department data can be restructured into two separate tables (DEPT and EMP), as shown in Tables 1-2 and 1-3.

Table 1-2	A Sample Relational DEPT Table
DeptNo	*DeptName*
10	Marketing
20	Purchasing

Table 1-3	A Sample Relational EMP Table	
EmpNo	*EName*	*DeptNo*
101	Abigail	10
102	Bob	20
103	Carolyn	10
104	Doug	20
105	Evelyn	10

By using this structure, you can examine the EMP table to find out that Doug works in department 20. Then you can check the DEPT table to find out that department 20 is Purchasing. You might think that Table 1-1 looks more efficient. However, retrieving the information you need in a number of different ways is much easier with the two-table structure. Joining the information in the two tables for more efficient retrieval is exactly the problem that relational databases were designed to solve.

When the tables are implemented in the database, the information in the two tables is linked by using special columns called *foreign keys*. In the example, the DeptNo column is the foreign key linking the Department and Employee tables.

Tables 1-4 and 1-5 show another common database structure, namely a purchase order (PURCH_ORDER table) for an item and the information details associated with the purchase order (PURCH_ORDER_DTL table).

Table 1-4	A Sample Relational PURCH_ORDER Table
PO_Nbr	*Date*
450	12/10/2006
451	2/26/2006
452	3/17/2006
453	6/5/2006

Table 1-5		A Sample Relational PURCH_ORDER_DTL Table		
PO_Nbr	*Line_Nbr*	*Item*	*Qty*	*Price*
450	1	Hammer	1	$10.00
451	1	Screwdriver	1	$8.00
451	2	Pliers	2	$6.50
451	3	Wrench	1	$7.00
452	1	Wrench	3	$7.00
452	2	Hammer	1	$10.00
453	1	Pliers	1	$6.50

A purchase order can include many items. Table 1-5 shows that Purchase Order 451 includes three separate items. The link (foreign key) between the tables is the Purchase Order Number.

Understanding basic database terminology

A database consists of tables and columns, as we describe in the preceding section. There are some other terms you need to know in order to understand how databases work. A database is built in two stages. First you create a *logical data model* to lay out the design of the database and how the data will be organized. Then you implement the database according to the *physical data model,* which sets up the actual tables and columns. Different terminology applies to the elements of the logical and physical designs. In addition, relational database designers use different words from object-oriented (OO) database designers to describe the database elements. Table 1-6 shows the words used in each of these cases.

Table 1-6	Database Design Terminology	
Logical/Relational	*Logical/Object-Oriented*	*Physical Implementation*
Entity	Class	Table
Attribute	Attribute	Column
Instance	Object	Row

The definitions of the words in Table 1-6 are as follows:

- **Entity:** An entity corresponds to something in the real world that is of interest and that you want to store information about. Examples of entities include things such as departments within an organization, employees, or sales. Each specific department or employee is considered an *instance* of that entity. For example, in Table 1-3, Doug is an instance of the entity Employee. (In the OO world, Doug would be an object in the Employee class.)

- **Attribute:** This word is used in both relational and OO databases to represent information about an entity instance or an object that will be tracked. An example of an attribute might be the birth date or Social Security number of an employee.

- **Entities (classes), their attributes, and instances (objects):** These are implemented in the database as tables, columns, and rows respectively.

One additional important concept to understand when dealing with relational databases is the primary key. A *primary key* uniquely identifies a specific instance of an entity. No two instances of an entity can have the same primary key. The values of all parts of the primary key must never be null. The most common types of primary keys in relational databases are ID numbers. For example, in Table 1-3, the EmpID can be the primary key. Sometimes more than one attribute (or sets of attributes) can be used as a primary key. These attributes are called *candidate keys,* one set of which must be designated as the primary key.

Introducing database normalization

A database is considered *normalized* when it follows the rules of normalization. Database normalization is useful for several reasons:

- It helps to build a structure that is logical and easy to maintain.

- Normalized databases are the industry standard. Other database professionals will find it easier to work with your database if it is normalized.

- Retrieving data will be easier. This is actually the formal reason to normalize. Graduate students in database theory courses often have to prove a theorem that roughly states, "If your database is normalized, you can be sure that any set of information you want to retrieve from your database can be done by using SQL."

You frequently need very complex procedural code to extract information from a non-normalized database. The rules of normalization will help you to design databases that are easy to build systems with.

Although a detailed discussion of normalization is beyond the scope of this book, there are three basic rules of normalization that every database professional should have memorized. Not so coincidentally, we tell you about them in the following three sections.

First Normal Form (1NF)

First Normal Form means that the database doesn't contain any repeating attributes. Using the Purchase Order example from Tables 1-4 and 1-5, the same data could be structured as shown in Table 1-7.

Table 1-7		PURCH_ORDER Table (1NF Violation)					
PO_NBR	*DATE*	*ITEM 1*	*QTY1*	*PRICE1*	*ITEM2*	*QTY2*	*PRICE2*
450	12-10-06	Hammer	1	$10.00			
451	02-26-06	Screwdriver	1	$8.00	Pliers	2	$6.50
452	03-17-06	Wrench	3	$7.00	Hammer	2	$10.00
453	06-05-06	Pliers	1	$6.50			

Although this table looks okay, what if a third item were associated with PO 451? Using the structure shown in Table 1-7, you can order only two items. The only way to order more than two items is to add additional columns, but then to find out how many times an item was ordered, you'd need to look in all the item columns. Table 1-7 violates First Normal Form.

You can build a good database that doesn't adhere to First Normal Form by using more complex collections such as VARRAYs and nested tables (which we discuss in Chapter 11).

Second Normal Form (2NF)

Violations of *Second Normal Form* occur when the table contains attributes that depend on a portion of the primary key.

To talk about Second Normal Form, you should know what we mean by an attribute being *dependent* on another attribute. Say attribute X is dependent upon attribute Y. Then if you know the value of attribute X, you have enough information to find the value of attribute Y. Logically, attribute Y can have only one value. For example, from the information in Table 1-1, if you know the Employee Number (EmpNo), you also know the employee's name, which department number he or she works in, and the number of that department. In this case, the EmpNo is the primary key. However, knowing the department number and department name doesn't tell you a specific employee's name or number. You can't use the department number/name combination as the primary key. You can't even use the name (Ename) as the primary key because a large organization might have more than one "John Smith" working there.

Second Normal Form violations can exist only when you have a multi-column primary key, such as the purchase order and the purchase order detail structure, as shown in Tables 1-8 and 1-9.

Table 1-8	PURCH_ORDER Table	
PO_NBR	*DATE*	*Vendor*
450	12-10-06	ABC Co.
451	02-26-06	XYZ Inc.
452	03-17-06	XYZ Inc.
453	06-05-06	ABC Co.

Table 1-9		PURCH_ORDER_DETAIL Table (2NF Violation)			
PO_NBR	*LINE*	*DATE*	*ITEM*	*QTY*	*PRICE*
450	1	12-10-06	Hammer	1	$10.00
451	1	02-26-06	Screwdriver	1	$8.00
451	2	02-26-06	Pliers	2	$6.50
452	1	03-17-06	Wrench	3	$7.00
452	2	03-17-06	Hammer	2	$10.00
453	1	06-05-06	Pliers	1	$6.50

In this structure, the PURCH_ORDER_DETAIL table uses both PO_NBR and LINE for the primary key. But DATE is dependent only on the PO_NBR (when you know the PO_NBR, you know the date that each item was ordered), so that column violates Second Normal Form.

Third Normal Form (3NF)

Third Normal Form violations occur when a *transitive dependency* exists. This means that an attribute ID is dependent on another attribute that isn't part of either a primary or candidate key. These are serious violations indicating errors in the database design that must be detected and corrected. Table 1-1 shows an example of Third Normal Form violation in a badly designed database. The DeptName column is dependent only on the DeptNo column (that is, if you know the department number, you know the name of the department). The EmpNo is the obvious primary key, so the existence of DeptName column violates Third Normal Form.

All attributes in entities (columns in tables) must be dependent upon the primary key or one of the candidate keys and not on other attributes.

For more information about normalization, look at books about database theory such as *Beginning Database Design,* by Gavin Powell (Wiley) and *A First Course in Database Systems,* by Jeffrey D. Ullman and Jennifer Widom (Prentice Hall), or numerous works by Chris J. Date.

What is a DBMS?

After you've designed a relational database, you need to implement it. The easiest way to do this is by using a product that's specifically designed for this purpose. Products that perform these operations are called Relational Database Management Systems (usually abbreviated to RDBMS or just DBMS). They allow you to easily create relational databases by defining and creating tables and then populating them with data. In addition, you could be provided with a special tool to modify and manipulate the data and write reports and applications to interact with the data.

DBMSs also handle all sorts of other important functions. They allow many people to access the database at the same time without interfering with one another or corrupting the data. They also make it easy to create backups in case of problems such as a power failure or other disasters.

A number of positions in Information Technology involve interaction with a DBMS:

- **Database designer:** This person analyzes the requirements for the system and designs an appropriate database structure to house the data.

- **Database administrator (DBA):** This person installs the DBMS, monitors it, and physically manages its operations.

- **Database application developer:** This person writes the code that resides within the DBMS and directly interacts with the database.

- **User interface (UI) application developer:** This person writes the code for the user interface, which enables users to communicate with the database.

Many other people, including project managers, software testers, and documentation specialists, also work with database systems. This book focuses on the skills required to be a database application developer.

The Scoop on SQL and PL/SQL

As a database application developer, you interact with the Oracle DBMS by using the programming languages Structured Query Language (SQL, pronounced *sequel*) and Programming Language/Structured Query Language (PL/SQL, pronounced either P-L-S-Q-L or P-L-*sequel*). In the following sections, we introduce how SQL and PL/SQL work together and how they are different. We also introduce what's new in the current versions.

The purpose of SQL and PL/SQL

SQL is the industry standard language for manipulating DBMS objects. Using SQL, you can create, modify, or delete database objects. This part of SQL is called Data Definition Language (DDL). You can also use SQL to insert, update, delete, or query data in these objects. This part of SQL is called Data Manipulation Language (DML).

Oracle's implementation of SQL isn't exactly industry standard. Virtually every DBMS (Oracle included) has invented items that are not part of the standard specification. For example, Oracle includes sequences and support for recursive queries that aren't supported in other DBMS products.

Oracle is more than a database

The Oracle environment doesn't consist solely of the DBMS. The Oracle environment itself is enormous and complex, and the large number of products that Oracle sells is a reflection of that. So how does the DBMS fit into the bigger picture? Here's a quick overview of the main categories of Oracle products:

✔ **Oracle DBMS:** This database management system runs on a variety of computers and operating systems. As we write this book, it's often considered to be the largest, fastest, most powerful, and fully featured database product on the market. The Oracle DBMS is the industry standard for big companies that need to store and manipulate large volumes of data. Oracle also provides versions of the DBMS to support small and medium-sized companies.

✔ **Application development software:** Oracle has many application development products.

The current main product is JDeveloper, a Java-based programming environment.

✔ **Oracle Application Server (OAS):** Web-based applications typically run on a dedicated computer. Oracle's version of this is called OAS.

✔ **Oracle Applications:** Oracle has created or acquired a number of enterprise-wide applications that work with the Oracle DBMS and help Accounting, Manufacturing, and Human Resources departments to perform their day-to-day functions more efficiently.

Oracle Corporation also includes consulting (Oracle Consulting) and education (Oracle University) divisions to round out its offering of products and services.

Getting to know SQL in an Oracle environment allows you to work in almost any DBMS environment, such as SQLServer or MySQL, but you'll encounter some differences in the DBMS environments. You should probably know SQL before trying to use PL/SQL. This book assumes that you already know SQL. If you haven't mastered SQL, take a good long look at *SQL For Dummies,* 5th Edition, by Allen G. Taylor (Wiley), before you dive into this book.

PL/SQL is unique to Oracle. It isn't industry standard. No other product uses it. Being able to use PL/SQL will help you work only within the Oracle database environment, but if you're familiar with any other programming language, you'll find that PL/SQL follows the same basic rules.

PL/SQL is similar to other non-object-oriented procedural programming languages, such as C or Pascal. Its intellectual roots go back to a programming language called Ada.

What makes PL/SQL unique is its tight integration with SQL. It is easier and more natural to embed SQL in PL/SQL than to do so in any other programming language. This makes PL/SQL ideal for writing large, complex programs that must interact with an Oracle database.

The difference between SQL and PL/SQL

SQL and PL/SQL are completely different languages. SQL is a limited language that allows you to directly interact with the database. You can manipulate objects (DDL) and data (DML) with SQL, but SQL doesn't include all the things that normal programming languages have, such as loops and IF...THEN statements.

That is what PL/SQL is for. PL/SQL is a normal programming language that includes all the features of most other programming languages. But it has one thing that other programming languages don't have, namely the easy ability to integrate with SQL.

What's new in Oracle SQL and PL/SQL?

Oracle SQL and PL/SQL are evolving languages that constitute the backbone of applications written for the Oracle environment. Every version of the Oracle database expands the features of these languages. The production version of Oracle 10*g* Release 2 has recently been released. As with previous versions, this release offers lots of new things, including the following:

✔ PL/SQL will probably run faster in the 10*g* version than it did in previous versions. You don't have to do anything extra to benefit from that improvement. Oracle has made PL/SQL code run faster without requiring any additional work on the part of the programmer.

✔ In SQL, many new commands allow you to retrieve information more easily than before. Information about these commands is beyond the scope of this book, but make sure you have a good Oracle SQL book, such as *Oracle Database 10g: The Complete Reference,* by Kevin Loney (McGraw-Hill), as a source for all the commands.

Because every release brings new capabilities, keeping up with the new features in Oracle is important. Many developers don't keep up with new features because "all the old features will still work," but those developers miss out on the great new features included in each version. If you do a search for "new features in PL/SQL" or "new features in Oracle SQL" in Google or your favorite search engine, you'll always find many articles and resources to show you the latest additions to these programming languages.

What Is PL/SQL Good For?

PL/SQL is the language to use when writing code that resides in the database. In the following sections, we introduce different situations in which you'll find PL/SQL useful.

Using database triggers

A *trigger* is an event within the DBMS that can cause some code to execute automatically. There are four types of database triggers:

✔ **Table-level triggers** can initiate activity before or after an INSERT, UPDATE, or DELETE event. These are most commonly used to track history information and database changes, to keep redundant data synchronized, or to enhance security by preventing certain operations from occurring. See Chapter 3 for more information about table-level triggers.

✔ **View-level triggers** are very useful. A *view* is a stored SQL statement that developers can query as if it were a database table itself. By placing INSTEAD OF triggers on a view, the INSERT, MODIFY, and DELETE commands can be applied to the view regardless of its complexity, because the INSTEAD OF trigger defines what can be done to the view. See Chapter 3 for more information about view-level triggers.

✔ **Database-level triggers** can be activated at startup and shutdown. For example, when the database starts up you might want to test the availability of other databases or Web services. Before a database shutdown, you might want to notify other databases and Web services that the database is going offline.

✔ **Session-level triggers** can be used to store specific information. For example, when a user logs on or off, you might want to execute code that contains the user's preferences and loads them into memory for rapid access. When the session closes, a trigger can save the preferences for future use.

Database and session-level triggers are usually handled by DBAs, and further discussion of their use is beyond the scope of this book.

Scripting with speed

When writing code, the ability to type a portion of code and execute it without first saving it to the database is useful. Oracle provides this capability, which is supported by all PL/SQL IDEs. We discuss this capability in Chapter 2.

Keeping code server-side

The majority of PL/SQL code is stored as program units in the server. A typical application has many lines of code.

Some programmers, particularly Web-based developers working in the J2EE or .NET environments, try to write most of their code in the application server in Java (for J2EE developers) or VB.NET (for .NET developers). This isn't good practice. In a database application, much of the logic is devoted to retrieving and updating information. If the code to accomplish this task resides in an application server, it must send a request to the database over a network. Then the database must process the request and send the information back across the network for the application to process. Because networks and computers are now very fast, you might think that this would take only fractions of a second. Although this is the case for a single request, if a very complex application requires millions or even hundreds of millions of interactions with the database, multiplying the number of interactions by even fractions of a second can lead to very poor performance.

Even relatively simple operations requiring only a few database requests can be problematic if the application is being accessed by hundreds, thousands, or tens of thousands of users simultaneously. It is much more difficult to build a database-intensive application without using server-side coding than it is to write all the code to run in an application server.

One of the arguments against writing server-side code is that the application won't be portable (can't be moved from one platform to another). However, most organizations using Oracle have been using it for a very long time (ten or more years) and aren't contemplating a switch to a different platform. Also, Web development is currently in a state of rapid flux. Organizations frequently change between .NET, J2EE, and other environments for their Web-based application development.

Both the .NET and J2EE environments are in flux, as well. In the J2EE environment, the industry standard for Web development a year or so ago was to create JavaServer pages (JSPs). Currently, the industry standard is to work in the JSP/Struts environment. In the next year or so, JavaServer Faces (JSFs) will likely become the industry standard. Therefore, code written in the middle-tier runs a high risk of needing to be rewritten in the future.

Server-side code runs faster, is easier to maintain and test, and is less susceptible to change than code placed in the middle tier. Therefore, creating significant portions of an application in the database is a better approach.

There are a number of places where you can write code that your applications can use. We discuss each in turn:

- **Portions of applications:** PL/SQL program units can return a set of values (functions), or PL/SQL routines can perform database operations (procedures). These functions and procedures may be called by other functions and procedures or (in the case of functions) used in SQL statements. PL/SQL routines may be as large and complex as you need them to be. Some complex routines may contain thousands of lines of code. Entire systems may contain millions of lines of code. Chapter 3 covers the creation of functions and procedures and how to place them into packages.

- **PL/SQL code embedded in views:** Oracle allows you to embed code in database views. The code might actually be located in one of two places in the view. First, you can place correctly crafted functions returning a value in the SELECT portion of a SQL statement to retrieve additional information, which might or might not be part of the tables being queried. For example, you can create a view of a Customer table with a function that would return the amount currently owed, even if this amount involves a complex calculation and is not stored in the Customer table.

  You can also embed PL/SQL in INSTEAD OF triggers on a view. These triggers allow you to perform INSERT, UPDATE, and DELETE operations on complex views, with PL/SQL programmatically handling how these operations should be handled. Chapter 6 tells you about embedding code in views.

- **Batch routines:** *Batch routines* run code that processes a large number of records at the same time. Generating invoices for every customer in a system or processing payroll checks for an entire organization are examples of batch routines. These routines are usually large, complex, and database intensive. This type of routine should assuredly be written in PL/SQL.

Programming for Oracle Developer

Oracle Developer used to be the Oracle Corporation's primary application development tool. More recently, Oracle's JDeveloper has been used for Java-based applications. However, many organizations still use Oracle Developer for internal application development — mostly development for systems that handle things like payroll.

Oracle Developer consists of two main parts:

- ✔ **Oracle Forms:** A user interface screen building tool
- ✔ **Oracle Reports:** A reporting tool

Both of these tools use PL/SQL as their programming language. The advantages to this are numerous, because the code used to create the applications is the same as that used in the database itself. Because the J2EE and .NET environments have emerged, developers must use one programming language for applications and a separate language for server-side development. Although Oracle made some efforts to make Java work within the Oracle database as PL/SQL does, the efforts weren't entirely successful.

If you're involved in a new project, the probability of using Oracle Forms is fairly low. Most new development isn't being done in Forms. However, many organizations are still using large Forms-based systems that require ongoing modifications and enhancements.

For reporting, Oracle Reports is still the primary tool for working with Oracle databases. It continues to be enhanced. Further discussion of Oracle Developer is beyond the scope of this book. For more information, see *Oracle Developer: Advanced Forms & Reports,* by Peter Koletzke and Dr. Paul Dorsey (McGraw-Hill).

Chapter 2

The PL/SQL Environment

*B*efore you can start working with PL/SQL, you need a place to write and run your programs as well as a database (preferably populated with some sample data) that your programs can interact with. You might be lucky enough to be working at a company where someone can help you set up and install everything. Or, you might be completely on your own and need to do everything yourself.

Installing an Oracle environment isn't the same as installing a simple Windows application. You can't just put the CD in the drive and have it all magically install for you. You need to set up the right environment. This involves installing the Oracle database and the necessary tools to allow you to write, edit, and debug the code. In this chapter, you discover what you need to do to start writing and testing your PL/SQL code.

Depending upon your particular system configuration and where you're working, you might need some help from a database administrator (DBA) to get everything set up correctly the first time.

Setting Up an Oracle Environment

When setting up your environment, you need several components (although you can create a pared down version if you just want to get up to speed with PL/SQL, which this chapter also explains how to do).

If you want to set up a typical PL/SQL environment, you need the following components:

- ✔ **Database server:** This is a computer (or set of computers) that runs the Oracle database. Oracle runs in many popular computer environments. The most commonly used with Oracle are UNIX, Linux, or some version of Microsoft Windows.

  PL/SQL usually runs on the database server. But Oracle also has a number of products that can use PL/SQL (Forms Developer 10*g*, Reports Developer 10*g*, and so on).

- ✔ **Database Management system (DBMS):** This is the Oracle software itself. This software is installed on the database server. You must have this installed prior to creating a database.

- ✔ **Database:** A database is primarily a set of tables and data that constitute the persistent (permanent) information for your system. You will also store many other things in the database such as code, indexes (to help queries run faster), and so on. Most of the interesting things you can do with a database (for example, Java classes, snapshots, and links to other databases) are beyond the scope of this book.

  When you install the database software, Oracle gives you the option of installing a sample database. If you take advantage of this option, it can help you get started.

- ✔ **Application server:** This is the computer where your application code is stored and executed. Now that most application development is done for the Web, you need a place to store and execute these programs. Those programs are usually executed on an application server. They can also be run on any common operating system, but are usually run on Microsoft Windows or UNIX.

- ✔ **Application server software:** To make applications work on an application server, you need special software to manage and run those programs. Various products that are available can do this. The most commonly used products are Orion and Apache. In an Oracle environment, you often see Oracle's own application server, called Internet Application Server (IAS), which is an extension of the Orion server software.

- ✔ **Client computer and software:** Batch routines are usually run directly on the database server, but client programs are run from a PC. Web applications are run on an Internet browser, and client/server programs execute directly on the client PC. Web applications mainly run on the application server and present the screen output to the client machine only through the browser.

- ✔ **Network:** The database server, application server and client computers have to be able to talk to each other through some kind of network or over the Internet. However, a discussion of how to network computers together is beyond the scope of this book. For an introduction to networking, *Networking For Dummies,* 7th Edition, by Doug Lowe (Wiley Publishing, Inc.) can help.

If you're setting up an environment just to figure out how PL/SQL works, you at least need access to a database server and a client PC. If you're trying to learn from home, you can put everything on the same computer. (This assumes that you have a fairly powerful PC; see the hardware and software requirements in the next section for details.) If you run everything from a PC, you can't build a really large database but you can build a big enough database to try every technique that this book demonstrates.

Hardware and Software Requirements

If you're connecting to an existing Oracle database on a dedicated server, you don't need a very powerful machine. However, if you want to run the entire Oracle environment on the same PC, you need a PC with sufficient resources to run smoothly. You can use Oracle's listed minimum requirements as a guideline for the required hardware and software. However, you'll have an easier time if you have the following hardware and/or software resources available:

- ✔ **CPU: Intel Pentium 4 or AMD Athlon 1.5 GHz and up.** Of course, faster processors are always better, but any reasonable CPU made in the last few years should be sufficient.

- ✔ **Memory: 1GB or more.** Memory is the most critical resource.

- ✔ **Hard disk drive: 2.5GB or more free.** The database by itself might use about 1.5GB, but it is also nice to have the entire documentation library on your local machine, which takes up about 1GB unzipped.

- ✔ **Operating system:**

    - *Microsoft-based: MS Windows 2000 or MS Windows XP.* Windows NT is a bit too old, and Windows 95/98/ME weren't designed to run such complex applications.

    - *UNIX-based:* If your workstation is UNIX-based, you're probably pretty technical already. We do suggest that you check the OTN (at `www.oracle.com/technology/support/metalink/index. html`) for any issues you will need to consider. (For details about OTN, see the following section.)

- ✔ **Security software:** Oracle uses multiple TCP/IP ports, so be careful when configuring firewalls. If the database is trying to access something via TCP/IP, don't block it. This issue arose recently when Microsoft provided a built-in firewall for Windows XP Service Pack 2, and many users had configuration problems. Therefore, expect some firewall messages to pop up after the installation.

Accessing the Oracle Technology Network

Oracle Corporation supports a forum to publicize technical information called the Oracle Technology Network (OTN). The OTN contains a wealth of information for Oracle professionals. Because PL/SQL is the language of Oracle databases, the OTN includes many valuable resources to help you discover how to use PL/SQL effectively.

The OTN Web site gives you access to learning materials, discussion forums, documentation libraries, and best of all, a place from which to download the software. Because of the large size of some of the files, a reasonably fast connection speed is probably a must.

Although you need an environment in which to practice using PL/SQL, your boss might not like you playing with a production database. And if you think that an Oracle license is too expensive to buy for home use, you're probably right. Luckily, you can set up everything you need at home. After registering on OTN, you can download all the necessary software for free.

To register, go to the OTN Web site (`www.oracle.com/technology/index.html`) and click the New OTN Visitors link. Then click the Join OTN link, and on the next page, click the line to create an account. Registration is free, very simple, and should take you only a minute or two.

After you register, you're all set to download whatever you need. The first thing you'll see on the download page is the following disclaimer:

> "All software downloads are free, and each comes with a development license that allows you to use full versions of the products only while developing and prototyping your applications. You can buy Oracle products with full-use licenses at any time from the online Oracle Store or from your Oracle sales representative."

So, you're allowed to download and use any of the Oracle software free of charge as long as you're just getting to know Oracle.

Installing the Database

Many versions of the Oracle database are in use all over the world, and combined with the various operating systems you might be using, it's beyond the scope of this book to explain the entire installation process in detail. However, we do offer some general information in this section to get you started.

As of this writing, the most current version is called Oracle Database 10*g*. For getting to know PL/SQL, you should install the latest version of 10*g* available for your environment. This will allow you to practice with all the available new features. With every release, Oracle improves the PL/SQL language by adding new features and improving performance.

Which version should you use? The Enterprise Edition is preferable because it includes some features that you might be interested in later during your work with PL/SQL.

After you've downloaded the appropriate version of the database, you need to install it. Here's some helpful information that you should be aware of during the database installation process:

✔ Be sure to record the service name of the database when you install it.

✔ A preconfigured database with example *schemas* is very helpful. (Schemas are sets of objects belonging to the particular database user. If an object belongs to the user SCOTT, it is part of schema SCOTT.) Anyone with at least some Oracle experience recognizes these schemas, because all the Oracle tutorials and manuals are based on them.

✔ Don't forget to unlock and set passwords for the most common schemas (SCOTT, HR, OE). The SCOTT schema is used often in examples in this book.

✔ The OTN contains a lot of useful information, including the whole Oracle documentation library (`www.oracle.com/technology/ documentation/index.html`). Check out the Quick Installation Guide (preferable for beginners) or the Installation Guide for installation details specific to your operating system. Both guides include steps that are fairly easy to follow.

If you've had some experience in installing other large products, you should be able to successfully install the database. Of course, as with any complex software, you might have some problems, but many Internet resources are available to help you if necessary.

Working with Code

After you have the database installed, the next question is, "Where will you run all these PL/SQL programs?" The answer isn't as simple as you might think. The ultimate goal is productivity, and you can create PL/SQL programs from numerous tools.

SQL*Plus

If you've already been working with Oracle, you've probably heard of SQL*Plus. This tool is installed with all versions of Oracle (both server and client). The main purpose of SQL*Plus is to provide quick and easy access to the database in both interactive and batch modes. Compared to the leading GUI development tools, SQL*Plus is a relatively primitive tool that most professional developers rarely use.

You can run SQL scripts, PL/SQL scripts, and other scripts by using the internal command language of SQL*Plus by itself. Many developers do all their work by using SQL*Plus because they don't trust the fancy GUI tools.

Several versions of SQL*Plus are available after completing the installation of the Oracle database:

✔ The **command line interface** shown in Figure 2-1 is the most widely used tool because it can be called from any operating system batch language.

✔ The **basic SQL*Plus GUI tool** consists of a wrapper around the same command line interface, as shown in Figure 2-2. It has some GUI features such as the ability to set options in the special form, but it can hardly be called very user friendly.

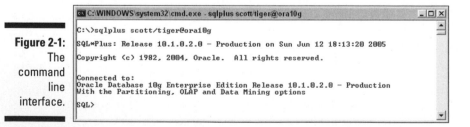

Figure 2-1:
The command line interface.

```
C:\>sqlplus scott/tiger@ora10g

SQL*Plus: Release 10.1.0.2.0 - Production on Sun Jun 12 18:13:20 2005

Copyright (c) 1982, 2004, Oracle.  All rights reserved.


Connected to:
Oracle Database 10g Enterprise Edition Release 10.1.0.2.0 - Production
With the Partitioning, OLAP and Data Mining options

SQL>
```

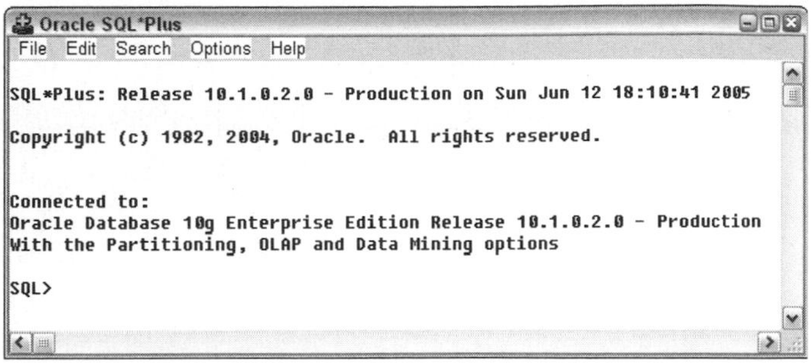

Figure 2-2:
The basic
PL/SQL
GUI tool.

▸ **iSQL*Plus** is the Web interface shown in Figure 2-3. It is the latest one
and has some nice features, but it also might require some workarounds
to deal with timeout settings and security patches.

Because SQL*Plus is included with all Oracle configurations, it remains
extremely popular despite its relatively minimal capabilities. For more details
about SQL*Plus, you can find a lot of documentation on OTN as well as many
custom scripts. It isn't necessary to know a lot about SQL*Plus, but understanding some basics about how to run/save/edit scripts could be useful in
case you're limited to SQL*Plus.

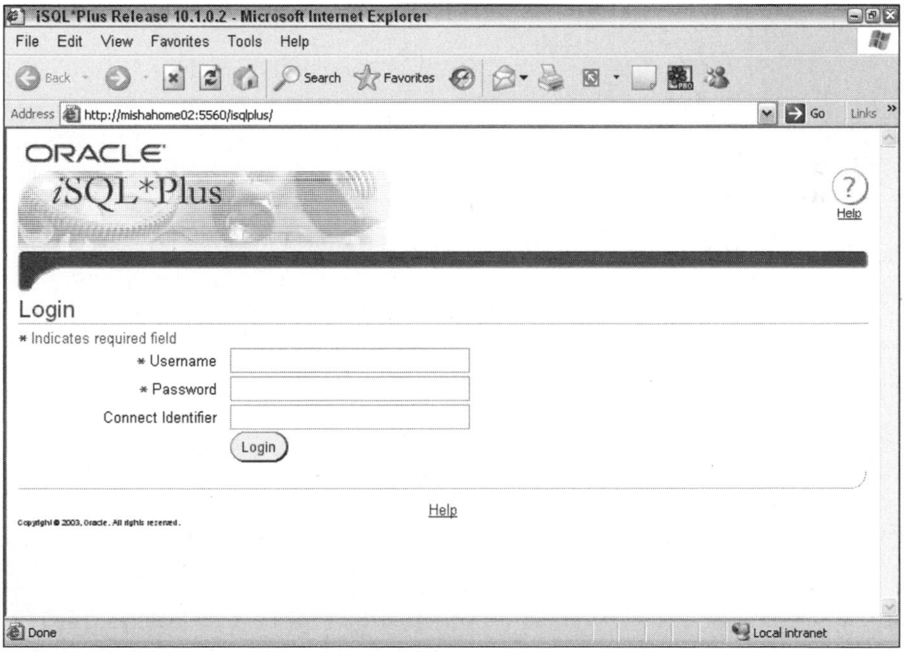

Figure 2-3:
The Oracle
*i*SQL*Plus
Web
interface.

Oracle SQL Developer

In the first part of 2006, Oracle added a new tool to the mix — Oracle SQL Developer (formerly known as Project Raptor). It's a free Java-based graphical environment targeted at database developers. With SQL Developer, you can browse database objects, run SQL statements and SQL scripts, and edit and debug PL/SQL statements. The Oracle SQL Developer interface is shown in Figure 2-4.

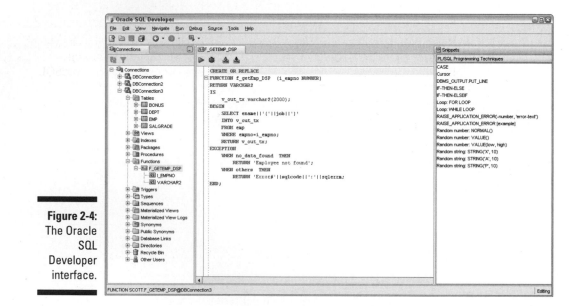

Figure 2-4: The Oracle SQL Developer interface.

Currently, this product it still in the "Early Adopter" phase, although it is a good alternative to the command line interface. The authors do not recommend using it in production systems without significant testing, but SQL Developer looks very promising. If you don't have access to a more mature third-party tool, we recommend trying it (see `http://www.oracle.com/technology/products/database/sql_developer/index.html` to download it).

Third-party tools

In addition to SQL*Plus and newly born Oracle SQL Developer, a number of other tools enable you to work with PL/SQL. The reason for using any one of these is to make your life easier. Of course, any GUI might have bugs/restrictions/issues, but overall the pros usually outweigh the cons. Here are a few popular options:

✓ **Toad from Quest Software:** Toad is the most popular PL/SQL coding tool on the market. It includes a nice editing environment for SQL and PL/SQL. However, the most distinctive feature of Toad is a very powerful set of administrative tools. Toad provides a full working environment for DBAs and power users.

✓ **SQL Navigator from Quest Software:** SQL Navigator, another product from Quest Software, has a more limited audience. It is built by Oracle developers for Oracle developers. Everything there is optimized for writing PL/SQL or SQL as quickly and effectively as possible. It isn't as useful for DBAs, but its add-ons and overall functionality make it a very attractive option for server-side developers.

✓ **RapidSQL from Embarcadero:** RapidSQL, another major development-centered tool, is focused on working with the whole IT environment. Because Embarcadero targets more enterprise-wide solutions, RapidSQL has many features that might just get in the way and be confusing for the PL/SQL beginner. However, RapidSQL does include everything you need to maximize your productivity.

For more information, you can read a set of reviews of these tools at www. orafaq.com/tools/index.htm. The site might not always discuss the most up-to-date versions, but it does include enough details to help you find the right tool for your needs.

Establishing a Database Connection

After you install the database, you need to perform a few more steps before you can connect to a database. In the sections that follow, we outline each step. Connecting to the database after installation is also the simplest way to verify that you have installed everything correctly.

Before you connect to the database, it's important to understand how Oracle handles user accounts. In Oracle, the concept of a *user* (and a set of objects that belong to user is called a *schema*, as you already know) is one of the major elements of the system. Here are the important points you need to understand about accounts and how they relate to connecting to a database:

✓ The only way of connecting to the database is by providing a username and password. So you need to know the user/password account to which you will connect. If you installed the database yourself, you will have a user account called SYSTEM with whatever password you specified during installation. Otherwise ask for help from your organization's DBA.

Oracle includes sample schemas (SCOTT, HR, and OE), and you should have unlocked them and set their passwords during the installation. If you didn't do it, a bit farther on you find commands for doing it manually.

✔ Users can be created/dropped/modified/locked from any administrative account.

✔ All objects in the database (tables, procedures, and so on) belong to some user.

✔ Users have privileges and roles (sets of privileges). These roles govern which users can do what. Users could have system privileges (for example, the right to connect) or object privileges (the right to create a table or to update data in somebody else's table).

✔ Users can grant privileges (such as the right to select the data from the table or execute the procedure) on their objects to other users.

Checking the operating services

First, you need to validate that the appropriate operating system services are running. In Windows-based systems, you can find the list of services running under `Control Panel\Administrative Tools\Services`. Oracle usually installs a lot of them but the core ones are

✔ `OracleService<your service name>`: This is the database itself and represents all processes and memory elements.

✔ `OracleOraDb10g_home1TNSListener` (That is a naming convention in Oracle 10*g*. In other versions, look for the service that has `TNSListener` in the name.) This is a special utility that listens for connection requests from the client applications and routes them to the appropriate database processes of the main service.

Connecting with your username

To verify the database connection, you must connect as user SYSTEM because you need all administrative privileges to perform the necessary tasks.

If you see the Connected To message shown earlier in Figure 2-1 (assuming you're using the 10*g* database), congratulations! You successfully connected to the database, which means that you have installed everything correctly.

The syntax to connect via SQL*Plus from the command line looks like the following:

```
C:\>sqlplus user/password@database
```

This is exactly the way you'll connect to the database to run the test scripts in this book, or you can use one of the third-party tools we mention earlier in this chapter.

Unlocking (or locking) accounts

Now it's time to unlock the accounts you'll need to use to master PL/SQL. The syntax of this command should be clear. It allows the user to lock or unlock any existing accounts. If an account is locked, this means that even if the user has all privileges, he/she still won't be able to connect. However, other users will be able to access objects of the locked account if they have the privileges to do so. Use the following line of code to lock or unlock your account:

```
alter user YOUR_USER account [unlock|lock];
```

You can unlock the HR, OE, and SCOTT schemas by using the following code:

```
SQL> alter user hr account unlock;
User altered.
SQL> alter user oe account unlock;
User altered.
SQL> alter user scott account unlock;
User altered.
SQL>
```

You should receive a "User altered" response after typing each line and pressing Enter.

Each of these accounts contains sample data that you can use with the examples in this book. The sample data connected with these accounts is described later in this chapter.

Resetting passwords

The next step is to reset passwords by using the syntax shown in the following line of code. (You don't need to do it for SCOTT — The password is always TIGER.)

```
alter user YOUR_USER identified by YOUR_PASSWORD;
```

After you fire the following code, you can connect as any of these users:

```
SQL> alter user hr identified by hr;
User altered.
SQL> alter user oe identified by oe;
User altered.
SQL>
```

 To reconnect as another user, you don't need to close SQL*Plus. Simply use the CONNECT command, as shown here for the HR schema (assuming that ORA10G is a service name of the database you specified during installation):

```
SQL> connect hr/hr@ora10g
Connected.
SQL>
```

You should receive the response "Connected."

Setting up the server to communicate

Before running anything, you have one more step to complete. You need to enter the following command:

```
Set serveroutput on
```

This special command allows the server to communicate back to you because, by default, server output is turned off. This communication will be critical in the future. In most third-party tools, you can enable server output by clicking an icon on the toolbar.

The Basics of PL/SQL Programs

With your environment set up, you're ready to explore some fundamentals of PL/SQL programs. The following sections describe some of the basic syntax you need to know in order to work with PL/SQL.

Writing a simple program

The simplest kind of PL/SQL code is called an *anonymous block*. An anonymous block is a block of code that has its own DECLARE/BEGIN/END structure. Anonymous blocks can either stand on their own (as shown here) or they can sit within any other PL/SQL program.

```
declare
    ...
      <Declaration part => Chapter 3,6>
    ...
begin
    ...
    <Procedural part => Chapter 4>
    ...
exception
    ...
    <Exception handler => Chapter 5>
    ...
end;
```

The *declaration* section defines all variables, cursors, subprograms, and other elements to be used in the code. This section is optional, and you may skip it if no variables or other program elements need to be declared. You find out how to declare variables and subprograms in the Chapter 3 — and about cursors in Chapter 6.

The *procedural* section contains the main body of the routine. It starts with the `begin` keyword and ends with the `exception` keyword or the `end` keyword if you have no exception section. This is the only mandatory part of the code.

You must have at least one line of executable code in the procedural section. If you don't want anything to execute in the program unit, you can use the NULL command to indicate that nothing should be executed.

The *exception* section is also optional. It allows the program to intercept and process special conditions that could happen at runtime (divide by zero, duplicate value of the primary key, and so on). We discuss exceptions in more detail in Chapter 5.

Now you're ready to write your first program. At the SQL*Plus prompt that you get after you successfully connect, type the following:

```
SQL> declare
  2     v_string_tx varchar2(256):='Hello, World!';
  3  begin
  4     dbms_output.put_line(v_string_tx);
  5  end;
  6
```

Each complete line of the PL/SQL code must end with a semicolon (;).

To run the code, type **/** at the beginning of the first blank line after the last line of the code This is a SQL*Plus command to execute the last SQL or PL/SQL statement. If you're using a third-party tool, you'll probably click a Run icon to accomplish the same task. The result is the following:

```
SQL> declare
  2     v_string_tx varchar2(256):='Hello, World!';
  3  begin
  4     dbms_output.put_line(v_string_tx);
  5  end;
  6  /
Hello, World!
PL/SQL procedure successfully completed.
SQL>
```

This code indicates that the command was successfully sent to the server and the server processed it. How will you know that the program did something? In the earlier section, "Setting up the server to communicate," you set SERVER OUTPUT to ON. This allows the server to "talk" to you. The DBMS_OUTPUT.

PUT_LINE command sends whatever text you passed as a parameter back to the client console. Because you received Hello, World! back, you have absolute proof of execution.

Of course, simply writing anonymous blocks isn't enough to make PL/SQL usable. Although you can store your routines as anonymous blocks and pass them to the command line, this is definitely not the most convenient method.

Creating stored procedures

You can store PL/SQL code inside the database. (See Chapter 3 for additional information about this topic.) For example, you could store the first PL/SQL routine from the preceding section as a standalone procedure. Stored procedures use a slightly different syntax, shown here:

```
create or replace procedure p_hello
is
    v_string_tx varchar2(256):='Hello, World!';
begin
    dbms_output.put_line(v_string_tx);
end;
```

These few lines of code constitute a PL/SQL program that creates a stored procedure in the database.

When the procedure exists in the database, you can easily call the routine and get the same result as before, as shown here:

```
SQL> create or replace procedure p_hello
  2  is
  3      v_string_tx varchar2(256):='Hello, World!';
  4  begin
  5      dbms_output.put_line(v_string_tx);
  6  end;
  7  /
Procedure created.
SQL>begin
  2      p_hello;
  3 end;
  4  /
Hello,World!
PL/SQL procedure successfully completed.
SQL>
```

Passing parameters to procedures

You could even go a step farther. Like any other programming language, PL/SQL allows you to pass parameters to procedures as shown here:

```
Create or replace procedure p_helloTo (i_tx varchar2)
is
    v_string_tx varchar2(256):='Hello, '||i_tx||'!';
begin
    dbms_output.put_line(v_string_tx);
end;
```

In this case, you can pass whatever string you want into the procedure and the server will pass the message back with the modified string:

```
SQL> begin
  2     p_helloTo('Everybody');
  3   end;
  4   /
Hello, Everybody!
PL/SQL procedure successfully completed.
SQL> _
```

Examining the Sample Data

The history of sample data sets in Oracle databases started when Oracle was still called the Software Development Laboratories. At that time, Oracle Corporation had a developer named Bruce Scott whose daughter had a cat named Tiger. As a result, even in the latest version of the Oracle database, you can still find the sample schema SCOTT with password TIGER. If you need more complicated sample data, the Human Resources (HR) and Order Entry (OE) schemas are also available.

The Scott/Tiger schema

Anyone who has ever worked with an Oracle database has used the Scott/Tiger schema tables. The information contained in those tables is very basic but will allow you to explore the relationships among the tables and understand how a relational database works. In the Oracle 10g database, that schema consists of the four tables shown in Figure 2-5.

The table descriptions for this schema are as follows:

- **DEPT** contains a list of departments in the organization.
- **EMP** contains a list of employees in the organization (including the organization tree).
- **SALGRADE** is a dictionary to identify the appropriate salary grade.
- **BONUS** contains bonuses for employees (empty by default).

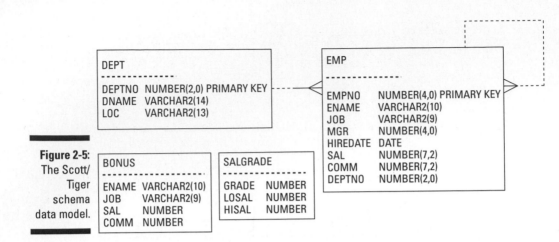

Figure 2-5:
The Scott/
Tiger
schema
data model.

Throughout this book, we help you interact with these tables as you discover how to communicate with the database by using PL/SQL.

The Human Resources (HR) and Order Entry (OE) schemas

As time passed and the Oracle database matured, the old Scott/Tiger schema was not robust enough to demonstrate many of the abilities of the DBMS. Currently, several schemas are available. The most popular ones are HR (Human Resources) and OE (Order Entry). Even though we are not using HR and OE schemas in this book, you should be aware of them, because the latest Oracle tutorials and manuals use HR and OE.

The HR and OE schemas are significantly more complex than good old SCOTT. HR is a direct descendant of SCOTT and targeted for beginners. It has seven tables with a relatively small number of rows in each and does not involve any complex datatypes.

The OE (Order Entry) schema is more complex, with emphasis placed on the multiple datatypes supported by Oracle. Objects from that schema reference ones in the HR schema, so using OE without HR is impossible.

Both of these schemas can provide sample data and tables as you write programs and discover the features of PL/SQL.

Part II
Getting Started with PL/SQL

The 5th Wave   By Rich Tennant

Oracle
PL/SQL
Manual
Publishing

"They're moving on to the OOP section. That should daze and confuse them enough for us to finish changing the tire and get the heck out of here."

In this part . . .

The four chapters in this part describe some of the important concepts that you need to understand in order to be a PL/SQL programmer.

Chapter 3 describes the PL/SQL programming language and how it fits into the overall database environment. There are brief sections about the different PL/SQL structures and how to create reusable portions of code. You also find out about important extras that you need to be a successful programmer.

Chapter 4 introduces the important concepts of control structures, conditions, and loops and how to use them effectively in your programming.

Chapter 5 explains how to handle many different types of code exceptions.

Chapter 6 shows you how PL/SQL and SQL work together and discusses the important topic of cursors.

Chapter 3

Laying the Groundwork: PL/SQL Fundamentals

*P*L/SQL is a procedural language that interacts with the Oracle database. It can access all the capabilities of SQL. In addition, it allows developers to use the functionality typically associated with programming languages. For example, PL/SQL supports variables, arrays, exceptions, and flow of control statements. It allows developers to structure their code into subprograms, which include packages, triggers, functions, and procedures. This chapter introduces the important concepts you need to understand when writing and working with PL/SQL code.

PL/SQL As a Programming Language

Computer languages allow people to give instructions to computers. There are generic languages (Java or C++) as well as functional languages (PL/SQL or COBOL). Generic languages allow programmers to implement just about anything, but functional languages have a more limited scope.

PL/SQL is a perfect example of a functional language because it is designed to provide easy and effective communication with a relational database. PL/SQL allows you to create procedural logic for data processing in the database.

Before you find out about PL/SQL in more depth, you need to recognize its limitations:

- ✔ If data can be manipulated via SQL, the logic to do so should be placed in SQL because the Oracle SQL engine is the most effective way to process data.

- ✔ Very large mathematical calculations should be taken out of the database. C++ is significantly more efficient for handling them.

- ✔ File operations are not the strongest feature of the database. The purpose of the DBMS is to process data, not to serve as a substitute for the operating system.

The point is to use PL/SQL for the tasks for which it was designed, namely to provide procedural programming by using relational data, and not try to stretch it beyond its intended purpose.

Anonymous PL/SQL Blocks

PL/SQL can be run as a fully interpreted language. (In the 9*i* Release2 and 10*g* versions, you can create compiled versions of your code, but that topic is beyond the scope of this book). This means that you can communicate with the database engine in real time without any explicit compilation steps. Therefore, if you've established an open connection to the database, you can send messages and get responses.

PL/SQL uses code constructs called *procedural blocks*. These blocks contain commands and sets of commands, which can be *named* or *anonymous*.

We introduce the basic structure of a procedural block in Chapter 2. For easy reference, we show it again here:

```
<<MAIN>>
declare
    ...
     Declaration section
    ...
begin
    ...
    Procedural section
    ...
exception
    ...
    Exception handler
    ...
end;
```

Anonymous blocks can be nested (in the procedure and exception blocks) in as many levels as you want, as shown in this simple example:

```
<<MAIN>>
declare
    ...
        Declaration section
    ...
begin
    ...
        Procedural section
    ...
        <<SUB1>>
        declare
        ...
        begin
        ...
        end;
    ...
exception
    ...
end;
```

Because Oracle doesn't process PL/SQL code line by line, but instead handles whole messages at one time, the root anonymous block containing all sub-elements is one logical unit. This means that all references and errors are analyzed in the context of that unit.

You can label all blocks (including nested ones) by using identifiers enclosed in << >>. This notation allows programmers to reference elements of different blocks.

Introducing the Lexical Set of Elements

The PL/SQL lexical set of elements consists of identifiers, delimiters, literals, and comments.

When you create these elements in PL/SQL, you use the standard English character set, so the valid characters are as follows:

- **Upper- and lowercase letters:** A–Z and a–z
- **Numerals:** 0–9
- **Symbols:** ( ) + - * / < > = ! ~ ^ ; : . ' @ % , " # $ & _ | { } ? [ ]
- **Tabs, spaces, and carriage returns**

We describe each briefly in the following sections.

Identifiers

Identifiers are names of PL/SQL program items and units. These items and units could be of different kinds — constants, variables, exceptions, cursors, cursor variables, subprograms, and packages. When creating identifiers, be sure to keep the following in mind:

✔ **An identifier cannot exceed 30 characters.** Every character, including dollar signs, underscores, and number signs, is significant. For example, `v_index_nr` and `vindex_nr` represent two different things.

✔ **An identifier consists of a letter optionally followed by more letters, numerals, dollar signs, underscores, and number signs.** Some examples of valid and invalid identifiers are shown here:

- `v_index_nr` (valid)
- `v$index_nr` (valid)
- `v index_nr` (invalid because of the space)
- `5_index_nr` (invalid because it starts with a number)
- `v-index_nr` (invalid because it contains –, a hyphen)

✔ **By default, identifiers are not case sensitive, so `v_index_nr` and `V_Index_NR` are the same.** Although you can now make some elements case sensitive in the Oracle environment, you shouldn't do this because Oracle has historically been case insensitive, and other programmers and developers won't expect the code to pay attention to case.

✔ **Identifiers may not be the same as reserved words (for example, you cannot use the word *end* as a variable name).** Check any PL/SQL manual for a complete list of reserved words.

Delimiters

A *delimiter* is a simple or compound symbol that has a special meaning in PL/SQL. For example, you use delimiters to represent arithmetic operations such as addition and subtraction. A list of PL/SQL delimiters is shown in Table 3-1.

Table 3-1	PL/SQL Symbols
Delimiter	**Description**
+, –, *, /	Addition, subtraction/negation, multiplication, division
%	Attribute indicator
'	Character string delimiter

Delimiter	Description
.	Component selector
(,)	Expression or list delimiter
:	Host variable indicator
,	Item separator
"	Quoted identifier delimiter
=	Relational operator
@	Remote access indicator
;	Statement terminator
:=	Assignment operator
=>	Association operator
||	Concatenation operator
^ ^	Exponentiation operator
<<, >>	Label delimiter (begin and end)
/*, */	Multi-line comment delimiter (begin and end)
--	Single-line comment indicator
. .	Range operator
<, >, <=, >=	Relational operators
<>, '=, ~=, ^=	Different version of NOT EQUAL

Literals

Literals are explicit numeric, character, string, or Boolean values not represented by an identifier. You can find more information about literals in the "Literals as variable values" section, later in this chapter.

Comments

Comments are used to indicate that what follows should be ignored by the PL/SQL interpreter. Comments usually serve the purpose of explaining some hidden rules or logic in the code to other developers.

PL/SQL allows two types of comments: single and multi-line.

Single-line comments start with a delimiter `--` and go to the end of the line, as shown here:

```
declare
-- here you should declare variables,
-- constants, etc.
   ...
begin
-- here you place your code
   ...
end;
```

Multi-line comments start with `/*` and end with `*/`. These delimiters may span as many lines as needed. An example is shown here:

```
declare
/* This code is written by Michael Rosenblum
   Dec 20 2005 */
   ...
begin
   ...
end;
```

Always include enough comments to make your code readable. When doing so, keep in mind that you can't nest comments. For pointers on how you can write effective comments that will help others understand your code, see Chapter 9.

Working with Constants and Variables

Constants and variables create a set of elements to be used in coding. Although constants and variables are common to almost all programming languages, the way a particular language handles them varies. This section outlines the basics of constants and variables in PL/SQL. You find out how to declare variables, assign values to them, define their scope, and more.

Declaring variables

In PL/SQL, variables must be included in the declaration block before they can be used. There are a number of ways to declare a variable. The most common way is by using a *direct declaration,* as shown here:

```
declare
     variable_name [constant] DATATYPE
                 [DEFAULT value |DEFAULT NULL];
begin
     ...
```

Variable names are PL/SQL identifiers. Therefore all the rules that apply to identifiers, which we explain earlier in this chapter, also apply to variable names.

The datatype of the variable may be a standard SQL datatype (NUMBER, VARCHAR2, DATE) or a PL/SQL datatype (BOOLEAN, BINARY_INTEGER).

The keyword *constant* means that the variable's value can't be changed in the body of the program. If you declare a variable as a constant, you must assign a default value to it by using the optional DEFAULT *value* clause.

If you don't use a DEFAULT clause, the variable will have a NULL value, indicating that the variable has been declared but not yet initialized. This means that, although you can reference the variable, it doesn't have any value, and all operations involving that variable have no meaning and produce no result. We share more information about working with NULL values in Chapter 4.

The following shows an example of correct declarations of variables:

```
declare
     v_sal_nr   NUMBER;
     v_name_tx  VARCHAR2(10) DEFAULT 'KING';
     v_start_dt DATE := SYSDATE; -- same as DEFAULT SYSDATE
begin
     ...
```

You can also declare a variable by reference (%TYPE for simple variables and %ROWTYPE for variables that can store the whole row) as shown in Listing 3-1:

Listing 3-1: Declaring a Variable by Reference

```
declare
     variable_name   table.column%TYPE;          →2
     variable_name2 variable_name%TYPE;           →3
     variable_row    table%ROWTYPE;               →4
begin
     ...
```

Here's what happens in Listing 3-1:

→2   Declares that the variable has the same datatype as the specified column.

→3   References a variable already defined in the code. (You can't do forward referencing.)

→4 Creates a record variable that can store all the columns from the row in the specified table. In addition to tables, views, cursors, and other record variables could be also used as a point of reference. (You can read more about record variables in Chapter 11.)

Defining datatypes by reference is extremely useful and decreases the amount of program maintenance required, because changing the datatype of a column in the database does not require searching for all the places where that column is referenced. Changes are inherited automatically and on the fly.

The following code shows some examples of defining datatypes:

```
declare
    v_empno1 emp.empNo%TYPE;
    v_empno2 v_empNo%TYPE;
    v_dept_rec dept%ROWTYPE;
begin
    ...
```

There are some restrictions on the declaration of variables:

✔ There is no forward declaration.

✔ Multiple declarations supported in some languages are not allowed in PL/SQL, as shown here:

```
declare
    v1_nr, v2_nr NUMBER; -- INVALID
    -- VALID
    v1_nr NUMBER;
    v2_nr NUMBER;
begin
    ...
```

Assigning values to variables

There are a number of ways to assign a value to a variable. A simple one is shown in Listing 3-2:

Listing 3-2:   Assigning a Value to a Variable

```
declare
    v_length_nr NUMBER DEFAULT 5;                    →2
    v_height_nr NUMBER := 4;                         →3
    v_width_nr  NUMBER;
    v_volume_nr NUMBER;
    v_min_nr    NUMBER;
```

```
begin
    v_width_nr := 3;                                              →8
    v_volume_nr:= v_length_nr*v_width_nr*v_height_nr;    →9
    v_min_nr := least(v_length_nr,v_width_nr,v_height_nr);
end;
```

Listing 3-2 works as described here:

→2   This is the default assignment. You can use either the keyword DEFAULT or an assignment operator :=).

→8   Assigns a literal to the variable.

→9   Assigns the result of the operation to the variable.

→10 Assigns the result of the SQL built-in function to the variable.

Taking a step farther, you can assign SQL query results to PL/SQL variables, as shown here:

```
declare
    v_name_tx VARCHAR2(256);
begin
    select eName
      into v_name_tx
      from emp
    where empNo=7369;
end;
```

Literals as variable values

All values in the text of the program are denoted as alphanumeric representations, or *literals*.

Two types of *numeric literals* exist:

- **Integer literals** represent optionally signed numeric values without decimal points.
- **Real literals** represent optionally signed whole or fractional numbers with decimal points.

SQL and PL/SQL aren't good at enforcing datatypes, and usually literals are dynamically converted to be the same type as the variables to which they are being assigned. However, the way in which you define the literal might have significant side effects, especially when communicating with languages like Java. Some examples of assigning literals of both types are shown in Listing 3-3.

Listing 3-3:   **Examples of Integer and Real Literals**

```
declare
    v_int1_nr BINARY_INTEGER :=5;   -- integer
    v_int2_nr BINARY_INTEGER :=-5;  -- integer
    v_int3_nr BINARY_INTEGER :=0;   -- integer
    v_int4_nr BINARY_INTEGER :=+5;  -- integer

    v_real1_nr NUMBER :=5.0; -- real          →7
    v_real2_nr NUMBER :=5.;  -- real          →8
    v_real3_nr NUMBER :=-7.123; -- real
    v_real4_nr NUMBER :=0.5; -- real          →10
    v_real5_nr NUMBER :=.5;  -- real          →11
    v_real6_nr NUMBER :=0.0; -- real          →12
    v_real7_nr NUMBER :=2/3; -- real
begin
   ...
```

The following are additional details about Listing 3-3:

→**7–8**   If you use a decimal point, the literal automatically becomes real even though the value could still be an integer.

→**10–11** In the Oracle environment, you don't have to place a zero before the decimal point, so 0.5 and .5 are exactly the same.

→**12**   Zero could also be represented as a real number, using the notation 0.0.

Numeric literals cannot contain dollar signs or commas, but they can be written in scientific notation, as shown here:

```
declare
    v_real1_nr NUMBER:=$123456.00;  -- INVALID
    v_real2_nr NUMBER:=123,456.00;  -- INVALID
    v_real3_nr NUMBER:=5e10;  -- VALID
    v_real3_nr NUMBER:=5e-3;  -- VALID
begin
   ...
```

Oracle supports scientific notation for numbers between 1.0×10^{-130} and 1.0×10^{126} (or between 1E-130 and 1E $\times$ 126, where E stands for "times ten to the power of.")

Character and string literals in the Oracle world are enclosed by single quotes, as shown here:

```
declare
    v_char_tx CHAR(1):='H';
    v_text1_tx VARCHAR2(10) :='Hello';
    v_text2_CHAR(1) :='';  -- the same as NULL
begin
   ...
```

Assigning an empty string to the character variable is exactly the same as assigning NULL to it.

Because the single quote character is used to enclose the whole string, the process of writing code can get a bit tricky if you need to have those characters as a part of the text, as shown in Listing 3-4.

Listing 3-4:   Using Single Quote Characters as Part of Text Strings

```
declare
    v_text1_tx VARCHAR2(50) :='It''s Misha''s text.';   →2
    v_text2_tx VARCHAR2(50) :=q'!It's Misha's text.!';   →3
    v_text3_tx VARCHAR2(50) :=q'[It's Misha's text.]';   →4
begin
    ...
```

Here's what Listing 3-4 is doing:

→2   Represents the old way of placing quotes inside the text, namely to double them.

→3   Starting with Oracle 10g, you can declare the whole string to be enclosed in quotes by using the construct q'!*text*!'. Using this approach, you can type the string exactly as you want it to appear.

→4   You can use other delimiters (not only !, but </>, [/], {/}, and (/)) to declare the start and end of a quoted string. In this line, the text does not end with a period but with a real exclamation point so you must replace the string delimiter with something else.

Text literals in Oracle are case sensitive. This means that 'text' and 'Text' are two different literals.

Understanding the scope of variables

By definition, the *scope* of a variable is a region of a program unit (block, subprogram, or package) from which you can reference the variable. As you work with variables in your programs, knowing their scope is important because you don't want variables to collide and either render your code unworkable or make your code perform in unexpected ways. You also need to understand where to declare your variable so that it works with all the relevant code.

Avoiding conflicts of variable scope

When considering how to avoid scope problems, the key guideline to follow is that all identifiers within the same scope must be unique. In some programming languages, you can have variables of the same name but different datatypes. PL/SQL doesn't allow this, as shown here:

```
declare
    v_amount_nr NUMBER;
    v_amount_nr BINARY_INTEGER; -- duplicate!!!
begin
    ...
```

Also, although it isn't explicitly prohibited, you should never use variable names that could match column names in the database. In SQL statements, the names of database columns take precedence over the names of local variables and formal parameters, as shown here:

```
declare
    ename VARCHAR2(10):='KING';
begin
    update emp
    set sal = sal * 10
    where eName = eName; -- WRONG!!!
end;
```

Running the preceding code updates everyone's salary because Oracle will compare the column to itself, not to your variable. To avoid this situation, use naming conventions as suggested in Chapter 8.

The bold line in the following code shows the proper way to perform the salary update:

```
declare
    v_eName_tx VARCHAR2(10):='KING';
begin
    update emp
    set sal = sal * 10
    where eName = v_eName_tx; -- CORRECT!
end;
```

Controlling scope with a variable declaration

When working with variables and scope, you need to understand what makes a variable visible, local, or global:

- A variable is *visible* only in blocks from which you can reference the identifier by using an unqualified name.

- A variable is *local* to the block where it is declared.

- A variable is *global* to all sub-blocks of the block where it is declared.

In the following code, variable V_STR1_tx is *local* for the block labeled <<MAIN>> and *global* for the block labeled <<SUB>>. Variable V_STR2_tx is *visible* only in the block <<SUB>>.

```
<<MAIN>>
declare
    v_str1_tx VARCHAR2(10);
begin
    v_str1_tx :='ABC'; -- local
    <<SUB>>
    declare
        v_str2_tx VARCHAR2(1);
    begin
        v_str1_tx:='ABC'; -- local
        v_str2_tx:='A'; -- global and visible
    end;
    v_str1_tx :='ABC'; -- local
end;
```

You can use the same variable name for multiple levels of anonymous blocks. However, labels on blocks are optional. The following example doesn't include them, but that doesn't change the behavior of the code. Only local variables are visible, as shown here:

```
declare
    v_str1_tx VARCHAR2(10);
begin
    declare
        v_str1_tx VARCHAR2(2);
    begin
        v_str1_tx:='ABC'; -- INVALID
        v_str1_tx:='AB';    -- valid
    end;
    v_str1_tx:='ABC'; -- valid
end;
```

Because variable V_STR1_tx is declared in both blocks, in the inner block only the local one is visible. This means that you can assign only a two-character value to it (in this case, AB). Outside the inner block, you can assign up to a ten-character value to the variable because now the visible variable V_STR1_tx is of type VARCHAR2(10).

Later in this chapter, you find out about the scope and visibility of other types of identifiers beyond variables in the PL/SQL environment.

Building Expressions with Operators

By definition, *expressions* are constructed by using operands and operators. An *operand* is a variable, constant, literal, or function call that contributes a value to an expression. An operator like + or – indicates what the program should do with the operands. An example of a simple expression is shown in Listing 3-5.

Listing 3-5:   An Example of a Simple PL/SQL Expression

```
declare
    v_i1_nr NUMBER;
    v_i2_nr NUMBER;
begin
    v_i1_nr:=10/3;                                        →5
    v_i2_nr:=-vi1_nr;                                     →6
end;
```

Check out what happens in Listing 3-5:

→5   Represents an example of a binary operator / which requires two operands.

→6   Represents a unary operator –, which requires only a single operand.

PL/SQL doesn't have an operator that can process three operands, so complex expressions are resolved as a sequence of unary and binary operations. That sequence is built based on the precedence of operators. Table 3-2 shows the precedence of operators in PL/SQL organized from highest to lowest.

Table 3-2	PL/SQL Operator Precedence
Operator	*Description*
**	Exponentiation
+, –	Identity, negation (unary operation)
*, /	Multiplication, division
+, –, | |	Addition, subtraction, concatenation
=, <, >, < =, > =, <>, ! =, ~= IS NULL, LIKE, BETWEEN, IN	Comparison
NOT	Logical negation
AND	Conjunction
OR	Inclusion

Operations with higher precedence are applied first. Operators with the same precedence are applied in their text order, as shown here:

```
Expression:   2+3*4 =>
Action:            ^     (multiplication has higher precedence)
Next step:    2+12
Action:            ^      (the last operation left)
Result:       14


Expression:    2*3*4 =>

Action:           ^      (first operation of the same type)
Next step:        6*4
Action:             ^ (the last operation left)
Result:        24
```

You can change the execution order by using parentheses. If the expression includes parentheses, the execution starts with the innermost pair, as shown here:

```
Expression:   ((2+3)*4+5)*6 =>
Action:           ^             (innermost parenthesis)
Next step:    (  5  *4+5)*6
Action:              ^    (highest precedence in parenthesis)
Next step:    (  20 +5)*6
Action:                ^  (operation in parentheses)
Next step:        25*6
Action:                ^   (the last operation left)
Result:               150
```

Don't be afraid to insert extra parentheses to logically separate parts of a statement or condition. By doing this, you can be sure that the code will execute correctly.

Logical operators in PL/SQL are based on exactly the same concepts as in any other language, as shown in Table 3-3.

Table 3-3		Logical Operators in PL/SQL		
x	y	x AND y	x OR y	NOT x
True	True	True	True	False
True	False	False	True	False
False	True	False	True	True
False	False	False	False	True

Cases involving NULL values are covered in Chapter 4, where you find out more about using logical expressions to build conditional logic.

All SQL logical operators (IN, LIKE, BETWEEN) are also valid in PL/SQL, and we discuss them in Chapter 4.

Running Anonymous Blocks of Code

As we explain earlier in "Anonymous PL/SQL Blocks," PL/SQL can use an interpreter to run code. This means that when you finish typing the code, it is ready to be executed. You have a number of ways to do this. The easiest is to use SQL*Plus (which we introduce in Chapter 2) and type everything there. An example is shown here:

```
SQL> set serveroutput on
SQL> declare
  2       v_length_nr NUMBER :=5.5;
  3       v_width_nr  NUMBER :=3.5;
  4       v_area_nr   NUMBER;
  5  begin
  6       v_area_nr:=v_length_nr*v_width_nr;
  7       DBMS_OUTPUT.put_line('Area:'||v_area_nr);
  8  end;
  9  /
Area:19.25
PL/SQL procedure successfully completed.
SQL>
```

As we discuss in Chapter 2, the command SET SERVEROUTPUT ON turns on the communication channel from the database back to the client session. Therefore, it's a waste of time to repeat it over and over again. Use it any time you're using the procedure DBMS_OUTPUT.PUT_LINE.

Identifying common mistakes

If you mistype something when you run code in your IDE, PL/SQL does a separate parsing step to check for errors. Then it tries to execute whatever you typed. If the parse fails, it returns an error, as shown here:

```
SQL> declare
  2       v_length_nr NUMBER :=5.5;
  3       v_width_nr  NUMBER :=3.5;
  4       v_area_nr   NUMBER;
  5  begin
```

```
6        v_area_nr:=v_length_nr*v_width_nr;
7        DBMS_OUTPUT.put_line('Area:'||area_nr);
8   end;
9   /
    DBMS_OUTPUT.put_line('Area:'||area_nr);
                                    *
ERROR at line 7:
ORA-06550: line 7, column 35:
PLS-00201: identifier 'AREA_NR' must be declared
ORA-06550: line 7, column 5:
PL/SQL: Statement ignored
SQL>
```

In this example, the name of the variable was incorrectly typed. As a result, the code can't be parsed. Oracle tried to provide as much information as possible about the source of the problem. Usually, you will receive a useful hint about where to look.

Oracle doesn't process one line at a time; you're sending the whole block at once, so Oracle checks the block as a whole for logical consistency. As a result, if you get a parsing error, you can be sure that nothing from the code you passed was executed. This point comes up again in Chapter 13 when building dynamic PL/SQL on the fly. In that case, you might encounter a parsing error at runtime, but all code before the line with the error will be executed.

Oracle error messages are usually very helpful for common structural issues such as:

✔ Missing parenthesis (We recommend that you count them.)

✔ Incorrect operators (such as = instead of : = for assignment of values)

✔ Mistyped names of operators or variables

Spotting compilation errors

Compilation errors are shown in an error stack. (See Chapter 5 for more information.) Using the length, width, and area example, you're looking for any error starting with PLS- indicating that you have something wrong with your code.

Recognizing semicolon-related errors

When you have a missing semicolon, the error message you see might not identify the problem as clearly as in earlier examples. Listing 3-6 is an example of this error and the resulting message.

Listing: 3-6:   Error Messages

```
SQL> declare
  2        v_length_nr NUMBER :=5.5;
  3        v_width_nr  NUMBER :=3.5;
  4        v_area_nr   NUMBER;
  5  begin
  6        v_area_nr:=v_length_nr*v_width_nr            →6
  7        DBMS_OUTPUT.put_line('Area:'||area_nr);      →7
  8  end;
  9  /
    DBMS_OUTPUT.put_line('Area:'||area_nr);
      *
ERROR at line 7:
ORA-06550: line 7, column 5:
PLS-00103: Encountered the symbol "DBMS_OUTPUT" when
           expecting one of the following:
. ( * @ % & = - + ; < / > at in is mod remainder not rem
<an exponent (**)> <> or != or ~= >= <= <> and or like
between || member SUBMULTISET_
The symbol "." was substituted for "DBMS_OUTPUT" to
           continue.
SQL>
```

→6-7   Oracle tries to give you as much information as possible. In this case, line 7 started with something strange. But the same message can be restated as "previous line did not end correctly." This is the most common mistake in the world of PL/SQL. There is no semicolon at the end of line 6, so Oracle doesn't know that the line ended. It tried to parse the next line as a part of the previous one and returned an error.

Another common error is a missing semicolon after the END statement, as shown here:

```
SQL> declare
  2        v_length_nr NUMBER :=5.5;
  3        v_width_nr  NUMBER :=3.5;
  4        v_area_nr   NUMBER;
  5  begin
  6        v_area_nr:=v_length_nr*v_width_nr;
  7        DBMS_OUTPUT.put_line('Area:'||area_nr);
  8  end
  9  /
end
  *
ERROR at line 8:
ORA-06550: line 8, column 3:
PLS-00103: Encountered the symbol "end-of-file" when
           expecting one of the following:
; <an identifier> <a double-quoted delimited-identifier>
The symbol ";" was substituted for "end-of-file" to
           continue.
```

Unfortunately, this error message isn't completely self-explanatory. If you didn't end the last line of the block with an appropriate symbol (`;`), Oracle tries to look for more code. Because there is no more code, `"end-of-file"` is returned.

Creating Reusable PL/SQL Code

When creating computer programs, you often need to repeat the same task over and over again. To automate this repetitive kind of activity, all complete computer languages include the idea of *reusable code modules* or *subprograms*.

Traditionally, two kinds of subprograms exist:

- **Procedures** are simply wrapped code containers that usually represent some task or part of a task. They don't have to return anything to the main routine. For example, if you need to process some textual information and print results, this could be defined as an independent task and implemented as a procedure.

- **Functions** serve as user-defined operators and return a value to the calling routine. For example, they can calculate the factorial value of an integer and return the value to the main routine or calculate whole expressions (validate text, substitute special characters) and return them to the main routine.

The only difference between procedures and functions is that functions return some value to the main routine.

There is one more critical element of subprograms to keep in mind regarding procedures. You shouldn't need to create a printing procedure for all the possible strings you're planning to pass. You should write a procedure that takes a value and processes it the way you want, or you can define a *parameter* of the procedure. In functions, you use parameters in the same way.

Wrapping a task into a procedure

Listing 3-7 shows an example of a PL/SQL procedure.

Listing 3-7:   A Procedure Example

```
declare
    v_tx VARCHAR2(50):= 'I just printed my <in> line!'; →2
    procedure p_print                                    →3
        (i_string_tx  in VARCHAR2,                       →4
```

(continued)

Listing 3-7 *(continued)*

```
           i_replace_tx in VARCHAR2 := 'new')
    is
    begin
        DBMS_OUTPUT.put_line(replace(i_string_tx,
                        '<in>', i_replace_tx));
    end;                                                →10
begin
    p_print (v_tx,'first');                             →12
    p_print (v_tx,'second');                            →13
    p_print (v_tx);                                     →14
end;
```

Here are the details about this listing:

→**2–3**   All variables must be declared before declaring any subroutines, such as this procedure.

→**3–6**   The procedure declaration starts with the keyword IS and is preceded by a specification. The specification consists of two parts:

- **Header:** You need to name a procedure according to the standard rules for PL/SQL identifiers.

```
procedure name
```

- **Optional Parameter List:** The list is enclosed in parentheses. Parameters are separated by commas and each has the form:

```
variable1 [type] datatype [DEFAULT value]
```

Parameter names will be used inside the procedure, so be sure to differentiate them from variables in the routine by using a distinctive naming convention. For example, you can prefix them, as we recommend in Chapter 8.

Procedures may have three types of parameters: IN (the default type; an input value will be passed by the calling routine), OUT, and IN OUT. We discuss these parameters in more detail later in this chapter.

Procedures may have up to 256 parameters. The datatypes of these parameters are more generic than the datatypes of regular variables. You don't need to define the length of strings as in line 4 of Listing 3-7. Parameters can have default values.

→**4–10**   In general, a procedure has the same structure as an anonymous block — namely an optional declarative block, mandatory procedural block, and optional exception block. Although the procedural and exception blocks are similar, the declaration of a procedure is very different. In an anonymous block, you can simply use DECLARE and you're ready to go.

→**12–14** Always place a semicolon at the end of each procedure call.

By default, you pass parameters into the procedure in the order in which they were declared. You can use variables, expressions, or literals as parameters as long as they are of the correct datatype or can be automatically converted to the correct datatype. So, 999 and '999' could be used in a lot of cases both as a string and as text.

If you want to stop the execution of the procedure because of some additional logic, you can use the RETURN command. For example, in Listing 3-7, if you don't want to process anything in case the main routine passed NULL, you can modify the p_print procedure as shown in Listing 3-8.

Listing 3-8:   Stopping Procedure Execution

```
procedure p_print (i_string_tx  in VARCHAR2,
                   i_replace_tx in VARCHAR2 := 'new') is
begin
   if i_string_tx is null                                    →4
   then
       return;                                               →6
   end if;
   DBMS_OUTPUT.put_line(replace(i_string_tx,
                                '<in>', i_replace_tx));
end;
```

Here are the details about the listing:

→4   Checks to see whether or not the passed string is null.

→6   Immediately finishes the routine.

Because of early condition checking, you can be sure that the code won't waste any machine resources on useless activities that could have significant performance effects on your code.

Returning values with functions

Listing 3-9 is an example of a function. This function calculates the differences between total areas of circles with a number of radii.

Listing 3-9:   A Function Example

```
declare
  v_pi_nr NUMBER:=3.14;                                       →2
  function f_getDiff_Nr(i_rad1_nr NUMBER,i_rad2_nr NUMBER)
  return NUMBER is
        v_area1_nr NUMBER;
        v_area2_nr NUMBER;
        v_out_nr NUMBER;
```

(continued)

Listing 3-9 *(continued)*

```
   function f_getArea_Nr (i_rad_nr NUMBER)              →9
   return NUMBER
   is
   begin
      return v_pi_nr*(i_rad_nr**2);                     →13
   end;

 begin
      v_area1_nr := f_getArea_Nr (i_rad1_nr);           →17
      v_area2_nr := f_getArea_Nr (i_rad2_nr);
      v_out_nr   :=v_area1_nr-v_area2_nr;
      return v_out_nr;                                  →20
 end;
begin
  DBMS_OUTPUT.put_line
        ('Diff between 3 and 4: '||f_getDiff_Nr(4,3));→24
  DBMS_OUTPUT.put_line
        ('Diff between 4 and 5: '||f_getDiff_Nr(5,4));
  DBMS_OUTPUT.put_line
        ('Diff between 5 and 6: '||f_getDiff_Nr(6,5));
end;
```

Here's what you see in Listing 3-9:

→**3, 9**   There are two nested functions, one inside the other. Each sub-program (procedures too) can have its own subprograms.

Like procedures, functions have a specification block that starts with the keyword FUNCTION and may include parameters. They also include a unique specification clause, RETURN *datatype*. That datatype declares what kind of data the function will return. As with procedures, you don't need to define the parameter precision or length.

→**13, 20**   Because the primary role of the function is to return something, the body of all functions must have at least one RETURN statement (line 13 for the inner function and line 20 for the outer function). Like procedures, that clause signals the immediate end of the execution of the subprogram. Unlike procedures (where you don't need to return anything, just end the routine), functions require you to return a variable (line 20) or expression (line 13) that is compatible with the declared datatype.

You need to be careful when defining conditional logic. (You can find more information about IF and CASE statements in Chapter 4.) If the function ends without executing a RETURN command, there will be an error.

→**17**   Directly assigns the result of the function to the variable. The result of the function can be used as any variable or expression (line 24).

Parameters of subprograms

In previous examples, we show you how data can be passed to subprograms by using parameters. But there are really two kinds of parameters:

- **Formal parameters** are variables that you define in the declaration part of the subprogram (for example, variables i_rad1_nr and i_rad2_nr are formal parameters of the function F_GetDiff_NR from Listing 3-9). These are the only elements of the subprogram visible to the outside world.

- **Actual parameters** are what you pass from the main program into the subprogram. (In Listing 3-8, you passed literals 3, 4, 5, and 6 to the function F_GetDiff_NR, so these were actual parameters of that function.) Depending upon the type of formal parameter, actual parameters could be literals, variables, expressions, and so on. If you have more than one layer of subprogram, the formal parameter on a higher level could be an actual parameter of the lower one (for example, variable i_rad1_nr is an actual parameter of function f_getArea_Nr and a formal parameter of function f_getDiff_Nr).

If possible, Oracle dynamically converts datatypes of actual parameters to match formal parameters.

There are three types of formal parameters in subprograms: IN, OUT, and IN OUT, which we discuss in the following sections.

IN Parameters

IN parameters are used to pass values into the subprogram. A variable serving as a formal parameter can be referenced inside the subprogram (its scope is the same as that of any local variable), but can't be changed, as shown here:

```
function f_getArea_Nr (i_rad_nr NUMBER)
return NUMBER
is
begin
   if i_rad_nr is null              -- legal
   then
     -- i_rad_nr:=10;               -- ILLEGAL
     return null;
   end if;
   return 3.14*(i_rad_nr**2);  -- legal
end;
```

Because the formal parameter of type IN is really a constant and works in only one direction (from the main program to subprogram), the actual parameter of the subprogram could be any PL/SQL element that contains a value (literal, constant, initialized variable, expression, result of function), as shown here:

```
declare
    v_out_nr NUMBER;
    v_in1_nr  CONSTANT NUMBER :=5;
    v_in2_nr   NUMBER :=4;

    function f_getArea_Nr (i_rad_nr NUMBER)
    return NUMBER is
    begin
        return 3.14*(i_rad_nr**2);
    end;
begin
    v_out_nr:=f_getArea_Nr(10);          -- literal
    v_out_nr:=f_getArea_Nr(v_in1_nr);  -- constant
    v_out_nr:=f_getArea_Nr(v_in1_nr);  -- variable
    v_out_nr:=f_getArea_Nr(2+3);         -- expression
    v_out_nr:=f_getArea_Nr(abs(2/3));  -- another function
end;
```

OUT Parameters

An OUT parameter returns a value to the main program and allows you to return more than one variable from the subprogram. In this case, the actual parameter is always a variable. It works as a placeholder and waits for a subprogram to return something. The formal parameter is also a variable initialized with NULL that could be used in any normal operation, as shown in Listing 3-10.

Listing 3-10: An OUT Parameter Example

```
SQL> declare
  2     v_hour_nr NUMBER:=12;                              →2
  3     v_min_nr  NUMBER:=20;                              →3
  4     procedure p_split (i_date_dt DATE,
  5         o_hour_nr OUT NUMBER, o_min_nr OUT NUMBER)
  6     is
  7     begin
  8       DBMS_OUTPUT.put_line(o_hour_nr||'/'||o_min_nr);
  9       o_hour_nr:=to_NUMBER(to_char(i_date_dt,'hh24'));
 10       o_min_nr :=TO_CHAR(i_date_dt,'mi');
 11       DBMS_OUTPUT.put_line(o_hour_nr||'/'||o_min_nr);
 12     end;
 13  begin
 14     p_split(sysdate, v_hour_nr, v_min_nr);
 15     DBMS_OUTPUT.put_line (
 16         'Total minutes:'||(v_hour_nr*60+v_min_nr));
 17  end;
 18  /
/
0/33
Total minutes:33
PL/SQL procedure successfully completed.
```

Here are additional details about Listing 3-10:

→**2–3** In the example, variables v_hour_nr and v_min_nr are actual parameters. The default values will be overridden when the procedure is executed.

→**8** From the logical side, o_hour_nr and o_min_nr are formal parameters that serve as variables and are initialized with NULL values.

→**9–10** Sets values of OUT parameters.

→**11** Gets output.

Changes to actual parameters happen only when the subprogram ends successfully. This means that if there are any errors inside a subprogram, the values of actual parameters don't change. Because actual parameters change only if a subprogram successfully completes, you can always be sure that you won't change something by mistake; however, this is possible with high-level global variables on lower programmatic levels.

IN OUT parameters

You can use IN OUT parameters for both input to and output from the subprogram. If the actual parameter already had some value, the formal parameter is initialized with that value, as shown here:

```
SQL> declare
  2     v_hour_nr NUMBER:=12;
  3     v_min_nr  NUMBER:=20;
  4     procedure p_split (i_date_dt DATE,
  5        o_hour_nr IN OUT NUMBER, o_min_nr IN OUT NUMBER)
  6     is
  7     begin
  8        DBMS_OUTPUT.put_line(o_hour_nr||'/'||o_min_nr);
  9        o_hour_nr:=to_NUMBER(to_char(i_date_dt,'hh24'));
 10        o_min_nr :=to_char(i_date_dt,'mi');
 11        DBMS_OUTPUT.put_line(o_hour_nr||'/'||o_min_nr);
 12     end;
 13  begin
 14     p_split(sysdate, v_hour_nr, v_min_nr);
 15     DBMS_OUTPUT.put_line (
 16        'Total minutes:'||(v_hour_nr*60+v_min_nr));
 17  end;
 18  /
12/20
0/33
Total minutes:33
PL/SQL procedure successfully completed.
```

Although you can include `OUT` and `IN OUT` parameters in functions, this practice isn't recommended. Doing this confuses not only other developers, but also the Oracle engine itself. There are also a number of side effects that might be very difficult to trace.

You can pass parameters into subprograms in a number of ways. Previously you saw *positional notation* where you pass parameters in the same order that they appear in the specification.

But you can also have default values for parameters. In that case, the question arises: How do you avoid passing parameters that you would like to keep as default? If these parameters are the last ones, you can just avoid them, as shown here:

```
declare
    procedure p_print
    (i_str1_tx VARCHAR2 :='hello',
     i_str2_tx VARCHAR2 :='world',
     i_end_tx VARCHAR2  :='!' ) is
    begin
        DBMS_OUTPUT.put_line(i_str1_tx||','
            ||i_str2_tx||i_end_tx);
    end;
begin
    p_print('Hi','anybody','...');  -- both parameters
    p_print('Hi','people');         -- without the last
    p_print('Hi');                  -- only the first
    p_print();                      -- no parameters
    p_print;                        -- no parenthesis
end;
```

All five function calls shown in the preceding code are legal. You can cut as many parameters as you want (one, two, or even all three) from the end. If you don't want to pass any parameters to a function/procedure, you don't need to type the parentheses. The last two `p_print` lines are semantically equivalent.

If you want to pass only the last parameter, you can do this by using *named notation,* where you explicitly define which actual parameter corresponds to each formal one, as shown in Listing 3-11.

Listing 3-11: Using Named Notation

```
declare
    procedure p_print
    (i_str1_tx VARCHAR2 :='hello',
     i_str2_tx VARCHAR2 :='world',
     i_end_tx VARCHAR2  :='!' ) is
    begin
        DBMS_OUTPUT.put_line(i_str1_tx||','
            ||i_str2_tx||i_end_tx);
    end;
```

```
begin
    p_print(i_str2_tx=>'people');   -- just the second
    p_print(i_end_tx=>'...');           -- just the third
    p_print(i_end_tx=>'...',i_str2_tx=>'people');  -- mix
                                                    →13
end;
```

> **→13**   The => operator indicates explicit pairs. Because you're naming parameters explicitly, you don't need to use any specific order.

To add flexibility, you could use *mixed notation* where you start defining actual parameters in order, but after some point, use explicit names. For example, you could use mixed notation to avoid the second parameter, but keep the first and third, as shown here:

```
declare
    procedure p_print
    (i_str1_tx VARCHAR2 :='hello',
     i_str2_tx VARCHAR2 :='world',
     i_end_tx VARCHAR2  :='!' ) is
    begin
        DBMS_OUTPUT.put line(i_str1_tx||','
               ||i_str2_tx||i_end_tx);
    end;
begin
    p_print('Hi',i_end_tx=>'...'); -- mixed
    p_print(i_str1_tx=>'Hi',i_end_tx=>'...'); -- pure named
end;
```

Storing PL/SQL in the Database

Although you can store PL/SQL programs in the file system as text files and execute them as needed, in a production environment, storing your code in the database is significantly more efficient.

To manage the storage of code in the database, keep the following important points in mind.

- Know what code already exists so you don't reinvent the wheel.

- Know which database objects (tables, views, or sequences) are used in what modules.

- Know what side effects could be caused by changes in PL/SQL logic.

- Know what side effects could be caused by changes in the database environment.

The best way to manage code in the database is by using *stored procedures*. They allow you to store your code in the database in a special "parsed" mode. This way, Oracle can easily extract all references to other database objects from the code and determine what code is referencing a particular object. In addition to database management tasks, stored procedures allow you to create Application Programming Interfaces (APIs) that client applications and other modules can use.

A number of types of stored procedures exist: procedures, functions, triggers, and packages. We discuss these briefly in the upcoming sections.

Database procedures and functions

We discuss procedures and functions earlier in this chapter (see "Creating Reusable PL/SQL Code"), but only as pure PL/SQL procedures. However, they can also be saved as database elements rather than text in the file system.

To store a procedure or function, you need to connect to the database (this example uses SQL*Plus) and execute a special command, as shown here:

```
create [or replace]
procedure procedure name (parameters)
is
  ...
begin
  ...
end;

create [or replace]
function function name (parameters)
return ...
is
  ...
begin
  ...
end;
```

The CREATE OR REPLACE procedure/function command tells Oracle to create a stored procedure. If the stored procedure with the specified name already exists, you will overwrite it. The first time, you can simply use CREATE, but the second time produces an error, as shown in the last case here:

```
SQL> create or replace
  2  function f_getArea_Nr (i_rad_nr NUMBER)
  3     return NUMBER
  4  is
  5        v_pi_nr NUMBER:=3.14;
```

```
  6  begin
  7     return v_pi_nr * (i_rad_nr ** 2);
  8  end;
  9  /
Function created.
SQL> create
  2  procedure p_print
  3  (i_str1_tx VARCHAR2 :='hello',
  4   i_str2_tx VARCHAR2 :='world',
  5   i_end_tx VARCHAR2  :='!' ) is
  6     begin
  7        DBMS_OUTPUT.put_line(i_str1_tx||','
  8                       ||i_str2_tx||i_end_tx);
  9  end;
 10  /
Procedure created.
SQL> create
  2  procedure p_print
  3  (i_str1_tx VARCHAR2 :='hello',
  4  i_str2_tx VARCHAR2 :='world',
  5  i_end_tx VARCHAR2  :='!' ) is
  6  begin
  7  DBMS_OUTPUT.put_line(i_str1_tx||','
  8                     ||i_str2_tx||i_end_tx);
  9  end;
 10  /
procedure p_print
          *
ERROR at line 2:
ORA-00955: name is already used by an existing object
```

By default, procedures and functions are created in the same Oracle schema as that of the user connected to the database. This means that if you were connected as SCOTT, your new function and procedure would belong to the SCOTT schema.

After functions are created, you can use them as you use built-in PL/SQL or SQL functions or procedures, as shown here:

```
begin
    p_print('Hi','anybody','...'); -- that is enough!
end;
```

Packages

A *package* is a container for your code. It can also contain cursors, types, global variables, and other constructs that we discuss in later chapters. As we mention in the preceding section, you can write functions or procedures and store them in the database. Packages allow you to place those functions and procedures in a container that helps manage all the program units.

A large system may contain hundreds or even thousands of functions and procedures. By using packages, you can place these program units into logical groups.

For example, because you know that both the previously created procedure and function will be used in the same application module (named TEST1), you can create the following package by using the CREATE OR REPLACE PACKAGE command:

```
create or replace package pkg test1
as
    function f_getArea_Nr (i_rad_nr NUMBER) return NUMBER;
    procedure p_print (i_str1_tx VARCHAR2 :='hello',
                       i_str2_tx VARCHAR2 :='world',
                       i_end_tx VARCHAR2  :='!' );
end;
/
create or replace package body pkg_test1
as
    function f_getArea_Nr (i_rad_nr NUMBER)
       return NUMBER
    is
       v_pi_nr NUMBER:=3.14;
    begin
       return v_pi_nr * (i_rad_nr ** 2);
    end;

    procedure p_print
    (i_str1_tx VARCHAR2 :='hello',
     i_str2_tx VARCHAR2 :='world',
     i_end_tx VARCHAR2  :='!' ) is
    begin
        DBMS_OUTPUT.put_line(i_str1_tx||','
                       ||i_str2_tx||i_end_tx);
    end;
end;
/
```

Notice how you created two database objects, a package (usually called the *package specification* or just *spec* for short) and a package body. The spec contains only the function header. This is the visible part of the function and contains all the information that any code accessing the function needs to know (the function name, its parameters, and its return type). The actual function code is placed in the package body.

You can find out more about using packages and package features in Chapter 7.

Triggers

Another way to store PL/SQL code in the database is by using a *trigger*. By definition, a trigger is a procedure stored in the database and implicitly run, or *fired,* when something happens.

Depending upon the version of Oracle you're using, different events may fire a trigger, but these events are always divided into three groups: DML triggers, INSTEAD OF triggers, and system event triggers. This section includes a brief overview of each type. For more details, see Chapter 7.

DML triggers

You can place triggers on INSERT/UPDATE/DELETE operations in any table, as shown in Listing 3-12.

Listing 3-12: DML Trigger Example

```
create or replace trigger emp_biu                          →1
BEFORE INSERT OR UPDATE                                     →2
of sal, comm                                               →3
on emp                                                      →4
for each row                                                →5
declare
    v_error_tx VARCHAR2(2000);
begin
    if :new.comm + :new.sal > 10000                         →9
    then
        v_error_tx:=:old.ename||' cannot have that much!';
        raise_application_error(-20999,v_error_tx);
    end if;
end;
```

The following are some additional details about Listing 3-12:

→1   Starts with CREATE OR REPLACE TRIGGER.

→2   Defines an event or group of events with timing of BEFORE or AFTER the event with which you want to fire the trigger.

→3–4 Defines the object (line 4) to which the trigger is applied. You can optionally (line 3) narrow the conditions. In this case, the trigger fires for updates only if the value of the SAL or COMM column of the EMP table has changed.

→5   The last part of the definition before the block of code is the optional FOR EACH ROW. If you don't use this clause, the trigger is executed only once for each statement. An INSERT or UPDATE

statement might affect a number of rows. For this reason, you
need to decide whether you want your trigger to be executed once
for the whole statement (in the case of checking additional privileges about whether the user can alter a specified table) or once
for each processed row (in the case of validating the business rule
that salary plus commissions for each employee can't exceed
some limit).

→**9–11** Row-level triggers place the old and new values of all columns in
the specified table into special variables, using the format :OLD.
variable_name and :NEW.*variable_name*. Now you are checking values before they are processed in order to retrieve the old
value after these values have already been overridden. In some
cases, not all variables are available. (For DELETE triggers, all :NEW
values are NULL; for INSERT triggers, all :OLD values are NULL.)

INSTEAD OF triggers

INSTEAD OF triggers are similar to DML triggers, but they exist only on
views. Their main purpose is to perform data modifications of views that are
not otherwise updatable. This feature is extremely powerful because now
you can present data to the end users in the way they want, but under the
hood you perform any activity based on user requests.

The following view isn't updatable because of the ORDER BY clause:

```
create or replace view v_emp as
select empNo, eName
from emp
order by eName
```

However, the end user wants to have a way of changing ENAME here because
there is no access to the real table. This task can be accomplished easily by
using an INSTEAD OF trigger, as shown here:

```
create or replace trigger v_emp_iu
INSTEAD OF UPDATE
on v_emp
declare
    v_error_tx VARCHAR2(256);
begin
    if updating('EMPNO')
    then
        v_error_tx:='You cannot update the PK!';
        raise_application_error (-20999,v_error_tx);
    else
        update emp
        set eName = :new.eName
        where empNo = :old.empNo;
    end if;
end;
```

All INSTEAD OF triggers are fired for each row (there is no such thing as a statement trigger) and you cannot narrow down the event by column. Instead you can check to see what columns are updated in the body of the trigger by using the UPDATING ('*column_name*') clause.

System triggers

There are a number of events where you can set system triggers such as ON LOGON, ON LOGOFF, ON STARTUP, ON DROP, ON TRUNCATE, and so on. You can even track when any DDL command (CREATE, DROP, ALTER, and so on) was executed in the database. You may place system triggers at the database level or schema level. At the database level, triggers fire for each event for all users. At the schema level, triggers fire for each event for a specific user.

Although system triggers are very useful for database administrators and system developers, we recommend that you avoid experimenting with them until you have a good understanding of how the Oracle environment works.

Interpreting and fixing compilation errors

If you mistype something in an anonymous PL/SQL block, you receive a compilation error. Listing 3-13 shows what happens when you mistype something when creating stored procedures.

Listing 3-13: Compiling Stored Procedures

```
SQL> create or replace
  2  function f_getArea_Nr (i_rad_nr)                        →2
  3     return NUMBER
  4  is
  5     v_pi_nr NUMBER:=3.14;
  6  begin
  7     return v_pi_nr * (i_rad_nr ** 2);
  8  end;
  9  /
Warning: Function created with compilation errors.          →10
SQL> show errors                                            →11
Errors for FUNCTION F_GETAREA_NR:
LINE/COL ERROR
-------- ------------------------------------------------------------
1/31     PLS-00103: Encountered the symbol ")" when
         expecting one of the following:
         in out <an identifier> <a double-quoted
         delimited-identifier> ... LONG_ double ref char
         time timestamp interval date binary national
         character nchar
         The symbol "<an identifier>" was substituted for
          ")" to continue.
```

Here's what you see in Listing 3-13:

→2   A common problem is forgetting to define the datatype for an input parameter.

→10   Oracle creates the function with compilation errors, which means that even though the function is stored in the database, you can't use it.

→11   The SQL*Plus environment doesn't automatically show you what the problem is with your function, but you can get the error status of the last command by using the special request SHOW ERRORS. Now you can try to decipher a real problem from the Oracle compiler message.

If a stored procedure was created with compilation errors, it has an INVALID status. The way to check the status for all stored procedures is by using the Oracle data dictionary view USER_OBJECTS, as shown here:

```
SQL> select object_type, object_name, status
  2  from user_objects
  3  where object_type in ('FUNCTION','PROCEDURE',
  4  'PACKAGE','PACKAGE BODY','TRIGGER')
  5  order by object_type,object_name
  6  /

OBJECT_TYPE          OBJECT_NAME          STATUS
-------------------  -------------------  -------
FUNCTION             F_GETAREA_NR         INVALID
PROCEDURE            P_PRINT              VALID
...
```

Now you have to fix the problem and re-create the function. When you get a response "Function created", you can start using it.

There is no easy way to view the current version of the function in SQL*Plus, but you can always query the Oracle data dictionary view USER_SOURCE, as shown here:

```
SQL> select text
  2  from user_source
  3  where name = 'F_GETAREA_NR'
  4  order by line;
TEXT
----------------------------------------
function f_getArea_Nr (i_rad_nr)
   return NUMBER
is
    v_pi_nr NUMBER:=3.14;
begin
   return v_pi_nr * (i_rad_nr ** 2);
end;
7 rows selected.
```

By using the USER_SOURCE view in SQL*Plus, you can copy the result into any text editor, modify it, and paste it back with the appropriate CREATE OR REPLACE prefix. Note that when you do a search in the Oracle data dictionary, all object names are in uppercase.

The reason why you need to know what objects are valid is simple: You might need to reference them in other stored procedures. Assume that you need to create another function that uses F_getArea_Nr, as shown here:

```
SQL> create or replace
  2  function f_getDiff_Nr
  3       (i_rad1_nr NUMBER, i_rad2_nr NUMBER)
  4  return NUMBER is
  5       v_area1_nr NUMBER;
  6       v_area2_nr NUMBER;
  7       v_out_nr NUMBER;
  8  begin
  9     v_area1_nr := f_getArea_Nr (i_rad1_nr);
 10     v_area2_nr := f_getArea_Nr (i_rad2_nr);
 11     v_out_nr   :=v_area1_nr-v_area2_nr;
 12     return v_out_nr;
 13  end;
 14  /
Warning: Function created with compilation errors.
SQL> show errors
Errors for FUNCTION F_GETDIFF_NR:
LINE/COL ERROR
-------- --------------------------------------------
8/3      PL/SQL: Statement ignored
8/17     PLS-00905: object SCOTT.F_GETAREA_NR is invalid
9/3      PL/SQL: Statement ignored
9/17     PLS-00905: object SCOTT.F_GETAREA_NR is invalid
```

Oracle detects that you're trying to reference an invalid object, and Oracle marks the new one as invalid. You can use the following code to fix the first routine and check the status of the new one:

```
SQL> create or replace
  2  function f_getArea_Nr (i_rad_nr NUMBER)
  3       return NUMBER
  4  is
  5       v_pi_nr NUMBER:=3.14;
  6  begin
  7     return v_pi_nr * (i_rad_nr ** 2);
  8  end;
  9  /
Function created.
SQL> select status
  2  from user_objects
  3  where object_name = 'F_GETDIFF_NR';
STATUS
-------
INVALID
```

Oops. . . . Even though you have fixed the problem, Oracle doesn't revalidate dependent objects. The way to manually recompile objects is to use the ALTER *object type object name* COMPILE command, as shown here:

```
SQL> alter function f_getDiff_Nr compile;
Function altered.
SQL> select status
  2  from user_objects
  3  where object_name = 'F_GETDIFF_NR';
STATUS
-------
VALID
```

For more information about compilation issues, check the Oracle documentation.

Checking Out PL/SQL Extras

There are many other interesting and useful features in PL/SQL that can enhance your programming expertise. The following is by no means an exhaustive list but includes a few more concepts that you should be aware of when working with PL/SQL.

Overloading calls

You can *overload* calls, which means that you can declare local or packaged stored procedures with exactly the same name, as long as their parameters are different by at least one of these factors: the number of parameters, names of parameters, order of parameters, or the datatype family of the parameters. This section shows some examples of each type.

Number of parameters

The following example shows how you can declare a different number of parameters:

```
declare
    function f_getArea_Nr
    (i_rad_nr NUMBER)
        return NUMBER
    is
        v_pi_nr NUMBER:=3.14;
    begin
        return v_pi_nr * (i_rad_nr ** 2);
    end;
```

```
      function f_getArea_Nr
      (i_length_nr NUMBER, i_width_nr NUMBER)
        return NUMBER
      is
      begin
        return i_length_nr * i_width_nr;
      end;
begin
   DBMS_OUTPUT.put_line('Area (R=3):'||f_getArea_Nr(3));
   DBMS_OUTPUT.put_line('Area (2x3):'||f_getArea_Nr(2,3));
end;
```

In the example, you have two functions with the same name, but the first one has a single parameter and the second has double parameters. We describe how Oracle can precisely resolve which function you really need in the section "Resolving calls to subprograms."

Names of parameters

You can overload program units simply by using different names of parameters as long as you use named notation when you call the program units, as shown here:

```
declare
    function f_getArea_Nr
      (i_rad_nr NUMBER, i_prec_nr NUMBER)
        return NUMBER
    is
        v_pi_nr NUMBER:=3.14;
    begin
        return trunc(v_pi_nr * (i_rad_nr ** 2),i_prec_nr);
    end;
    function f_getArea_Nr
      (i_length_nr NUMBER, i_width_nr NUMBER)
        return NUMBER
    is
    begin
        return i_length_nr * i_width_nr;
    end;
begin
   DBMS_OUTPUT.put_line('Area (R=3): '
          ||f_getArea_Nr(i_rad_nr=>3,i_prec_nr=>1));
   DBMS_OUTPUT.put_line('Area (2x3): '
          ||f_getArea_Nr(i_length_nr=>2,i_width_nr=>3));
end;
```

Datatype family of parameters

Datatype families are groups of similar datatypes. For example, CHAR and VARCHAR2 are used to describe exactly the same kind of textual data, so they belong to the same family.

Distinguishing between datatypes from the same family is a bit difficult. That's why you can overload only between different families. The following code is an example of declaring a different datatype family:

```
declare
  function f_getArea_Nr
  (i_rad_nr NUMBER, i_prec_nr NUMBER) return NUMBER is
      v_pi_nr NUMBER:=3.14;
  begin
      return trunc(v_pi_nr * (i_rad_nr ** 2),i_prec_nr);
  end;
  function f_getArea_Nr
  (i_rad_nr NUMBER, i_ignore_yn VARCHAR2) return NUMBER is
      v_pi_nr NUMBER:=3.14;
  begin
      if i_ignore_yn='Y' and i_rad_nr < 5 then
        return 0;
      else
        return v_pi_nr * (i_rad_nr ** 2);
      end if;
  end;
begin
  DBMS_OUTPUT.put_line('Area (R=3):'
          ||f_getArea_Nr(3,1));
  DBMS_OUTPUT.put_line('Area (R=3):'
          ||f_getArea_Nr(3,'N'));
end;
```

You can find more information about datatypes in Chapter 10. For now, you simply need to understand that DATE, VARCHAR2, and NUMBER are from different families.

There are some restrictions on overloading:

✔ You can't overload standalone procedures or functions. The second definition simply overwrites the first one.

✔ You can't overload functions that differ only by the datatype of the return value. If you need to implement this requirement, use overloaded procedures with OUT parameters.

Resolving calls to subprograms

Calling subprograms is critical to understanding how overloading works. This activity happens not at the moment of compiling your code, but at *runtime*, which is the moment when the Oracle engine is prepared to execute your subprogram. There are several steps in this process:

1. The Oracle compiler searches for the declaration of the routine that matches a call starting from the current block up the chain of blocks. Next, it looks at the list of stored procedures that are either owned or can be accessed by the current user. If no corresponding names are found, an error will be returned, such as `"PLS-00201: identifier .. must be declared"`.

2. If you're using named notation to pass parameters, Oracle tries to find a subroutine with the appropriate parameter names. At this point, you can narrow the search by cutting out overloads with mismatched names. If you used positional notation, Oracle skips this step.

3. If, in the previous steps, Oracle found a number of matches (as it should if you overloaded a subroutine), it should try to find a unique match between the actual parameters you're trying to pass to the subroutine and the formal parameters of each found subprogram. You will get one of three outcomes:

   - **An exact match was found and Oracle executed the detected subroutine.**

   - **An exact match was not found, so Oracle will extend the search to all possible permutations of implicit data conversions and start from the very beginning.** (For example, `'3'` is originally a string, but also could be implicitly converted to number 3.) Here's an example:

```
declare
   function f_getArea_Nr
   (i_rad_nr NUMBER)
      return NUMBER
   is
      v_pi_nr NUMBER:=3.14;
   begin
      return v_pi_nr * (i_rad_nr ** 2);
   end;
   function f_getArea_Nr
   (i_length_nr NUMBER, i_width_nr NUMBER)
      return NUMBER
   is
   begin
      return i_length_nr * i_width_nr;
   end;
begin
   DBMS_OUTPUT.put_line('Area (R=3): '
   ||f_getArea_Nr(3));
   DBMS_OUTPUT.put_line('Area (R=3): '
   ||f_getArea_Nr('3'));
end;
```

Because there is no overload of the function f_getarea_nr with string parameter, the next valid match is found by successfully converting a string into a number. In that case, Oracle can find a unique match.

- **More than one match was found so Oracle raised a special error.** Usually this happens if you use default variables in the declaration of overloaded subroutines (a bad habit) or Oracle wasn't able to find any direct matches. Your actual parameter could be implicitly converted into a number of datatypes at the same time (for example, you could convert DATE to both NUMBER and VARCHAR2). In the following example, Oracle tried to set the default value of the second parameter in the overloaded function but was unsuccessful:

```
SQL> declare
  2      function f_getArea_Nr
  3      (i_rad_nr NUMBER)
  4          return NUMBER
  5      is
  6          v_pi_nr NUMBER:=3.14;
  7      begin
  8          return v_pi_nr * (i_rad_nr ** 2);
  9      end;
 10      function f_getArea_Nr
 11      (i_length_nr NUMBER, i_width_nr NUMBER:=3)
 12          return NUMBER
 13      is
 14      begin
 15          return i_length_nr * i_width_nr;
 16      end;
 17  begin
 18      DBMS_OUTPUT.put_line('Area (R=3):'
 19          ||f_getArea_Nr(3));
 20  end;
 21  /
    ||f_getArea_Nr(3));
     *
ERROR at line 19:
ORA-06550: line 19, column 9:
PLS-00307: too many declarations of 'F_GETAREA_NR'
   match this call
ORA-06550: line 18, column 4:
PL/SQL: Statement ignored
```

Recursion

Oracle PL/SQL supports the coding technique called *recursion,* which means that you can call the routine from itself. This technique is used a lot in mathematics.

The most famous example is calculating the factorial of any integer. Because a factorial is a product of all integer numbers between 1 and a specified integer, it is defined using the recursive formula (n!=n*(n-1)!). In PL/SQL, this is written as follows:

```
create or replace function f_factorial_nr (i_nr NUMBER)
return NUMBER
is
begin
    if i_nr = 1
    then
        return 1;
    else
        return i_nr*f_factorial_nr(i_nr-1);
    end if;
end;
```

Recursive code can be dangerous; if you forget to specify the moment when the recursion should stop, you can easily create an *infinite loop*. An infinite loop occurs when the logical flow of the program never ends. For this reason, you should always think about the *termination point* of the recursion. You should include a precise termination point (in the example, i_nr=1).

Be sure that you have a precise way of reaching the termination point by using any branch of logic. In the factorial example with the termination point defined as i_nr = 1, i_nr would eventually be equal to 1 only if a positive number were initially passed to the function. If the initial value of i_nr were 0 or a negative number, the program would continue to execute until PL/SQL runs out of memory. Stable code to handle the preceding factorial example should look like this:

```
create or replace function f_factorial_nr (i_nr NUMBER)
return NUMBER
is
begin
    if sign(i_nr)=-1 or abs(i_nr)!=i_nr
    then
        return null;
    else
        if i_nr = 1
        then
            return 1;
        else
            return i_nr*f_factorial_nr(i_nr-1);
        end if;
    end if;
end;
```

Each time you call the next level of a recursive routine, a new instance of the routine is created. This means that it consumes resources (memory, CPU, network, and so on), so be careful. Even though your program might be logically correct, you need to keep the limitations of your hardware in mind.

Compiler hints and directives

In low-level computer languages, you can pass variables from a program into a subprogram in one of two ways:

- **By value:** This means that a full copy of the variable values is made in memory. Now the subprogram has its own "clone" of the variable that can be changed without a major impact on the main one.

- **By reference:** This means that only a pointer to the location of the original variable is passed to the subprogram. The subprogram can access the value using that pointer. Because it is a real pointer and not a clone, all the changes to the variable in the subprogram without any extra activity will be visible to the main program.

Although PL/SQL doesn't provide this level of granularity, you can give the compiler a *hint* (recommendation) that reference memory management could be used in certain conditions. This is useful if you need to pass a large amount of data in a procedure that does some kind of validation of textual data, as shown here:

```
create or replace procedure p_validate
    (io_string_tx IN OUT NOCOPY VARCHAR2)
is
    v_invalid_tx VARCHAR2(8):='!@#$%^&';
begin
    io_string_tx:=replace (io_string_tx,v_invalid_tx);
    if length(io_string_tx)>4000
    then
        io_string_tx:=substr(io_string_tx,1,3997)||'...';
    end if;
end;
```

As shown in this example, it makes sense to pass the parameter with the hint NOCOPY. This hint is applicable only to OUT and IN OUT types of variables.

We discuss the restrictions and side effects involved with the NOCOPY hint in Chapters 11 and 15. For now, you need to remember that you can pass variables by reference, even in PL/SQL.

In addition to compiler hints in PL/SQL, you can also use compiler directives (orders). These orders are processed only at runtime. Usually they serve to enforce special runtime rules or modify runtime conditions. The keyword PRAGMA *command* is used for that purpose. You see how this directive is used in Chapters 5 and 12.

Built-in packages

In addition to the list of standard packages and functions you already might know from SQL, Oracle provides a group of PL/SQL packages that extend the capabilities of the language. These packages can send e-mail, schedule jobs, work with large objects, and more. We describe few of the most commonly used packages here. For more detailed information about Oracle's built-in packages, see *Professional Oracle Programming,* by Rick Greenwald, Robert Stackowiak, Gary Dodge, David Klein, Ben Shapiro, and Christopher G. Chelliah (Wiley Publishing, Inc.) and *Oracle Built-In Packages,* by Steven Feuerstein, Charles Dye, and John Beresniewicz (O'Reilly).

DBMS_OUTPUT

This package sends text messages from stored procedures, packages, and triggers to your PL/SQL environment.

The Oracle engine creates a text buffer (by default, it's 20,000 characters, but it can be modified up to 1,000,000) where your procedure could send any text by using the following commands:

- DBMS_OUTPUT.PUT (text) places your text in the buffer.
- DBMS_OUTPUT.PUT_LINE (text) places your text in the buffer and ends the line with the standard line separators.

Prior to Oracle RDBMS 10*g* Release 2, you couldn't send more than 255 characters at once by using either of these commands.

There are a number of ways to retrieve data from the buffer: either explicitly via the command DBMS_OUTPUT.GET_LINE or automatically in some environments. For example, in SQL*Plus, if you have SET SERVEROUTPUT ON, Oracle checks the buffer after the end of the execution of a standalone DML or an anonymous block.

UTL_FILE

The UTL_FILE package allows you to read and write files from the operating system. Although there are many restrictions and limitations, it can still be a very useful tool. Before using this package, check other sources of documentation for more complete information.

DBMS_UTILITY

DBMS_UTILITY is one of the oldest utility packages in the Oracle environment. It contains a number of very useful tools from retrieving the current time accurate to $\frac{1}{100}$ of a second to a full analysis of any PL/SQL name.

DBMS_JOB

The DBMS_JOB package allows you to schedule and manage any task to be executed at a precise point in time. Oracle 10*g* includes the more flexible DBMS_SCHEDULE. However, for older Oracle versions DBMS_JOB is an important package to be familiar with, especially for administrators.

DBMS_JAVA

This package includes the whole set of Application Programming Interfaces (APIs) that allow you to define the Java environment (privileges, compiler options, debugging, and so on) from within the Oracle database.

DBMS_RANDOM

Although the DBMS_RANDOM package isn't intended for cryptography, it is a reasonable random-number generator for any other use.

Chapter 4

Controlling Program Flow

● ●

● ●

*E*very programming language has the ability to use logic to control what statements execute next. PL/SQL is no different in this regard. PL/SQL supports IF. . .THEN, CASE, and LOOP statements.

If you're an experienced programmer, you can probably just skim this chapter for the PL/SQL-specific syntax. You won't be missing anything important.

If you have studied programming only in school or are a novice programmer, you should probably read this chapter carefully to make sure that you understand all these structures.

To solve a programming problem, you can write programs by using one of two types of control structures:

✔ **Conditional statements:** In this case, the execution path is divided into branches depending upon the condition. If the condition is true, one path is followed; if false, a different path is used. These true or false conditions are called *Boolean* (meaning they can only have two states, such as on/off, yes/no, true/false) conditions.

✔ **Loops (iterations):** This execution path repeats a group of statements as long as the condition is satisfied (that is, it returns a Boolean value of TRUE).

Creating Condition Statements

Condition statements are among the most common statements used in PL/SQL. This section discusses how to use conditions in IF and CASE statements.

IF...THEN statements

The most common logical element is the conditional execution of a statement or group of statements. For example, to write a function that checks whether the specified day is Sunday, you could use the code shown in Listing 4-1.

Listing 4-1:   A Simple Condition Statement

```
create or replace function f_isSunday_tx (in_dt DATE)
return VARCHAR2
is
    v_out_tx VARCHAR2(10);
begin
    if to_char(in_dt,'d')=1 then
        v_out_tx:='Y';
        DBMS_OUTPUT.put_line('IsSunday=Y');
    end if;
    return v_out_tx;
end;
```

The syntax is very simple, namely:

```
if <condition> then
    ...<<set of statements>>...
end if;
```

The syntax is very simple, namely:

```
if <condition> then
    ...<<set of statements>>...
end if;
```

Within an IF...THEN statement (as in any logical block of PL/SQL code), there must be at least one valid statement. The following code is invalid:

```
if salary < 1000 then
end if;
```

If you want to comment out everything within an IF...THEN statement, you need to add a NULL (do nothing) statement. So, the following code is perfectly fine:

```
if salary < 1000 then
  null;
  /*
  salary = 5000;
  */
end if;
```

The condition may be either a Boolean expression (as in the example) or Boolean variable. Listing 4-2 accomplishes the same thing as Listing 4-1.

Listing 4-2:   A Simple Condition Statement

```
create or replace function f_isSunday_tx (in_dt DATE)
return VARCHAR2
is
    v_out_tx VARCHAR2(10);
    v_flag_b BOOLEAN;
begin
    v_flag_b := to_char(in_dt,'d')=1;
    if v_flag_b then
        v_out_tx:='Y';
        DBMS_OUTPUT.put_line('IsSunday=Y');
    end if;
    return v_out_tx;
end;
```

You can execute as many statements as you want inside an IF...THEN statement. There are no restrictions.

IF...ELSE statements

The code in Listing 4-2 returns 'Y' for all days that are Sundays; but for all others it returns NULL. Because passing back NULL isn't very useful, you can change the code to return 'Y' if the date is Sunday and 'N' in all other cases. This is the same as saying that if the condition is true, do one thing, and otherwise do something else. PL/SQL has an ELSE construct to support this type of condition shown in Listing 4-3.

Listing 4-3:   Using ELSE in a Condition Statement

```
create or replace function f_isSunday_tx (in_dt DATE)
return VARCHAR2
is
    v_out_tx VARCHAR2(10);
    v_flag_b BOOLEAN;
begin
    if to_char(in_dt,'d')=1 then
        v_out_tx:='Y';
    else
        v_out_tx:='N';
    end if;
    return v_out_tx;
end;
```

As specified:

```
IF <condition> then
    ...<<set of statements>>...
else
    ...<<set of statements>>...
end if;
```

Now you can take this principle one step farther. In the real world, few situations have conditions with only two outcomes. Assume that you need to create a function that returns `'HOLIDAY'` for all holidays, `'SATURDAY'` or `'SUNDAY'` for weekend days (unless they are holidays), and `'WEEKDAY'` for all weekdays (unless they are holidays). For this code, you're still working with the same value, namely the date that was passed into the function. But instead of two outcomes, you now have a *logical group of alternatives* (representing the whole selection process). That group consists of a number of *branches* (each representing one condition and corresponding code to be executed if the condition is true). In this case, you can use the code shown in Listing 4-4.

Listing 4-4:   Using an ELSIF Statement

```
create or replace function f_getDateType_tx (in_dt DATE)
return VARCHAR2
is
    v_out_tx VARCHAR2(10);
begin
    if to_char(in_dt,'MMDD') in ('0101','0704') then
        v_out_tx:='HOLIDAY';
    elsif to_char(in_dt,'d') = 1 then
        v_out_tx:='SUNDAY';
    elsif to_char(in_dt,'d') = 7 then
        v_out_tx:='SATURDAY';
    else
        v_out_tx:='WEEKDAY';
    end if;
    return v_out_tx;
end;
```

Listing 4-4 includes more advanced logic in comparison to the first examples:

```
if <condition> then
    ...<<set of statements>>...
elsif <condition> then
    ...<<set of statements>>...
elsif <condition> then
    ...<<set of statements>>...
else
    ...<<set of statements>>...
end if;
```

Oracle evaluates conditions starting at the beginning until it finds a valid one. Although only one branch is executed, you can have as many ELSIF statements as you want, as long as you include all the possible conditions in the set. Your conditions don't have to be exactly the same type, as in Listing 4-4 where two ELSIF statements are checking the day of the week, while the first IF checks the date explicitly.

In the case of multiple conditions, the ELSE clause means "if all conditions above are false." That clause is optional, but it is a good idea to include it in order to explicitly list the complete logical set of conditions.

Because Oracle doesn't allow a branch without any statements inside, you could rewrite Listing 4-1 by using a NULL command as follows:

```
create or replace function f_isSunday_tx (in_dt DATE)
return VARCHAR2
is
    v_out_tx VARCHAR2(10);
begin
    if to_char(in_dt,'d')-1 then
        v_out_tx:='Y';
    else
        null;
    end if;
    return v_out_tx;
end;
```

Writing the code this way explicitly indicates that if the day of the week is not Sunday, nothing should be done. This doesn't change the logic, but it makes the code significantly more readable and maintainable.

CASE statements

Oracle 9*i* version R2 introduced another mechanism for handling conditional choices, namely, CASE statements. Using the days of the week example, assume that you need to return one of the following results: 'SATURDAY', 'SUNDAY', or 'WEEKDAY'. The IF/THEN/ELSE way to do this might be something like Listing 4-5:

Listing 4-5: A Traditional Condition Statement

```
create or replace function f_getDateType_tx (in_dt DATE)
return VARCHAR2
is
    v_out_tx VARCHAR2(10);
```

(continued)

Listing 4-5 *(continued)*

```
begin
    if to_char(in_dt,'d') = 1 then
        v_out_tx:='SUNDAY';
    elsif to_char(in_dt,'d') = 7 then
        v_out_tx:='SATURDAY';
    else
        v_out_tx:='WEEKDAY';
    end if;
    return v_out_tx;
end;
```

A CASE statement can replace code with multiple ELSIF statements, as shown in Listing 4-6.

Listing 4-6:   A Condition Using a CASE Statement

```
case <selector>
    when <valueA> then
        ...<<set of statements>>...
    when <valueB> then
        ...<<set of statements>>...
    else
        ...<<set of statements>>...
end case;
```

Using this structure, the previous example could be rewritten as shown here:

```
create or replace function f_getDateType_tx (in_dt DATE)
return VARCHAR2
is
    v_out_tx VARCHAR2(10);
begin
    case to_char(in_dt,'d')
        when 1 then
            v_out_tx:='SUNDAY';
        when 7 then
            v_out_tx:='SATURDAY';
        else
            v_out_tx:='WEEKDAY';
    end case;
    return v_out_tx;
end;
```

This code is exactly equivalent to Listing 4-1 (shown earlier), but it uses a selector instead of a set of Boolean expressions. The *selector* (the driving part of the CASE statement) is either a variable or function, the value of which should be evaluated against values from branches. (As you see in the example, branches are represented by using a single value, but not a condition.) The selector is executed only once, after which its value is compared to all the values in the WHEN clauses, one after another, until it finds a match. If any WHEN clause is executed, control passes to the next statement after the logical group.

The ELSE clause in a CASE statement works like the ELSE clause in an IF statement but with one critical difference. If you don't use ELSE in an IF statement, Oracle doesn't do anything. But in a CASE statement, if no condition is satisfied and ELSE is missing, the execution fails. (For more information about errors and exceptions, see Chapter 5.)

Oracle also introduced another kind of CASE statement (*searched CASE*) to meet the requirements of ANSI standards. Instead of testing that a variable is equal to some value, a searched CASE statement can test on any condition:

```
case
   when <condition> then
         ...<<set of statements>>...
   when <condition> then
         ...<<set of statements>>...
   else
         ...<<set of statements>>...
end case;
```

It looks and works exactly like IF/THEN/ELSE, but the code is much easier to read.

Comparing with NULL

To successfully work with conditions in PL/SQL, you need to know about comparing with NULL. As we discuss earlier, a newly initialized variable is always equal to NULL unless you assign a default value. (An empty string ' ' is also interpreted as NULL.)

The NULL value is special. It is neither equal nor unequal to any non-NULL value. It is even unequal to itself, as shown in Listing 4-7.

Listing 4-7:   Comparisons Using NULL

```
SQL> declare
  2       v_nr NUMBER;                                      →2
  3  begin
  4       if v_nr = 1 then                                  →4
```

(continued)

Listing 4-7 *(continued)*

```
 5              DBMS_OUTPUT.put_line('*Equal to 1');
 6         elsif v_nr!= 1 then
 7              DBMS_OUTPUT.put_line('*Not equal to 1');
 8         elsif v_nr = v_nr then
 9              DBMS_OUTPUT.put_line('*Equal to itself');
10         else
11              DBMS_OUTPUT.put_line('*Undefined result');
12         end if;                                          →12
13         v_nr:=v_nr+1;                                    →13
14         DBMS_OUTPUT.put_line('New value: <'||v_nr||'>');
15    end;
16    /
*Undefined result                                          →17
New value: <>                                              →18
PL/SQL procedure successfully completed.
```

Here's the scoop on Listing 4-7:

→2 An uninitialized variable always has a value of NULL.

→4–12 Checks to see if variable v_nr is equal to 1, not equal to 1, or equal to itself.

→17 Surprisingly, only the ELSE branch was executed. This means that none of these conditions returned TRUE.

→18 Prints the result of the computation in line 13, which increased the value of variable v_nr by 1. The output shows nothing.

There are a number of rules that clarify the previous results:

✔ All logical operations (including NOT) involving NULL always return NULL

✔ If, in a logical group of IF/THEN/ELSE or CASE statements, a condition of some branch returns NULL, then statements belonging to that branch are not executed. In that case, NULL is interpreted as FALSE.

✔ Most operations (built-in functions, arithmetic) with any NULL operand return NULL with the following exceptions:

• Concatenations of strings ignore NULL.

• DECODE (which we discuss later) can compare values with NULL.

• The REPLACE function can take NULL as a third parameter.

If you expect that some variable, value, or function could have a NULL value, you should check for NULL values by using the syntax:

```
variable|expression|function IS [NOT] NULL
```

This structure evaluates the value against NULL. (You can check equality by using IS NULL or inequality by using IS NOT NULL.) That clause is the only condition that always returns either TRUE or FALSE if NULL values are involved. Now you can change Listing 4-7, as shown here:

```
SQL> declare
  2      v1_nr NUMBER;
  3      v2_nr NUMBER :=1;
  4  begin
  5      if v1_nr is null then
  6          DBMS_OUTPUT.put_line('*V1 is NULL');
  7      elsif v1_nr is not null then
  8          DBMS_OUTPUT.put_line('*V1 is not NULL');
  9      else
 10          DBMS_OUTPUT.put_line('*Undefined result');
 11      end if;
 12
 13      if v2_nr is null then
 14          DBMS_OUTPUT.put_line('*V2 is NULL');
 15      elsif v2_nr is not null then
 16          DBMS_OUTPUT.put_line('*V2 is not NULL');
 17      else
 18          DBMS_OUTPUT.put_line('*Undefined result');
 19      end if;
 20  end;
 21  /
*V1 is NULL
*V2 is not NULL
PL/SQL procedure successfully completed.
```

Oracle correctly detected that v1_nr is NULL and v2_nr is not NULL. There are no more unpredictable results.

The syntax IS NULL works fine for comparisons, but you might not always have the option of checking each variable and assigning appropriate values. To make programmers' lives easier, Oracle provides a very useful function, NVL, as shown here:

```
variable:=nvl(value1,value2);
```

The idea is very simple. If the first value is not NULL, then return it; otherwise return the second value. You can use expressions, variables, functions, and literals in NVL, as long as both variables are of the same datatype, as shown in Listing 4-8.

Listing 4-8:   Using NVL

```
SQL> declare
  2      v_nr NUMBER;
  3  begin
  4      v_nr:=nvl(v_nr,0)+1;                                →4
  5      DBMS_OUTPUT.put_line('New value: <'||v_nr||'>');
```

(continued)

Listing 4-8 *(continued)*

```
  6  end;
  7  /
New value: <1>
PL/SQL procedure successfully completed.
```

→4   The NVL function checks to see whether the value of v_nr is NULL, and because it is NULL, returns 0 (the second value). Because NULL is no longer involved in the addition operation, a result is returned.

One more thing to remember about NULL is that when creating selector CASE statements, you cannot have NULL in the list of possible values. For example, although the following code is correct from the syntax point of view, it doesn't work:

```
create or replace function f_getDateType_tx (in_dt DATE)
return VARCHAR2
is
    v_out_tx VARCHAR2(10);
begin
    case TO_CHAR(in_dt,'d')
        when null then
        -- value will be null if in_dt is null
            v_out_tx:='<NULL>';
        when 1 then
            v_out_tx:='SUNDAY';
        when 7 then
            v_out_tx:='SATURDAY';
        else
            v_out_tx:='WEEKDAY';
    end case;
    return v_out_tx;
end;
```

The reason that this code fails is that the selector works by comparing one value to another. However, in PL/SQL the Boolean expression NULL=NULL evaluates to FALSE. You need to wrap the selector in an NVL expression to be sure that it could never be NULL, as shown next:

```
create or replace function f_getDateType_tx (in_dt DATE)
return VARCHAR2
is
    v_out_tx VARCHAR2(10);
begin
    case nvl(to_char(in_dt,'d') , 0)
        when 0 then
        -- value will be null if in_dt is null
            v_out_tx:='<NULL>';
        when 1 then
            v_out_tx:='SUNDAY';
        when 7 then
```

```
            v_out_tx:='SATURDAY';
        else
            v_out_tx:='WEEKDAY';
    end case;
    return v_out_tx;
end;
```

Handling conditions

You need to keep a few details in mind when working with conditions in PL/SQL.

In Oracle (as in most other programming languages), conditions can be connected by using logical operations (AND, OR, and NOT). In these cases, the default order of evaluation is standard. First any parentheses are resolved, and then operators are executed on the same level in order of precedence: NOT (highest precedence), AND, and OR (lowest precedence), as shown here:

```
SQL> declare
  2     v_day_nr NUMBER :=
  3         TO_CIIAR(TO_DATE('20060101','YYYYMMDD'),'D');
  4  begin
  5     if v_day_nr in (1,7)
  6     or (v_day_nr not in (1,7)
  7         and (v_day_nr between 0 and 6
  8              or v_day_nr between 19 and 23
  9              )
 10         )
 11     then
 12         DBMS_OUTPUT.put_line(v_day_nr||': Off-peak');
 13     else
 14         DBMS_OUTPUT.put_line(v_day_nr||': Peak');
 15     end if;
 16  end;
 17  /
1: Off-peak
PL/SQL procedure successfully completed.
```

In this example, you have four different conditions connected into one complex condition to be evaluated. January 1, 2006, was indeed a Sunday, and the condition returned Off-peak exactly as expected.

But not everything is that simple. Oracle uses a very interesting mechanism called *short-circuit evaluation* to work with conditional structures. PL/SQL stops evaluating the expression as soon as the result can be determined. If you have several conditions connected with OR and you already know that one of them is TRUE, why do you need to check any others? To validate this concept, the previous example has been changed, as shown here:

```
SQL> declare
  2      v_day_nr NUMBER :=
  3          TO_CHAR(TO_DATE('20060101','YYYYMMDD'),'D');
  4
  5      function f_DayNr return NUMBER is
  6      begin
  7          DBMS_OUTPUT.put_line('Called function');
  8          return v_day_nr;
  9      end;
 10  begin
 11      if f_DayNr in (1,7)
 12      or (f_DayNr not in (1,7)
 13          and (f_DayNr between 0 and 6
 14              or f_DayNr between 19 and 23
 15              )
 16          )
 17      then
 18          DBMS_OUTPUT.put_line(v_day_nr ||
                  ': Off-peak');
 19      else
 20          DBMS_OUTPUT.put_line(v_day_nr || ': Peak');
 21      end if;
 22  end;
 23  /
Called function
1: Off-peak
PL/SQL procedure successfully completed.
```

Even though the function f_dayNr appears four times, it is executed only once. The very first condition is TRUE, so Oracle doesn't fire anything else. This feature can be critical for tuning because by simply using the appropriate ordering of conditions, you can avoid executing unnecessary code.

Oracle also has one function, called DECODE, that's available only in SQL, where you can also achieve the benefits of short-circuit evaluation, as shown here:

```
select DECODE(expression,
              Value1, result1,
              Value2, result2
                 ...
              [ResultElse]) from dual
```

In this case, you're specifying the expression and evaluating it against a number of values. If it is equal, it returns the result associated with the value. Also, you could set the result to be returned if all other conditions failed.

Many programmers are unaware of this functionality in PL/SQL, so they invent their own DECODE functions like this:

```
create or replace function f_decode
                (in_value VARCHAR2,
                 in_compare VARCHAR2,
                 in_success_value VARCHAR2,
                 in_fail_value VARCHAR2) return VARCHAR2
           is
begin
  if in_value=in_compare then
    return in_success_value;
  else
    return in_fail_value;
  end if;
end;
```

Although this code will functionally behave the same way as using DECODE, hand-written decode short-circuit evaluations don't work. As a result, if you call that function, all expressions to calculate values and results will be fired at the very beginning (before passing values into the function).

Looping the Loop

A very common logical structure in PL/SQL code is *loops,* which allow for repeated execution of a set of commands. There are three types of iterations:

- ✔ **Simple loops** include a starting loop, execute a set of commands, and then check the condition. If the condition is satisfied, the loop is exited and the program returns to the beginning of the loop. You can nest simple loops, so that several loops occur within a loop.
- ✔ **WHILE loops** check the condition and execute a set of commands. This process is repeated until the loop is exited.
- ✔ **FOR loops** have a fixed and predefined number of iterations to execute a set of commands N times.

This section will discuss each of these loop types with some examples.

Simple loops

The syntax of a typical simple loop looks like the following:

```
loop
    ...<<set of statements>>...
    exit when <<conditionA>>;
    ...<<set of statements>>...
end loop;
```

or

```
loop
    ...<<set of statements>>...
    if <<conditionB>> then
        ...<<set of statements>>...
        exit;
    end if;
    ...<<set of statements>>...
end loop;
```

The set of commands enclosed in the LOOP/END LOOP is repeated until the EXIT command is fired. The preceding example shows both ways for exiting a loop: EXIT WHEN and EXIT.

When you use the EXIT command, as soon as Oracle encounters it, the loop is immediately terminated. Therefore, you will usually place the EXIT command inside an IF...THEN statement, which we introduce earlier in this chapter. As a result, when the condition in the IF statement is true, the EXIT command will be fired. It is recommended that you use the EXIT command when you want to execute some other code within the IF...THEN statement just before the loop ends.

The EXIT WHEN statement is a bit more elegant. You place the condition right alongside the EXIT command. You use EXIT WHEN if the only thing you want to do when the condition is true is to exit the loop.

Always check your code for valid exits from the loop; otherwise, you might very easily create an endless loop.

Using the previous example of days of the week, if you want to show all the Saturdays in January, the logical steps would be

1. Find the first Saturday in January.

2. Print the date.

3. Add 7 to the detected date.

4. If the new date is not in January, exit; otherwise, repeat Steps 2 and 3.

Programmatically, this would look like the following:

```
declare
    v_start_dt date:=to_date('01-01-2006','MM-DD-YYYY');
    v_end_dt   date:=to_date('02-01-2006','MON-DD-YYYY');
begin
    v_start_dt:=v_start_dt+
            (7-to_number(TO_CHAR(v_start_dt,'d')));
```

```
-- detect first Saturday
loop
    DBMS_OUTPUT.put_line
        (to_char(v_start_dt,'MM-DD-YYYY'));
    v_start_dt:=v_start_dt+7;
    exit when v_start_dt >=v_end_dt;
end loop;
end;
```

Nested loops

You can also create multiple loops nested within each other. These are called *nested loops*. Nested loops occur frequently when you're dealing with hierarchical data. Some examples of how to loop through records in the database are included in Chapter 6. Assume that you want to print out the following list of numbers (each on its own line):

0 0 0 0 5 5 5 5 10 10 10 10 15 15 15 15 20 20 20 20 25 25 25 25

In this case, you want to step from 0 to 25 by fives and print each number four times. Specifying the task this way, you will need two loops (see Listing 4-9) one inside of another. This example illustrates a few different kinds of loops (with both EXIT and EXIT WHEN).

Listing 4-9:   Loop inside of a Loop

```
declare
    v_ind_nr        NUMBER;
    v_current_nr NUMBER;
begin
    v_current_nr:=0; -- should not be null!
    loop                                                        →6
        v_ind_nr:=0; -- reset each time
        loop                                                    →8
            v_ind_nr:=v_ind_nr+1;
            DBMS_OUTPUT.put_line(v_current_nr);
            exit when v_ind_nr=4;
        end loop;                                               →12
        v_current_nr:=v_current_nr+5;
        exit when v_current_nr=25;
    end loop;                                                   →15
end;
```

→8–12 The exit from the internal loop does not break the external one (lines 6–15).

There is a way to exit an outer loop from an EXIT statement in an inner loop. To do this, you must name the loop by using a label. You indicate labels by enclosing them in << and >> as in <<myLabel>>. For this example, assume that you have a parameter to indicate how many records should be printed and to stop when a certain number is reached. You could use Listing 4-10 to accomplish this.

Listing 4-10:   Exiting from Nested Loops

```
declare
    v_ind_nr        NUMBER;
    v_current_nr NUMBER;
    v_max_printed_nr NUMBER :=10;
    v_printed_nr NUMBER:=0;
begin
    v_current_nr:=0; -- should not be null!
    <<Main>>
    loop
        v_ind_nr:=0; -- reset each time
        <<Inner>>
        loop
            v_ind_nr:=v_ind_nr+1;
            DBMS_OUTPUT.put_line(v_current_nr);
            v_printed_nr:=v_printed_nr+1;
            exit Main when v_printed_nr = v_max_printed_nr;
            exit when v_ind_nr=4;
        end loop Inner;
        v_current_nr:=v_current_nr+5;
        exit when v_current_nr=25;
    end loop Main;
end;
```

Both loops are marked with the labels <<Main>> and <<Inner>>. These lines must immediately precede their respective loops. Using this strategy, you can explicitly reference the external loop via its label to indicate which loop to exit from because of the condition. You need to place the labels only where appropriate, and the rest of the commands will work normally.

WHILE loop

If you can write your loop with EXIT WHEN as the first statement after the LOOP command, you can use a WHILE loop. A WHILE loop is exactly equivalent to a regular loop with an EXIT WHEN as the first statement. There is absolutely no difference. Keep in mind that the condition is checked before the code in the loop is executed. So, if the condition is false, the code in the loop will never be executed. You use a WHILE loop because the syntax makes your code a little easier to read than with a normal loop. The syntax is shown in Listing 4-11.

Listing 4-11:   WHILE Loop

```
while <<condition>>
loop
   ...<<set of statements>>...
end loop;
```

For example, Listing 4-11 could be rewritten as shown in Listing 4-12.

Listing 4-12:   Nested WHILE Loop

```
declare
    v_ind_nr        NUMBER;
    v_current_nr NUMBER;
begin
    v_current_nr:=0; -- should not be null!
    while v_current_nr<=25
    loop
        v_ind_nr:=0; -- reset each time
        while v_ind_nr<4
        loop
            v_ind_nr:=v_ind_nr+1;
            DBMS_OUTPUT.put_line(v_current_nr);
        end loop;
        v_current_nr:=v_current_nr+5;
    end loop;
end;
```

If you compare Listings 4-9 and 4-12, most people would agree that Listing 4-12 is a little easier to read. You should also notice that the conditions to terminate the loops are a bit different. In Listing 4-9, the loops terminated at the end of the LOOP...END statement. In Listing 4-12, you had to change the equalities (=4, =25) to inequalities (<4, <=25).

Getting the loop ending condition just right so that it doesn't execute one time too many or too few can be tricky. You need to very carefully think through what will happen with your code.

It is possible to add an emergency EXIT inside the loop. If an EXIT statement is encountered inside a WHILE loop, the loop will terminate independent of the WHILE condition.

Be very careful about using an EXIT statement inside a WHILE loop. By using a WHILE loop, the loop will only terminate when the WHILE condition is false. If you also allow the loop to terminate with a conditionally executed EXIT statement, it can make your code very hard to modify and debug.

FOR loop

In many cases, you will know exactly how many times to repeat a set of commands. Oracle handles these situations by using a FOR loop. The syntax for a FOR loop is as follows:

```
for <counter> in <lower_bound>..<higher_bound>
loop
    ...<<set of statements>>...
end loop;
```

This code will execute these steps:

1. In the background Oracle defines the counter as a PLS_INTEGER and assigns it the lower bound.

2. If the counter does not exceed the higher bound, a set of statements is executed.

3. The counter is incremented by 1 (the default step of the regular loop).

4. If the counter does not exceed the higher bound, the set of statements is executed.

In Listing 4-11 (shown earlier), the inner loop is always executed four times. This example is also appropriate to demonstrate a FOR loop:

```
declare
    v_current_nr NUMBER;
begin
    v_current_nr:=0; -- should not be null!
    loop
        for inner_c in 1..4
        loop
            DBMS_OUTPUT.put_line(v_current_nr);
        end loop;
        v_current_nr:=v_current_nr+5;
        exit when v_current_nr>25;
    end loop;
end;
```

The main loop is a bit difficult to replace with a FOR loop, because you would need to go from 0 to 25 with a step increment of 5. But in PL/SQL, there is no way to increment the loop counter by anything other than 1. (You can also decrement the loop counter by one each time. Many languages allow you to specify the step increment in a loop. But you can still use a FOR loop with our example. You just have to manipulate the loop counter (and assign it to a new variable) inside the loop as shown here:

```
declare
    v_main_nr NUMBER;
begin
    for main_c in 0..5
    loop
        v_main_nr := main_c * 5;                    →6

        for inner_c in 1..4
        loop
            DBMS_OUTPUT.put_line(v_main_nr);
        end loop;
    end loop;
end;
```

▌ →6   Adjusts main_c so it will have the correct values.

The counter variables' visibility is what you would expect. The counter from the main loop is visible in the internal loop, but the counter from the internal loop isn't visible in the external loop.

There is no way to modify the loop counter. It is read-only. If you need to add some conditional logic and move the counter one way or another, you won't be able to use a FOR loop.

There is one other option with a FOR loop. You can reverse directions and go from the upper bound to the lower one, as shown here:

```
SQL> begin
  2      for main_c in reverse 1..3
  3      loop
  4          DBMS_OUTPUT.put_line(main_c);
  5      end loop;
  6  end;
  7  /
3
2
1
PL/SQL procedure successfully completed.
SQL>
```

The upper or lower bounds of the FOR loop can be defined as variables or functions. The following code will first round off the values into integers at runtime:

```
SQL> declare
  2      V_lower_nr NUMBER:=2/3;
  3  begin
  4      for main_c in reverse v_lower_nr..10/3
  5      loop
  6          DBMS_OUTPUT.put_line(main_c);
  7      end loop;
  8  end;
  9  /
3
2
1
PL/SQL procedure successfully completed.
```

In this case, the cursor was executed successfully three times because ⅔ was rounded to 1 and ¹⁰⁄₃ was rounded to 3. Therefore the last example works exactly the same way as the previous one, but the second one used both a variable and calculated value that were converted to PLS_INTEGER.

It is also possible to use EXIT in the FOR loop. However, not only is it poor programming practice, it will also make your code run slower. Oracle's compiler runs FOR loops very quickly. When you have an EXIT statement in your FOR loop, the compiler creates a routine that runs slower.

Chapter 5

Handling Exceptions

*A*lmost any program has uncommon situations that need to be handled. These situations are sometimes caused by data entry problems. Imagine that a user enters several pieces of information into an online-book-order application. Maybe one or more pieces of information are missing or incorrectly entered. For example, in the case where the person forgot to indicate the shipping method on their order, the application responds with a user-friendly error message, such as `You must enter a shipping method for your order`. This is an example of user-defined exception handling in action.

You also want to have a nice way to handle programming errors and exceptions so that users don't see incomprehensible messages such as `Unhandled Program Exception — ORA 600`. If you have ever encountered a message such as `An unexpected program error has occurred. Please contact the help desk and report this problem`, you have experience with a program where the designers tried to come up with a general way to handle unexpected situations.

In PL/SQL, you can handle these problems by using a special construct called an *exception*. The command `RAISE` is used to indicate that an exception has occurred, as in "the program raised an exception." Many exceptions are automatically raised by PL/SQL when improper situations occur. For example, an exception is raised if you try to divide a number by zero.

In addition to the automatic exceptions, you can define your own exceptions to handle any unusual or improper situations. For example, having a start date of a project that takes place after the end date makes no sense. If this situation arises, you can raise your own exceptions by using the `RAISE` command.

When an exception is raised in a PL/SQL program, it means that something unusual has occurred and the normal processing of the program unit should stop. This chapter explains how to define and work with exceptions in PL/SQL.

Understanding Exception Basics

PL/SQL has a specific set of commands to support exceptions. First, it is important to understand the different parts of the exception.

1. **Declare the exception.**

   By declaring the exception, you're creating a new type of exception. Many Oracle predefined exceptions also exist (for example, ZERO_DIVIDE), and you don't need to explicitly declare them.

2. **Raise an exception.**

   After the exception is declared, it can be raised within the program. For user-defined exceptions, you raise the exception in response to something that happens in your program (for example, if the application detects that no shipping method was specified on a book order). For predefined exceptions, the exceptions are automatically raised when the problem occurs. For example, if you try to divide by zero, the ZERO_DIVIDE exception is automatically raised.

3. **Handle the exception.**

   After an exception has occurred, the program stops normal execution and control is transferred to a special part of the program unit called the *exception handler.*

In addition to the parts of an exception, you also need to understand that an exception has four attributes:

- ✔ **Name** provides a short description of the problem.
- ✔ **Type** identifies the area of the error. (It could be PL/SQL language, Oracle kernel, and so on.)
- ✔ **Exception Code** gives a numeric representation of the exception.
- ✔ **Error message** provides additional information about the exception.

For example, the predefined divide-by-zero exception has the following values for the attributes:

- ✔ Name = ZERO_DIVIDE
- ✔ Type = ORA (from the Oracle engine)
- ✔ Exception Code = -01476
- ✔ Error message = divisor is equal to zero

We cover these parts and attributes in more detail later in this chapter.

Adding Exception Handlers to Your Code

As an example of an exception handler, assume that you're using a program that divides distance by time to get speed. If someone enters 0 for time, dividing distance by time raises the ZERO_DIVIDE exception.

First look at the program without an exception handler (see Listing 5-1) to see how the program behaves.

Listing 5-1:   Code with No Exception Handler

```
SQL> create or replace function f_get_speed_nr
  2  (i_distance_nr NUMBER, i_timeSec_nr NUMBER)
  3  return NUMBER
  4  is
  5     v_out_nr NUMBER;
  6  begin
  7     v_out_nr:= i_distance_nr/i_timeSec_nr;        →7
  8     return v_out_nr;
  9  end;
 10  /
Function created.
SQL> declare
  2       v_speed_nr NUMBER;
  3  begin
  4       v_speed_nr:=f_get_speed_nr(10,0);           →15
  5  end;
  6  /
declare                                              →18
*
ERROR at line 1:
ORA-01476: divisor is equal to zero
ORA-06512: at "SCOTT.F_GET_SPEED_NR", line 7
ORA-06512: at line 4
```

Here are the details on Listing 5-1:

→7 This statement raises the ZERO_DIVIDE exception if i_timeSec_nr = 0 and i_distance_nr is not null.

→15 This statement calls the function f_get_speed_nr with 0 as the second parameter.

→18 The program works fine as long as no one enters 0 for Time. When that happens, Oracle complains about an "unhandled exception." Exception information starts as a result of division by zero in the code. It includes the exception code, error message, and the location of the error.

Unhandled exceptions should never happen in a program. They generally indicate that, as a programmer, you really haven't thought through all the things that could happen in your program. This problem can be solved by using conditional logic like that shown in Listing 5-2.

Listing 5-2: Code with Conditional Control to Avoid an Exception

```
create or replace function f_get_speed_nr
  (i_distance_nr NUMBER, i_timeSec_nr NUMBER)
return NUMBER
is
  v_out_nr number:=0;
begin
  if i_timeSec_nr!=0 then                              →7
    v_out_nr:= i_distance_nr/ i_timeSec_nr;
  end if;
  return v_out_nr;
end;
```

→7   This line tells the program not to perform the speed calculation if it would mean dividing by zero.

This code will avoid the unhandled exception. However, from looking at the code, it isn't clear that you're trying to avoid a ZERO_DIVIDE exception. Of course, if your code were well commented, a comment might explain what you are doing. However, the code can be even clearer if the exception logic is handled in the block's own exception handler. As shown in Listing 5-3, when the exception is raised, that information is entered into the LogError table.

Listing 5-3: Code with Explicit Handler for Predefined Exception

```
SQL> create table t_logError(                          →1
  2      error_tx VARCHAR2(4000),
  3      date_dt date default sysdate,
  4      loggedby_tx VARCHAR2(32) default user)
  5  /
Table created.
SQL> create or replace function f_get_speed_nr
  2    (i_Distance_nr NUMBER, i_timeSec_nr NUMBER)
  3  return NUMBER
  4  is
  5    v_out_nr NUMBER;
  6  begin
  7    v_out_nr:= i_distance_nr/i_timeSec_nr;           →13
  8    return v_out_nr;                                 →14
  9  exception                                          →15
 10    WHEN ZERO_DIVIDE THEN                            →16
 11      insert into t_logError (error_t)               →17
 12      values ('Divide by zero in the
          F_GET_SPEED_NR');
```

```
13          return null;                                    →19
14   end;
15   /
Function created.
SQL>
```

Here is some additional information about Listing 5-3:

→**1** You need a special table to store your logging information.

→**13** If a zero time and a distance that isn't null are encountered, this line will throw an exception.

→**14** If an exception is raised in line 7, this line won't execute.

→**15** Exception indicates the start of the exception handler.

→**16** For each exception to be handled, use a line like this. The when zero_divide then line means that when a ZERO_DIVIDE exception is raised, the program should execute the code following it until the next WHEN clause or the END of the block, which in this case is in lines 11–13.

→**17** When a ZERO_DIVIDE exception is raised, put an entry into the t_logError table.

→**19** The function returns a value of NULL. Remember that a function must always return a value (or Oracle will raise its own exception).

Table 5-1 compares a few different execution scenarios based on the time and distance example in Listing 5-3 to show how different scenarios are handled.

Table 5-1	Comparing Output Scenarios for Listing 5-3	
Scenario	*What Happens*	*Result*
Case A: distance = 10, time = 2	The divisor is not 0 and nothing unpredictable happened. The function will return the expected result.	The function returns 5.
Case B: distance = 10, time = 0	Case B attempts to divide by 0. The database raised an exception, but successfully intercepted it in the exception handler, because that exception was specifically expected. As a result, the program logged a failure by inserting a record into the log.	The function's exception handler detects the ZERO_ DIVIDE exception, logs the error, and returns NULL to the calling routine.

(continued)

Table 5-1 *(continued)*

Scenario	What Happens	Result
Case C: distance = 10, time = 0, but there was not enough space on the hard drive to log the exception	Even though the exception was handled, the insert failed, because of inadequate hard drive space.	An additional exception is raised because of the insert failure and the function terminates without returning any value. Because you did not handle that new exception, it will be raised to the calling program.

Understanding Different Exception Types

Earlier in this chapter, we mention that exceptions are identified by type, code, name, and error message. This section explains those types in more detail so you can quickly identify the kind of exception being raised.

Exception types can be identified by the error code prefixes, as outlined in Table 5-2.

Table 5-2	**Identifying Exception Types**
Error Code Prefix	*Indicates This Exception Type of Error*
ORA	Core RDBMS errors
PLS	PL/SQL errors
FRM	Oracle Forms errors (If you're using an Oracle product, the product might use its own exception type.)
REP	Oracle Reports errors

You will rarely see exception types other than ORA. Situations governing other types of exceptions are beyond the scope of this book.

Exception codes are negative and are always displayed with five digits. The code, in conjunction with the exception type, uniquely defines the exception. The Oracle function SQLCODE returns the type and code of the most recently raised exception. For example, SQLCODE returns ORA-01476 when the ZERO_DIVIDE exception is raised.

Exception names are usually associated with exceptions that you create yourself. Only a small number of predefined exceptions (about 20) are named. If the exception is named, you can use its name in the exception handler. For example in Listing 5-3, line 16 referred to the divide-by-zero exception by including WHEN ZERO_DIVIDE THEN in the code. We discuss how to handle unnamed predefined exceptions in the next section.

The *exception message* is a text string that describes the exception in more-or-less user-friendly terms. Many Oracle exceptions (and most of the ones you're likely to encounter) have some exception message associated with them. The function SQLERRM returns the text of the error message for the most recently raised exception.

The easiest way to get more information about an Oracle exception is to search for it on the Web. For example if you google **ORA-01476**, you'll find dozens of sites that describe the divide-by-zero error, how to fix it, odd things that might have caused it, and more information than you ever wanted to know about it.

Predefined Exceptions in PL/SQL Code

Oracle includes a large set of predefined exceptions. A few of the most common predefined exceptions are named (like ZERO_DIVIDE).

All named exceptions have codes, but in the exception-handling block, you will usually refer to them by using their more user-friendly names. Different versions of the Oracle RDBMS might include different sets of these named exceptions. A few of the most important ones are mentioned here:

✔ INVALID_NUMBER (ORA-01722): Conversion of string to number failed.

✔ VALUE_ERROR (ORA-06502): Generic error indicating that there is an inconsistency between the variable and its value (for example, you are trying to assign a string with 15 characters into a variable with a maximum length of 10).

✔ DUP_VAL_ON_INDEX (ORA-00001): The program is attempting to store duplicate values in a database column that is constrained by a unique index.

Only some predefined exceptions have names. Even if the exception is unnamed, you still need to be able to handle the exception when it is raised. For this purpose, you will use the SQLCODE function we discuss in Listing 5-4.

One situation where you need to refer to an unnamed exception is to detect deadlocks. Deadlocks occur when two sessions are both waiting for the other to complete. It is possible for any DML statement that changes data to cause a deadlock. (For further discussion of deadlocks, see Chapter 12.) Oracle is able to detect deadlocks and, when it does, it raises the associated exception. In this example, the exception is simply logged if a deadlock is detected. Any other unanticipated errors are logged and re-raised, as shown in Listing 5-4.

Listing 5-4:   Handling an Unnamed Exception

```
procedure p_updateLoc
  (i_deptno_nr NUMBER, i_new_loc_tx VARCHAR2)
is
    v_error_nr NUMBER;
    v_error_tx VARCHAR2(4000);
begin
  update dept                                              →7
  set loc=i_new_loc_tx
  where deptno=i_deptno_nr;
exception
  when others then                                        →11
        v_error_nr :=sqlcode;                             →12
        v_error_tx := sqlerrm;                            →13
        insert into t_LogError(error_tx)                  →14
        values(i_deptno_nr||'-'||
              v_error_nr||':'|| v_error_tx );
  if sqlcode=-60 then-- deadlock error is ORA-00060       →17
     null;
  else
     raise;                                               →20
  end if;
end;
```

The following are additional explanations for Listing 5-4:

→7   The UPDATE statement might cause a deadlock. If it occurs, the deadlock exception is raised.

→11   You cannot directly handle an unnamed exception, so instead use WHEN OTHERS to handle the error.

→12–14 You cannot use SQLCODE and SQLERROR inside an SQL statement. First return the functions into temporary variables that pass the information to the UPDATE statement.

→17   if sqlcode=-60 detects the deadlock.

→20   For all errors other than deadlock, it is a good idea to re-raise the error so it isn't hidden.

The WHEN OTHERS THEN NULL and WHEN OTHERS THEN RETURN NULL commands can handle many situations, but be very careful when using them because they might mask a serious problem. There might be cases when you need to debug multi-level "spaghetti code" where other real activity is hidden under these generic exception handlers. It's tempting to use WHEN OTHERS NULL when you're first developing your code, but be sure to go back and write code to actually handle the exception. Most experienced PL/SQL developers consider use of WHEN OTHERS THEN NULL as a very poor programming practice.

Oracle lets you assign a name to a predefined exception by using a PRAGMA command (see Chapter 12 for a discussion of PRAGMAs). An exception handler that checks for the e_deadlock_detected exception is easier to understand and maintain than code that is checking for SQLCODE 60. A sample is shown in Listing 5-5.

Listing 5-5:   Assigning a Name to Predefined Exception Code

```
procedure p_updateLoc
(i_deptno_nr NUMBER, i_new_loc_tx VARCHAR2)
is
  v_error_nr NUMBER;
  e_deadlock_detected exception;                           →5
  pragma exception_init(e_deadlock_detected,-60);          →6
begin
 update dept
 set loc=i_new_loc_tx
  where deptno=i_deptno_nr;
exception
  when e_deadlock_detected then                            →12
    v_error_nr:=sqlcode;
    insert into t_LogError (error_tx)
        values(i_deptno_nr||':'||v_error_nr);              →15
    raise;                                                 →16
end;
```

Here's a little more detail about some of the lines in the preceding code block:

→**5–6**   This line created a custom exception e_deadlock_detected and associated it with existing exception code -60.

→**12**   The exception is handled, using its name.

→**15**   When the exception is logged, the number -60 is passed.

→**16**   Re-raise the same exception, because you need only to log the event without preventing the exception to be raised.

Adding User-Defined Exceptions

In addition to predefined exceptions, which were discussed in the preceding section, you can add *user-defined* exceptions. The exception usually corresponds to the breaking of some rule and works as a red flag to notify you about the infraction. With user-defined exceptions, you can use PL/SQL to clearly identify exception conditions in your business logic.

Before raising a user-defined exception, you must first declare the exception in the declaration section of the program. The syntax is

```
<exception_name> exception;
```

When you raise the exception, you do it by using the RAISE command. The syntax is:

```
raise <exception_name>;
```

Handle your exception just as if it were a named predefined exception. The syntax is:

```
when <exception_name> then
```

For example, a business might have a rule that "A salary increase may not exceed 300 percent." If someone tries to implement an increase larger than 300 percent, the whole application module should be halted for a security investigation. Of course, you could use IF...THEN logic to support this requirement, but the code is clearer when using an exception handler, as shown in Listing 5-6.

Listing 5-6:   A User-Defined Exception

```
function f_ValidateSalary
  (i_empNo_nr NUMBER, i_new_Sal_nr NUMBER)
  return VARCHAR2
is
  v_current_Sal_nr NUMBER;
  e_increaseTooLarge exception;                          →6
begin
  select sal into v_current_Sal_nr
  from emp
  where empNo=i_empNo_nr;
  if (i_newSal_nr/v_current_Sal_nr)*100>300
  then
    raise e_increaseTooLarge;                            →13
end if;

--- maybe lots of other tests here
```

```
      return 'Y';                                      →18
   exception
      when e_increaseTooLarge then                     →20
         insert into t_LogError ...
         return 'N';                                   →22
   end;
```

The following list explains some of the lines in Listing 5-6:

→**5**   The exception declaration.

→**13**   The salary is too large, so the exception is raised. If the exception is raised, the program jumps to the exception handler.

→**18**   If no exceptions are raised, the function returns `'Y'` (salary modification is valid).

→**20**   Detects the `e_increaseTooLarge` exception after the exception has been raised.

→**22**   Because an exception was raised, the function returns `'N'` (salary modification is invalid).

Assigning a code to a user-defined exception

User-defined exceptions don't have associated codes. (See "Understanding Different Exception Types" earlier in this chapter for an introduction to codes.) Therefore SQLCODE will return NULL if a user-defined exception is raised. However, there is a way to associate user-defined exceptions with a specific code number, using a `pragma exception_init` statement.

For consistency, and to keep your exceptions organized, it is helpful to assign a code to each user-defined exception. You can insert this code into your log table, as shown in Listing 5-7.

Listing 5-7:   **Code Assigned to a User-Defined Exception**

```
procedure p_validateSalary
   (i_empNo_nr NUMBER, i_new_sal_nr NUMBER)
is
   v_current_sal NUMBER;
   v_error_nr NUMBER;

   e_increaseTooLarge exception;
   pragma exception_init(e_increaseTooLarge,-20999);    →6
begin
...
```

(continued)

Listing 5-7 *(continued)*

```
exception
  when increase_too_much then
    v_error_nr := sqlcode;
    insert into t_LogError (error_tx)
        values(i_empNo_nr||':'||v_error_nr);
    raise;
end;
```

→6   This line associates the previously defined exception with a number: -20999.

The EXCEPTION_INIT statement is placed in the declaration section of the block. It is a good practice to always place the EXCEPTION_INIT right next to the exception declaration.

Also, when assigning a code to a user-defined exception, choose a code between –20999 and –20000 only. Codes in this range distinguish user-defined exceptions from predefined exceptions. Oracle has promised that it will *never* use the numbers between –20999 and –20000 for any Oracle exceptions, so you can safely use them for your applications. Although you could conceivably use any other number, we don't recommend doing so, just in case Oracle decides to use that number in the future.

You can still run into trouble by using these numbers for your exceptions if you're writing an extension to packaged software. The packaged software vendor might have already used some of those exceptions. You have to be very careful if you're using packaged software to avoid using the same numbers that the software uses.

If a user-defined exception is raised and not handled, Oracle will return the error code you have assigned. If no code number was assigned to the user-defined exception and that exception was not handled, Oracle uses the exception ORA-06510 (PL/SQL: unhandled user-defined exception) to notify the program about the error.

Including error messages in user-defined exceptions

As mentioned earlier in this chapter, Oracle usually not only provides an error code or name, but also an explanation of what happened. That explanation is called an *error message*.

In your user-defined exceptions, you can specify error messages. The only limitation is that you can only specify error messages for exceptions that have already been assigned a code. Using the example of not allowing any salary increase of over 300 percent, you want to add a user-friendly error message to the user-defined exception, as shown in Listing 5-8.

Listing 5-8:   Assigning an Error Message for a User-Defined Exception

```
procedure p_validateSalary
(i_empNo_nr NUMBER, i_new_sal_tx NUMBER)
is
   v_current_sal NUMBER;
   e_increaseTooLarge EXCEPTION;                            →5
   pragma exception_init (e_increaseTooLarge,-20999)        →6
begin
   select salary into v_current_sal
   from emp
   where empNo=i_empNo_nr;
   if (i_newsal_nr/v_current_sal)*100>300
   then
      raise_application_error (-20999, 'Cannot triple →14
        salary for employee #'||i_empNo);
   end if;
   <....some validation...>
exception
   when e_increaseTooLarge then
     insert into t_logError ...
     raise;
end;
```

Here are explanations for the called-out lines in the code:

→5   The exception is declared.

→6   The exception is associated with a numbered code.

→14   The built-in procedure RAISE_APPLICATION_ERROR is used instead of RAISE, because it allows passing not just the exception itself, but the whole error message. The syntax of that procedure is very simple, as shown here:

```
raise_application_error
    (<exception code>,<error message>);
```

This procedure can be extremely helpful, especially for user-defined exceptions because now you can explain the problem in greater detail.

The error message must be specified each time the exception is raised. It isn't attached directly to the user-defined exception. If that same exception is raised again by using the RAISE command (rather than RAISE_APPLICATION_ERROR), SQLERRM will return NULL.

Propagation of Exceptions

The preceding sections give you enough knowledge to work with exceptions in real life. In complex programs, some procedures within packages might call functions in different packages that, in turn, call other functions, and so on. It is important to understand how exceptions propagate between calling program units. If an exception is raised in a function called by a procedure, how does it affect the calling procedure?

How you handle (or choose not to handle) an exception can cause odd behavior in your program if you don't understand how exceptions propagate. If an error occurs in some function being called by your program, your program might have to handle that exception.

For example, when loading large amounts of data into a data warehouse, there are typically very complex rules about how to handle different kinds of errors. Simple errors (like a missing State code value) are perhaps passed through and logged for later manual cleanup. Other errors (like an invalid State code) might cause a referential integrity failure so the record is not loaded at all. If too many errors exist in a small number of records, this might indicate that the file being loaded is corrupted and processing should stop. In each case, the exception is being raised in one program unit and probably being assessed in an entirely different program unit.

Seeing propagation of exceptions in action

Trying to use a real-world data-migration code example would be a little hard to follow, so, we have made a simple (though less realistic) example to illustrate the principles.

Assume that you have two program units, `f_makeAddress_tx` and `p_validateZip`. The function `f_makeAddress_tx` takes several text strings (address, city, state, and zip) and groups them into a single string. The procedure `p_validateZip` makes sure that the ZIP code is valid. The function `f_makeAddress_tx` calls `p_validateZip`, as shown in Listing 5-9.

Listing 5-9:   Propagating Exceptions between Program Units

```
create or replace function f_makeAddress_tx (
      i_address_tx VARCHAR2,
      i_city_tx VARCHAR2,
      i_state_tx VARCHAR2,
      i_zip_tx VARCHAR2)
return VARCHAR2
is
```

```
    e_badZip EXCEPTION;                              →8
    pragma EXCEPTION_init(e_badZip,-20998);          →9
    v_out_tx VARCHAR2(256);
begin
  p_validateZip (i_zip_tx);                          →12
  v_out_tx:= i_address_tx||', '||                    →13
        i_city_tx ||', '||
        i_state_tx ||', '||
        i_zip_tx;
    return v_out_tx;                                 →17
exception
  when e_badZip then                                 →19
     return i_zip_tx || ': Invalid zip code.';
end;
/
create or replace
procedure p_validateZip (i_zipCode_tx VARCHAR2)
is
    e_tooShort EXCEPTION;                            →26
    e tooLong   EXCEPTION;                           →27
    e_badZip    EXCEPTION;                           →28
    pragma exception_init(e_badZip,-20998);          →29
    v_tempZip_nr NUMBER;
Begin
    if length(i_zipCode_tx)< 5 then
      Raise e_tooShort;                              →33
    elsif  length(i_zipCode_tx)> 6 then
      Raise e_tooLong;                               →35
    end if;

    v_tempZip_nr := to_number(i_zipCode_tx);         →38

exception
  when e_tooLong then                                →41
     insert into t_LogError (error_tx)
        values('long zip');
     raise e_badZip;
  when e_tooShort then                               →45
     insert into t_logError (error_tx)
        values('short zip');
     -- raise e_badZip SHOULD be here
  when value_error then                              →48
     insert into t_LogError (error_tx)
        values('non-numeric zip');
     raise; -- re-raising the same exception
end;
```

The following list explains particular lines from Listing 5-9:

→8   The `e_badZip` exception is never raised in the function
      `f_makeAddress_tx`. It will be passed from the procedure
      `p_validateZip`.

→**9**   The e_badZip exception should be associated with the code throughout all routines using it; otherwise, there is no way to indicate that it is exactly the same exception.

→**12**   Here is where the program calls p_validateZip.

→**13–17** This is the standard return statement. It will be skipped if an exception is raised by p_validateZip.

→**19**   In the exception handler, if the e_badZip exception is raised by p_validateZip, the error string address is returned.

→**26–28** Various exceptions are declared within p_validateZip.

→**29**   This line associates e_badZip exception with its code.

→**33, 35** These lines raise exceptions in response to the rule violations.

→**38**   This line raises a predefined VALUE_ERROR exception if there are any non-numeric characters in i_ZipCode_tx.

→**41**   Logs the error and raises an e_badZip exception that will propagate back to the calling routine.

→**45**   Logs the error but *forgets* to raise e_badZip. If this exception is raised, the calling program will never know about it.

→**48**   Intercepts a predefined exception and re-raises the same exception after logging the problem.

It is helpful to examine how this program behaves with various inputs. The following scenarios do just that.

Scenario 1: No rule violations

```
SQL> declare
  2      v_out_tx VARCHAR2(2000);
  3  begin
  4      v_out_tx:=f_makeAddress_tx('123 Main Str',
  5          'Redwood City','California','94061');
  6      DBMS_OUTPUT.put_line(v_out_tx);
  7  end;
  8  /
123 Main Str, Redwood City, California, 94061          →9
PL/SQL procedure successfully completed.
```

→**9**   The function returned the full address string as expected.

No exceptions are raised. Everything follows the normal execution path.

Scenario 2: Short ZIP code

```
SQL> declare
  2       v_out_tx VARCHAR2(2000);
  3  begin
  4       v_out_tx:=f_makeAddress_tx('123 Main Str',
  5'Redwood City', 'California','940');
  6       DBMS_OUTPUT.put_line(v_out_tx);
  7  end;
  8  /
123 Main Str, Redwood City, California, 940          →9
PL/SQL procedure successfully completed.
SQL>
```

→9   The function returned the full address even though the ZIP code is invalid.

The exception e_tooShort is raised in the p_validateZip procedure. However, in the exception handler for e_tooShort, you are just adding a record in the log without raising any other exception (e_badZip is commented out). Therefore, f_MakeAddress_tx treats the ZIP code as valid.

Scenario 3: Non-numeric ZIP code

```
SQL> declare
  2       v_out_tx VARCHAR2(2000);
  3  begin
  4       v_out_tx:=f_makeAddress_tx('123 Main Str',
  5           'Redwood City' , 'California','9406A');
  6       DBMS_OUTPUT.put_line(v_out_tx);
  7  end;
  8  /
declare
*
ERROR at line 1:
ORA-06502: PL/SQL: numeric or value error:               →12
    character to number conversion error                 →13
ORA-06512: at "SCOTT.P_VALIDATEZIP", line 36             →14
ORA-06512: at "SCOTT.F_MAKEADDRES", line 11              →15
ORA-06512: at line 12                                    →16
SQL>
```

The predefined exception value_error is raised in p_validateZip, which in turn raises itself after logging an error. The error is propagated back to f_makeAddress_tx. But there is no exception handler for the value_error exception in f_makeAddress_tx. In this case, execution is halted.

What shows in the SQL*Plus window (lines 12–16) is an *error stack*. Oracle remembers the whole chain of exception calls. This means that if any exception is raised, you can see all the exceptions raised and the program units where they were raised.

The stack tells a story that is easily read:

→**12–14** On line 38 (`v_tempZip_nr := to_number(i_zipCode_tx);`) of `p_validateZip`, a numeric or value error was encountered. (Oracle uses only uppercase for code elements in exceptions, that's why you see `P_VALIDATEZIP`.)

→**15–16** Either that exception was not handled or it was re-raised in the exception handler. In this case, it was re-raised on line 12 (`p_validateZip (i_zip_tx);`) of `f_makeAddress_tx`.

Scenario 4: Long ZIP code

```
SQL> declare
  2      v_out_tx VARCHAR2(2000);
  3  begin
  4      v_out_tx:=f_makeAddress_tx('123 Main Str',
  5  'Redwood City','California','940612345');
  6      DBMS_OUTPUT.put_line(v_out_tx);
  7  end;
  8  /
940612345: Invalid zip code.                              →9
PL/SQL procedure successfully completed.
```

→**9** The function `f_makeAddress_tx` returned the invalid message showing that the `e_badZip` exception was raised in `f_make Address_tx`.

In Scenario 3, you see that exceptions are shown in the error stack in the reverse order of calls. This means that exceptions are handled from the lowest to the highest level. The exception `e_tooLong` was raised in `p_validate Zip`, which in turn raised `e_badZip`, which is propagated back to `f_make Address_tx`.

Because the exception `e_badZip` in both program units is associated with the same code (–20998), the exception handler of the parent routine is able to detect that `e_badZip` refers to the same exception in both cases.

Handling exceptions without halting the program

At times you want to immediately detect and handle the exception and then continue in your code. You might not want to stop execution of your program unit. Of course, you can always make the "exception-risky" part of code into its own program unit to isolate the exception, but sometimes it is convenient just to make the area of the program an anonymous PL/SQL block (as we discuss in Chapter 3) and handle the exception right in that block.

Assume you are validating a ZIP code as part of a much larger routine. You want to detect that there was a bad ZIP code and log the problem but you don't want to stop the whole execution of the program. Listing 5-10 is a rewrite of Listing 5-3 crafted to use this technique.

Listing 5-10:   Raising an Exception Local PL/SQL Block

```
function f_get_speed_nr
(i_distance_nr NUMBER, i_timeSec_nr NUMBER)
return NUMBER
is
  v_out_nr NUMBER;
begin                                                         →6
-- could be lots of code here

  begin                                                       →9
    v_out_nr:= i_distance_nr/i_timeSec_nr;
  exception
     when zero_divide then
        insert into t_logError (error_tx)
        values ('Divide by zero in the F_GET_SPEED_NR');
  end;                                                        →15

  -- could be lots of more code here
  return v_out_nr;                                            →18
end;
```

The following list gives more details about Listing 5-10:

→**6**   This is the beginning of the main routine. There can be any amount of code here prior to the anonymous PL/SQL block.

→**9–15** This is the anonymous PL/SQL block with its own exception handler.

→**18**   This is the RETURN statement. Notice how you do not need a RETURN in the anonymous PL/SQL block. After the exception is handled, processing continues after the block and the RETURN will be encountered as long as the exception raised in the anonymous PL/SQL block is handled within its exception handler. If any exceptions other than ZERO_DIVIDE were raised in the anonymous PL/SQL block, the main routine would detect it and the RETURN statement would not be executed.

Avoiding exceptions raised in declaration part and exception handler

Exceptions can be handled only if they're raised in the body of the program unit. Exceptions raised in the declaration section or in the exception handler cannot be handled within the same program unit. You should avoid placing any code declaration section or exception handler that can raise an exception anywhere other than in the body of your program where it can be explicitly handled.

We discuss exceptions raised in the declaration part first. Assume that you decided to simplify your code by moving the assignment of the variable v_tempZip_nr in the procedure p_validateZip from the body to the declaration, as shown in Listing 5-11. This means that you might raise an exception in the declaration section of the program.

Listing 5-11: Raising an Exception in the Declaration Section

```
procedure p_validatezip (i_zipCode_tx VARCHAR2)
   is
     e_tooShort EXCEPTION;
     e_tooLong  EXCEPTION;
     e_badZip   EXCEPTION;
     pragma exception_init(e_badZip,-20998);
     v_tempZip_nr number:=to_number(i_zipCode_tx);          →7
   begin
     if length(i_zipCode_TX)< 5 then
       raise e_tooShort;
     elsif  length(i_zipCode_TX)> 6 then
       raise e_tooLong;
     end if;
   exception
     when e_tooLong then
         insert into t_LogError (error_tx)
            values('long zip');
        raise e_badZip;
     when e_tooShort then
         insert into t_logError (error_tx)
            values('short zip');
        -- raise e_badZip SHOULD be here
     when VALUE_ERROR then
         insert into t_logError (error_tx)
            values('non-numeric zip');
        raise e_badZip;
   end;
```

→7   This line of code moved the assignment statement from the body of the program to the declaration section and a variable initialization.

Note that the exceptions raised in the declaration section are not handled by
the exception handler.

```
SQL> declare
  2      v_out_tx VARCHAR2(2000);
  3  begin
  4      v_out_tx:=f_makeAddress_tx
  5      ('123 Main','Redwood City','California','9406A');
  6      DBMS_OUTPUT.put_line(v_out_tx);
  7  end;
  8  /
declare
*
ERROR at line 1:
ORA-06502: PL/SQL: numeric or value error: character to
           number conversion error
ORA-06512: at "SCOTT.P_VALIDATEZIP", line 7
ORA-06512: at "SCOTT.F_MAKEADDRES", line 12
ORA-06512: at line 4
SQL>
```

The exception handler for value_error in p_validateZip (remember
that Oracle displays object names in uppercase which is why you see P_
VALIDATEZIP) was never executed. When the exception was raised, control
did not pass to the exception handler. The exception handler is used only
when the exception is raised in the body of the program unit. Exceptions
raised in the declaration section cannot be handled by the exception handler
in that unit.

Exactly the same problem is applicable to exceptions raised in the exception
handlers. The example shown in Listing 5-12 proves that case.

Listing 5-12: Exceptions Raised in the Exception Handler

```
procedure p_validatezip (i_zipCode_tx VARCHAR2)
   is
     e_tooShort EXCEPTION;
     e_tooLong  EXCEPTION;
     e_badZip   EXCEPTION;
     pragma exception_init(e_badZip,-20998);
     v_tempZip_nr NUMBER;
   begin
     if length(i_zipCode_tx)< 5 then
       Raise e_tooShort;
     elsif  length(i_zipCode_tx)> 6 then
       Raise e_tooLong;
     end if;
     v_tempZip_nr :=to_number(i_zipCode_tx);
   exception
     when e_tooLong then
```

(continued)

Listing 5-12 *(continued)*

```
      raise e_badZip;
   when e_tooShort then
      raise e_badZip;
   when VALUE_ERROR then
      raise e_badZip;                                    →23
   when e_badZip then                                    →24
      insert into t_LogError (error_tx)
         values('problem with Zip');
      raise;
 end;
```

Here's what's going on at the end of Listing 5-12:

→**23**   Raises the e_badZip exception.

→**24**   Should handle any e_badZip exceptions, but it does not handle
          the e_badZip exception raised in 23.

Writing Exceptional Exceptions

Any PL/SQL block can contain an exception handler. Keep the following rules
in mind to help you write exception handlers. The exception handler:

✔ Is the last part of the program unit between the last statement of the
  main body and the END; statement.

✔ Always starts with the word EXCEPTION.

✔ Handles one or more exceptions with the following structure:

```
   when <exceptionA> then
       statement1A;
       statement2A;
   when <exceptionB> then
       statement1B:
       statement2B;
```

✔ Can have any number of statements in each exception block.

✔ May conclude with a catchall exception to intercept all exceptions not
  otherwise handled, using the following structure:

```
   when others then
       statement1:
       statement2;
```

But you should be very careful to never use WHEN OTHERS THEN NULL;.

✔ May include a special statement RAISE that raises the same exception
  that was intercepted.

Chapter 6

PL/SQL and SQL Working Together

*T*he main reason to use PL/SQL as a programming language is that it works really well with SQL. PL/SQL works better with SQL than any other programming language does. This cooperation works both ways; you can embed SQL in PL/SQL code, and you can call PL/SQL functions within SQL structures. This chapter shows you how to use both languages together more effectively. For example, you find out

✓ **How to integrate SQL into PL/SQL with cursors:** Cursors are one of the most efficient portions of the PL/SQL language. The ability to use SQL to define a set of information and then create a cursor to loop through this information is one of the main reasons for using PL/SQL.

✓ **How cursors allow PL/SQL to retrieve information from an Oracle database:** PL/SQL's ability to easily and efficiently handle this task is one of its core strengths as a programming language. A PL/SQL program with effective cursor handling can execute many times faster than a Java program written to perform the same task running on an application server.

✓ **How to call PL/SQL functions in SQL:** Calling these functions gives you the power to have queries return almost any information you can imagine. Any column in a SQL query can be calculated from a PL/SQL function stored in the database.

Cursors: What They Are and How to Use Them

Cursors are special PL/SQL objects that you define in the declaration section of a program. But declaring a cursor is just the beginning. The code in a PL/SQL block opens the cursor, fetches data from the cursor, and then closes the cursor. A simple program demonstrating these cursor operations is shown in Listing 6-1.

Listing 6-1:   Declaring a Cursor

```
declare                                                         →1
    cursor c_countEmps is
      select count(*)
        from emp;
    v_out_nr NUMBER;                                            →5
begin
    open c_countEmps;                                           →7
    fetch c_countEmps into v_out_nr;                           →8
    close c_countEmps;                                          →9
    DBMS_OUTPUT.put_line('number of emps is:'||v_out_nr);
end;
```

Listing 6-1 declares a cursor that will return a single record. This cursor is called an *explicit* cursor, meaning that you explicitly declare it in a declaration section of the program and manipulate the cursor elsewhere in the program. We discuss another kind of cursor (called *implicit*) later in this chapter.

→**1–5**   The DECLARE section defines the cursor and the variable where you will store the returned result.

→**7**   First, you need to open the cursor by using the OPEN command.

→**8**   When the cursor is open, the FETCH command fetches the cursor's contents into an output variable.

→**9**   Finally, clean up after yourself and close the cursor by using the CLOSE command

This sequence of operations represents the basic cursor-routine theme, but variations on this theme allow you great flexibility in where you declare cursors and how you manipulate and use them. In addition to a single piece of information (the count of employees), you can use cursors to

✔ **Retrieve many rows of data by setting up cursors that return the information from multiple columns in a SQL query.** This technique lets you use any SQL query in your program no matter how many tables or columns it references.

✔ **Loop through, examine, and manipulate the database records returned by a SQL query.** For example, you might want to loop through all your customers and generate an invoice for each one.

✔ **Loop through cursor records within other cursors by using the programming technique known as *nesting*.** For example, you would use one cursor to loop through departments and a nested cursor to find the employees in each department.

✔ **Change cursor behavior based on passed parameters.** This allows you to better encapsulate the logic of the cursor without having to reference global variables.

The sections that follow explain how you use cursors in these four different ways, so read on for details.

Returning more than one piece of information

A cursor can return one or more pieces of information. SQL statements may have lots of columns in the SELECT portion of the query, and cursors certainly support this.

In Listing 6-1 for counting employees, only one value was returned by the cursor. Specifying where the information was returned was simple because only one variable was defined and it was passed to an output variable in the INTO clause. But what if your cursor returns a whole list of values? In this case, you have two options:

✔ Explicitly declare as many variables as you need for all the values that the cursor returns and list those variables after the INTO in the FETCH command.

✔ Explicitly define a *record variable* consisting of all the variables you need and then just list the name of the record variable in the INTO clause of the FETCH command. If you use a record variable, you can use Oracle's %ROWTYPE declaration to get Oracle to automatically define a record variable with the right number of variables in the right order.

In the following sections, you find out how these two options work.

Option 1: Listing the variables separately

Listing variables separately is the quick and dirty option. You can explicitly declare where you want the values of the cursor returned by using a comma-delimited list after the INTO keyword in the FETCH statement.

Be sure that the number of variables you return to is exactly the same as the number retrieved and that they're listed in the same order as the elements in the cursor. Also make sure that the variables you're fetching into are the correct datatype, as shown in Listing 6-2.

Listing 6-2: Returning Cursor Variables the Quick and Easy Way

```
declare
    cursor c_countemps is
      select count(*), sum(sal)
        from emp;
    v_count_nr NUMBER;
    v_sum_nr NUMBER;                                      →6
begin
    open c_countEmps;
    fetch c_countEmps into v_count_nr, v_sum_nr;
    close c_countEmps;
    DBMS_OUTPUT.put_line
        ('number of emps is:'||v_count_nr);
    DBMS_OUTPUT.put_line
        ('sum of emp salaries is:'||v_sum_nr);           →14
end;
```

▮ →14   Shows the number retrieved.

Option 2: Defining a record type

You can declare a record variable that consists of one or more elements and fetch the cursor into that variable. You can find out more about record variables in Chapter 11. For now, you need to know that record variables in PL/SQL are a way of representing a single row from the table, where you define attributes in the same way that you would define attributes in the table definition.

When you declare a record, the list of elements is in the declaration section and not in the FETCH command in the middle of the executable code. This has two advantages:

✔ Your code is easier to read.

✔ If you want to use the same cursor in two different places, you don't have to repeat the whole list of elements, only the name of one record variable.

Listing 6-3 shows an example of this option.

Listing 6-3: Retrieving Cursor Variables with a Record Variable

```
declare
    cursor c_countEmps is
      select count(*) , sum(sal)
        from emp;
```

```
    type rt_testRecType is record                        →4
        (v_count_nr NUMBER,
         v_sum_nr NUMBER);
    r_testRec rt_testRecType;                            →7
begin
    open c_countEmps;
    fetch c_countEmps into r_testRec;                    →10
    close c_countEmps;
    DBMS_OUTPUT.put_line('number of emps is:'||
        r_testRec.v_count_nr);
    DBMS_OUTPUT.put_line('sum of emp salaries is:'||
        r_testRec.v_sum_nr);
end;
```

Check out these details about the code:

→4   This code declares the RECORD datatype, indicating that you need a place to store a row of data consisting of two numbers.

→7   Here you declare a record variable of the newly created datatype.

→10   This line fetches the cursor into the record variable.

Keep in mind that the record and the cursor must have the same variables, with the same datatype, listed in the same order. Also note how the components of the record are referred to in the DBMS_OUTPUT statements. Because each variable is now part of a record, you need to refer to it by using dot notation. For example, r_testRec.v_sum_nr refers to the number field v_sum_nr, which is declared to be part of the record r_testRec.

In both previous options (declaring independent variables and declaring a special RECORD type) you still have to laboriously list all the elements to which the cursor data was being returned. Oracle provides a shortcut that eliminates this tedious work. You can allow the cursor to specify the record for you by using %ROWTYPE. Instead of having to list all the elements in a record, you simply declare it to be the same structure as a cursor that you've previously declared or the same type as a table in the database, provided that you are retrieving all the columns in the table into the cursor. This has the following advantages:

✔ You have less code to write, read, and correct.

✔ If you need to change the data that the cursor retrieves, you have to make only one change to your code in the SELECT clause of the cursor declaration. Any record referencing the cursor via %ROWTYPE automatically changes so that the record always matches the cursor.

Listing 6-3 written using a %ROWTYPE declaration would look like Listing 6-4.

Listing 6-4:   Defining a Record Type for a Cursor by Using %ROWTYPE

```
declare
    cursor c_countEmps is
        select count(*) count_nr, sum(sal) sum_nr          →3
        from emp;
    r_testRec c_countEmps%ROWTYPE;                         →5
begin
    open c_countEmps;
    fetch c_countEmps into r_testRec;
    close c_countEmps;
    DBMS_OUTPUT.put_line('number of emps is:'||
        r_testRec.count_nr);                               →11
    DBMS_OUTPUT.put_line('sum of emp salaries is:'||
        r_testRec.sum_nr);
end;
```

Here's what's happening in the listing:

→3   Because you're planning to use a cursor as a reference for datatype, you must assign aliases to columns in the resulting list that don't have real names. (For example, all function results require aliases, but EMPNO is valid by itself.) These aliases will be used as column names in the resulting record.

→5   Because the record r_testrec takes its structure from the cursor c_counttemps, you can be sure that r_testrec has exactly the right structure for the cursor. If you change the cursor, you don't need to modify the record structure of r_testrec. It will adjust itself automatically!

→11   The field name in the record variable is the same as the alias you assigned in the cursor.

Looping through multiple records

In Listing 6-4, only a single row of data is retrieved. However, in the real world, most situations require you to loop through many records and process them. For example, a payroll system must loop through all employees and write checks for all of them.

These real-world systems might have to deal with thousands or even millions of records retrieved by a single query. The process must not only read those thousands or millions of rows, but also, in most cases, modify the information in a record or use the information in the record to do something else entirely, such as generate an invoice or statement. You can manage such a process by integrating the use of a cursor with any of the looping mechanisms we describe in Chapter 4.

Listing 6-5 shows the basic syntax for looping through the records in a cursor.

Listing 6-5: Looping through Records in a Cursor

```
declare
    cursor c_emp is
      select *
        from emp;
    r_emp c_emp%ROWTYPE;
begin
    open c_emp;
    loop
        fetch c_emp into r_emp;
        exit when c_emp%NOTFOUND;                    →10
        DBMS_OUTPUT.put_line(r_emp.eName);
    end loop;
    close c_emp;                                     →12
end;
```

Whenever you have a loop, it must have a beginning, a middle, an end, and, most important, a way to get out of the loop. The program needs to know when to get out of the loop. With cursors, the time to exit the loop is usually when there are no more records to process.

→10   Detects that there are no more records to process and ends the looping. %NOTFOUND is a special *cursor variable* that returns TRUE when the last fetch to that cursor does not return any records. In Listing 6-5, the program prints out the name of each employee. When there are no more employees to process, the FETCH command won't return any data, and c_emp%NOTFOUND will return TRUE. This ends the loop and immediately jumps to the first line of code after the END LOOP statement.

→12   This code line will execute when the loop terminates.

Placing cursors in nested loops

You can loop through cursor records within other cursors. For example, suppose you want to print a roster of all employees in your company, listed by department. To do this, you would loop through records for each department in your company and, within each department, loop through the employees. You can set up two cursors and loop through all department and employee records in a very efficient way, as shown in Listing 6-6.

Listing 6-6: **Cursors in Nested Loops**

```
declare
    cursor c_dept is                                       →2
      select *
        from dept;
    r_dept c_dept%ROWTYPE;
    cursor c_empInDept (cin_deptNo NUMBER) is              →6
      select *
        from emp
        where deptNo = cin_deptNo;                         →9

    r_emp c_empInDept%ROWTYPE;
begin
    open c_dept;
    loop
        fetch c_dept into r_dept;
        exit when c_dept%NOTFOUND;
          --<... do something with each department
          --<... such as initialize total salary

        open c_empInDept (r_dept.deptNo);
        loop
            fetch c_empInDept into r_emp;
            exit when c_empInDept%NOTFOUND;
          --<... do something with each employee
            --<... such as change their salary
        end loop;
        close c_empInDept;

    end loop;
    close c_dept;
end;
```

Here are some more details about Listing 6-6:

→**2-5**   This line declares the department cursor and record.

→**6-9**   These lines declare the employee cursor and record.

→**9**   How are these cursors different? The employee cursor specifies the parameter in `cin_deptNo` (department number to be passed in). Each time the cursor `c_empInDept` is called, it returns only the employees in the department specified by the parameter.

Passing parameters to cursors

Cursors are very useful constructs. They're the primary method of retrieving information from the database. One of the things you need to be able to do is dynamically control the cursor when the program is running.

For example, if you want to run your payroll for only a single department, it would require a lot of work to create separate cursors for each department. Instead, you can use a single cursor that will return the employee records for *any* department you specify. The way you tell the cursor which department to return records for is by passing the department ID to the cursor as a parameter.

Usually, parameters are used in the WHERE clause of the query to filter what data are returned.

To illustrate the basic syntax of passing parameters in the WHERE clause, Listing 6-7 counts the number of employees in a specified department.

Listing 6-7:   Basic Syntax for Passing Parameters in a Cursor

```
declare
    cursor c_emp (cin_deptNo NUMBER) is              →2
      select count(*)
        from emp
        where deptNo = cin_deptNo;
    v_deptNo dept.deptNo%type:=10;
    v_countEmp NUMBER;
begin
    open c_emp (v_deptNo);                           →9
    fetch c_emp into v_countEmp;                     →10
    close c_emp;                                     →11
end;
```

When passing a parameter to a cursor, the syntax is different from your basic cursor in the following ways:

→2   You must declare the parameter as part of the cursor definition.

→9   When you open the cursor, you need to pass a parameter (of the correct type) to the cursor.

→10, 11 When fetching and closing the cursor, you don't specify the parameter.

As illustrated in Listing 6-7, the most common use of a parameter is as a variable referenced in the WHERE clause. You can pass a value to the parameter in various ways.

You can pass a literal value, as in

```
open c_emp (10);
```

or a variable, whether it is a simple variable like

```
open c_emp (v_deptNo)
```

or part of a record, like this:

```
open c_emp (r_emp.deptNo);
```

Use parameters to avoid references to variables outside the cursor. Good structured programming style involves trying to make your code *modular,* meaning that it is self-contained and has no references to anything outside the module. By using cursor parameters, not only is your code more flexible, it is easier to read and maintain.

There are various places in the SELECT statement where you reference a parameter. A few examples follow in Table 6-1. All parameters are prefixed with cin (cursor in).

Table 6-1	SELECT Statement Examples
Part of SQL Statement	*Example*

Where	`select ...`
	`from emp`
	`where deptNo = cin_deptNo`

Group by . . . having	`select count(*)`
	`from emp`
	`group by deptNo`
	`having deptNo > cin_deptNo`

Connect by . . . start with	`select ...`
	`from emp`
	`start with empNo = cin_empNo`
	`connect by prior empNo =`
	`prior manager`

Other than the WHERE clause, the HAVING clause, and the START WITH clause, a parameter cannot change the query. For example, you can't change what is returned in the SELECT clause by using a parameter. Neither can you change the columns in the ORDER BY clause by using a parameter. For example, if you wanted the records returned to be in order by employee last name instead of by Social Security number, that would require you to change the name of a column listed in the ORDER BY clause:

```
order by lname
```

instead of

```
order by ssn
```

Because parameters can change only values and not names of columns or tables in the query, you can't use them to change the FROM, ORDER BY, or GROUP BY clauses. If you want to modify these parts of the query dynamically, you need to use a REF cursor or dynamic PL/SQL (which are described in Chapter 13).

Knowing Where to Declare Cursors

You can declare cursors in many different places. Where you place the cursor definition depends upon where and how you're going to use the cursor. If you're going to use a cursor only once, you can declare it right next to where it is called. (But are you very sure you are only going to use it once? Famous last words. . . .) If you plan to reuse the same query many times in the application, you shouldn't have to declare the same cursor every time you want to run the query. You should declare the cursor in a place where it can easily be called by all parts of the application.

The discussion of functions and procedures in Chapter 3 covers program scope. The point where you declare the function or procedure determines where you are able to call that function or procedure. The same principle applies to cursor declaration. Table 6-2 offers an overview of what we mean. In the following sections, you can find out how to place a cursor declaration in these various locations. For more information about packages, please see Chapter 3.

Table 6-2	Where to Define the Cursor?
If . . .	*. . . Then Define the Cursor Here*
You use the cursor only once in program unit	The header of the program unit
The program unit is large and you need the cursor in a limited scope	The local (anonymous) PL/SQL block (for more information about anonymous PL/SQL blocks, see Chapter 3)
You use a cursor throughout a package, but not elsewhere	The package body (for more information about packages, see Chapter 7)
You need to access the cursor anywhere	The package specification

Always define your cursor in as restrictive a scope as possible, but as generally as needed. Cursors should be accessible enough that you can avoid having to define the same cursors over and over again.

Defining cursors in the header of the program unit

The header of the program unit (a function or procedure) is the most common place to declare a cursor. If you declare the cursor in the header of the program unit, you can call it only within that program unit.

Even if a cursor is used only once in a program unit, it is common to define all the cursors used in a program unit in the declaration header of that unit. Declaring a cursor in an anonymous PL/SQL block is quite rare. You should probably avoid doing so because it adds lines to your code body and can make it hard to find the cursor declaration. (Most programmers immediately look in the declaration section of a program for cursor declarations.)

If you have so many cursors that you start to lose track of them, the program unit is probably too big and should be broken up into smaller units.

Listing 6-8 is an example showing a cursor declared within a PL/SQL procedure.

Listing 6-8:   Declaring a Cursor within a Procedure

```
create or replace procedure p_printEmps is          →1
    cursor c_emp is                                 →2
      select *
        from emp;
    r_emp c_emp%ROWTYPE;
begin
    open c_emp;
    loop
      fetch c_emp into r_emp;
      exit when c_emp%NOTFOUND;
      DBMS_OUTPUT.put_line(r_emp.eName);
    end loop;
    close c_emp;
end;
```

Note that there is no DECLARE used in a procedure. This clause is only needed for anonymous blocks. The declaration (line 2) begins right after the CREATE OR REPLACE PROCEDURE statement (line 1).

Defining cursors in the local PL/SQL block

If your program unit is very large and you need the cursor only in a very limited scope, you can define a small local PL/SQL block and define the cursor to exist only within that scope.

Listing 6-9 is an example of how you define a cursor in an anonymous PL/SQL block.

Listing 6-9:   Defining a Cursor in an Anonymous PL/SQL Block

```
create or replace procedure p_printEmps is          →1
begin -- for main function

...Lots of other code could go here                 →4

   declare                                           →6
      cursor c_emp is                                →7
         select *
            from emp;
         r_emp c_emp%ROWTYPE;
   begin
      open c_emp;                                    →11
      loop
         fetch c_emp into r_emp;
         exit when c_emp%NOTFOUND;
         DBMS_OUTPUT.put_line(r_emp.eName);
      end loop;
      close c_emp;
   end; -- for local block                           →18

   ...Lots of other code could go here, too

end; --p_printEmps
```

Here are some details about Listing 6-9:

→**1**   This is the beginning of the program unit you're creating.

→**4, 18** The cursor isn't defined here and can't be referenced.

→**6**   This line starts the anonymous PL/SQL block.

→**7**   Here, you declare the cursor to be visible only within the anonymous block.

→**11**   This line opens the cursor.

Defining cursors in the package body

If you plan to reuse a cursor throughout a package but don't anticipate using it outside that package, you can define the cursor in the package body, as shown in Listing 6-10.

Listing 6-10:   Declaring a Cursor in the Package Body

```
create or replace package body bigUtil is
    cursor c_emp is                                        →2
      select *
        from emp;
    r_emp c_emp%ROWTYPE;

    procedure p_printEmps is
        r_emp c_emp%ROWTYPE;
    begin
        open c_emp;                                        →10
        loop
            fetch c_emp into r_emp;
            exit when c_emp%NOTFOUND;
            DBMS_OUTPUT.put_line(r_emp.eName);
        end loop;
        close c_emp;
    end; --p_printEmps

    --- lots of other functions or procedures              →19
    ---could be defined here

end; --bigUtil
```

Here are the details about Listing 6-10:

→2   This is where the cursor is declared.

→10   This is where the cursor is referenced. Notice that the cursor isn't
        declared within the procedure.

→19   The same cursor could be referenced in other program units
        within the package body.

If you declare the cursor in the package body (outside any function or procedure), the same cursor can be used by any procedure or function in the package body.

Defining cursors in the package spec

If you have a cursor that needs to be accessible anywhere, you need to declare it in the package specification. That way, any program unit in the same schema can use the cursor. If you grant privileges on the package to other schemas, anyone who can see the package can execute the cursor. For more information about packages, see Chapters 3 and 7. Consult any good Oracle SQL book (for example, *Oracle Database 10g: The Complete Reference,* by Kevin Loney, McGraw-Hill, 2004) for information about granting privileges to other schemas.

When you reference the cursor within the same package where it was declared, you can do it without any qualifier, the same way as shown earlier in the package body example (refer to Listing 6-10).

If you're using the cursor in a different package from where the cursor was declared, you need to prefix the cursor with the package name, as shown in Listing 6-11.

Listing 6-11:   Calling a Cursor Declared in a Different Package

```
--Here is the package spec where the cursor is declared.

create or replace package pkg_Util is
    cursor c_emp is                                          →2
      select * from emp;
    r_emp c_emp%ROWTYPE;
end;

--Here is a different package that references the cursor

create or replace package body pkg_aDifferentUtil is
    procedure p_printEmps is
    begin
        open pkg_Util.c_emp;                                 →11
        loop
            fetch pkg_Util.c_emp into pkg_Util.r_emp;   →13
            exit when pkg_Util.c_emp%NOTFOUND;          →14
            DBMS_OUTPUT.put_line(pkg_Util.r_emp.eName);→15
        end loop;
        close pkg_Util.c_emp;                                →17
    end;
end;
```

Details about Listing 6-11 are shown here:

→2	Declares the cursor in the first package.
→11	References the cursor in an entirely different package. Note that you have to preface the cursor name with the first package name (pkg_Util.c_emp).
→11, 13–15, 17	Note that all references to the cursor must be prefaced with the package name where the cursor was declared.

Placing cursors in package specifications means that any program unit can use them. You should do this only when you expect the cursor to be used outside of the package. This has the significant advantage of code reuse, but it also has disadvantages. What happens if a developer wants to modify the cursor at a later date? You should perform a full impact analysis to ensure that any changes to the cursor won't adversely affect other code.

Being Explicitly Smart with Implicit Cursors

In some cases, Oracle doesn't require you to manually create a cursor as a way of accessing existing data. Instead of *explicit cursors,* it uses *implicit cursors* and drives them automatically so that no more OPEN/FETCH/CLOSE commands are needed. You need to do less coding than the explicit cursors (which we discuss in the rest of this chapter), and implicit cursors sometimes even execute a tiny bit faster than the corresponding explicit cursor.

Although implicit cursors make coding easier in some regards, they can be tricky to work with unless you're careful. In the following section, you find out how to use a basic implicit cursor and how to avoid problems when using them.

Retrieving a single row: The basic syntax

If you're retrieving a single row of data (like information for a single employee, or for a count of employees in a single department), you can use an implicit cursor. You do not even need to specify the cursor. You can use a SELECT INTO command. For example, to get the count of all employees in an organization, you might write something like the following example:

```
declare
    v_out_nr NUMBER;
begin
    select count(*) into v_out_nr              →4
    from emp;
    DBMS_OUTPUT.put_line
        ('the number of emps is:'||v_out_nr);
end;
```

→4   Takes the place of the explicit cursor declaration as well as opening, fetching, and closing the cursor. All cursor activity is replaced by a single SELECT INTO command.

This code is much easier to write than an explicit declaration of the cursor with an associated OPEN/FETCH/CLOSE code sequence. Behind the scenes, Oracle is still creating a cursor called an implicit cursor.

To use a SELECT INTO command, the query must return exactly one row. If the SELECT statement returns no rows, the code will throw a NO_DATA_FOUND exception. If it returns more than one row, the code will throw the TOO_MANY_ROWS exception. Fortunately, you can still use implicit cursors even if your code might not return any row or more than one row. The next section has the details.

Handling exceptions in implicit cursors

You can still use an implicit cursor with the SELECT INTO command even if there is a possibility of returning no rows (or more than one row) from the query. For example, if you want to have a function that returns the name of a department given its department number, there's a chance someone might enter a nonexistent department number, and you need a way to handle that scenario. In that situation, you might write your function like this:

```
create or replace
function f_getdName_tx (in_deptNo NUMBER)
return VARCHAR2 is
    v_out_tx dept.dName%TYPE;
begin
    select dName into v_out_tx
    from dept
    where deptNo =  in_deptNo;
    return v_out_tx;
exception
    when no_data_found then
        return 'NO SUCH DEPARTMENT';
end f_getdName_tx;
```

In this example, because deptNo is the primary key of the table, you don't have to worry about the query returning too many rows. But if a user asked for the name of a department that doesn't exist, the situation would be addressed in the exception handler.

Returning an implicit cursor into a record

One downside of an implicit cursor is that there is no easy way to declare a record into which to return the cursor. There are two workarounds that you might find useful.

First, if the query columns from the cursor are the same as the columns in a single table, you can use the %ROWTYPE clause on the table name as shown Listing 6-12.

Listing 6-12:   Using the %ROWTYPE Clause on the Table Name

```
declare
    r_emp emp%ROWTYPE;                                        →2
begin
    select emp.* into r_emp                                  →4
    from emp,
        dept
    where emp.deptNo = dept.deptNo
```

(continued)

Listing 6-12 *(continued)*

```
    and   emp.deptNo = 20
    and emp.job = 'MANAGER';
    DBMS_OUTPUT.put_line
        ('Dept 20 Manager is:'||r_emp.eName);
end;
```

Check out the details about lines 2 and 4:

> **→2**   Declares a record based on the EMP table because the cursor uses the same structure for the records returned by the cursor.

> **→4**   Fetches the implicit cursor into the record defined in line 2.

In Listing 6-12, the query returns only the columns from the EMP table, so you could specify the cursor record by using the EMP table.

Another possible workaround might be needed if the cursor returns many columns from different tables. In this case, you could explicitly declare a record variable, as we discuss in the previous section "Returning more than one piece of information."

Accessing Status Info by Using Cursor Variables

Oracle can tell you the status of a cursor. Specifically, you can find out

✔ Whether the cursor is open

✔ Whether a row was found the last time the cursor was accessed

✔ How many records have been returned

All cursors have properties that report their state of operation. For example, in Listing 6-5, earlier in this chapter, the syntax %NOTFOUND is used to terminate a loop. Because the syntax used to capture the state of or information about cursors enables you to make decisions in your code, they are called "cursor variables." There are four variables:

✔ %FOUND checks whether a fetch succeeded in bringing a record into a variable. Returns TRUE if the fetch succeeded, FALSE otherwise.

✔ %NOTFOUND the reverse of %FOUND. Returns FALSE if the fetch succeeded, TRUE otherwise.

✔ %ISOPEN checks whether a cursor is open.

✔ %ROWCOUNT returns the number of rows processed by a cursor at the time the %ROWCOUNT statement is executed.

The variable properties of explicit cursors are referenced as

```
cursor_name%VARIABLE_NAME
```

Specifically, to reference the `c_emp` cursor with the `%FOUND` variable, you'd do it like this:

```
c_emp%FOUND
```

For implicit cursors, the syntax is always `sql%variable_name`. The following section explains how to use cursor variables with both explicit and implicit cursors in more detail.

The last variable, `%ROWCOUNT`, is a regular number variable, but the first three are Boolean variables that return a logical `TRUE` or `FALSE`. They can be used together with other logical expressions. For example, if you want to ensure that the fetch succeeded and then check the value returned, you can combine them as follows:

```
if c_empInDept%FOUND and r_emp.eName = 'King'...
```

Checking the status of explicit cursors

The following example illustrates how to use cursor variables with explicit cursors. Listing 6-13 shows the values of cursor variables on a cursor that loops through employee names in a department.

Listing 6-13: Using Explicit Cursors

```
Declare
    cursor c_emp (cin_deptNo NUMBER) is
      select eName
        from emp
        where deptNo=cin_deptNo;
    v_eName VARCHAR2(256);
begin
    if not c_emp%ISOPEN then                           →8
        DBMS_OUTPUT.put_line('Cursor is closed');
    end if;

    open c_emp(10);

    if c_emp%ISOPEN then                               →14
        DBMS_OUTPUT.put_line('Cursor is opened');
    end if;

    loop
        fetch c_emp into v_eName;
```

(continued)

Listing 6-13 *(continued)*

```
        if c_emp%NOTFOUND then                          →20
            DBMS_OUTPUT.put_line('No rows to fetch!');
            exit; -- the same as exit when c1%NOTFOUND;
        end if;

        DBMS_OUTPUT.put_line
            ('Processed:'||c_emp%rowcount);              →26
    end loop;

    close c_emp;

    if not c_emp%ISOPEN then                             →31
        DBMS_OUTPUT.put_line('Cursor is closed');
    end if;
end;
```

In this case, the output of Listing 6-13 would be:

```
Cursor is closed
Cursor is opened
Processed:1
Processed:2
Processed:3
No rows to fetch!
Cursor is closed
```

Using %ISOPEN showed exactly when the cursor was opened; %ROWCOUNT showed the number of currently fetched rows; and %NOTFOUND showed when there were no more rows to fetch.

There are some issues to be aware of:

- ✔ If you use the %FOUND, %NOTFOUND, and %ROWCOUNT cursor variables before the cursor is opened or after the cursor is closed, they will raise an exception. If you see an exception from this situation, you probably made a mistake in your code.

- ✔ Values of %FOUND, %NOTFOUND, and %ROWCOUNT are changed after every fetch. So, the status of these variables refers to the status of the cursor after the last fetch from the cursor.

- ✔ If there are no more rows to fetch, %ROWCOUNT keeps the number of successfully fetched records until the cursor is closed. No matter how many unsuccessful fetches you make from a cursor, the value of this variable won't change.

Checking the status of implicit cursors

You can use the same cursor variables for implicit cursors, too. When used with an implicit cursor, the value of a cursor variable corresponds to the last statement needing an implicit cursor that was fired in the current procedural block (the area between BEGIN and END). Because there is no cursor name, you use SQL rather than the cursor name. In the following example, look at the value of cursor variables on an implicit cursor that updates an employee's salary:

```
SQL> begin
  2        update emp
  3        set sal=sal*1
  4        where eName='KING';
  5
  6        DBMS_OUTPUT.put_line('Processed:'||sql%rowcount);
  7
  8        if sql%FOUND then
  9            DBMS_OUTPUT.put_line('Found=true');
 10        else
 11            DBMS_OUTPUT.put_line('Found=false');
 12        end if;
 13  end;
 14  /
Processed:1
Found=true
PL/SQL procedure successfully completed.
SQL>
```

As you can see from this example, cursor variables are wonderful tools for knowing exactly how many records were processed and whether any were processed at all.

In the preceding example, if you change the WHERE clause to where eName='TEST'; the output changes, as shown here:

```
SQL> begin
  2        update emp
  3        set sal=sal*1
  4        where eName='TEST';
  5
  6        DBMS_OUTPUT.put_line('Processed:'||sql%rowcount);
  7
  8        if sql%FOUND then
  9            DBMS_OUTPUT.put_line('Found=true');
 10        else
 11            DBMS_OUTPUT.put_line('Found=false');
 12        end if;
 13  end;
 14  /
Processed:0
Found=false
PL/SQL procedure successfully completed.
SQL>
```

Because there is no employee with the specified name, no row was updated. You don't need to requery the table to find out how many records were updated. This last point is especially critical for batch processing. By taking advantage of `SQL%ROWCOUNT`, you can reduce the amount of code you have to write to detect whether your DML operations were successful.

As usual, there are some caveats in using implicit cursor variables:

✔ `%ISOPEN` is always false because implicit cursors are opened as needed and closed immediately after the statement is finished. Never use `%ISOPEN` with implicit cursors.

✔ Both `%FOUND` and `%NOTFOUND` are false before any statement is executed. Using them in your code in this way is a waste of time and space.

✔ Any DDL or transaction control commands (commit or rollback) will clear implicit cursor variables. You can check the value of your cursor variables only prior to doing a commit or rollback.

Updating Records Fetched from Cursors

As you loop through a set of records, you'll frequently want to update each of the records. For example, you might want to loop through all employees and adjust their salaries or loop through purchase orders and update their statuses.

You can update records in a few different ways. When you need to use more complex logic, be sure to evaluate whether to lock the records so that other actions don't interfere with your update. The following sections explain the different methods and considerations in more detail.

Using a simple UPDATE statement

Often, you can update records with a simple SQL UPDATE statement like

```
update emp
set salary = salary * 1.1
where deptNo = 10;
```

This statement would add 10 percent to everyone's salary in department 10.

However, sometimes you need to use more complex logic.

Updating with logical operators

When you need to look at each record individually and decide what to do with it, logical operators come into play. You usually don't want to simply update all the records the same way. One way to do this is by embedding a simple UPDATE statement in your code. For example, the following code gives a raise to everyone with a salary below $5,000:

```
declare
  cursor c_empInDept is
    select * from emp;
  begin
  for r_emp in c_empInDept loop
    if r_emp.sal < 5000 then
      update emp
      set sal = sal * 1.1
      where empNo = r_emp.empNo;
    end if;
  end loop;
end;
```

But this isn't very safe code. While your routine is running, someone else might be updating employee salaries. You might give a raise to someone whose salary, in the last split second, has already been raised above $5,000.

To solve this problem, you need to lock all the records while you're working on them. This is done using a SELECT FOR UPDATE command, as shown in Listing 6-14. You can find out more about locking, sessions, and transaction control in Chapter 12.

Listing 6-14:   Using the SELECT FOR UPDATE Command

```
declare
  cursor c_empInDept is
    select * from emp
    for update of sal;                               →4
begin
  for r_emp in c_empInDept loop
    if r_emp.sal < 5000 then
      update emp
      set sal = sal * 1.1
      where current of c_empInDept;                  →10
    end if;
  end loop;
end;
```

Here are the details about lines 4 and 10:

→4   Notice that the code uses FOR UPDATE OF SAL;. This lock means that others can't delete records or modify the salary column but are allowed to modify other columns. You need to lock not only the column that you're modifying, but also any other column that might determine what record you will process. If you don't specify any column, the clause FOR UPDATE locks the entire record.

→**10** Notice that the WHERE clause was changed to use where current of c_empInDept. This code updates the exact record that the cursor is referencing by using the internal Oracle record identifier (rowid). It will execute very fast.

If you lock the records, no one else will be allowed to modify the records until your cursor closes. This can be a problem. If your routine takes a long time to execute, you can affect other users of your system.

Whether to use SELECT FOR UPDATE or just UPDATE for the current record by using the primary key is a difficult decision to make. You need to balance the safety of SELECT FOR UPDATE against the impact that it might have on other parts of the system.

Taking a Shortcut with CURSOR FOR Loops

The technique of looping through all the records in a cursor is so common that PL/SQL has a nifty shortcut, the CURSOR FOR loop. This is an alternative to the OPEN/FETCH/CLOSE sequence introduced in "Looping through multiple records," earlier in this chapter.

Of course, if there's a shortcut, you might wonder why anyone still uses OPEN/FETCH/CLOSE at all. And the reason is an important one: There are some exception-handling issues to consider before choosing to use a CURSOR FOR loop implementation. If something goes wrong inside the CURSOR FOR loop, Oracle closes the cursor, which can affect your procedural logic.

The following sections introduce how this shortcut works and help you decide when to take the shortcut and when the long way is better.

Comparing CURSOR FOR loops to cursors with the LOOP command

As we explain in the "Looping through multiple records" section earlier in this chapter, cursors help process multiple records at once in a block of code. For example, if you need to access all the records in department 10, increase the salary of all employees in department 10 by 50 percent, and print out a report with the old and new salary values, the code would look something like Listing 6-15.

Listing 6-15:   Looping through a Cursor by Using the LOOP Command

```
declare
    cursor c_emp (ci_deptNo NUMBER) is
      select *
        from emp
        where deptNo = ci_deptNo;
    r_emp c_emp%ROWTYPE;
begin
    open c_emp(10);
    loop
        fetch c_emp into r_emp;
        exit when c_emp%NOTFOUND;
        update emp
        set sal=sal*1.5
        where empNo=r_emp.empNo;
        DBMS_OUTPUT.put_line('Emp '||r_emp.eName||
            ' - salary change:'||r_emp.sal||
            '->'||r_emp.sal*1.5);
    end loop;
    close c_emp;
end;
```

Although Listing 6-15 will work, if you want to process all the rows in the query, you don't need to bother with the full OPEN/FETCH/EXIT/CLOSE syntax. You can make your code more compact by telling Oracle to manage a CURSOR FOR loop based on the cursor, as in Listing 6-16.

Listing 6-16:   Looping through a Cursor by Using a CURSOR FOR Loop

```
declare
    cursor c_emp (ci_deptNo NUMBER) is
      select *
        from emp
        where deptNo = ci_deptNo;
begin
    for r_emp in c_emp(10) loop
        update emp
        set sal=sal*1.5
        where empNo = r_emp.empNo;
        DBMS_OUTPUT.put_line('Emp '|| r_emp.eName||
            ' - salary change:'||r_emp.sal||'-
            '- >'||r_emp.sal*1.5);
    end loop;
end;
```

The method shown in Listing 6-16 is much more convenient than Listing 6-15. The code is much shorter. Several tasks you previously needed to do by hand are handled automatically:

✔ You don't have to declare the r_emp record variable. In a CURSOR FOR loop, the record variable is automatically declared when it is used in the FOR statement, and it automatically has the same row type as the cursor.

✔ There is no EXIT statement. The program automatically exits the loop when there are no more records to process.

✔ There are no OPEN or CLOSE statements. The CURSOR FOR loop automatically opens the cursor and closes it when there are no more records to fetch.

✔ If a SQL query returns no records, the code inside the loop won't be executed at all.

✔ The record that holds data retrieved by the cursor exists only inside the loop and provides temporary storage of each fetched record. Individual columns can be referenced as variable.column_name.

Listing 6-16 is much easier to read and understand, but it will spin through the dataset and process all its records just the same as the longer version.

When do CURSOR FOR loops simplify exception handling?

By using CURSOR FOR loops, you don't need to worry about an accumulation of open cursors that could eventually reach the maximum number of cursors allowed for the database. For example, if you were looping through employees doing payroll and encountered an error, you would have to stop processing your payroll and gracefully recover. The following example illustrates the simplification of code made possible by the CURSOR FOR loop's automatic housekeeping:

```
declare
    cursor c_emp is ...
begin
    for r_emp in c_emp loop
      <...something that could fail ...>
    end loop;
exception
    when others then
        /* The cursor is already closed - don't do
         anything*/
        ...
end;
```

If you write the same example with OPEN/FETCH/CLOSE, you need to know whether failure can occur before the cursor is closed.

```
declare
    cursor c_emp is ...
    r_emp c_emp%ROWTYPE;
begin
    open c1;
    loop
        fetch c_emp into r_emp;
        exit when c_emp%NOTFOUND;
        <... .something that could fail #1..>
    end loop;
    close c_emp;
        <... .something that could fail #2..>
exception
    when others then
        /* Cursor is opened at #1 and closed at #2 */
        if c_emp%ISOPEN is true
        then
            close c_emp; -- close the cursor
        end if;
        raise;
end;
```

If failure occurs during loop processing (in the first example), you must close the cursor in the exception block. But you need to check %ISOPEN beforehand, because the failure could have occurred in processing the second example code block, and the cursor would already be closed.

Make it a habit to place such exception-handling logic into any code that uses explicit cursors (not CURSOR FOR loops). Otherwise, you risk intermittent and unpredictable database collapse.

When should you use a CURSOR FOR loop instead of a looping through the cursor by using a LOOP command? The answer is pretty simple: Always start by using a CURSOR FOR loop. If you then end up needing very precise control that prevents you from using a CURSOR FOR loop, change your code to the traditional technique. Only rarely will you need to switch to the traditional way.

When CURSOR FOR loops make your life harder

There are times when you want to use the standard OPEN/FETCH/CLOSE syntax in a loop. In a CURSOR FOR loop, if you want to know the last record retrieved, you have to do some extra work. In the basic OPEN/FETCH/CLOSE sequence, the last fetched value before failure is sitting in the record variable, but that isn't the case in a CURSOR FOR loop. In a CURSOR FOR loop, the record variable is null after the cursor closes.

A shortcut in a shortcut

If you want to push the envelope to the extreme, you can rewrite Listing 6-13 without explicitly declaring a CURSOR FOR loop at all. Although we don't recommend this strategy, because of the decreased readability of the code and lack of reusability of a cursor, you can still do it, as shown here:

```
begin
    for r_emp in (select *
                    from emp
                    where deptNo = 10) loop
        <... do something ...>
    end loop;
end;
```

To solve this problem, you could store part or all of the current record in a variable visible outside the CURSOR FOR loop, and then you could perform whatever processing you need. If a failure occurs, you can use that record in the exception handler, as shown in Listing 6-17.

Listing 6-17:   Adding an Exception Handler to a CURSOR FOR Loop

```
declare
    cursor c_emp (ci_deptNo NUMBER) is
      select empNo, deptNo, empName
        from emp
        where deptNo = ci_deptNo
        order by empNo; --helps ID failure point       →6
    v_empNo NUMBER;
begin
    for r_emp in c_emp(10) loop
        v_empNo := r_emp.empNo; --record identifier     →10
          <... .something that could fail #1..>
    end loop;
exception
    when others then
      raise_application_error
        (-20999,'Update failed on the emp#'||v_empNo||
        ' with error :'||sqlerrm);                      →17
end;
```

Here's how Listing 6-17 works:

→10   Saves EMPNO into a variable (v_empNo) that will still exist after the cursor is closed.

→**17**   References `v_empNo` in the error handler. You know that all records with `empNo < V_empNo` were processed successfully because of the `order by` (line 6) in the query.

Knowing what record is processing

Cursor variables were introduced earlier in the section "Accessing Status Info Using Cursor Variables." Although the `%ISOPEN`, `%FOUND`, `%NOTFOUND` variables aren't useful at all in `CURSOR FOR` loops, you can use `%ROWCOUNT` to detect what record you are processing at a given point, as shown in the following example:

```
declare
    v_recordCount_nr NUMBER;                              →2
    cursor c1 is ...
begin
    for r in c1 loop
        v_recordCount_nr:=c1%rowcount;                   →6
        <... do something ...>
    end loop;
    DBMS_OUTPUT.put_line('Rows processed:'||
        v_recordCount_nr);                               →10
end;
```

Here are some additional details about this code:

→**2**   Declares a variable that will hold the number of records processed.

→**6**   Copies the number of records fetched into the variable.

→**10**   References the number of records retrieved after the cursor is closed.

Because you need to know the value of the cursor variable outside the loop, you have to use an additional variable to store that value. If you don't do this, after the loop is closed you can't answer the question "How many records were processed?" Because the cursor is already closed, there is no way to access its information. As usual, if you need something done, just do it yourself.

Referencing Functions in SQL

In SQL, you already know that you can retrieve columns as well as expressions that reference those columns. What you may not know is that you can also write your own functions that can then be referenced within the query.

You find out about writing functions in Chapter 4. If you haven't read that chapter yet, you might want to read it now.

Why some cursor variables work, and some don't

%ISOPEN, %FOUND, %NOTFOUND variables aren't useful at all in CURSOR FOR loops:

✔ The CURSOR FOR loop is always closed before and after the loop and open inside the loop. There is no reason to ever use %ISOPEN.

✔ Inside the loop, records are always found (or else the program would never go inside the loop). So %FOUND is always true inside

the loop. Outside the loop, %FOUND, %NOT FOUND would return an error.

%ROWCOUNT is useful:

✔ %ROWCOUNT can be referenced inside the loop in CURSOR FOR loops or if you used an explicit cursor to define the loop. You can't use it with implicit cursors.

✔ %ROWCOUNT can't be used before or after the loop. It will return an error.

Start with a simple example of creating a Departments/Employees report sorted by department, with a comma-separated list of employees in each department. Your report should look like this:

Department	*Employees*
Accounting	Smith, Jones
Finance	Benson, Marks, Carson
Marketing	Johnson, Chu

There are actually two tasks required here: preparing the comma-separated list and displaying the report.

1. **To prepare the comma-separated list, create the following PL/SQL function, named f_get_Emps:**

```
create or replace function f_getEmps_tx
    (i_deptNo NUMBER)
return VARCHAR2
is
    cursor c_emp is
      select eName
        from    emp
        where   deptNo = i_deptNo;
    v_out_tx VARCHAR2(4000);
begin
    for r_emp in c_emp loop
        if v_out_tx is null
        then
            v_out_tx:=r_emp.eName;
        elsif length(v_out_tx)+
            length(r_emp.eName)>3999
        then
```

```
              null;
          else
              v_out_tx:=v_out_tx||', '||r_emp.eName;
          end if;
      end loop;
      return v_out_tx:
end;
```

2. **Display the report:**

```
select deptNo, dname, f_getEmps_tx(deptNo) emps
from dept
order by dname;
```

That's all you need to do. You can use PL/SQL functions inside SQL code, which gives you the power to go beyond pure SQL functionality. You can use "industrial strength" procedural logic to work with requirements that you couldn't implement otherwise.

Important facts to remember

Everything always comes with a price, and using functions in SQL is no exception. There are a number of drawbacks and restrictions to using these functions.

Datatypes

PL/SQL datatypes don't always correspond directly to SQL datatypes (more details about PL/SQL datatypes can be found in Chapters 10 and 11):

- ✔ BOOLEAN and REF CURSOR types do not exist in SQL at all.
- ✔ VARCHAR2 can only go up to 4,000 in SQL rather than 32,000 in PL/SQL (note this limit in the preceding example).

Read/write restrictions

The PL/SQL reference manual includes some fairly strict rules:

- ✔ When called from a SELECT statement, the function cannot modify any data (no DML except SELECT).
- ✔ When called from an INSERT, UPDATE, or DELETE statement, the function cannot query or modify any data.
- ✔ When called from a SELECT, INSERT, UPDATE, or DELETE statement, the function cannot execute SQL transaction control statements (such as COMMIT), session control statements (such as SET ROLE), or system control statements (such as ALTER SYSTEM). Also, it cannot execute DDL statements (such as CREATE) because they are followed by an implicit COMMIT.

The reason for these rules is simple. Oracle can't be sure that modifying data, the session, the system, or object structure doesn't have any impact on the data you're querying or even on objects you're processing. If such activity isn't blocked, a logical loop or conflict that can't be resolved might result.

Think about what should happen if the function in the next example is called in SQL. This function updates the salary of the specified employee and tells you whether the update was successful:

```
create or replace
function f_giveRaise_tx (i_empNo NUMBER, i_pcnt NUMBER)
return VARCHAR2 is
begin
    update emp
      set sal=sal*(i_pcnt/100)+sal
      where empNo = i_empNo;
    return 'OK';
exception
    when others then
        return 'Error:'||substr(sqlerrm,1,256);
end f_giveRaise_tx;
```

Instead of the update confirmation, the result of the query is an Oracle error, which is caught by the exception handler of the function:

```
SQL> select f_giveRaise_tx(7369,100)
  2  from dual;

F_GIVERAISE_TX(7369,100)
------------------------------------------------------------
Error:ORA-14551: cannot perform a DML operation inside a
          query
SQL>
```

Oops! Oracle just told you that you cannot make that UPDATE.

Performance impact

How does the Oracle know what exactly is happening "under the hood" of the function that you placed inside the query? How can it determine what impact that function could have on overall execution? It can't.

In terms of performance, using functions in SQL is risky. With functions in SQL, the whole idea of SQL optimization gains another dimension; namely, decreasing the impact of function calls.

There are some guidelines you can follow. The next example shows a display function for an employee that returns name and job. It also includes a view that uses this display function for managers:

```
create or replace
function f_emp_dsp (i_empNo NUMBER)
return VARCHAR2 is
    v_out_tx VARCHAR2 (256);
begin
    DBMS_OUTPUT.put_line('Inside of F_EMP_DSP');
    select initcap(eName)||': '||initcap(job)
      into v_out_tx
      from emp
      where empNo = i_empNo;
    return v_out_tx;
end f_emp_dsp;
/
create or replace view v_emp as
select empNo, eName, mgr, f_emp_dsp(mgr) mgr_name, deptNo
from emp;
/
```

When you query the view, it may run much more slowly than a query that accesses the EMP table directly. If performance is important (and performance is always important), you need to be careful. Here are some guidelines:

Don't ask for what you don't need

If you only need EMPNO and ENAME, the following statement is inefficient:

```
select *
from v_emp;
```

Use this statement instead:

```
select empNo, eName
from v_emp;
```

Remember that one of the columns in the view v_emp is defined as a function. In the first case, that function will be executed for each record to be processed. The asterisk (*) means that you are retrieving all columns listed in the view including the column defined as a function. You do not need that extra data, but it will still be unnecessarily calculated when the query is executed, making your query run more slowly than necessary.

Don't ask for what you already have

Function f_emp_dsp will return exactly the same value for the same employee each time it is called. This behavior is called "deterministic." Knowing about this behavior can help Oracle avoid redundant function calls. If a deterministic function was called previously with the same arguments, the optimizer can elect to use the previous result. Thus, the function could be modified as follows:

```
create or replace function f_emp_dsp (in_empNo NUMBER)
return VARCHAR2
DETERMINISTIC is
...
```

Declaring a function DETERMINISTIC is only a hint, and there is no guarantee that the optimizer will use it. However, it can be very handy.

Don't run the function all the time when you only need it some of the time

Assume that you need to take some action for every record in department 10, which includes using the display function for employees. You could start by writing your query this way:

```
declare
    cursor c_emp is
      select *
        from v_emp;
begin
    for r_emp in c_emp loop
        if r_emp.deptNo = 10 then
            ...
        end if;
    end loop;
end;
```

You should assume that any number of calls greater than the number of employees in department 10 is a waste of resources. The following query works exactly as expected:

```
declare
    cursor c_emp is
      select *
        from v_emp
        where deptNo=10;
begin
    for r_emp in c_emp loop
    ...
    end if;
end;
```

Function calls can be expensive from a system resource perspective. Do your best to ensure that the calls you use are efficient and do only what you want them to do.

Getting good performance with functions

Oracle can't do everything for you. For example, it can't guess exactly what you want from your system. The human mind can always outsmart a computer, but the trick is not to outsmart yourself.

Sticking to the following rules will make your life and your database performance significantly better.

- **As you write any function, ask yourself, "Will it be used in SQL or not?"** If so, verify that SQL works with the datatypes you're passing in and out.

- **Verify that you are not performing illegal reads/writes.** For how to cheat if needed, see Chapter 12, which covers transaction control.

- **Think about performance at design time, not later, when users start to complain about it.** Write your code with its future use in mind. Sometimes saving a keystroke or two in implementation might seem like a good idea, but it can result in hours of necessary tuning when your system is in production.

Part III
Standards and Structures

The 5th Wave   By Rich Tennant

The program Roy is testing is so poorly documented, he fails to notice that the game rules for "Twister" have accidentally been included.

In this part . . .

Part III provides guidance about how to structure the code you write and useful standards for naming and coding.

Chapter 7 discusses the many options of where to place PL/SQL code within a system and provides information to help you make the right decision.

Chapters 8 and 9 cover the importance of establishing standards for both naming and coding and list standards that we use in our own work to assist you in creating your own.

Chapter 7

Putting Your Code in the Right Place

*W*riting good code that runs efficiently isn't enough to guarantee the success of a project. Deciding where to put the code is just as important as writing it. Code can be written in lots of different places within a system, but each of these places has pro and cons. Frequently, depending upon what the code needs to do, you can make a clear, correct decision about where the code should reside. At other times, you have a variety of acceptable alternatives for placing the code.

Deciding how and where to place code has been a hotly debated topic in the application development world. In client/server development, you had to decide what logic belonged in the database and what logic belonged within the user interface. Since the advent of Web-based systems that run code on an application server, code can reside in even more places. With all these options, the question remains: Which code should be placed where?

This chapter attempts to give you the answers by taking a look at the pros and cons of your options. First, you find out about storing code in the database. Then we explain why implementing logic in the middle tier should only be done very carefully.

Putting Code in the Database

The most common code container in the database is a stored procedure. *Stored procedures* refer to functions and procedures stored in isolation or grouped into packages. Opting for packages has a number of benefits, including the ability to store large functions or procedures and better code maintenance. In other cases, you might want to store code as a trigger or an `INSTEAD OF` trigger view. The following sections take a look at all these options.

Managing code

Before modern PL/SQL editors were developed, searching the database and retrieving code from the database for editing were inconvenient, but these are now simple tasks. If you're having difficulty finding a specific piece of code, most IDEs have efficient search capabilities that allow you to search all the code stored in the database and retrieve the desired section of code.

Some organizations maintain their source code in documents rather than in the database. This is particularly true of large organizations using formal configuration management architectures where code must be checked in and out before it can be worked on. However, from the developer's perspective, looking through code in the database is easier rather than trying to dig through files maintained by configuration management software. However, this won't be possible if the code in the database is obfuscated, so that it isn't human-readable. This is a measure that may be used in some security-conscious sites and by application packagers.

The most popular IDEs used to search and maintain PL/SQL code are Toad and SQL*Navigator, both developed by Quest Software. For many years, Oracle seemed content not to compete in this market. However, Oracle has recently released SQL Developer (formerly called Raptor and also mentioned in Chapter 2). This tool is a fully featured PL/SQL code editor that might easily dominate the market in the future.

Packaging code in the database

Packages (as we discuss in Chapter 3) are the most common place to put code in the database. There are some differences between placing code in a package and making it an isolated routine beyond its logical organization; we discuss these differences here.

From a code maintenance perspective, putting database code into packages is always better. This allows you to logically group and manage the code much more easily, assuming that you're using an IDE that allows you to view a list of the functions and procedures within a package and quickly navigate to them. However, putting all your functions and procedures into packages has a few disadvantages.

Code scope and visibility in packages

If you place a function or procedure inside a package, it isn't necessarily accessible from outside the package. It will be accessible outside the package only if it is declared in the package specification. Even within the package, it is accessible only to other functions and procedures that are declared after it.

Similarly, within packages, you can declare variables or any objects in the package that either are visible only within the package or can be referenced from outside the package.

Listing 7-1 shows a package to handle login functions. Some functions are accessible only within the package; others can be seen outside of the package.

Listing 7-1:   The Login Function Package

```
create or replace package pkg_emp is
    gv_current_empNo NUMBER;                                  →2

    procedure p_setCurrentEmpNo (i_empNo NUMBER);
    function   f_getCurrentEmpNo return NUMBER;

    procedure p_giveRaise (i_pcnt NUMBER);
end;

create or replace package body pkg_emp is
    gv_LOGUSER_tx VARCHAR2(256);                              →11

    procedure p_validateUser is                              →13
    begin
        if gv_LOGUSER_tx is null then
            raise_application_error
                (-20999,'no valid user!');
        else
            if gv_LOGUSER_tx not like 'SCOTT%' then
                raise_application_error
                    (-20999,'not enough privileges!');
            end if;
        end if;
    end;

    procedure p_setCurrentEmpNo (i_empno number)is
    begin
        gv_LOGUSER_tx:=user||'|'||
                sys_context('userenv','ip_address');
        gv_current_empno:=i_empNo;
    end;

    function f_getCurrentEmpno return NUMBER is
    begin
        return gv_current_empNo;
```

(continued)

Listing 7-1 *(continued)*

```
    end;

    procedure p_giveRaise (i_pcnt NUMBER) is
    begin
        p_validateUser;

        update emp
        set sal=sal*(i_pcnt/100)+sal
        where empno = f_getCurrentEmpno;
    end;
end;
```

The following are additional details about Listing 7-1:

→2   The variable is declared in the package specification. It is visible both inside and outside the package.

→11   The variable is declared in the package body. It will be visible only for procedures/functions after the declaration.

→13   The procedure is declared in the package body. It won't be visible from outside of the package.

Package values are session-specific

Values that are set in objects declared in the package specification are session-specific. This means that until you disconnect your session from Oracle, these values will persist. Traditional database development often uses variables declared in the package specification to act as globals for application code. This approach is valid for client/server development. When Web development began, a problem arose. With a Web application, you don't usually maintain a single persistent connection with the database throughout the entire user session.

Every time users interact with the database, they typically are grabbing an available connection from a persistent pool of connections to perform the database operations. This means that session variables that are set in one operation by a user might not return the same value if examined at a later point in time.

If you want to have a global variable that remains valid throughout a user session, you can't use a package specification variable. What are the alternatives? We discuss several in the following sections.

Storing global values in database tables

If you store the value in a table in the database, when a user begins a processing session, a unique session number is passed from the database. You can then store the global value in a table in the database by using that session identifier. Each time the user makes a system request, this session identifier is passed back to the database. When the user session is terminated, the database must be informed so that the session-specific global values are deleted.

You might also want to create a routine that periodically deletes any old global values in case sessions were abnormally terminated. This happens frequently in a Web environment.

Pros: Storing global values in the database is fast, easily organized by using packages, and has very little overhead.

Cons: The only problem with this approach is that it isn't transparent to the application developer who needs to know that an ID will be passed to him or her. Every time a reconnection to the database is made, this ID must be passed back to the database.

Storing global variables in the middle tier

You can store a copy of all the global variables in the middle tier in some sort of generic structure, in a vector array, or as individual values. To use this approach, you need to minimize the number of round trips between the database and the application server. If you're using a PL/SQL-centric approach, this is difficult because a PL/SQL routine can't access a value stored on the application server. The global values must be passed to the database before they are referenced, using one of the following methods:

- ✔ **You can pass all the global variables to the database when the session is initiated,** which can potentially adversely affect performance if the number is too many.

- ✔ **Or you can pass the variables as needed, depending upon the database action required.** This can be a very complex piece of logic to support. Oracle's Application Development Framework - Business Components (ADF BC) will handle all this complexity quite efficiently. If you're using ADF BC, you can safely use a modest number of package variable references in your code with relatively little performance impact. This method won't be as efficient as storing the code in the database, but it might be adequate for your needs.

If you're placing all the code in the middle tier anyway, storing the global references in the same place makes sense. If the code is divided between the database and the middle tier and you need to have a consistent copy of the global variables, you should also use the application server as the primary storage mechanism.

Pros: Placing global variables in the middle tier makes the global variable references visible from either the middle tier or the database. The middle tier can reference the database, but not vice versa.

Cons: This storage option causes minimal performance impact but the main drawback is complexity. If the code isn't completely stored in the middle tier, you will need to maintain and synchronize multiple copies of the global variables.

Compiling code in a database package

One of the disadvantages of using a package is that you can't compile a portion of a package. Fortunately, you can compile the specification independent of the package body. If you're making changes only to the package body, you aren't required to compile the package specification. Keep in mind the following details about package compilation:

- When recompiling a package specification, any code referencing this package specification must also be recompiled. If you don't recompile, Oracle invalidates the code containing the reference the next time that code is run, and you receive an error message regarding the invalid existing state of packages. Typically, after encountering this initial problem, Oracle automatically recompiles the code (or package body containing the reference), so that the next time the code is run, you don't get an error message. In a development or test environment, this situation is a minor annoyance. However, the compilation of a package specification in a production environment might potentially inconvenience any user logged into the system.

- Another effect of compiling a package specification is that global values stored in the package specification by any open sessions will be lost.

Because compiling a specification leads to these problems, you need to be careful about recompiling packages in a production environment. The good news is that recompiling a package body doesn't affect the package specification.

To illustrate this point, here is a brief example. Keep in mind that the invalidation of code during compilation cascades, meaning that if stored procedure A references stored procedure B which, in turn, references stored procedure C, and stored procedure C is recompiled, both A and B will be invalid.

If procedure A references procedure B and simultaneously B also references A, how can you ever get both compiled at the same time? The answer is that you can't. Oracle will detect the deadlock and nothing will compile.

If you have two packages (P1 and P2) and the body of P2 references something in the specification of P1, recompiling the specification of P1 will invalidate only the body of P2. Therefore, any code referencing the specification of P2 won't be invalidated, as shown in Listing 7-2, in which we create two packages where the package body of PKG_A references PKG_B.

Listing 7-2:   Referencing Package Specifications

```
create or replace package pkg_a is
    v_a NUMBER;
    function a1 return NUMBER;
end;
create or replace package body pkg_a is
    function a1 return NUMBER is
    begin
        return 0;
    end;
end;

create or replace package pkg_b is
    function b1 return NUMBER;
end;
create or replace package body pkg_b is
    function b1 return NUMBER is
    begin
        return pkg_a.a1+1;
    end;
end;
```

Now recompile the package spec of PKG_A and see what happens:

```
SQL> create or replace package pkg_a is
  2        v_a number:=0;
  3        function a1 return NUMBER;
  4  end;
  5  /

Package created.

SQL> select object_name||' '||object_type
  2  from user_objects
  3  where status = 'INVALID';

OBJECT_NAME||''||OBJECT_TYPE
----------------------------------------------------------
PKG_A PACKAGE BODY
PKG_B PACKAGE BODY
SQL>
```

The first time you access package elements, the package bodies would be recompiled:

```
SQL> select pkg_a.a1, pkg_b.b1 from dual;

        A1          B1
---------- ----------
         0           1

SQL> select object_name||' '||object_type
```

```
  2   from user_objects
  3   where status = 'INVALID';

no rows selected

SQL>
```

Controlling access to packages

When using packages to store code in the database, you need to understand how to control access to that code. You can do this in one of two ways: a simple command or a wrapper package.

To grant a user rights to access a particular package, you need to explicitly grant those rights by using the following command:

```
grant execute on package_name to user
```

Note that you can't grant rights to execute a portion of a package. Rights must be granted to an entire package.

To revoke grants from a user, use the following command:

```
revoke execute on package_name from user
```

The following code shows some examples of granting and revoking privileges:

```
SQL> grant execute on pkg_emp to hr;
Grant succeeded.
SQL> revoke execute on pkg_emp from hr;
Revoke succeeded.
SQL>
```

You can limit access to objects in package specification by creating *wrapper packages* by using the capability of procedures in packages to call procedures in other packages. In a complex system, you might have a few large code modules (A, B, and C). Within module A, there might be many different packages. However, there are relatively few functions and procedures in package A that need to be referenced outside of package A. Instead of requiring module B developers to completely understand the structure of module A, you can create a wrapper package to expose only the routines needed to be public to module B. It will be necessary to look only in one wrapper package in module A to access the desired code, as shown in Listing 7-3.

Listing 7-3:   Using a Wrapper Package

```
create or replace package pkg_clientPrint is
    procedure p_print (i_deptNo NUMBER);
    ...
end;

create or replace package body pkg_clientPrint is
    procedure p_print (i_deptNo NUMBER) is
    begin
        pkg_empPrint_pkg.p_printempfile                    →9
                (i_deptNo,'list.txt','IO');
    end;
    ...
end;
```

→9   In the original package PKG_EMPPRINT, the user can specify the output filename and directory. But you want to force the client to use the precise directory and file. That's why you create a special wrapper package with hard-coded values passed to the original P_PRINTEMPFILE. Now if you make only the PKG_CLIENTPRINT package accessible, you can be sure of the output.

If you don't want a user to have access to a particular function or procedure, you can create a separate wrapper package that includes only the portions of the package that the user is allowed to access.

Placing packages for optimal performance

Placing code in packages has mixed impacts on performance. The first time a package is referenced, the entire package is brought into memory. For very large packages (20,000 lines of code or more), this might mean a delay of a full second or more the first time that the package is referenced. When the package is in memory, other users can reference it very quickly. Oracle doesn't reload a new copy of the package for each user on a system.

However, there is only so much room in memory for storing PL/SQL code. If this memory fills up, Oracle is forced to swap out any code that hasn't been used recently. The next time that this code is referenced, it must be reloaded into memory, potentially swapping out other code. Therefore, if you have a large amount of PL/SQL in your system and not a lot of memory allocated for its storage, the performance of the system might rapidly degrade when many users are accessing it.

Sometimes, you need to restructure which procedures reside in which package in order to minimize wasted space in memory. This is particularly true in systems with very large packages, where only a very small number of these packages is being used. Say Package 1 (P1) contains two procedures: procedures A and B. Procedure A is very small and is used often. Procedure B is very large but runs only once each month. Each time procedure A is accessed, the entire package including procedure B is loaded into memory where it consumes space for no good reason.

When functions and procedures are executed, they're individually loaded into memory. This results in much more efficient memory management. However, if you have several dozen functions and procedures that are frequently used, placing them into a package and loading this package one time is more efficient than loading the relevant function or procedure into memory each time it is referenced.

Avoiding size limitations with packages

Here's another important consideration when you're deciding whether to place code into packages: Functions and procedures can be much bigger when placed into packages. An individual function or procedure in Oracle is limited to 32,000 characters (including spaces). This might sound like a lot, but in large routines, this can be used up very quickly.

Packages have no such limitation. You can create a package that is as large as you want. For very large routines, it isn't uncommon to have a package that has nothing in it other than a single function or procedure as a workaround to the size limitation of unpackaged functions and procedures in Oracle.

Placing triggers on tables

Placing triggers on tables is a very common practice that causes more headaches for developers than any other technique. As a result, in many organizations only DBAs are allowed to add triggers to tables.

This section can't present a full treatment of table triggers, but we show you a few useful trigger examples.

For the last 20 years, table triggers have been used to enforce data validation business rules completely independent from the application layer. Conditions specified in the triggers will still be checked, even if they aren't enforced in the user interface. Therefore, you're protected from corrupted data.

Table triggers can be of two types: row-level or statement-level.

Statement-level triggers

Use statement-level triggers when you need to check business rules that are not row dependent. For example, say you have a rule stating that nobody can delete or create new employees over a weekend. This rule concerns the behavior of the whole EMPLOYEE table. That's why you could implement it as a statement-level trigger, as shown in Listing 7-4.

Listing 7-4:   A Statement-Level Trigger

```
create or replace trigger emp_bid
 before insert or delete
 on emp                                                      →2
 referencing new as new old as old
begin
    if to_char(sysdate,'Dy') in ('Sat','Sun') then
        raise_application_error
        (-20999,'No create/delete employees on weekend!');
    end if;
end;
```

→2   By default, triggers are statement-level so you don't need to spec-
      ify the trigger type.

Row-level triggers

If you're concerned about the data in each row, you need to use row-level triggers. Assume that you have the following rule: A manager may not receive a commission that exceeds his or her salary. This rule is about the data in each row, so it should be implemented as row-level trigger as in Listing 7-5.

Listing 7-5:   Row-Level Trigger

```
create or replace trigger emp_biu
 before insert or update
 on emp
 referencing new as new old as old
 for each row                                                →4
begin
    if :new.job = 'MANAGER'                                  →6
    and nvl(:new.sal,0)<nvl(:new.comm,0) then
        raise_application_error (-20999,'Managers should
          not have commissions higher then salary!');
    end if;
end;
```

The following are some additional details about Listing 7-3:

→4   Here you explicitly indicate that you want a row-level trigger.

→6   The major advantage of row-level triggers is that you can use
      :OLD and :NEW prefixes on each column of the table to reference
      the original and modified values.

Not all business rules are so easy to implement because there are restrictions on what you can and cannot do in triggers. Assume that you need to check the following rule: The commissions of any employee may not exceed the salary of his/her manager. The problem here is that you don't have the salary of the employee's manager in the same row. Therefore, you need to query a different row in the same table inside of the trigger. But that is prohibited because of the possibility of table mutation (you can't query the same table you're updating). There are various ways to cheat and query the table you're placing the trigger on. One of these cheats is to declare the trigger as an autonomous transaction, as we discuss in Chapter 12.

Controlling when a trigger fires

You may set triggers to execute either before or after the database event to which they are tied. BEFORE EVENT triggers, as shown in the preceding code, are for preventing the event from actually happening. AFTER EVENT triggers are also very useful. For example, you could use them to create an audit trail when sensitive data in a record was successfully changed. You should not record that information in BEFORE EVENT triggers, because before the database event, you don't know whether your activity will succeed. (Foreign keys or check constraints could fail). An example of an AFTER EVENT trigger is shown in Listing 7-6.

Listing 7-6:   Using an AFTER EVENT Trigger

```
alter table emp add note_tx varchar2(2000)
/
create or replace trigger emp_aiu
 after insert or update of comm, sal                    →4
 on emp
 referencing new as new old as old
 for each row
begin
    update emp
    set note_tx = note_tx||chr(10)||
                  'Update of '||:new.empNo
    where empNo = :new.mgr;                             →12
end;
```

Here's what you need to know about this code:

→4   The trigger is fired after INSERT or UPDATE if the columns COMM or SAL are modified. Therefore, you can be sure that the change already occurred.

→12   In AFTER EVENT row-level triggers you can use :NEW and :OLD variables, but you can't change the value of the NEW variable. That's why you need to fire an explicit UPDATE command. In the current example, we are placing an update notification to the manager of the current employee.

Because you're updating the same table where you have the trigger, the column you're changing should be excluded from the list of columns that cause the trigger to fire. Otherwise, you'll create an infinite loop.

Never place validation rules in AFTER EVENT triggers. Any error raised in an AFTER EVENT trigger causes all previous changes to roll back. This can be an extremely time-consuming error to recover from.

Building INSTEAD OF trigger views

You probably already know that a view is nothing more than some stored SQL that you can query as if it were a table. Only views that are single table or "row ID preserved" allow INSERT UPDATE and DELETE commands. With an INSTEAD OF trigger you can define the behavior of INSERT, UPDATE, and DELETE for any view (no matter how complex).

The INSTEAD OF triggers override the default Oracle behavior of the INSERT, UPDATE, or DELETE command and substitute your custom code.

Assume that you have a customer table and a separate address table in your database. We don't assert that this is a perfect data model, but it will help to illustrate the value of INSTEAD OF trigger views. Tables 7-1 and 7-2 show the columns and datatypes of the CUSTOMER and ADDRESS tables.

Table 7-1	A Sample CUSTOMER Table
CUSTOMER	
customer_id NUMBER	
lastName_tx VARCHAR2(20)	
firstName_tx VARCHAR2(20)	

Table 7-2	A Sample ADDRESS Table
ADDRESS	
address_id NUMBER	
street_tx VARCHAR(200)	
stateProvince_cd VARCHAR2(10)	
postal_cd VARCHAR2(10)	
country_tx VARCHAR2(10)	
customer_id NUMBER — **foreign key to** CUSTOMER	
type_cd VARCHAR2(20)	

In the system we describe here, each customer always has exactly one work address and one home address. If you want to build a screen to enter customer and address information, it would be convenient to have a single CUSTOMER table upon which to base your application. With INSTEAD OF trigger views, you can build a view that does exactly that, as shown in Listing 7-7.

Listing 7-7:   Using an INSTEAD OF Trigger View

```
create or replace view v_customer
as
select c.customer_id,c.lastname_tx,c.firstname_tx,
       w.address_id         work_id,
       w.street_tx          work_street_tx,
       w.stateprovince_cd   work_state_cd,
       w.postal_cd          work_postal_cd,
       w.country_tx         work_country_tx,
       h.address_id         home_id,
       h.street_tx          home_street_tx,
       h.stateprovince_cd   home_state_cd,
       h.postal_cd          home_postal_cd,
       h.country_tx         home_country_tx
from customer c
left outer join address w
    on c.customer_id = w.customer_id
    and w.type_cd = 'W'
left outer join address h
    on c.customer_id = h.customer_id
    and h.type_cd = 'H'

/
create or replace trigger v_customer_id
instead of delete on v_customer
referencing new as new old as old
begin
    delete from address
    where customer_id=:old.customer_id;
    delete from customer
    where customer_id=:old.customer_id;
end;
/
create or replace trigger v_customer_ii
instead of insert on v_customer
referencing new as new old as old
declare
    v_customer_id NUMBER;
begin
    if :new.lastname_tx is not null
    or :new.firstname_tx is not null then
      -- create new customer if name is populated
      insert into customer (customer_id,
        lastname_tx, firstname_tx)
```

```
      values (object_seq.nextval,
        :new.lastname_tx, :new.firstname_tx)
    returning customer_id into v_customer_id;
    -- create work address if street is populated
    if :new.work_street_tx is not null then
      insert into address (address_id,street_tx,
        stateprovince_cd, postal_cd,
        country_tx, type_cd, customer_id)
      values (object_seq.nextval,:new.work_street_tx,
        :new.work_state_cd,:new.work_postal_cd,
        :new.work_country_tx, 'W', v_customer_id);
    end if;
    -- create home address if street is populated
    if :new.home_street_tx is not null then
      insert into address (address_id,street_tx,
        stateprovince_cd,postal_cd,
        country_tx,type_cd,customer_id)
      values (object_seq.nextval,:new.home_street_tx,
        :new.home_state_cd,:new.home_postal_cd,
        :new.home_country_tx, 'H', v_customer_id);
    end if;
  else
      raise_application_error (-20999, 'Cannot create
        customer without name');
  end if;
end;
/
create or replace trigger v_customer_iu
instead of update on v_customer
referencing new as new old as old
begin
  -- update customer
  update customer
  set lastname_tx  = :new.lastname_tx,
      firstname_tx = :new.firstname_tx
  where customer_id = :old.customer_id;
  -- insert/update/delete work addres
  if :old.work_id is not null
  and :new.work_street_tx is null then
    delete from address
    where address_id = :old.work_id;
  elsif :old.work_id is null
  and :new.work_street_tx is not null then
    insert into address (address_id,street_tx,
      stateprovince_cd, postal_cd,
      country_tx, type_cd, customer_id)
    values (object_seq.nextval,:new.work_street_tx,
      :new.work_state_cd,:new.work_postal_cd,
      :new.work_country_tx, 'W', :old.customer_id);
  else
    update address
```

(continued)

Listing 7-7 *(continued)*

```
          set street_tx=:new.work_street_tx,
              stateprovince_cd=:new.work_state_cd,
              postal_cd=:new.work_postal_cd,
              country_tx=:new.work_country_tx
          where address_id = :old.work_id;
      end if;
   -- insert/update/delete home address
      if :old.home_id is not null
      and :new.home_street_tx is null then
         delete from address
         where address_id = :old.home_id;
      elsif :old.home_id is null
      and :new.home_street_tx is not null then
         insert into address (address_id, street_tx,
            stateprovince_cd, postal_cd,
            country_tx, type_cd, customer_id)
         values (object_seq.nextval,:new.home_street_tx,
            :new.home_state_cd,:new.home_postal_cd,
            :new.home_country_tx, 'H', :old.customer_id);
      else
         update address
         set street_tx=:new.home_street_tx,
             stateprovince_cd=:new.home_state_cd,
             postal_cd=:new.home_postal_cd,
             country_tx=:new.home_country_tx
         where address_id = :old.home_id;
      end if;
end;
/
```

With these triggers, you can INSERT, UPDATE, and DELETE from your view, and the data is correctly maintained in the database.

Some developers might argue that you should have built your database table just like the view we created in the first place. Most good designers would design the database in exactly the way we have here. This way you can easily modify the database to hold additional kinds of addresses. You could also easily extend the structure so your address table could attach to different types of objects (like employees). A database isn't designed to support a single application, but rather it must be built to support multiple uses and easily adapt over time. INSTEAD OF trigger views look just like what your developers want to see without compromising good database design principles.

You can create a view for each application screen that looks exactly like the screen you want. You can place validation logic in the view that is specific to the application, and you can add any other logic that means writing less code. There is a big movement in the industry to move code from the database to the application server, but we've found that logic that is implemented in the database runs faster, is less prone to errors, and is easier to maintain.

Understanding INSTEAD OF trigger view performance

If you're using views to drive your user interface, there is no reason to have any concerns about performance. The code in the triggers will almost surely run faster than any other alternative (like code in the application server). And if it is possible for the code to run faster in the application server, it will be faster only by hundredths or even thousandths of a second. This isn't a performance degradation your users are ever likely to notice.

INSTEAD OF trigger views can cause a performance problem if you try to use them to support batch routines. There isn't much overhead in the INSTEAD OF trigger, but the way in which Oracle executes UPDATE commands can cause problems because it takes about ten times as long to update 100 columns as it does to update a single column in a table. If you're updating a single value by using an INSTEAD OF trigger view that is updating a 100-column table, it will take twice as long as updating the table directly. Because Oracle can execute about 10,000 such update statements in a second, this performance problem becomes apparent only if you're doing bulk updates to thousands (or millions) of records. We avoid INSTEAD OF triggers for views that have to support a great deal of data manipulation.

Locking in INSTEAD OF trigger views

The conventional wisdom for locking used to be that you need to lock all your objects before updating any of them. The technique for doing this was to use a SELECT FOR UPDATE command. Experience has shown that using SELECT FOR UPDATE usually causes many more problems than it prevents.

You'll want to keep in mind a few modifications of this old conventional wisdom about locking:

- ✔ In the UPDATE and DELETE triggers in Listing 7-7, it is theoretically possible to cause a deadlock for Oracle to resolve. Because of this possible but logically unlikely event, some developers would place a SELECT FOR UPDATE command in the UPDATE and DELETE triggers. Such measures are almost never necessary.

- ✔ Usually you can ignore locking altogether.

- ✔ If you want to lock the object when it is open in your user interface, you have to lock only the customer record. However, in Web applications, this is hard to do because your session isn't persistent.

- ✔ One alternative to locking the record is to place your own persistent lock as a column in the database. Then your application effectively checks out a record for editing, and when the application is done, it checks the record back in. To do this, pass a unique session ID to each session when it is initiated. The session uses that ID to lock objects. In this case, you would add a LockedBySession_ID to the CUSTOMER table that's populated when the object is checked out and that's set to

NULL when the object is checked back in. Be sure to write a routine to clear out any locks that might have been left when the session terminated abnormally.

Advantages of putting code in the database

In most cases, we recommend keeping code in the database. Using a database-centric approach to creating applications has the following advantages:

- **This approach is the most comfortable for experienced Oracle developers.** It uses basically the same philosophy as creating any front-end application for an Oracle database.

- **The system isn't closely tied to an application development framework (ADF).** Most of the non-UI code resides in the database. We explain why in more detail later in this chapter.

- **User interface work becomes much simpler.** For example, if you use Oracle's JDeveloper, almost all development can be supported through the JDeveloper wizards. Little hand-coding is required. You can build the ADF BC project for an application module in a few hours or less because you're using only one default entity object definition for each database view.

Disadvantages of putting code in the database

The following are some of the disadvantages of creating applications by using a database-centric approach:

- **This approach ignores all the power and flexibility of user interface tools.** If you use JDeveloper and the Oracle ADF, you will have a sophisticated framework that you aren't taking full advantage of.

- **You don't take advantage of the data caching in the user interface.** This is one of the main strengths of Oracle's ADF BC because it offloads database activity to another location and thus saves the CPU cycles of the database server to fulfill its primary purpose — to manage data. The ADF BC layer can cache rows and maintain consistency with the database. This reduces the number of network messages and the amount of database activity required to serve data that has already been served.

✔ **Many products support the J2EE notion that splitting out some application code to another server is beneficial.** If the database is called upon to handle application code, its efficiency to fulfill the primary directive will be compromised by having to handle complex business logic.

✔ **Your application is heavily tied to the Oracle DBMS idea of views with INSTEAD OF triggers.** You can't use this approach to build cross-database applications unless the other database provides a structure similar to views with INSTEAD OF triggers.

Putting Code in the Application Server (Middle-Tier Approach)

Coding in the application server is usually done by using Java in the J2EE environment or VB.NET or C# in the .NET environment. PL/SQL isn't used in middle-tier coding.

Many developers see placing data in the database as old fashioned. It is clearly "cool" to move all your application code into the *middle tier* (the cool way to say "application server"). But if you want your application to run quickly, scale well, and actually work, be careful about moving too much to the application server.

If you're thinking of moving data to the middle tier, you'll want to consider the following points, especially in the early stages of your decision-making:

✔ **If your code needs to access the database, it has to go get that data over the network.** That shouldn't take very long, but if you're processing millions of records, grabbing each one over the network one at a time can turn a smoothly running application into an unusable program.

✔ **It's possible to pull lots of logic into the middle tier and still have a fast running application.** If you can move all the data you need into the middle tier and then do lots of complex processing and push relatively little data back to the database, then moving your code to the middle tier might actually help performance.

In practice, however, this technique is very hard to use. You're counting on the benefits of partitioning work away from an overworked database server to offset the cost of moving data around unnecessarily. Such a benefit is realized only if your database server is being heavily utilized, which isn't a common situation.

✔ **The main impetus for moving data into the middle tier is that the developers are Java or .NET programmers who don't know how to program well in the database.** This lack of skill isn't a good reason for placing data in the middle tier.

✔ **Some amount of code should be placed in the middle tier.** Code needed by the user interface will perform better in the middle tier.

✔ **One way that PL/SQL is used in the middle tier is when building applications using the Oracle Developer suite that includes Oracle Forms and Oracle Reports.** Forms isn't used for much new development because it has been eclipsed by J2EE (JDeveloper in the Oracle environment) and .NET-based products. However, Reports is still one of the best reporting tools on the market. Both Forms and Reports allow you to write PL/SQL to support all your logic in those products. This is very convenient because you can move code between the database and the middle tier easier than with any other language. It's a shame that no current development product uses PL/SQL on the application server, nor can you write Java (at least not very well) or some .NET language in the database.

In addition to the preceding points, we sum up the pros and cons of working with the middle tier and explore a couple of cases when using this tier might be to your advantage.

Advantages of the middle-tier approach

The following advantages can be gained by using the middle-tier approach:

✔ Data caching, code reuse, and independence from the database are useful aspects of this approach.

✔ If used correctly, this approach provides development efficiencies because of the increased modularity of the persistence/business logic layer.

✔ You can take advantage of the ability to offload activity from the database server.

Disadvantages of the middle-tier approach

The following are some of the disadvantages of the middle-tier approach:

✔ It is a conceptually difficult approach because the business rules of the system might reside in different places. For example, the rules might reside in the database or in code in the application server. Standards and guidelines for the use of the different code locations must be developed and enforced.

✔ Organizations embracing this strategy should be careful to formalize the design rules. The rules need to answer questions such as "How will objects be constructed and how will they interact?"

✔ Without careful planning, the additional flexibility afforded by this approach can result in systems where bugs are difficult to track down. This is because the logic error might reside in many places. Well-designed error messages can assist in reducing this problem.

✔ If you change your UI architecture (or if the architecture evolves), you will have to rewrite your application.

Placing code in the view layer

You can use client-side (view layer) coding involving languages like JavaScript to enforce business rules. This should be done very carefully (and rarely). By adding code to a Web application, you can greatly increase the size of the application, causing it to load very slowly. Making round trips from the client to the application server or database usually takes (at least) a significant fraction of a second, making multiple round trips impossible.

Where Should You Place the Business Logic?

As long as the development team has some requisite PL/SQL skills and isn't attempting to create a database-platform independent system, whenever possible, business logic should be placed in the database, either in functions and procedures or encapsulated as complex views (perhaps with INSTEAD OF triggers).

Whether through the evolving J2EE stack or the political arbitrariness of organizations, architectures change. Organizations might give up and decide to change their entire development platforms from Oracle to .NET. Drastic changes in the UI architecture are protected by placing as much logic as possible into the database. In addition, even though improving performance by using a middle-tier approach such as ADF BC (where data is cached in the middle tier instead of the database) is logically possible, in most cases, systems where business logic is stored in the database will outperform those where this same logic is stored in the middle tier. The industry standard (particularly in the OO community) is to pull logic out of the database and place it in the middle tier. Rarely does this strategy have any beneficial impact on system performance.

Logic should never be placed in the view layer when it will require a round trip to the database or application server. If any logic is placed in the view layer of Web applications, developers will have to be very careful to avoid performance problems caused by the increased size of the applications being loaded to the client machines.

Chapter 8

Creating Naming Standards

· ·

· ·

*N*aming and coding standards are among the most important, albeit contentious, topics we cover in this book. (We discuss coding standards in Chapter 9.) Most developers agree that being consistent in both naming code structures and organizing code is vitally important for two key reasons:

  ✔ Applying standards consistently makes your code easier to read and allows other developers to maintain the code much more easily.

  ✔ Using good naming standards can actually help you write code faster because you won't have to stop and think about how to name elements every time you encounter them.

Despite the almost universal agreement that standards are necessary, there is little agreement about what these standards should be. Every organization tends to evolve its own style. If you move from one organization to another, you'll find very different naming styles and standards.

The goal of this chapter is to provide some examples of useful PL/SQL naming conventions. In addition, we present explicit naming and coding examples to provide a clear understanding of the naming concepts and how you can implement them.

What's in a Naming Standard?

When creating or reviewing naming standards, most organizations attempt to examine the development environment as a whole rather than define the PL/SQL (or any other) part of their standards in isolation. A number of factors are related to the programming languages and tools that influence the most widely used naming conventions. You should be aware of these before setting your standards.

Oracle database influences

One influence that affects PL/SQL naming and coding standards is the database itself. Oracle includes some naming limitations that you must carry over into your naming standards. Among your key considerations are the following:

- PL/SQL is an Oracle database programming language. As a result, you will refer to Oracle database objects such as tables, columns, and stored procedures. So your naming conventions need to take into consideration the naming limitations and rules within Oracle.

- Oracle has a length limitation on object names. Most database objects (tables, columns, views, and so on) must have names that are less than 32 characters long.

- Names of objects are stored all in uppercase (as evidenced in the database view USER_OBJECTS) even if they were created with lowercase or mixed case. Although later versions of Oracle enable you to create objects with mixed case, this functionality is rarely used.

- It is particularly challenging to name things appropriately when writing PL/SQL code to modify or extend existing software or packaged software where you have no control over the previously established naming standards. Try to make your PL/SQL naming standards consistent with the existing database naming standards. Unfortunately, much of the available packaged software demonstrates inconsistent or nonexistent use of naming standards. In these situations, we recommend creating your own naming standards for new code and making the best of existing oddly named database objects.

Java influences

Writing database applications usually involves some programming language in addition to PL/SQL. Most user interfaces use Java or .NET to create Web-based applications. These languages have evolved their own naming conventions. One big difference is that these languages support mixed-case naming. To create a consistent set of standards throughout your environment, you might want to use standards similar to those used by most Java (or other language) programmers to avoid conflicts between the PL/SQL code and these other languages.

Modern application development tools and their influences

Unfortunately, many organizations are unwilling to invest in tools to make their developers more productive. Oracle's SQL*Plus is a no-frills tool with few of the nice features of products that try to support PL/SQL development. Some developers even prefer SQL*Plus for development (just as some Java or C++ developers who prefer using basic text editors to write code).

However, most developers use code development products such as Quest Software's Toad or SQL Navigator, rather than SQL*Plus, to write code. Only recently did Oracle release a sophisticated, user-friendly graphical PL/SQL development tool called Oracle SQL Developer (formerly called Project Raptor). Tools like these, which we introduce in Chapter 2, tend to automatically highlight language reserved words in a contrasting color and might even do a reasonable job of laying out the code with consistent indentation. When you're creating both naming and coding standards, take into consideration the way these tools operate. For example, before the widespread use of code development tools, many organizations made all locally named objects lowercase and language reserved words uppercase to easily distinguish them. This standard is irrelevant when using code development tools. If you're using a tool that automatically formats code according to a reasonable standard, be sure to adopt this style as your standard.

Setting Naming Standards for Common Code Elements

You need to create a coherent set of naming standards based on your environment, the programming languages involved, and the database software. The standards shouldn't be so detailed and complex that they're impossible to follow. Neither should they be so lax that they fail to impose some structure and guidelines for developers to follow.

Because everyone has different ideas about the best standards, many experienced PL/SQL developers might not be comfortable with the examples in this chapter. So just consider these rules and examples a starting point or jumping-off point for creating your own standards. The point is to create a set of standards and rigorously enforce them. No matter what standard you use, it should include approximately the level of detail proposed in the following pages.

Basic objects

Naming an object is not as simple as it sounds. You must address the following factors:

- ✔ **Capitalization:** As already mentioned, capitalization of reserved words isn't necessary because you can usually rely on your development tool to color all reserved words for you.

  Using mixed case makes your code much more readable. In general, lowercase or mixed-case text is easier to read than uppercase text.

  In Java, all classes begin with a capital letter, but objects start with a lowercase letter. To be consistent with this standard, elements such as tables and views should start with a capital letter. Columns and variables should start with a lowercase letter.

- ✔ **Usage of prefixes and suffixes:** Prefixes and suffixes typically indicate some attribute of the object being named, usually the object's type or the type of data that it stores or returns. Many people think that prefixes and suffixes greatly help in the readability of code. Others find them to be a useless annoyance.

  On the positive side, prefixes and suffixes tell you something about the element. Another significant advantage of prefixes and suffixes is that they prevent you from naming an element the same as a reserved word or a similar object of a different type. On the negative side, prefixes and suffixes make the element name longer.

  We believe that the advantages of prefixes and suffixes outweigh their disadvantages. The standard we propose in this chapter uses prefixes to indicate the type of the object and suffixes to indicate the types of data associated with the element. For example, v_name_tx indicates an internal variable (v_) that stores text (_tx).

- ✔ **Degree of abbreviation:** All names of elements in Oracle must be less than 32 characters. This means that very long names aren't possible in PL/SQL. Therefore, you have to abbreviate because you simply cannot use a name like totalPayrollSocialSecurityWithholdingTax.

  In general, try to be consistent. If you abbreviate the word Total to Tot in one context, you might want to seriously consider using Tot for Total everywhere. This way, you won't have to remember whether Total is spelled out in any particular name. To support consistency in naming, keep a list of abbreviations that all developers will use.

  Set a size limit for words (usually six characters). All words with more than six characters must be abbreviated. Words shorter than six characters are never abbreviated. Very common short words (such as Total) that have widely understood common abbreviations can also be abbreviated.

✔ **Separating individual words (underscore, initial-letter capitalization, and so on):** You can't name elements with embedded spaces in PL/SQL. If the element name includes several words, you need some way to indicate the start of each word. Because Oracle doesn't support mixed-case naming very well, many developers use an underscore (_) as a method of separating words, as in FIRST_NAME. Although the underscore adds a character to the name (remember, all names must be less than 32 characters), this method has the advantage of clearly indicating different words in the element name.

The other method used for separating words is to use initial-letter capitalization (init-caps) for each word, as in firstName. This is the standard in Java and other languages that support mixed-case names.

Our proposed standard suggests using the init-caps method. The benefits of shorter names and conforming to the Java standard outweigh the difficulty in reading the names of database elements. It isn't usually a problem to discern beginnings of words in names of database elements even though they always appear in uppercase (for example, FIRSTNAME).

Variables

At this point, you may not have used all the datatypes that are mentioned in Tables 8-1 and 8-2 (most of them are covered in Chapters 10, 11, and 13) but you need to be aware of the standards set for them.

The following guidelines should be used when naming variables:

✔ Every variable name must have an attached prefix (see Table 8-1 for examples).

✔ Variables (where applicable) are suffixed with an abbreviation to denote datatype (see Table 8-2).

✔ Between the prefix and suffix, the name of the variable is one or more words separated by init-caps.

✔ If a variable is semantically equivalent to a column in a database table (whether or not that variable will directly read or write data from the database column), it should be named the same as the database column with an appropriate prefix.

Table 8-1	PL/SQL Variable Prefixes
Prefix	*Variable Type*
v_	Local variables declared within a function or procedure
c_	Cursor
r_	Record variable for CURSOR FOR loops
gv_	Global variables declared within a package
gl_	Global constants declared within a package
gc_	Global cursors declared within a package

Table 8-2	PL/SQL Variable Suffixes
Suffix	*Variable Type*
_yn	Pseudo-Boolean items using 'Y' and 'N' for values
_cd	Variables restricted to a set of "codes"
_tx	All other text formats not covered by cd or yn
_id, _oid	Variables to store unique IDs / object IDs
_nr	Any numeric datatype not covered by _id or _oid
_dt	Date
_ts	Timestamp datatype
_tf	Boolean variable (TRUE/FALSE values)
_rec	Record defined via %ROWTYPE reference to existing table/view/cursor
_ref	REF CURSOR defined via SYS_REFCURSOR datatype
_cl	CLOB datatype
_bl	BLOB datatype
_bf	BFILE datatype

The following examples show how you might apply these prefixes and suffixes to create variable names:

✔ A variable storing a customer's name: `v_custName_tx`

✔ A global variable storing an employee's death date: `gv_death_dt`

✔ A Boolean evaluation variable: `v_eval_tf`

Many larger organizations extend the idea of variable prefixes and suffixes to contain even more information. For example, we have listed only six suffixes for our variables. Some organizations use many more suffixes. They have separate suffixes to denote a person's name field (`nm`), currency (`cy`), percentage (`pc`), and so on.

The bottom line: The more complex you make your variable names, the easier it is to read the code. However, a complex standard takes longer to master, and complying with the standard becomes more difficult for the developers.

Program units: Procedures, packages, functions, triggers

The following guidelines should be used when naming program units:

✔ Every procedure or function name should have a prefix (see Table 8-3).

✔ Every package or trigger name should have a suffix (see Table 8-4).

✔ Functions are suffixed by the datatype of the value they return. In some cases, you can use special suffixes to indicate a class of the function (`_DSP` for display functions rather than generic `_TX`).

✔ Between the prefix and suffix, the name of the variable will be one or more words separated by initial capital letters (init-caps).

✔ Trigger names are always a composite. The last part indicates the type of event (`I` for insert, `U` for update, `D` for delete, or combinations of these letters). The first part of the trigger indicates its type.

Table 8-3	PL/SQL Object Prefixes
Prefix	*Object Type*
`p_`	User-defined procedure
`f_`	User-defined function
`pkg_`	User-defined package

Table 8-4	PL/SQL Trigger Suffixes
Suffix	*Object Type*
`<table>_B[I,U,D]`	Row-level BEFORE triggers
`<table>_SB[I,U,D]`	Statement-level BEFORE triggers
`<table>_A[I,U,D]`	Row-level AFTER triggers
`<table>_SA[I,U,D]`	Statement-level AFTER triggers
`<table>_I[I,U,D]`	INSTEAD OF trigger

In the following examples, you can see how these prefixes work with actual procedures and functions:

- A procedure that runs employee payroll: `p_empPay`
- A package that stores employee related functions and procedures: `pkg_empUtil`
- A function that returns an employee's birthday: `f_empBirth_dt`. Note that because the variable uses the date suffix (`_dt`), you don't need to include the word `Day` or `Date` in the name.
- A function that returns a VARRAY of all managers: `f_mgr_va`
- A row-level BEFORE UPDATE trigger on table EMP: `emp_bu`
- An INSTEAD OF trigger on the view V_EMP to handle inserts, updates and deletes simultaneously: `v_emp_iiud`

Parameters in code objects

Use the following guidelines for naming parameters:

- Every parameter will be prefixed by one to three characters that indicate its input/output type and context. (See Table 8-5.)
- Otherwise parameters are named the same as regular data variables. (See the section "Variables," earlier in this chapter.)

Table 8-5	Parameter Prefixes
Prefix	*Variable Type*
`i_`	Procedure and function IN variable
`o_`	Procedure OUT variable

Prefix	Variable Type
io_	Procedure IN OUT variable
ci_, co_, cio_	Parameter (IN, OUT, and IN OUT) called in a cursor
fi_, fo_, fio_	Parameter (IN, OUT, and IN OUT) in a local function
pi_, po_, pio_	Parameter (IN, OUT, and IN OUT) in a local procedure

Rather than giving specific examples, illustrating parameter naming in the context of a small program might be clearer. Listing 8-1 assumes that you want a program to return the address of an employee, given the employee's ID.

Listing 8-1:   A Parameter Naming Example

```
create or replace function
     f_currAddr_tx (i_emp_id NUMBER                         →2
   return VARCHAR2 is
cursor c_currAddr (ci_emp_id NUMBER) is                     →4
     select addr.addr_tx
       from addr, emp
     where addr.emp_id = emp.emp_id
     and emp.emp_id = ci_emp_id;
     v_currAddr_rec  c_currAddr%ROWTYPE;

     v_addr_tx addr.addr_tx%TYPE;

     --local function to get employee name
     --for line 1 of addr display
     function f_empName_tx (fi_emp_id NUMBER)               →15
         return VARCHAR2 is
       v_out_tx VARCHAR2(2000);
     begin
       select ename
         into  v_out_tx
         from emp
       where emp_id = fi_emp_id;
       return  v_out_tx;
     end  f_empName_tx;

begin  -- f_currAddr_tx
  open c_currAddr (i_emp_id);
  fetch c_currAddr into v_currAddr_rec;
  close c_currAddr;
  v_addr_tx := r_currAddr.addr_tx;
  return v_addr_tx;
end f_currAddr_tx;
```

Check out the following explanations of lines from Listing 8-1:

→**2**   `i_emp_id` is declared as an input parameter for the main function.

→**4**   `ci_emp_id` is declared as an input parameter for a cursor.

→**15**   `fi_emp_id` is declared as the input parameter for a local function.

Exceptions

User-defined exceptions will include a prefix string `e_` to identify exceptions, followed by a descriptive name. The name should contain two parts: what went wrong, and what thing failed. For example, if a procedure to run payroll (`p_runPay`) failed, you might call the exception `e_failRunPay`.

The exception might have a datatype suffix if it refers to a variable with a datatype suffix. For example, if you want an exception for an incorrect format of the Social Security number (`SSN_tx`), you could call it `e_BadSSN_tx`.

The following examples illustrate how you might apply these exception-naming standards:

✔ An exception for a too-long name field: `e_longName_tx`

✔ An exception for a function (`f_getSalary`) that should have returned a value but didn't: `e_noValueFromGetSalary`

User-defined datatypes

The name of all user-defined datatypes should include a composite suffix as shown in Table 8-6.

Table 8-6	User-Defined Datatypes
Suffix	*Type*
`_oty`	User-defined object type
`_rty`	User-defined record type
`_sty`	User-defined subtype
`_rcty`	User-defined `REF CURSOR` type

All variables of user-defined datatypes should have appropriate prefixes (`v_`, `gv_`, and so on) and corresponding suffixes. Listing 8-2 shows the proper use of naming standards:

Listing 8-2:   An Example of Proper Naming Standards Usage

```
create or replace TYPE custAddress_oty as object(
      street_tx VARCHAR2(50),
      city_tx   VARCHAR2(30),
      state_cd  CHAR(2),
      zip_tx    VARCHAR2(10));

create or replace package pkg_commonType
is
    gv_addres_oty custAddress_oty;

    type custAddress_rty is record(
      street_tx VARCHAR2(50),
      city_tx   VARCHAR2(30));
    type WeakRefCursor_rcty is ref cursor;

    subtype smallString_sty is VARCHAR2(10);

    gl_region_sty constant smallString_sty:='North-East';
end;
```

Collections

Oracle supports three types of collections:

- Associative arrays
- Nested tables
- VARRAYs

The name of the collection type will include a suffix string to identify the type. Table 8-7 shows the list of suffix strings for collection types.

Table 8-7	Collection Suffixes
Suffix	**Collection Type**
_aa	Associative arrays
_nt	Nested tables
_va	VARRAYs

Instances of object collections or VARRAYs are prefaced with in the same way as variables (v_, gv_ and so on) and have the same suffixes as their datatypes (see Listings 8-3 and 8-4).

Listing 8-3:   An Associative Array

```
declare
     type emp_rty is record (                          →2
         name_tx VARCHAR2(50),
         age_nr INT);

     type emp_aa is table of emp_rty                   →6
     index by binary_integer;

      v_emp_aa emp_aa;                                 →9
begin
 -- code goes here
end;
/
```

Here's what's going on in Listing 8-3:

→2   Declaration of record type to help define the associative array.

→6   Declaration of the associative array type.

→9   Declaration of an instance of the associative array.

Listing 8-4:   A VARRAY

```
declare
    type integer_va                                    →3
       is varray (10) of integer;
    v_integer_va integer_va;                           →5
begin
  -- code goes here
end;
```

Like the code in Listing 8-3, lines 3 and 5 in Listing 8-4 also use prefixes and/ or suffixes.

Filenames

When you write code, it is stored in the database. However, most organizations also store the script to create the object in a text file. You can then archive these files in a configuration management system to efficiently manage software versioning.

The name of the file will be the name of the database object being created.

The file type (or *extension*) indicates the type of object created. A three-letter suffix will be used as the file extension to identify the type of DDL stored in the file. Table 8-8 shows some common object type abbreviations.

Table 8-8	Object Type Abbreviations
Object Type Abbreviation	*Object Type*
pks	Package specification
pkb	Package body
fnc	Function
prc	Procedure
trg	Trigger
tys	Type specification
tyb	Type body

The following examples show how these abbreviations might work with actual files:

✔ The script for creating the function f_getEmp_dsp will be stored in the file f_getemp_dsp.fnc.

✔ The script to create a utility package specification might be pkg_util.pks.

✔ The script to create the same package body might be pkg_util.pkb.

Making Sure Your Organization Follows Standards

Most organizations recognize the need for standards. They take the time to create and distribute naming standards. However, relatively few organizations actively enforce those same standards. To enforce standards, all code must be reviewed prior to delivery. Code review may be done less formally by a coworker or it may be a formal step in the code delivery process. Each organization must decide the best way to enforce the standards that it sets.

When standards are in place, you need to be vigilant to make sure that developers follow them consistently. All it takes is one project that deviates from an organization's standards to change the culture from one that strictly adheres to standards to one where developers code any way they want. The extra work involved in creating and enforcing the naming standards will definitely pay off in the long run by making all your code easier to read and maintain over time.

Chapter 9

Creating Coding Standards

● ●

In This Chapter

▶ Uncovering universal truths

▶ Discovering SQL development rules

▶ Examining PL/SQL development rules

▶ Checking out stored PL/SQL program units

● ●

*T*his chapter provides some useful coding standards for PL/SQL developers. Setting and adhering to standards creates a uniform environment that makes it much easier to read and later modify code. Standards can also decrease the cost of the initial development of the code. Well-designed code is easier to write and debug.

Coding standards are as hotly contested a topic as naming conventions. How to capitalize, where to break up lines, and how to comment the code can inspire lively debates within organizations.

This chapter explains the important benefits of standards and provides useful coding standards for PL/SQL developers. Throughout the book, we talk about how to write good code. This chapter summarizes many of the rules and suggestions to help you write code that is easier to read and maintain. Because many of the same standards are applicable in both SQL and PL/SQL contexts, this chapter also includes a discussion of how to lay out your SQL code.

Why Standards Are Important

Coding standards, by and large, don't directly affect how the code behaves. However, they do have some important benefits:

✔ **Standards can make your code less prone to errors.** For an example, see the later section, "Use explicit data conversion for dates."

✔ **Standards make the code easier to read and maintain.** Setting and adhering to standards creates a uniform environment. This is important because code that goes into production has a bad habit of living for many years in a system. In the Y2K (year 2000) crises that hit the software industry in the late 1990s, millions of lines of COBOL code used a 2-digit field for the year. When the calendar rolled around to 2000, all that code was going to stop working. No one worried about this problem when the code was written in the 1960s and 1970s (up to 40 years previously). Count on the fact that the code you write will still be in production long after you retire.

✔ **Standards can decrease the cost of the initial code development.** Well designed code is easier to write and debug.

When programmers follow standards, they can more easily find errors, debug code while testing, and maintain code by quickly zeroing in on the problem spots.

Universal Truths

Developers can disagree about the right way to do things. However, the following guidelines are well accepted as good coding practices by most senior developers (even though many of these guidelines might not be very carefully followed).

These standards aren't unique to PL/SQL. Any programming language code should also follow these rules.

Don't hard-code any constant value

Never reference a constant in your code. This is especially true if the value is already stored in the database. For example, if you have special code that you need to execute for employees who live outside the United States and you have a column called `country_cd` that refers to the country `USA` in your `EMPLOYEE` table, you could create a constant that could be referenced throughout the application. As a result, it might be reasonable to consider these as *global* constants. Without the idea of such global constants, your code will look something like the examples in Listings 9-1 and 9-2.

Listing 9-1:   Hard-Coded Data Value

```
declare
  cursor c_employee is
    select emp_id,
           name
    from employee
    where country_cd != 'USA';                    →6
begin
```

```
     for r_employee in c_employee loop
       -- process non-US employees
     end loop;
  end;
```

■ **➝6**   Hard-coded reference to USA.

Imagine that the code in Listing 9-1 is part of a large system and that USA is referenced hundreds of times. Then your boss comes in and tells you to change the USA code to US throughout the database. This means that all of your code is going to stop working!

As a second example, imagine that you want implement a rule to limit purchases to no more than $10,000. To do this, you might include something like Listing 9-2.

Listing 9-2:   Hard-Coded Rule Parameter

```
if v_amount_nr > 10,000 then
  -- do something about the large amount
end if;
```

Raising the limit to $15,000 might seem like a simple task. However, if your system has hundreds or even thousands of program units, finding this specific rule might take days.

You can avoid these problems by placing all referenced values in a special package like the one shown in Listing 9-3. (We discuss packages in Chapter 7.)

Notice that you can't simply make the values variables in the package specification. Instead, create the variables in the package body and reference them through a procedure that sets the value (the *setter*) and a function that retrieves the value (the *getter*). The reason to do this is that there are limitations to using package variables. The biggest problem is that you can't directly reference them in SQL.

Listing 9-3:   Globals Stored in a Package

```
create or replace
package pkg_global
  is
 procedure p_countryUSA_cd (i_CD VARCHAR2);              ➝4
 function f_countryUSA_cd return VARCHAR2;               ➝5

 procedure p_purchaseLimit_nr (i_nr NUMBER);
 function f_purchaseLimit_nr return NUMBER;

end; -- PKG_GLOBAL
```

(continued)

Listing 9-3 *(continued)*

```
create or replace
package body pkg_global
is
--- data variables
  gv_countryUSA_cd VARCHAR2(3) := 'USA';                    →16
  gv_purchaseLimit_nr NUMBER := 10000;


 procedure p_countryUSA_cd (i_cd VARCHAR2) is               →20
 begin
   gv_countryUSA_cd := i_cd;
 end;                                                       →23

 function f_countryUSA_cd return VARCHAR2 is                →25
 begin
   return gv_countryUSA_cd;
 end;                                                       →28

 procedure p_purchaseLimit_nr (i_nr NUMBER) is
 begin
   gv_purchaseLimit_nr := i_nr;
 end;

 function f_purchaseLimit_nr return NUMBER is
 begin
   return gv_purchaseLimit_nr;
 end;

end;
```

Here are the details about Listing 9-3:

→**4, 5**   The setter and getter for `country_cd`.

→**16**   The package body variable that stores `country_cd`.

→**20–23** The setter code for `country_cd`.

→**25–28** The getter code for `country_cd`.

Using the `pkg_global` package in Listing 9-3, Listings 9-1 and 9-2 could be rewritten with the globals stored in the `pkg_global` package to produce Listings 9-4 and 9-5.

Listing 9-4:   Replace Hard-Coded Data Value with Reference

```
declare
  cursor c_employee is
    select emp_id,
           name
    from employee
```

```
      where country_cd != pkg_global.f_countryUSA_cd;
begin
   for r_employee in c_employee loop
     -- process non-US employees
   end loop;
end;
```

Listing 9-5:   Replace Rule Parameter with Reference

```
if v_amount_nr > pkg_global.f_purchaseLimit_nr then
  -- do something about the large amount
end if;
```

Despite the advantages of replacing hard-coded values with globals, this guideline is seldom followed. It takes an extra few seconds each time for the programmer to write the code that references a value to check that the value is in the global package and ready to be referenced. Most programmers will never take that extra time unless forced to do so.

In large organizations, individual programmers are usually not allowed to modify the global package to make sure that no one makes a mistake that could potentially impact hundreds of other programs.

Don't make your program units too big or too small

Inexperienced programmers don't always segment their code into discrete program units. Instead, they write individual routines that include hundreds or even thousands of lines of code. On the other hand, some inexperienced programmers learned about "structured programming" in a college class. These programmers might break every 20 lines of code into its own program unit, creating unreadable, unmaintainable "spaghetti" code, with routines calling other routines which call still other routines 10–20 levels deep.

Whenever a routine stretches over a few hundred lines of code and resides in a single program unit with no local functions or procedures, ask yourself whether you can break up the code into smaller chunks. On the other side of the spectrum, if your code has dozens of little routines of 20 or fewer lines each calling each other with more than 5 levels of nesting, think about consolidating the code more efficiently.

The only way to get a feel for the right size of a program unit is to have someone else review your code. You wrote the routine, so the logical structure is clear to you. However, if someone else has to maintain your code, will he or she able to do it? To verify that your code is maintainable, have someone else look over it. If that person can't figure out the logic just by looking at your code, you have a problem.

As in all things, there are exceptions to the rules. Some routines don't lend themselves easily to being divided and can get quite large. However, if a single program unit is longer than 1,000 lines, something is probably wrong.

Put each data element on its own line

When declaring cursors and calling functions with lots of parameters, put each data element on its own line. The SQL INSERT statement in Listing 9-6 illustrates this standard.

Listing 9-6: Place Data Elements on Separate Lines

```
insert into emp (
    empNo
    eName,
    sal)
  values (
    123,    --empNo
    Fred,   --eName,
    1000); --sal)
```

Notice how easy it is to see the different values. The column names are also repeated next to each of the values. This makes it very easy to be sure that you are assigning your values into the right column. The following are some simple guidelines to follow:

- Always repeat the column names in the values section of the INSERT statement.
- Write the top half of the code statement with all the column names, and then copy and paste those names into the bottom half of the code.
- Add values as you comment out the column names in the bottom half.

Some programmers like to put commas at the start of each line rather than at the end. That way, you can more easily comment out any particular line of the code without having to worry about removing the comma at the end of the previous line. This practice makes the code look somewhat funny, but it is a popular practice. There is no right answer to the question of which side of the element to add the comma. But whichever side your organization chooses, everyone needs to follow the standard consistently.

Too many comments are much better than too few comments

Every programming class you will ever take and every programming book you will ever read says that you should comment your code. Few resources address the issue of what, exactly, needs to be commented and how to do it.

To indicate comments, use the double dash (`- - comment`) rather than the `/*comment*/` construct. This makes it easy to comment out large blocks of code by using `/* */` when debugging.

Realistically, the only way you are likely to comment your code carefully is if you're forced to do so by your organization. This is another reason why organizations should set and enforce clearly defined standards. Code should always be reviewed by someone other than the person who wrote it before the code is used in a production system. Code should fail the review if it doesn't contain enough comments.

How many comments are enough?

To help you understand what we mean by "enough" comments, use the following guidelines:

✔ First and foremost, note who wrote the code and when it was written or modified. Many organizations insist on placing an author comment block at the top of each routine to show who has modified it. Listing 9-7 shows a sample author comment block.

Listing 9-7:   An Author Comment Block

```
--Author                  Date         What
--jsmith@dulcian.com      1/1/2005     Initial coding
--tjones@dulcian.com      2/2/2005     Performance tune SQL
--jsmith@dulcian.com      3/3/2005     Added date filter
```

✔ Inside the code routine, add a comment every time you modify code that is in use or was written by someone else.

✔ Every routine should have a comment at the top that explains what the routine does.

✔ You should also add comments at the beginning of every major section and whenever there is anything interesting or not obvious in your code. A good rule is that if you're looking at a screen's worth of code and don't see any comments, you probably have too few.

✔ Automatically comment all `BEGIN` and `END` statements (`END`, `END IF`, and `END LOOP`). Doing so makes it much easier to see the structure of the code with such comments. These comments need not be very long. They're just there to assist readability.

The goal is to make your code readable by another developer who might have to modify it. Therefore, the best way to know whether your code is adequately commented is to show it to another developer to see whether he or she can understand how your code works. Although it's tempting to look at one's own code and say, "This code is so simple, it's self-documenting," the author of the code can hardly be objective about his or her own work. If the other developer cannot easily follow your code, it needs more comments.

Writing useful comments

Writing a good comment is an art in itself. In addition to explaining when to comment, we also include helpful guidelines for *how* to comment:

✔ **Keep in mind what information is useful to a future reader of your code.** A comment `Start of loop` next to a statement that initiates a `LOOP` statement is a wasted comment. However, if the comment says `main customer loop`, it clearly indicates what the loop is and helps the programmer who will have to later read or maintain your code.

✔ **Some "obvious" comments can be very helpful.** Commenting the `END` statement of every program unit seems pretty silly. If the line is the last line in the program, it must be the final `END;` statement. However, when you're debugging, you might have several `END` statements in a row. Being able to see which is which is very helpful.

✔ **Try to keep your comments to no more than a line or two.** Comments shouldn't be so long as to make the code harder to read. Some programmers get carried away and write paragraphs in the middle of routines explaining their rationale for why the code is written in a certain way. Rarely is such explanation needed within the code.

Many different comments sprinkled throughout the code are much better than a few verbose descriptions.

Looking at example comments

Listing 9-8 is an example of well-commented code that illustrates the good coding standards described in this section.

Listing 9-8: Well-Commented Code

```
declare
--Routine to process payroll.                              →2
--Author          Date           What                     →3
--jsmith@dulcian.com 1/1/2005     Initial coding
```

```
      cursor c_emp is  -- main emp cursor                 →6
        select
            eName,
            sal,
            deptNo
        from emp;
    v_dName_tx dept.dName%TYPE;
    function f_dName_tx (fi_deptNo NUMBER)                →13
      return VARCHAR2 is
  --Get dName for each emp.                               →15
  --No exception handling needed.
      --temp output variable                             →17
      v_out_tx dept.dName%TYPE;
    begin -- f_dName_tx                                    →19
      -- prevents no data found exception                 →20
      if fi_deptNo is not null then
        select dName
            into v_out_tx
            from dept
        where deptNo = fi_deptNo;
      end if;                                              →26
      return v_out_tx; -- return null if no deptNo         →27
    end f_dName_TX;                                        →28


begin  --main                                             →31
    for r_emp in c_emp loop
      v_dName_tx := f_dName_tx(r_emp.deptNo);
      --
      --  lots of code here to process payroll
      --
    end loop; -- main emp loop                            →37
end; --main                                               →38
```

The following list explains lines from Listing 9-8:

→**2**   The main description of routine.

→**3**   An author block.

→**6**   A comment describing the cursor.

→**15**   A description of the local function.

→**17**   A description of v_out_tx.

→**19**   Indicates the start of the function.

→**20**   Describes the function if fi_deptNo is not null.

→**27**   The fact that the function will return NULL if deptNo is NULL isn't obvious and therefore needs a comment.

→**28**   No comment is needed on this END statement because the function name is part of the END statement.

→**31**   The beginning of the main program.

→**37**   The end of main `EMP` loop.

→**38**   The end of the program.

Avoid global variables

In well-structured programs, the only variables referenced within a routine are defined within that routine or are passed to the routine as parameters, except for comments, as we discuss earlier. Any time you reference a variable outside the scope of a routine, you're using a *global* variable. A true global variable would be one that could be accessed anywhere in the whole system. However, the term *global* applies anytime a routine uses variables declared outside the scope of the routine.

Note that not all global variables are necessarily bad. The method we describe here to avoid hard-coded variables encourages you to use global references to avoid hard-coded values. Each of those values could be passed to the program as a parameter but would probably make the code very awkward.

In general, structuring program units to be completely self-contained is the best strategy. You can more easily test the code. You know that if there is a bug in the routine, it is definitely in the routine and not being caused by some other part of the code that is inappropriately manipulating a global variable.

In Listing 9-8 earlier in this chapter, lines 13–28 completely encapsulated the function `f_dName_tx`. It doesn't reference any values that were not declared or passed to the function as parameters.

Sometimes, you should use true global variables. Even though you should do your best to avoid global variables, if avoiding them makes the code harder to read, by all means, use them. For example, if you have many program units in a package that all are performing validations on the same record, rather than passing the same record variable into each routine, just declaring the record once at the top of the package body is probably clearer. This allows each routine to refer to the record rather than pass it into each program unit.

Indent carefully

Indenting your code is probably one of the easiest ways to make it more readable. Listing 9-8, shown earlier, is an example of properly indented code. For each code block, the `BEGIN` and `END` commands are at the same level of indentation (lines 19 and 28). Within a code block, everything else is indented (lines 21 and 26). Fields are indented within a `SELECT` statement (lines 8 and 9).

The easiest way to apply indenting standards consistently is to let your PL/SQL editor do it for you. Most popular products do a fairly good job of indenting the code automatically. If you aren't using such a product or you dislike the way in which your product indents your code automatically, you need to do it manually. We discuss popular third-party editors in Chapter 2.

Be careful with capitalization

Reserved words (BEGIN, END, SELECT, and so on) have specific meanings and must stand out, but there are two schools of thought about *how* reserved words should stand out. To capitalize or not to capitalize, that is the question.

There is no accepted consensus about whether reserved words should be capitalized. Steven Feuerstein, the best-known PL/SQL expert, prefers to capitalize them. But capitalized words make the code harder to read, take up more space, and take more time for less able typists to enter. Most modern PL/SQL editing tools color-code reserved words. This way, you don't need to do anything special in order to make them stand out.

A good standard to follow is to use lowercase for all reserved words unless you don't have a PL/SQL editor that colors the reserved words. In that case, capitalize your reserved words. Either way, you need to be consistent with capitalizing all the reserved words in PL/SQL. For a more in-depth discussion of capitalization in user-created objects, see Chapter 8.

Use generic variable datatype declarations

Most variables in your code retrieve data from columns in the database or store data in those columns. Because you're always moving data from one variable to another, if your data variables aren't of the correct type, some very strange problems can occur. DML statements can fail because you're trying to put data into a variable that is too small for it, and you can get rounding errors by assigning numeric data into inconsistent types.

The best way to avoid such problems is to never directly assign datatypes to your data. For variables that can be the same datatype as a column in the database, the solution is simple. You can set the datatype of the variable to be the same as that of the database column. For example, to write code to retrieve the last name of an employee (emp.eName), you can define your variable by using the %TYPE or %ROWTYPE reference declaration in PL/SQL, as shown in Listing 9-9.

Listing 9-9: The %TYPE Command Illustrated

```
declare
  v_eName_tx emp.eName%TYPE;                                    →2
  v_emp_rec emp%ROWTYPE;                                        →3
begin
  v_eName_tx := 'Smith';                                       →5
  v_emp_rec.eName := 'Chan';                                   →6
end;
```

Here's what's going on in Listing 9-9:

→2   Declares `v_eName_tx` based on a column in the table.

→3   Declares record variable based on the whole table.

→5   The references variable.

→6   The references record component.

There are times when you need to declare a variable that isn't based on a table column. For example, if you create a `v_fullName_tx` variable that will concatenate first and last names together, the variable needs to be wider than either the first or last name field. You can always define your variable to be the maximum possible length of the variable; but if, at a later time, the maximum length of the last name field changes in the database, your code will be out of date.

You can solve this problem by never hard-coding datatypes. You can place a set of generic data widths in a package and reference them there. That way, if things change in the database, you have to access only one package to update your datatypes. Many programmers think of such structures as variable *domains*. PL/SQL implements domains in a structure called *subtypes* (and you can read more about them in Chapter 11).

Listing 9-10 shows a subtype package to store the datatypes so that you use only those subtypes in the code.

Listing 9-10: A Subtypes Example

```
create or replace
package pkg_subtype is
  --Employee First + Last + 1
  subtype fullName_sty is VARCHAR2(61);                        →4
end pkg_subtype;

declare
  v_fullName_sty pkg_subtype.fullName_sty;                     →8
begin
  v_fullName_sty := 'Margaret Chan';
end;
```

Here are more details about Listing 9-10:

→4   This line defines the new type in a package.

→8   This line declares a variable based on the new type.

This is another guideline that few organizations follow. Not even all the examples in this book use this technique. However, this technique produces code with significantly fewer problems due to datatype mismatch errors.

Limit line length

To improve the readability of the code, lines should not exceed 80 characters so that you can print out your code on paper.

Use explicit data conversion for dates

When storing or displaying dates, never use implicit date conversion. The default date format is a database parameter (NLS_DATE_FORMAT) that could possibly be changed by a DBA. Also, be aware that the standard date format differs from country to country. An example of explicit date conversion is shown in Listing 9-11.

Listing 9-11:   Explicit Date Conversion

```
declare
  v_temp_dt DATE;
  v_count_nr NUMBER(10);
begin
  -- Implicit date conversion. NEVER do this!
  v_temp_dt := '01-JAN-03';

  -- Explicit declaration of format mask.  ALWAYS do this!
  v_temp_dt := to_DATE('01-JAN-2003','dd-mon-yyyy');

  -- Explicit declaration of format mask in where clause.
  select count(*) into v_count_nr
  from emp
  where hiredate < to_DATE('01-JAN-2003','dd-mon-yyyy');
end;
```

Use synonyms

Because the schema where objects are found might change between environments, you shouldn't explicitly state the owner of an object. For objects not found in that schema, use private or public synonyms to provide schema independence.

Developing SQL Code Consistently

This section provides guidelines for creating a uniform SQL code base.

Using a new line

All the main parts of a SQL statement (for example, SELECT, FROM, WHERE, INSERT, and so on) and phrases (for example, GROUP BY, ORDER BY, BETWEEN...AND) must start on a new line indented to the proper position.

The reserved words AND and OR should usually begin on a new line. An exception to this rule is when the reserved words appear in a complex expression or the non-leading part of a phrase (that is, BETWEEN...AND).

Using explicit column lists

Using SELECT * should be avoided, but can be used in rare circumstances. Some cursor SELECT statements are appropriate places to use SELECT *.

If you want to query all the columns in a table or view and you're going to base a record on the cursor, using SELECT * is perfectly appropriate. If the structure of the table changes (for example, when a new column is added), depending upon the circumstances, you might not have to change your code at all. If you need to change the code, using this technique reduces the number of changes required.

Listing 9-12 is an example of where you might want to use SELECT *. In this case, you declare a cursor based on the EMP table and manipulate the data in that cursor in the program.

Listing 9-12:   Using SELECT * in a Cursor

```
declare
  cursor c_emp is
    select *
    from emp;

  v_empName_tx emp.eName%TYPE;
  v_empSal_nr  emp.Sal%TYPE;
  v_empDept_nr emp.deptNo%TYPE;
```

```
begin
  for r_emp in c_emp loop
    v_empName_tx := r_emp.eName;
    v_empSal_nr  := r_emp.Sal;
    v_empDept_nr := r_emp.deptNo;
  ..
  end loop;
end;
```

Prefixing (and suffixing) column names from multiple tables

To improve the readability of a SQL statement, all columns should be prefixed with the table name or table alias if multiple tables are used. Some guidelines for table aliases are as follows:

✔ The alias for a table name consisting of a single word should not be abbreviated.

✔ The alias for a table name consisting of multiple words should be created by using the first letter of each word in the table name. For example, if the table is called `PurchaseOrderDetail`, you can alias the table `POD`.

✔ Append a sequence number or some text identifier to the alias if the table is used multiple times in the same query (for example, `POD1` and `POD2` or `PODbig` and `PODsmall`).

✔ In the case of nested queries, suffix the outer query table alias with `_out` and/or inner query table alias with `_in`.

To demonstrate these guidelines, create a query to return the names of employees and their managers in departments with more than five employees. The appropriate column prefixes are shown in Listing 9-13.

Listing 9-13:   A Table Prefixing of Columns

```
select  empMgr.eName mgrName,                        →1
        emp.eName empName                            →2
  from
    emp empMgr                                       →4
  join emp                                           →5
  on empMgr.empNo = emp.empNo
  where empMgr.deptNo in
        (select dept_in.deptNo from                  →8
          emp emp_in                                 →9
          join dept dept_in                          →10
        on emp_in.deptNo = dept_in.deptNo
        group by dept_in.deptNo
        having count(*) > 5)                         →13
```

The following list further explains the code in Listing 9-13:

→1, 2 Both eName columns are prefaced with their table or table aliases.

→4, 5 The emp column appears in the query twice, so at least one must be aliased.

→8–13 A subquery to limit the returned departments to those with five or more employees.

→8 Alias deptNo by using the subquery alias.

→9, 10 Alias the two subquery tables.

Giving columns aliases

There are two situations when you must use an alias for a column, in the SELECT statement:

✔ When the selected value is an expression, you should use a logical name that describes the purpose of the expression.

✔ When you're selecting columns with the same name from two different tables (or two instances of the same table), the column must be prefixed with the underlying table name or table's alias.

In Listing 9-13, lines 1 and 2, the eName column was aliased because it was selected twice, once from each instance of the EMP table.

Using parentheses in complex mathematical and logical expressions

To avoid logic and syntax mistakes, you should use parentheses in all complex expressions. Unfortunately, it is fairly common for developers to be lazy about this practice. Table 9-1 shows how not using parentheses in logical expressions can be dangerous.

Table 9-1	Parentheses in Logical Expressions
Predicate Conditions	**Evaluation Result**
'a' = 'c' AND 'a' = 'b' OR 'a' = 'a'	TRUE
('a' = 'c' AND 'a' = 'b') OR 'a' = 'a'	TRUE
'a' = 'c' AND ('a' = 'b' OR 'a' = 'a')	FALSE

Using white space intelligently

White space plays an important role in keeping your code easy to read, so generously space all code. A blank line should precede and follow a new procedure block and all comment blocks.

Writing save exception handlers

No exception handler should ever have just the statement WHEN OTHERS THEN NULL;. Errors should be expected, trapped, and recorded, or allowed to propagate to the calling program. If you want to ignore a specific error, you can trap it and ignore it, but never use WHEN OTHERS THEN NULL; by itself. See Chapter 5 for more about handling errors. By ignoring errors in your code, you can introduce bugs that are very hard to find.

Packaging stored program units

Program units stored in the database (procedures, functions, and so on) should reside inside a PL/SQL package. You should usually avoid functions and procedures that are not stored in a package. That's because you'll probably have hundreds of program units supporting your system, and as the number of program units grows, managing them becomes more and more difficult. Placing all program units in a package right from the start is a good practice. That way, the number of program units always stays manageable.

Like all rules, this one has exceptions. In one project, we had to replace most calls to the sysdate function in our program with a special function that adjusted the values to compensate for the time zone where the user was located. So, we wrote our function and stored it as a function (not stored in a package) called f_sysdate. Then we just replaced the calls to sysdate with f_sysdate. The code also contained many places that needed to *not* be time-zone adjusted. By naming our function f_sysdate, we could change from one command to the other by just changing two characters.

We discuss packages in more detail in Chapter 7.

Part IV
PL/SQL Data Manipulations

The 5th Wave   By Rich Tennant

"I said I wanted to know more about
data types, Martin, not date types."

In this part . . .

This part builds on the knowledge you have gained in earlier chapters and discusses both basic (Chapter 10) and advanced (Chapter 11) data types.

This part also includes explanations of large objects (CLOB, BLOB, and BFILE) as well as collections and bulk operations. You need to understand these concepts when working on more complex systems.

Chapter 10

Basic Datatypes

● ●

In This Chapter

▶ Processing numeric data

▶ Working with DATE and TIMESTAMP datatypes

▶ Using the BOOLEAN datatype

▶ Working with characters and strings

● ●

A *datatype* is a construct that defines the storage format, constraints, and range limitations of constants, parameters, and variables. In addition to all the datatypes available in SQL (for example, NUMBER, VARCHAR2, DATE, and so on), PL/SQL includes some variations on these datatypes as well as some additional types not available in SQL. This chapter provides an overview of the basic datatypes that PL/SQL supports.

Introducing the Main Datatype Groups

In previous chapters, you use a number of built-in PL/SQL datatypes. There are four main groups:

✔ **Scalar datatypes** represent single values that can't be divided into parts. Scalar datatypes are divided into families:

- *Numeric datatypes* encompass information that can be represented as digits.

- *Character datatypes* are used for textual information (up to 32K).

- *Date/time information* is specified by using a group of datatypes that allow you to store a timestamp of some event or time interval.

- *Boolean datatypes* are a common element of logical operations.

✔ **Composite datatypes** include internal components that can be manipulated independently. (In Chapter 6, you use %ROWTYPE, which is an example of the PL/SQL RECORD datatype.)

> ✔ **References** contain pointers to other program items.
>
> ✔ **Large objects** store or point to large amounts of textual or binary information, such as images, movies, or books.

In this chapter, you find out about scalar datatypes. The other datatype groups available in PL/SQL are covered in Chapter 11.

Working with Numeric Datatypes

Since the beginning of the computer era, many complex calculations have been used to process scientific data that involved many numbers. This is the reason that, historically, numeric datatypes have the widest and most comprehensive representation in most programming languages.

PL/SQL supports a large number of numeric datatype variations. However, as a programmer, you'll realistically only use a few of them: NUMBER, BINARY_INTEGER/PLS_INTEGER (for versions lower than 9.2), and BINARY_FLOAT/BINARY_DOUBLE. We describe each briefly in the following sections.

Using the NUMBER datatype

NUMBER is the most generic datatype. It is used to support all but the most intensive scientific calculations. Numbers can have a maximum of 38 significant digits. The syntax is simple, as shown here:

```
declare
  variable1_nr NUMBER [(precision[, scale])];
...
```

Precision is the total number of digits in the number. The value of precision can be between 1 and 38.

Scale is the number of digits to the right of the decimal point. Scale might also be negative. In that case, rounding will take place to the left of the decimal point. The value of scale can be between –84 and 127.

Both precision and scale are optional. Therefore, the NUMBER datatype is overloaded to include three different numeric groups:

> ✔ **Integers** (you specify just precision) are between -10^{38} and 10^{38} not including either of the bounds.

✔ **Fixed-point values** (you specify both precision and scale) are between -10^{122} and 10^{122}, not including either of the bounds and can be as small as 10^{-127}.

✔ **Floating-point values** (you don't specify anything) are between -10^{130} and 10^{130}, not including either of the bounds and can be as small as 10^{-127}.

If you need to deal with numbers smaller than 10^{-38} or larger than 10^{38}, you have to use scientific notation (for example, 128000 should be written as 1.28E5). Working with these very large and very small numbers is not very common and it is unlikely that you will encounter them very often when working with PL/SQL.

Examples of all regular cases are shown in Listing 10-1.

Listing 10-1:   NUMBER Datatype

```
declare
    v1_nr NUMBER(10);     -- integer              →2
    v2_nr NUMBER(10,0);   -- also integer         →3
    v3_nr NUMBER(5,5);    -- fixed point
    v4_nr NUMBER(5,-3);   -- also fixed point
    v5_nr NUMBER;         -- floating point
...
```

→2–3   Both cases allow you to declare an integer variable because the scale is set to 0, either explicitly or by default. If you try to assign a real literal to that type of value, it is rounded to the nearest integer, as shown in Listing 10-2.

Listing 10-2:   Assigning a Fraction to an Integer

```
SQL> declare
  2      v1_nr NUMBER(10) := 2.567;                →2
  3  begin
  4      DBMS_OUTPUT.put_line('v1_nr='||v1_nr);
  5  end;
  6  /
v1_nr=3                                            →7
PL/SQL procedure successfully completed.
SQL>
```

Here are the details about Listing 10-2:

→2   A real numeric literal is assigned to a variable defined as an integer.

→7   The output shows that the value was rounded.

Some basic examples of fixed-point variables are covered in Listing 10-3.

Listing 10-3:   Setting Precision and Scale

```
SQL> declare
  2        v1_nr NUMBER(5,2) := 123.567;                    →2
  3        v2_nr NUMBER(5,-2) := 123.567;                   →3
  4  begin
  5        DBMS_OUTPUT.put_line(v1_nr||' and '||v2_nr);
  6  end;
  7  /
123.57 and 100                                              →8
PL/SQL procedure successfully completed.
SQL>
```

Additional information about Listing 10-3 is shown here:

→2   This line of code specifies a fixed-point number with 5-digit preci-
        sion and positive scale of 2, and assigns a numeric literal to it with
        3 digits before and after the decimal point.

→3   Here you are specifying a fixed-point number with 5-digit precision
        and negative scale of –2, and assigning a numeric literal to it with
        3 digits before and after the decimal point.

→8   If you specify positive precision, rounding occurs on the right side
        of the decimal point to the required number of digits (123.567 was
        rounded to 123.57). But if you specify negative precision, rounding
        occurs on the left side of the decimal point (123.567 was rounded
        to 100).

If you need to store floating-point data (for example, if you need to store a real
value of ⅔, unrounded) you can use the NUMBER datatype without specifying
either precision or scale. This allows you to work with numeric data without
fear that your data could be rounded. This is especially critical with financial
operations. An example using the NUMBER datatype is shown in Listing 10-4.

Listing 10-4:   Using the NUMBER Datatype

```
SQL> declare
  2        v1_nr NUMBER      := 2/3;                         →2
  3        v2_nr NUMBER(5,2):= 2/3;                          →3
  4  begin
  5        DBMS_OUTPUT.put_line(v1_nr*3||' and '||v2_nr*3);
  6  end;
  7  /
2 and 2.01                                                  →8
PL/SQL procedure successfully completed.
SQL>
```

Here's is what's going on in Listing 10-4:

→**2**   Specifies a floating-point number *without* precision and scale, and assigns the result of the division ⅔.

→**3**   Specifies a fixed-point number with precision and scale, and assigns the result of the division ⅔.

→**8**   Output shows that using floating-point division and multiplication didn't change the number's value. However, fixed-point operations give a different result, because the floating-point value of ⅔ is 0.6666666 . . ., but the fixed-point value of ⅔ is 0.67.

Boosting performance with BINARY_INTEGER

Although NUMBER is a convenient datatype, it isn't always the most efficient. Each digit in a NUMBER variable requires a single byte to be stored. That's why number 255 will use 3 bytes, even though in binary format, it requires only 1 byte (255 decimal = 11111111 binary). Therefore, using NUMBER is a waste of space (the default length is 38 bytes), especially if you store integer values. Also, Oracle can use its highly optimized machine arithmetic only on binary data. Otherwise, additional operations are required to transform numeric information into machine-readable format.

To improve performance and reduce space consumption for tasks involving massive processing of integer values, Oracle introduced the BINARY_INTEGER datatype. The PLS_INTEGER datatype works in a similar way, but is supported mostly for backward compatibility with Oracle versions prior to 9.2. A simple declaration of these datatypes is shown here:

```
declare
    variable1_nr BINARY_INTEGER;
    variable2_nr PLS_INTEGER;
```

Beginning with Oracle 10*g*, these datatypes are interchangeable. In earlier versions of Oracle, PLS_INTEGER provided better performance. Both of these datatypes exist only in PL/SQL, and you cannot create a column of these types.

BINARY_INTEGER variables are between -2^{31} and 2^{31}. Because of this datatype's binary nature, it's the fastest possible way of processing numeric data in Oracle. However, because of its limited range (2^{31} = 2,147,483,648), its usage is a bit restrictive.

Listing 10-5 shows both NUMBER and BINARY_INTEGER datatypes.

Listing 10-5:   NUMBER and BINARY_INTEGER Datatypes

```
SQL> set timing on                                            →1
SQL> declare
   2      v_nr number;
   3  begin
   4      for i in 1..1000000 loop
   5          v_nr:=v_nr+i-i+i*2-i*2;
   6      end loop;
   7  end;
   8  /
PL/SQL procedure successfully completed.
Elapsed: 00:00:00.35                                          →11
SQL> declare
   2      v_nr binary_integer;
   3  begin
   4      for i in 1..1000000 loop
   5          v_nr:=v_nr+i-i+i*2-i*2;
   6      end loop;
   7  end;
   8  /
PL/SQL procedure successfully completed.
Elapsed: 00:00:00.09                                          →21
SQL>
```

Here are additional details about Listing 10-5:

→1   This command turns on timing in order to measure execution
          time. Some PL/SQL coding environments (such as SQL
          Navigator) provide it automatically, but in SQL*Plus, it is set to
          Off by default. In these cases, you need to use the SQL*Plus
          command SET TIMING ON.

→11, 21   These lines show the results of using BINARY_INTEGER.
          Performance is significantly improved.

Using BINARY_FLOAT and BINARY_DOUBLE for complex calculations

If you have a program that needs to make high-speed scientific computations,
the BINARY_FLOAT and BINARY_DOUBLE datatypes offer significant performance improvement over other datatypes.

You shouldn't use BINARY_FLOAT and BINARY_DOUBLE datatypes for calculations where very high precision is required because they maintain only a
limited number of digits. As a result, some unexpected rounding might occur.

These datatypes can offer improved speed because they represent floating-point numbers in IEEE 754-format. Behind the scenes, these datatypes behave much like the native floating-point types on many hardware systems (4-byte and 8-byte operations).

To illustrate the most efficient usage of BINARY datatypes, examine the procedure that calculates pi (π) with reasonable accuracy (currently set to 0.000001 for pi/4 – 0.0000004 for pi) using the Leibniz formulae.

```
create or replace function pi return number
 as
      last_pi number := 0;
      delta   number := 0.000001;
      pi      number := 1;
      denom   number := 3;
      oper    number := -1;
      negone  number := -1;
      two     number := 2;
 begin
      loop
          last_pi := pi;
          pi := pi + oper * 1/denom;
          exit when (abs(last_pi-pi) <= delta );
          denom := denom + two;
          oper := oper * negone;
      end loop;
      return pi * 4;
 end;
```

This procedure is taken from one of the discussions on http://asktom. oracle.com, which is a very useful Web site for anyone working in the Oracle environment.

You should try all three cases with variables of type NUMBER, BINARY_FLOAT, BINARY_DOUBLE, and execute a basic SELECT PI FROM DUAL command. The results are interesting to observe, as shown in the following table:

Type	Time	Output
NUMBER	1.30	3.14159465358579324446263938327350288021
BINARY_FLOAT	0.18	3.14159775
BINARY_DOUBLE	0.22	3.1415946535856922

It is clear that BINARY datatypes have a major performance impact, which is even greater for BINARY_FLOAT. Because the number of decimal places for binary datatypes is less than it is for the NUMBER datatype, you might be forced to use a generic datatype for higher precision calculations.

Handling numeric datatypes in built-in functions

PL/SQL supports the same built-in numeric functions as SQL. Most numeric functions are accurate to 38 decimal places. Functions COS, COSH, EXP, LN, LOG, SIN, SINH, SQRT, TAN, and TANH are accurate to 36 decimal digits. Functions ACOS, ASIN, ATAN, and ATAN2 are accurate to 30 decimal digits.

Most built-in Oracle functions that work with numeric data can be overloaded to work with BINARY_DOUBLE and BINARY_FLOAT datatypes. But sometimes, you might have to force them to use the appropriate datatypes, as shown in the following examples, which calculate square roots:

Example 1:

```
SQL> declare
  2      v_nr number;
  3  begin
  4      for i in 1..1000000 loop
  5          v_nr:=sqrt(i);
  6      end loop;
  7  end;
  8  /
PL/SQL procedure successfully completed.
Elapsed: 00:00:01.35
```

Example 2:

```
SQL> declare
  2      v_nr binary_float;
  3  begin
  4      for i in 1..1000000 loop
  5          v_nr:=sqrt(i);
  6      end loop;
  7  end;
  8  /
PL/SQL procedure successfully completed.
Elapsed: 00:00:09.70
```

In the first case, the destination variable is type NUMBER, and the procedure was completed in 1.35 seconds:

In the second case, the variable is type BINARY_FLOAT and the time is slower. This change to BINARY_FLOAT slowed down the procedure to 9.7 seconds because the loop variable i is, by definition, PLS_INTEGER. In the hierarchy of automatic resolution of overload calls, Oracle picks up the version of SQRT function to work with NUMBER rather than with BINARY_FLOAT because the NUMBER datatype is higher in the resolution order (see Chapter 3 and Oracle manuals for more details about resolving overloads). As a result, Oracle not only uses a slower function, but afterward also has to implicitly convert the result from NUMBER to BINARY_FLOAT, which takes more time.

To force the appropriate overload, you need to explicitly declare that you are passing a variable of the appropriate datatype by using one of these two conversion functions:

```
v_float_nr:= to_binary_float(numeric variable)
v_double_nr:= to_binary_double(numeric variable)
```

In each case, you should select the appropriate conversion function based on the expected length and precision of the passed value. In the following example, BINARY_FLOAT is enough, because the highest possible number is 1,000,000 and the performance improvement is obvious:

```
SQL> declare
  2      v_nr binary_float;
  3  begin
  4      for i in 1..1000000 loop
  5          v_nr:=sqrt(to_binary_float(i));
  6      end loop;
  7  end;
  8  /
PL/SQL procedure successfully completed.
Elapsed: 00:00:00.48
SQL>
```

The conversion from NUMBER to BINARY_FLOAT/DOUBLE is not exact. Because NUMBER data is rounded to a decimal point and BINARY data is rounded to a binary value, differences at the rounding point could accumulate. So although you could use BINARY datatypes to speed up high-end financial reports, these datatypes shouldn't be used for day-to-day accounting.

Keeping Track of Date and Time

Oracle provides three groups of datatypes (DATE, TIMESTAMP, INTERVAL) and a number of built-in functions, which we describe in the following sections.

Selecting the info you want from DATE

Before Oracle 9*i*, only one datatype (DATE) allowed storing *point-in-time values* (generic term which includes both date and time information), because even now Oracle doesn't have independent datatypes for just date or just time, as in some other languages. Although Oracle has since added other time-related datatypes, DATE is still considered the most convenient and simple in that group.

DBMS_RANDOM

While you're working with numeric datatypes, you often need to generate some random values. Oracle provides a built-in package DBMS_RANDOM for this purpose. Although it isn't suited to cryptographic tasks, it's fine for all other purposes.

The two most important functions using DBMS_RANDOM are as follows:

```
v_random_nr:= dbms_random.
   random;
v_value_nr:= dbms_random.
   value[(min, max)];
```

The first one returns a random integer value in the range of -2^{31} to 2^{31}. The second one generates a random value between the MIN and MAX numbers passed as parameters (between 0 and 1 if parameters are omitted) with 38 digits after the decimal point. Simple examples of each type are shown here:

```
SQL> declare
  2      v1_nr number:=dbms_
    random.value(10,15);
  3      v2_nr binary_
    integer:=dbms_random.
    random;
  4  begin
  5      DBMS_OUTPUT.put_line
    ('Float:'||v1_nr);
  6      DBMS_OUTPUT.put_line
    ('Int:'||v2_nr);
  7  end;
  8  /
Float: 12.4996844577596455528
    554463900590540428
Int:   963693078
PL/SQL procedure successfully
    completed.
SQL>
```

The DATE datatype includes all the following information: century, year, month, day, hour, minute, and second. Valid dates range from January 1, 4712 BC to December 31, AD 9999. Use the following code to declare the DATE datatype:

```
declare
    variable1_dt DATE;
...
```

Declaring a variable of datatype DATE is very simple. You don't need to use any other parameters. However, to take any part of information out of the DATE variable, you need to use the TO_CHAR function with a date format, as shown in Listing 10-6.

Listing 10-6:   Displaying Date and Time

```
SQL> declare
  2      v_dt DATE :=sysdate;                              →2
  3      v_tx VARCHAR2(2000);
  4  begin
  5      v_tx:=to_char(v_dt,'mm/dd/yyyy');                 →5
  6      DBMS_OUTPUT.put_line(v_tx);
```

```
 7        v_tx:=to_char(v_dt,'hh24:mi');              →7
 8        DBMS_OUTPUT.put_line(v_tx);
 9        v_tx:=to_char(v_dt);                         →9
10        DBMS_OUTPUT.put_line(v_tx);
11   end;
12   /
02/12/2006
13:06
12-FEB-06
PL/SQL procedure successfully completed.
SQL>
```

The following are additional details about Listing 10-6:

→**2**   The built-in function SYSDATE returns the current date and time
for the server on which the database resides.

→**5**   Here you can see how to get just the date from the variable.

→**7**   This line retrieves just the time, in military (24-hour) format.

→**9**   No format mask is specified, so Oracle uses its default date format
from the database initialization parameter NLS_DATE_FORMAT
('DD-MON-RRRR').

NLS stands for National Language Support, also known as Globalization
Support. NLS allows to you configure the database to conform to the requirements of countries that use different date and time formats. These settings
can be viewed in the NLS_SESSION_PARAMETERS and NLS_DATABASE_
PARAMETERS dictionary views.

Applying format masks

To display the date in a meaningful way, you need to use the TO_CHAR function, as shown here:

```
v_string_tx := to_char(DATE variable[,format mask])
```

TO_CHAR converts the date value into the string by using a specified format
mask. Table 10-1 shows the most commonly used formatting options.

Table 10-1	Commonly Used Format Masks
Format	*Meaning*
Y, YY, YYYY, YYYY	Year (from one to 4 digits)
RR, RRRR	Rounded year (accepts 2- or 4-digit values and converts 2-digit values into the appropriate century)

(continued)

Table 10-1 *(continued)*

Format	Meaning
MM, MONTH, MON	Month of the year, name of the month, abbreviated name
W, WW	Week of the month, week of the year (not a calendar week, because the first week starts at the 1st of the month/year and ends at the 7th)
D, DD, DDDD	Day of the week, day of the month, day of the year
DAY, DY	Name of day (fixed length: 9 char), abbreviated name of day
HH, HH24	Hour of the day (1–12), hour of the day (0–23)
A.M./ AM	Meridian indicator with or without periods
MI	Minutes (0–59)
SS, SSSSS	Seconds (0–59), seconds from midnight (0–86399)

You can use some characters as separators (for example, comma, dot, space, and semicolon) within the format mask, but everything else has to be enclosed in double quotes, as shown in Listing 10-7.

Listing 10-7:   Using Format Masks

```
SQL> declare
  2      v_dt DATE :=sysdate;
  3      v_tx VARCHAR2(2000);
  4  begin
  5      v_tx:=to_char(v_dt,'"Today is": DAY');          →5
  6      DBMS_OUTPUT.put_line(v_tx);
  7  end;
  8  /
Today is: SUNDAY
PL/SQL procedure successfully completed.
SQL>
```

▌ →5   You can use the semicolon (:) without quotes, but the string
          "Today is" must be inside the quotes.

You can reverse the process, using the TO_DATE function to convert string values into date values by using an appropriate format mask (masks are the same as in TO_CHAR), as shown here:

```
v_date_dt := to_date(string variable[,format mask])
```

The DATE format allows you to store everything from centuries to seconds. You need to specify only the desired units, as shown in Listing 10-8.

Listing 10-8: Using the DATE Format Mask

```
SQL> declare
  2       v_dt DATE;
  3       v_tx VARCHAR2(2000);
  4  begin
  5       v_dt := to_date('19:40','HH24:MI');            →5
  6       v_tx := to_char(v_dt,'YYYY-MM-DD HH24:MI:SS');
  7       DBMS_OUTPUT.put_line(v_tx);
  8       v_dt := to_date('11-FEB-2006','DD-MON-YYYY');  →8
  9       v_tx := to_char(v_dt,'YYYY-MM-DD HH24:MI:SS');
 10       DBMS_OUTPUT.put_line(v_tx);
 11  end;
 12  /
2006-02-01 19:40:00
2006-02-11 00:00:00
PL/SQL procedure successfully completed.
SQL>
```

Understanding the defaults

Oracle uses the following rules to set default values:

→5   A missing date defaults to the first day of the current month.

→8   A missing time defaults to midnight of the day.

Other rules include:

- A missing year or month defaults to the current year or month.
- A missing day defaults to the first day of the month used (either current or specified).
- Missing hours, minutes, or seconds default to 00 value.

Validating format masks

Oracle can't detect format mask errors when compiling PL/SQL. Even if you've used an invalid format mask, the procedure or function will successfully compile. It fails only at runtime, as shown in Listing 10-9.

Listing 10-9: A Format Mask Failure

```
SQL> create or replace procedure p_format
  2  is
  3       v_dt DATE :=sysdate;
  4       v_tx VARCHAR2(2000);
  5  begin
  6       v_tx:=to_char(v_dt,'Today is: DAY');           →6
  7       DBMS_OUTPUT.put_line(v_tx);
  8  end;
```

(continued)

Listing 10-9 *(continued)*

```
   9   /
Procedure created.
SQL> exec p_format
BEGIN p_format; END;
*
ERROR at line 1:
ORA-01821: date format not recognized                    →15
ORA-06512: at "SCOTT.P_FORMAT", line 6
ORA-06512: at line 1
SQL>
```

Here are some additional details about Listing 10-9:

→6   There are no double quotes around the string "Today is" in the
       format mask, but the procedure is still successfully created.

→15   If you try to run the procedure P_FORMAT, you get the Oracle error.

Be sure to check format masks carefully for validity. It is significantly easier
to review your code during design than to figure out why the whole module
fails at runtime.

Using TIMESTAMP

Although the DATE datatype has been used for years, it has a number of limitations. That is why Oracle introduced the TIMESTAMP datatype, which we
discuss here.

Simple TIMESTAMP allows you to specify fractions of a second. (DATE precision is limited to seconds.) You can declare this datatype as shown here:

```
declare
    variable1_ts TIMESTAMP[(precision)];
...
```

This feature can be very useful if you need more detailed information on
sequential processing because now you can order events which occur in the
same second. By default, Oracle stores 6 digits of precision, but you can specify precision within the range from 0 to 9. TIMESTAMP(0) is equivalent to
DATE. Listing 10-10 shows how to declare the TIMESTAMP datatype.

Listing 10-10:   Declaring TIMESTAMP Datatype

```
SQL> declare
  2      v_ts TIMESTAMP(6):=systimestamp;                    →2
  3      v_tx VARCHAR2(2000);
  4   begin
```

```
   5       v_tx:=to_char(v_ts,'HH24:MI:SS.FF6');           →5
   6       DBMS_OUTPUT.put_line(v_tx);
   7  end;
   8  /
15:39:51.812000
PL/SQL procedure successfully completed.
SQL>
```

Listing 10-10 works as shown here:

→2   To initialize the variable, you use SYSTIMESTAMP, not SYSDATE.

→5   The new format mask element FF [1-9] represents fractions of a
      second. If you specify fewer digits than are stored, Oracle uses the
      same rounding technique as for floating-point numeric data.

Using TIMESTAMP WITH TIME ZONE

Another limitation of the DATE datatype is that even though you have a point-
in-time value, storing the time zone in which it was created is impossible. You
can explicitly store the time zone for TIMESTAMP datatypes, as shown here:

```
declare
    variable1_ts TIMESTAMP[(precision)] WITH TIME ZONE;
...
```

Oracle can detect the time zone of both database server and the client
computer. You can see these values yourself by using the built-in functions
DBTIMEZONE and SESSIONTIMEZONE, as shown in Listing 10-11.

Listing 10-11:   Declaring Time Zone Variables

```
SQL> declare
   2      v_ts TIMESTAMP(6) WITH TIME ZONE                →2
   3                 :=CURRENT_TIMESTAMP;                 →3
   4      v_tx VARCHAR2(2000);
   5  begin
   6      v_tx:=to_char(v_ts,'HH24:MI:SS.FF6 TZR');       →6
   7      DBMS_OUTPUT.put_line(v_tx);
   8      v_tx:=to_char(v_ts,'TZH TZM');
   9      DBMS_OUTPUT.put_line(v_tx);
  10  end;
  11  /
17:50:42.828000 -05:00                                   →12
-05 00
PL/SQL procedure successfully completed.
SQL>
```

Here is some additional information about Listing 10-11:

WARNING!

→**2–3** The built-in function CURRENT_TIMESTAMP provides the timestamp in the session (client) time zone but not the database time zone.

With Web-based applications, all database sessions occur between the application server and the database server. As a result, you can't use the TIMESTAMP WITH ZONE datatype to capture client region information because the client module is just a Web-browser, which doesn't have a dedicated connection to Oracle. It connects only to the application server that resolves all client requests.

→**6** The format mask TZR returns the time zone region information. Depending upon the database settings, it could be either the difference in hours and minutes between the session time zone and the UTC (Coordinated Universal Time, formerly Greenwich Mean Time) or name of the region.

→**7** If you only need the time difference, you could also use TZH and TZM, which return just hours and just minutes of difference.

→**12** This line shows the output of the command on line 6. For a computer in the Eastern Standard Time zone, it is minus 5 hours.

If you have a system running across multiple time zones, storing the information from CURRENT_TIMESTAMP allows you to determine that some activity was happening at a precise moment of the client time. Otherwise, you don't have a way to differentiate between 3 p.m. Eastern and 3 p.m. Pacific.

Storing elapsed time with INTERVAL

Another useful datatype introduced in Oracle 9*i* to extend the functionality of the DATE datatype is INTERVAL. Very often, you don't need to store a point in time, but the time elapsed between points in time, a duration.

For example, if you need to support phone cards services, you want to store the day on which the call took place and the duration of the call, but you don't care about the exact start time and end time of each call. In that case, there is not much difference between when each phone call started and when it ended. The only information you're interested in is how much time the person spent on the call. Of course, you could always use two variables (start and end date/time) or some other workaround like storing hours, minutes, and seconds in independent numeric columns. But as an alternative, you can store the interval itself, so it can be independently processed later, as shown here:

```
SQL> declare
  2      v_start_ts   TIMESTAMP:=
  3          to_timestamp('14:00:00','HH24:MI:SS');
  4      v_end_ts     TIMESTAMP:=
  5          to_timestamp('15:12:24','HH24:MI:SS');
```

```
  6        v_delta_int INTERVAL DAY TO SECOND;
  7   begin
  8        v_delta_int:=v_end_ts-v_start_ts;
  9        DBMS_OUTPUT.put_line(v_delta_int);
 10    end;
 11   /
+00 01:12:24.000000
PL/SQL procedure successfully completed.
```

INTERVAL includes two datatypes that allow you to set appropriate durations more precisely, as shown here:

```
declare
    variable1_int INTERVAL YEAR[(precision)] TO MONTH;
    variable2_int INTERVAL DAY[(precision)] to
            SECOND[(precision)];
...
```

The INTERVAL YEAR TO MONTH datatype allows you to store and manipulate intervals of years and months. You can specify the number of digits in years that you want to store (by default 2, available range is 0–4).

The INTERVAL DAY TO SECOND datatype allows you to store and manipulate intervals of days, hours, minutes, and seconds. In this case, day precision allows you to set the number of digits you want to store, and second precision identifies the number of digits used to store fractions of seconds.

Working with dates and built-in functions

Oracle provides a number of built-in functions that are useful for working with point-in-time values. We discuss the most commonly used functions in the following sections.

EXTRACT

The EXTRACT function allows you to take a single part of a date/interval/timestamp (year only, month only, and so on, up to the second) as shown here:

```
v_nr:= EXTRACT (TYPE from DATE/TIMESTAMP/INTERVAL value);
```

EXTRACT always returns a numeric value, so if you need the text name of the month, you should use TO_CHAR. But if you need to extract a month from the date value, EXTRACT is faster and more efficient than TO_CHAR. A basic example is shown here:

```
SQL> declare
  2        v_nr number;
  3   begin
  4        v_nr:=EXTRACT(MONTH from sysdate);
```

```
  5        DBMS_OUTPUT.put_line(v_nr);
  6  end;
  7  /
2
PL/SQL procedure successfully completed.
SQL>
```

The possible types you can pass into EXTRACT are YEAR, MONTH, DAY, HOUR, MINUTE, and SECOND. You can also use time zone types with timestamps.

As a good PL/SQL coding technique, using EXTRACT is strongly recommended. Although you can get the same results by using TO_CHAR (for example, TO_CHAR(SYSDATE, 'MM')),it is harder to detect a problem if you mistype a format mask.

TRUNC and ROUND

The TRUNC and ROUND built-in functions, typically applied to numbers, also work with dates and timestamps exactly as if they were numbers. The TRUNC function truncates the date to some level of precision, whereas ROUND rounds the date to a specified point:

```
v_dt:= TRUNC (DATE|TIMESTAMP|INTERVAL value[,PRECISION]);
v_dt:= ROUND (DATE|TIMESTAMP|INTERVAL value[,PRECISION]);
```

Rather than numeric precision, here you use date format masks (refer to Table 10-1). For example, 'YYYY' truncates the date to years, and 'MM' to a month. If you don't specify any precision, the default is day ('DD'). You can't specify a combination of format masks. Only one can be specified at a time. An example of using the TRUNC and ROUND functions is shown in Listing 10-12.

Listing 10-12:   Using TRUNC and ROUND Built-In Functions

```
SQL> declare
  2      v_dt DATE;
  3      v_form_tx VARCHAR2(25):='YYYY-MM-DD HH24:MI:SS';
  4  begin
  5      v_dt:=trunc(sysdate);                              →5
  6      DBMS_OUTPUT.put_line(to_char(v_dt,v_form_tx));
  7      v_dt:=trunc(sysdate,'YYYY');                       →7
  8      DBMS_OUTPUT.put_line(to_char(v_dt,v_form_tx));
  9      v_dt:=round(sysdate,'HH');                         →9
 10      DBMS_OUTPUT.put_line(to_char(v_dt,v_form_tx));
 11  end;
 12  /
2006-02-12 00:00:00
2006-01-01 00:00:00
2006-02-12 19:00:00
PL/SQL procedure successfully completed.
SQL>
```

The following information is relevant to Listing 10-12:

→5   TRUNC without a format mask rounds the current date to midnight.

→7   The same call with a 'YYYY' format mask rounds to midnight of the new year.

→9   ROUND with format 'HH' rounds the date to the beginning of the hour.

TRUNC (*value*,'W') is the easiest way of getting the first day of the week.

Here's another extremely critical detail to remember about dates: If the time isn't going to be significant and you want to use queries that sort rows in the database by a particular date, always truncate the date.

A reasonable alternative would be to build a function-based index (see the Oracle manuals) on TRUNC(*value*). This provides you with a perfect mechanism to improve performance on search requests where time is not significant, but you still want to store time for other kinds of requests.

ADD_MONTHS

Because the lengths of months differ, working with precisions higher than days isn't all that simple. Twenty-nine days could be more than one month, less than one month, or equal to one month, depending upon the month and year. Oracle makes your life easier by supporting a number of functions to help in this area: ADD_MONTHS, MONTHS_BETWEEN, and LAST_DAY. The ADD_MONTHS function adds a number of months to the specified date:

```
v_dt:= ADD_MONTHS(date,integer);
```

Listing 10-13 shows how ADD_MONTHS might be used.

Listing 10-13:   Using ADD_MONTHS

```
SQL> declare
  2      v_dt DATE;
  3      v_form_tx VARCHAR2(25):=
  4                   'DD-MON-YYYY HH24:MI:SS';
  5  begin
  6    v_dt:=add_months(sysdate,1);                        →6
  7    DBMS_OUTPUT.put_line(to_char(v_dt,v_form_tx));
  8    v_dt:=add_months(to_date('030130','RRMMDD'),1);   →8
  9    DBMS_OUTPUT.put_line(to_char(v_dt,v_form_tx));
 10  end;
 11  /
12-MAR-2006 19:13:51                                     →12
28-FEB-2003 00:00:00                                     →13
PL/SQL procedure successfully completed.
SQL>
```

Here are the details for the preceding code:

   →6   This code adds one month to the current day.

   →8   This code adds one month to January 30, 2003.

   →12   As a result of the first operation, you have the date with the same time, but one month ahead.

   →13   The second operation is significantly more interesting because you're adding a month to a date that doesn't exist in the resulting month. (There is no such thing as February 30). In that case, Oracle returns midnight of the last day of the resulting month. This behavior is the most important reason to use ADD_MONTHS. Otherwise, if you just added 30 days, you would get a date in March.

LAST_DAY

The LAST_DAY function retrieves the last day of the month in the specified date.

```
v_dt:= LAST_DAY (date);
```

An example of using the LAST_DAY function is shown in Listing 10-14.

Listing 10-14: Using LAST_DAY

```
SQL> declare
  2       v_dt DATE;
  3       v_form_tx  VARCHAR2(25):=
  4               'DD-MON-YYYY HH24:MI:SS';
  5  begin
  6       v_dt:=last_day(sysdate);
  7       DBMS_OUTPUT.put_line(to_char(v_dt,v_form_tx));
  8  end;
  9  /
28-FEB-2006 19:21:55                                      →10
PL/SQL procedure successfully completed.
SQL>
```

   →10   Remember that even though you're getting the last day of the month, time will be preserved.

Don't forget to truncate the date if you need midnight of the last day of the month.

MONTHS_BETWEEN

The MONTHS_BETWEEN function is shown here:

```
v_nr:= MONTHS_BETWEEN(date1,date2);
```

This function returns the number of months between two dates. If this difference is not exact, you get a floating-point number where the decimal portion represents the fraction N/31 where N is the number of remaining days. If SYSDATE were near the beginning of February, you would get results similar to those shown here:

```
SQL> declare
  2       v_nr number;
  3  begin
  4       v_nr:=months_between(sysdate,trunc(sysdate,'Y'));
  5       DBMS_OUTPUT.put_line(v_nr);
  6  end;
  7  /
1.3810748954599761051373954599761051374
PL/SQL procedure successfully completed.
SQL>
```

Because the number of months is represented by a floating-point number, you could always figure out days, hours, minutes, and even seconds from the result, but this technique isn't recommended. Use INTERVAL datatypes instead. Normally, the result of this function is either rounded or truncated as needed.

Storing Logical Values with BOOLEAN

PL/SQL has a BOOLEAN datatype to store logical condition values: TRUE, FALSE, or NULL. You declare it as shown here:

```
declare
    variable1_b BOOLEAN;
...
```

Because there is no corresponding SQL datatype, you cannot use Boolean variables outside of pure PL/SQL. For example, you can declare a function that would return a Boolean value, but you can't use that function in SQL code. Also, not all the built-in functions (like TO_CHAR) or built-in packages understand the BOOLEAN datatype.

Boolean variables can be assigned either directly by using values TRUE, FALSE, or NULL or as the results of logical expressions, as shown in Listing 10-15.

Listing 10-15:   Assigning Boolean Variables

```
declare
    v_b BOOLEAN:=false;                                    →2
begin
    v_b:=extract(year from sysdate)>2000;                  →4
    if v_b
```

(continued)

Listing 10-15 *(continued)*

```
    then
        DBMS_OUTPUT.put_line('21st Century!');
    end if;
end;
```

Here are the details for code listing 10-15:

→**2, 4**   Be careful to use values, not strings and no quotes for results of logical expressions.

You can use Boolean variables for all conditional structures (IF, CASE, EXIT WHEN, and so on).

→**4**   There was no need to include v_b = TRUE because the result of the comparison will also be a Boolean value, so using it would be redundant.

Processing Characters and Strings

Although early computers processed mostly numeric information, significantly more textual data is represented in the current data processing environment.

Textual information consists of the set of alphanumeric characters used to store any data that can be defined by them. Because this is the least restrictive data format, you can easily store textual or numeric information in one form or the other.

Depending upon the programming language you're using and the native language whose strings you plan to store in the database, you might have a ratio of 1:1, 1:2, or 1:3 between characters and the number of bytes required to store them. (Working with multibyte character sets such as Chinese is beyond the scope of this book.)

Limiting variable length with CHAR versus VARCHAR2

Historically, the first character datatype had a fixed length. In the Oracle world, it is called CHAR(*N*) where *N* is the maximum number of characters. If the actual value is shorter than the defined length, Oracle pads the value with blanks to reach the required length. You can declare this datatype as shown here:

```
declare
    variable1_tx CHAR(number of characters);
...
```

In SQL, the maximum length of the CHAR datatype is limited to 2,000 whereas in PL/SQL, the maximum length is 32,767 bytes. Listing 10-16 shows some ways to use CHAR.

Listing 10-16:   Using the CHAR Datatype

```
SQL> declare
  2        v_tx char(5);
  3  begin
  4        v_tx:='A';                                         →4
  5        DBMS_OUTPUT.put_line(length(v_tx));
  6        DBMS_OUTPUT.put_line('<'||v_tx||'>');
  7        v_tx:='A   ';                                      →7
  8        DBMS_OUTPUT.put_line(length(v_tx));
  9        DBMS_OUTPUT.put_line('<'||v_tx||'>');
 10  end;
 11  /
5                                                             →12
<A   >                                                        →13
5
<A   >
PL/SQL procedure successfully completed.
SQL>
```

The following details further explain Listing 10-16:

→**4**   This line of code assigns the fixed-length variable V_TX a literal with just one letter 'A'.

→**7**   This code tries to assign a 3-character string with a single letter and 2 spaces. The result is a bit surprising because after the assignment, there is no way to differentiate both cases. Strings are treated the same way, as shown here:

```
SQL> declare
  2        v_tx char(5);
  3  begin
  4        v_tx:='A';
  5        if v_tx = 'A' and v_tx = 'A   '
  6        then
  7              DBMS_OUTPUT.put_line('Equal!');
  8        end if;
  9  end;
 10  /
Equal!
PL/SQL procedure successfully completed.
SQL>
```

→**12–13** Oracle uses all defined characters. The output shows that the total length is 5 characters with 4 blanks on the right.

The CHAR datatype allows you to precisely define the amount of memory that your variables use. However, CHAR comes with drawbacks. You cannot tell the amount of meaningful data in the variable, nor can you use values with trailing spaces because those spaces are impossible to detect afterwards.

To overcome the problems of fixed-length variables, Oracle introduced the variable-length datatype VARCHAR2(*N*). Now you can declare the maximum possible length of the string that can be stored in the variable, but the actual string will not be padded in any way. The maximum length of a string declared as VARCHAR2 is also 32,767 bytes (with a SQL restriction of 4,000 bytes), as shown here:

```
declare
    variable1_tx VARCHAR2(number of characters);
...
```

The VARCHAR2 datatype has a number of advantages. First, you can be sure that you'll end up with exactly what you placed in the variable. Second, you can now detect the actual amount of data you're working with. The following code takes the previous example and changes the datatype:

```
SQL> declare
  2      v_tx VARCHAR2(5);
  3  begin
  4      v_tx:='A';
  5      DBMS_OUTPUT.put_line(length(v_tx));
  6      DBMS_OUTPUT.put_line('<'||v_tx||'>');
  7      v_tx:='A   ';
  8      DBMS_OUTPUT.put_line(length(v_tx));
  9      DBMS_OUTPUT.put_line('<'||v_tx||'>');
 10  end;
 11  /
1
<A>
3
<A  >
PL/SQL procedure successfully completed.
SQL>
```

These two cases provide completely different results, exactly as intended.

Useful character built-in functions

Oracle provides a number of built-in functions to work with text data.

CHR and ASCII

These functions are opposites. CHR(*code*) returns a character from the current character set identified by its binary equivalent, whereas ASCII (*character*) returns the binary equivalent of the character passed into the function, as shown in Listing 10-17.

Listing 10-17: CHR and ASCII Built-In Functions

```
SQL> declare
  2       v_nr number;
  3       v_tx char(1);
  4  begin
  5       v_nr:=ascii('A');                              →5
  6       DBMS_OUTPUT.put_line(v_nr);
  7       v_tx:=chr(v_nr);                               →7
  8       DBMS_OUTPUT.put_line(v_tx);
  9  end;
 10  /
65                                                       →11
A                                                        →12
PL/SQL procedure successfully completed.
SQL>
```

Here are additional details about Listing 10-17:

→**5, 11** These lines of code show a binary representation of the character 'A' via the function ASCII.

→**7, 12** This code applies the function CHR to the binary representation of a character and returns the character representation ('A').

From our experience, the most useful character specifications are

✔ CHR(10): Line feed

✔ CHR(13): Carriage return

✔ CHR(9): Tab

CHR(10) and CHR(13) usually implement the "next line" command. In some cases, just CHR(10) is enough. CHR(9) uses the default tab spacing of the current text environment. Using these characters makes generating strings to be displayed significantly easier, as shown here:

```
SQL> begin
  2       DBMS_OUTPUT.put_line('Line#1'||
  3                    chr(10)||chr(9)||'Line#2');
  4  end;
  5  /
Line#1
        Line#2
PL/SQL procedure successfully completed.
SQL>
```

SUBSTR and INSTR

Knowledge of the SUBSTR (substring) and INSTR (instring) functions is important for everyone working with strings either in SQL or PL/SQL.

SUBSTR is needed if you want to retrieve part of existing string, as shown here:

```
v_tx:= substr(string, start position[,number of chars]);
```

The start position could be either a positive or negative integer. This would start counting the position from the beginning or from the end of the string, as shown here:

```
SQL> declare
  2        v1_tx VARCHAR2(5):='ABCDE';
  3        v2_tx VARCHAR2(5);
  4  begin
  5        v2_tx:=substr(v1_tx,2);
  6        DBMS_OUTPUT.put_line(v2_tx);
  7        v2_tx:=substr(v1_tx,-2);
  8        DBMS_OUTPUT.put_line(v2_tx);
  9  end;
 10  /
BCDE
DE
PL/SQL procedure successfully completed.
SQL>
```

As shown in these examples, you can omit the third parameter (requested number of characters). In that case, Oracle returns everything from the point you specified to the end of the string. If your starting point is more than the total number of characters in the string, Oracle returns NULL.

The number of characters requested from the string might not always be the length of the resulting string. It could be less, because you might request more characters than the string has. In that case, Oracle just returns everything up to the end of the string, as shown in Listing 10-18.

Listing 10-18:   Using SUBSTR

```
SQL> declare
  2        v1_tx VARCHAR2(5):='ABCDE';
  3        v2_tx VARCHAR2(5);
  4  begin
  5        v2_tx:=substr(v1_tx,2,2);                              →5
  6        DBMS_OUTPUT.put_line(v2_tx);
  7        v2_tx:=substr(v1_tx,2,7);                              →7
  8        DBMS_OUTPUT.put_line(v2_tx);
  9  end;
 10  /
BC                                                               →11
BCDE                                                             →12
PL/SQL procedure successfully completed.
SQL>
```

Additional information about Listing 10-18 is shown here:

→**5, 11** The code works perfectly because you requested two characters and two characters were returned.

→**7, 12** This line requested 7 characters, and 4 were returned because only 5 characters were in the original string.

The function INSTR allows you to locate one string/character in the other one. You can declare it as shown here:

```
v_nr:= instr(string,substring[,position,occurrence]);
```

At the simplest level, INSTR returns the number of characters in the original string where the desired substring starts. But you can also specify the position from which you want the search to start (by default from the first character) and what occurrence of the desired string is required (by default, the first one), as shown in Listing 10-19.

Listing 10-19: Using INSTR

```
SQL> declare
  2       v1_tx VARCHAR2(20):='Hello, World!';
  3       v_nr  binary_integer;
  4  begin
  5       v_nr:= instr (v1_tx,'l');                        →5
  6       DBMS_OUTPUT.put_line(v_nr);
  7       v_nr:= instr (v1_tx,'l',-2);                     →7
  8       DBMS_OUTPUT.put_line(v_nr);
  9       v_nr:= instr (v1_tx,'l',2,2);                    →9
 10       DBMS_OUTPUT.put_line(v_nr);
 11  end;
 12  /
3                                                          →13
11                                                         →14
4                                                          →15
PL/SQL procedure successfully completed.
SQL>
```

Listing 10-19 works as shown here:

→**5, 13** There are three occurrences of the letter 'l' in the original string. In the first case, you're getting the position of first letter starting from the beginning (default).

→**7, 14** These lines of code retrieve the first occurrence of the letter 'l' starting from the second character at the end in reverse order. You can have both positive and negative starting positions as in SUBSTR, but here it means not only the starting point, but also the direction of the search.

→9, 15 These lines get the second occurrence of the letter `'l'`, starting from the second character.

You'll often use both SUBSTR and INSTR at the same time, especially for parsing text. For example, to print out the last word in the string, you can use the following code:

```
SQL> declare
  2      v1_tx VARCHAR2(20):='Hello to everybody';
  3      v2_tx VARCHAR2(20);
  4  begin
  5      v2_tx:= substr (v1_tx, instr (v1_tx,' ',-1)+1);
  6      DBMS_OUTPUT.put_line(v2_tx);
  7  end;
  8  /
everybody
PL/SQL procedure successfully completed.
SQL>
```

Even though this is an oversimplified case (you are taking everything from the last blank character to the end), it is absolutely correct. First, you need to find the position of the last space character by using INSTR, and second, you need to use SUBSTR to grab the rest of the string — starting with the next character from the one you found and going to the end of the original string.

REPLACE and TRANSLATE

The REPLACE and TRANSLATE functions allow you to transform text by using the specified pattern shown here:

```
v_tx:= replace(string,search[,replacement]);
v_tx:= translate(string, search, replacement);
```

Although these functions look similar, there is a major difference. The REPLACE function changes one string to another string, as shown here:

```
SQL> declare
  2      v1_tx VARCHAR2(20):='To be or not to be';
  3      v2_tx VARCHAR2(20);
  4  begin
  5      DBMS_OUTPUT.put_line('Before: ' || v1_tx);
  6      v2_tx:= replace (v1_tx,'be','eat');
  7      DBMS_OUTPUT.put_line('After: ' || v2_tx);
  8*  end;
  9  /
Before: To be or not to be
After: To eat or not to eat
PL/SQL procedure successfully completed.
SQL>
```

If you don't specify the third parameter, Oracle just removes all occurrences of the search string. This is very useful if you want to remove all the spaces from the text.

The `TRANSLATE` function takes search and replacement strings and creates character-to-character maps (the first character from the search string should be replaced with first character from the replacement string, and so on), as shown here:

```
SQL> declare
  2       v1_tx VARCHAR2(20):='To be or not to be';
  3       v2_tx VARCHAR2(20);
  4  begin
  5       v2_tx:= translate (v1_tx,'bo ','BO');
  6       DBMS_OUTPUT.put_line(v2_tx);
  7  end;
  8  /
TOBeOrnOttOBe
PL/SQL procedure successfully completed.
SQL>
```

If you have more characters in the source string than in the replacement string, those characters are removed. As in the example, because the replacement string has only two characters, the third character from the source string is gone. No spaces appear in the result.

With the `TRANSLATE` function, the third parameter (the replacement characters) can't be `NULL` or an empty string. Otherwise, the result is always `NULL`.

*PAD and *TRIM

A number of functions allow you to either add (`PAD`) or remove (`TRIM`) characters to an existing string: `LPAD`/`LTRIM` do it from the left side of the string, `RPAD`/`PTRIM` from the right side. Also, a wrapper function, `TRIM`, allows you to select the trimming mode (left side – leading /right side – trailing /both) as shown in Listing 10-20.

Listing 10-20:   Using LPAD and LTRIM

```
v_tx:= lpad(string,length,extra string);
v_tx:= ltrim(string [,character]);
v_tx:= trim(LEADING|TRAILING|BOTH character from string);

SQL> declare
  2       v1_tx VARCHAR2(20):='Hello!';
  3       v2_tx VARCHAR2(20);
  4       v3_tx VARCHAR2(20);
  5  begin
```

(continued)

Listing 10-20 *(continued)*

```
 6        v2_tx:= rpad(lpad(v1_tx,10,'*'),15,'*');          →6
 7        DBMS_OUTPUT.put_line(v2_tx);
 8
 9        v3_tx:= trim (both '*' from v2_tx);               →9
10        DBMS_OUTPUT.put_line(v3_tx);
11        v3_tx:= trim (leading '*' from v2_tx);            →11
12        DBMS_OUTPUT.put_line(v3_tx);
13        v3_tx:= trim (trailing '*' from v2_tx);           →13
14        DBMS_OUTPUT.put_line(v3_tx);
15   end;
16   /
****Hello!*****
Hello!
Hello!*****
****Hello!
PL/SQL procedure successfully completed.
SQL>
```

Here's what you see in Listing 10-20:

→6   This code pads the original string with * from the left and right sides.

→9   This code represents the most popular way of using the function TRIM by trimming specified character from both sides.

→11   This code represents trimming of leading characters using exactly the same functionality as LTRIM.

→13   This code represents trimming of trailing characters using exactly the same functionality as RTRIM.

Unless you are using Oracle 8*i*, the TRIM function is recommended instead of the older LTRIM/RTRIM because it provides greater flexibility and readability of the code.

Extending your options with regular expressions

In 10*g*, Oracle introduced *regular expressions,* which allow you to search for patterns in string data by using a very rich syntax. This syntax is becoming standard throughout the IT industry.

Regular expressions cannot be used as parameters in the standard Oracle built-in text search functions: LIKE, SUBSTR, INSTR, and REPLACE. Instead,

regular expressions have their own versions of the same functions: REGEXP_
LIKE, REGEXP_SUBSTR, REGEXP_INSTR, and REGEXP_REPLACE.

As an example, in regular expressions, the special character | defines an OR
condition for the characters surrounding it, as shown here:

```
SQL> declare
  2       v1_tx VARCHAR2(2000):='*ABC*BBC*';
  3  begin
  4       DBMS_OUTPUT.put_line('First hit:'||
  5       REGEXP_INSTR(V1_TX,'A|BBC',1,1));              →5
  6       DBMS_OUTPUT.put_line('Second hit:'||
  7       REGEXP_INSTR(V1_TX,'A|BBC',1,2));              →7
  8  end;
  9  /
First hit:2
Second hit:6
PL/SQL procedure successfully completed.
```

→**5, 7** These lines search for either 'ABC' or 'BBC' in the specified
string.

A detailed discussion of regular expressions is beyond the scope of this book.
If you need to perform advanced processing of textual information, a good
place to start is *Oracle Regular Expressions Pocket Reference,* by Jonathan
Gennick and Peter Linsley (O'Reilly).

Chapter 11

Advanced Datatypes

· ·

· ·

*T*o be able to handle many of the complex programming situations that can arise in building database systems, Oracle includes some advanced datatypes and ways to handle large objects, user-defined types and subtypes, and collections.

It is important to understand how to use these datatypes correctly and efficiently in your code, and in the sections in this chapter, we show you how.

Handling Large Objects in the Database

Less-experienced database professionals might think that the three major datatypes (DATE, NUMBER, VARCHAR2) are enough to build most systems. However, this is rarely the case. In modern systems, you might want to store pictures, movies, documents, and sounds. The basic Oracle character datatype (VARCHAR2) can hold only 4,000 characters (about the size of a page of text).

Imagine that you want to create an online shopping catalog of electronic goods. Each record should contain the name of the item, the full text of the user manual, a picture of the front page of the manual, and a reference to the original text file with the manual stored on the server.

Oracle technology provides the solution to this problem with a class of datatypes designed to store up to 8-128TB of binary/textual information. These datatypes are called LOBs (or *large objects*). However, in some cases, (depending upon the environment) you are restricted to 4GB.

When using large objects, the issues of performance and storage always arise. To address these concerns, Oracle provides two options:

- ✔ **You can store the large objects internally, within the database itself (called *internal* large objects in this book).** If you store large objects in the database, they can be retrieved quickly, and you don't have to worry about managing individual files. However, with these objects in the database, the database will get *very* large. If you don't use a good backup utility, it can take hours (or even days) to do a full database backup.

- ✔ **You can keep the objects in the file system and just store the filenames in the database (*external* large objects).** Storing large objects in the file system has its own risks. Some operating systems perform very slowly when thousands of files are in a single directory. And you have to worry about people moving, deleting, or otherwise changing the contents of the objects outside your database-based programs. The database is restricted to read-only access to these objects.

Using internal large objects (CLOB, BLOB)

With internal large objects, Oracle stores the data within the database. However, the data is physically stored separately from the rest of the columns in the table, and the table actually contains pointers to the data in the LOBs. Two types of internal large objects exist:

- ✔ **CLOB (character large object):** The most common use of CLOBs is to store large amounts of character (text) information.

- ✔ **BLOB (binary large object):** BLOBs are used to store binary (mostly video/audio) information in the database.

When saying "CLOB" or "BLOB" out loud, some people say *see-lob* and *bee-lob,* and others say *klob* and *blob.* You should be able to recognize either pronunciation.

Creating pointers with external large objects

With external large objects, the pointer (also called LOB locator) to the object is stored in a BFILE column in the database. The pointer is an internal reference that Oracle can understand, indicating the location where the real data is stored (in that case to the file in file system). It provides read-only access to files on the server. The most common use for BFILE is to provide a convenient way of referencing objects maintained outside the database (for example, a collection of photos).

Using the example of an online shopping catalog for electronic goods, you can use the advanced datatypes to create a table, as shown here.

```
create table catalog
(item_id number,
 name_tx VARCHAR2(2000),
 manual_cl CLOB,
 firstpage_bl BLOB,
 mastertxt_bf BFILE);
```

The amount of information needed to work with large objects is beyond the scope of this book. We provide some simple examples here, but you can find more information in the Oracle Database Documentation library available online in the section *Oracle Database Application Developer's Guide - Large Objects* of the OTN Web site (www.oracle.com/technology/index.html).

Working with Large Objects

The following sections explain the steps needed to create a system such as the online catalog of electronic goods mentioned earlier.

Populating BFILE

Oracle accesses files on the server by using a *directory,* which is just a pointer to an operating system folder. If you're in a normal Oracle working environment, your organization's DBA will probably have to create a directory for you. Assuming that a folder C:\IO exists on your server, and you want to call that folder IO within Oracle, the DBA would execute the following SQL commands:

```
create directory IO as 'C:\IO';
grant read, write on directory IO to public;
```

Now, when you refer to IO in any commands, you're referring to the C:\IO folder in the file system.

To create a pointer to the file on the server and place that pointer in the table on an existing record, use something like Listing 11-1.

Listing 11-1:   Creating a Pointer

```
declare
    v_bf BFILE;                                              →2
begin
    v_bf:=BFILENAME ('IO', 'text.htm');                      →4
    insert into  t_catalog                                   →5
      (item_id, name_tx, mastertxt_bf)
    values (1, 'TEXT.HTM', v_bf);                            →7
end;
```

Here are the details about the preceding code:

→2   Declares a variable of type BFILE to store a file pointer.

→4   Creates a pointer to the text.htm file stored in C:\IO.

→5–7   Inserts a row, including the mastertxt_bf column with the pointer.

Loading data to the CLOB by using BFILE

CLOBs are very useful structures. You can store lots of text information in a CLOB. Listing 11-2 shows how to read data from a file and place it in a CLOB column.

Listing 11-2:   Loading Data to a CLOB

```
declare
    v_file_bf        BFILE;
    v_manual_cl      CLOB;
    lang_ctx         NUMBER := DBMS_LOB.default_lang_ctx;
    charset_id       NUMBER := 0;
    src_offset       NUMBER := 1;
    dst_offset       NUMBER := 1;
    warning          NUMBER;
begin
    update t_catalog                                         →10
      set manual_cl = EMPTY_CLOB()                           →11
    where item_id = 1;                                       →12

    select mastertxt_bf, manual_cl                           →14
      into v_file_bf, v_manual_cl
      from t_catalog
    where item_id = 1;                                       →17
```

```
    DBMS_LOB.fileopen
           (v_file_bf, DBMS_LOB.file_readonly);          →20
    DBMS_LOB.loadclobfromfile (v_manual_cl,
                        v_file_bf,
                        DBMS_LOB.getlength (v_file_bf),
                        src_offset, dst_offset,
                        charset_id, lang_ctx,
                        warning);
    DBMS_LOB.fileclose (v_file_bf);                       →27
end;
```

The following list provides additional details about Listing 11-2:

→**10–12** Oracle works with CLOBs via pointers. For this reason, you must first update the field MANUAL_CL from NULL to EMPTY_CLOB ( ). This is a built-in function that creates a CLOB with a length of 0 bytes.

→**14–17** Now you have a real CLOB in the row (trying to reference NULL won't work) so you can retrieve its pointer into the local variable V_MANUAL_CL. You're also retrieving the pointer to the external BLOB (BFILE) into the local variable V_FILE_BF.

→**14** The next part of the code involves a package that works with all types of large objects — DBMS_LOB. Using the V_FILE_BF pointer, you have access to the file.

→**20–27** These lines of code read the file content into the CLOB V_MANUAL_CL. You can safely ignore some parameters in this command most of the time: src_offset, dst_offset, charset_id, and lang_ctx. Many of the things you can do with these parameters will never be needed in most systems.

There is one very important detail to notice in the preceding example. Although you're working with the local variable, it is actually a pointer to the real CLOB in the database. This means that all modifications to the CLOB that are made by using the local pointer go directly to the table. This is the reason why no update statements exist at the end of the routine. The text from the file went directly to the appropriate column.

Loading a page to a BLOB

Continuing with the example of creating an online catalog for electronic goods, imagine that you want to load an image that is the front page of a manual to the database.

The process of loading a BLOB is similar to that of a CLOB, as shown in Listing 11-3.

Listing 11-3: Loading a Page to the BLOB

```
declare
    v_file_bf  BFILE:= BFILENAME ('IO','picture.gif');   →2
    v_firstpage_bl    BLOB;
    src_offset_nr        NUMBER := 1;
    dst_offset_nr        NUMBER := 1;
begin
    update t_catalog                                      →7
      set firstpage_bl = EMPTY_BLOB()
    where item_id = 1;

    select firstpage_bl
      into v_firstpage_bl
      from t_catalog
    where item_id = 1;

    DBMS_LOB.fileopen (v_file_bf, DBMS_LOB.file_readonly);
    DBMS_LOB.loadblobfromfile (v_firstpage_bl,
                              v_file_bf,
                              DBMS_LOB.getlength (v_file_bf),
                              dst_offset_nr, src_offset_nr);
    DBMS_LOB.fileclose (v_file_bf);
end;
```

Here's a bit more detail about Listing 11-3:

→2   The BFILE pointer is created on the fly. The core logical flow is the same:

- Initialize an empty LOB in the database.

- Get the pointer to the local variable.

- Modify the LOB via the pointer.

→7   The changes from Listing 11-2 are minor. EMPTY_BLOB ( ) creates a new CLOB pointer in the table.

Performing basic string operations on CLOBs

You can use many regular string operations on CLOBs (search for the patterns, get length, get part of the code, and so on) to create advanced application logic. For example, you can implement a search or indexing routine for all large text files loaded in the database exactly the same way as you would for regular strings, as shown in Listing 11-4.

Listing 11-4:   CLOB String Operations

```
declare
    v_manual_cl     CLOB;
    v_nr            NUMBER;
    v_tx            VARCHAR2 (2000);
    v_add_tx        VARCHAR2 (2000)
      :='Loaded: '||TO_CHAR(SYSDATE,'mm/dd/yyyy hh24:mi');
begin
    select manual_cl                                         →8
      into v_manual_cl
      from t_catalog
    where item_id = 1
    for update;                                              →12

    DBMS_LOB.writeappend (v_manual_cl,                       →14
        LENGTH (v_add_tx), v_add_tx);                        →15

    v_nr := INSTR (v_manual_cl, 'Loaded:', -1);              →17
    v_tx := SUBSTR (v_manual_cl, v_nr);
    DBMS_OUTPUT.put_line (v_tx);
end;
```

Keep in mind that LOB pointers are transaction dependent. This means that if you have a COMMIT command in your code, the LOB pointer could become invalid (not pointing to anything) and you may not be able to perform some operations by using that locator.

In Listing 11-3 (populating the CLOB) a new pointer (EMPTY_CLOB( )) was created and retrieved to obtain the data via BFILE. Everything happened within the same logical group called a *transaction*. For more about locks and transactions, see Chapter 12.

→**8–12**   The SELECT...FOR UPDATE method (which we discuss in Chapter 6) guarantees that you're the only person working with the record at a given time.

→**14–15** Uses the writeappend built-in function to add text to the end of an existing CLOB.

→**17**   Searches for the string 'Loaded' starting from the end.

→**18**   Prints out the remainder of the string.

Keeping Code Consistent with User-Defined Subtypes

It is always a challenge to create and enforce standards for different teams working on the same project. For example, one group might define large text variables as VARCHAR2(2000) while another uses VARCHAR2(4000). These types of inconsistencies can cause problems. However, Oracle can help resolve these issues with a PL/SQL element called a *subtype*. The idea is that several column "types" are agreed upon (for example, ShortString, LongString, or Currency). Then all variables and database columns are defined by using only those types. This way, you can enforce a certain level of consistency across the system. The basic syntax for defining a subtype is simple:

```
declare
subtype newSubtype is standardType [NOT NULL];
```

In this case, you aren't creating something new but simply adding restrictions to the basic type. You can create subtypes in the declaration portions of procedures, functions, anonymous blocks, packages, or package bodies. You could use something like the following code:

```
create or replace package pkg_global
is
    subtype large_string   is VARCHAR2(2000);
    subtype medium_string  is VARCHAR2(256);
    subtype small_string   is VARCHAR2(10);
    subtype flag_yn        is VARCHAR2(1) not null;
end;
```

Developers can now simply reference these subtypes in their code, as shown in Listing 11-5.

Listing 11-5:   Referencing Subtypes

```
declare
    v_medium_tx pkg_global.medium_string;
    v_small_tx  pkg_global.small_string := 'ABC';
    v_flag_yn   pkg_global.flag_yn :='N';
begin
    v_medium_tx:=v_small_tx||'-'||v_flag_yn;
end;
```

Defining Your Own Datatypes

The preceding section describes how you can create your own subtypes as more specialized versions of existing Oracle datatypes. In addition, it is possible to create entirely new types. Some user-defined types are for PL/SQL only, and some can be used in both PL/SQL and SQL.

You can create PL/SQL datatypes in the declaration portions of procedures, functions, root anonymous blocks, package bodies, and package specs. The basic syntax is shown here:

```
declare
type newType is definitionOfTheType;
```

You create SQL types by using a DDL operation with the following syntax:

```
Create type newType is definitionOfTheType;
```

The following sections describe several kinds of user-defined types. Records are PL/SQL-only types, and you can use object types in PL/SQL or SQL.

Records

We discuss the record datatype in Chapter 6. The idea is to be able to store a whole set of variables as one entity in a single variable (not as a number of separate variables). By definition, a *record* is a group of related data items stored in attributes, each with its own name and datatype. You can think of a record as a locally stored row from the table with attributes rather than columns.

Records types are used in PL/SQL code (for example, as parameters of functions/procedures), but not in any SQL (views, table definitions, stored datatypes, and so on).

A record type can be defined either explicitly or implicitly.

An *explicit* declaration means that you first define your own datatype and then create a variable of that type, as shown in Listing 11-6.

Listing 11-6:   Explicit Record Type

```
declare
    type emp_ty is record (emp_tx VARCHAR2(256),        →2
                        deptNo emp.deptNo%TYPE);          →3
    v_emp_rty emp_ty;                                     →4
begin
    select empNo||' '||eName,  deptNo into v_emp_rty     →6
      from emp                                            →7
    where empNo=7369;
    DBMS_OUTPUT.put_line                                  →9
      ('Emp:'||v_emp_rty.emp_tx||
        '('||v_emp_rty.deptno||')');                      →11
end;
```

Here are the details about the preceding code:

→**2, 3**   These lines declare the type, which can contain one or more fields. You can define the datatype of each field explicitly, exactly the same as defining columns in a table (line 2), or by reference to the type of a previously defined object, typically a column in a table (line 3).

→**4** Declares the variable.

→**6** Fetches data from the implicit cursor into that variable.

→**7–9** Uses the new type.

As shown above, the way to reference fields in the record type variables is by using *variable.attribute* (as in line 11).

An *implicit* declaration uses an existing table, view, or cursor as a reference. An example is shown in Listing 11-7. (See Chapter 6 for additional information).

Listing 11-7:   Implicit Declaration

```
declare
    v_emp_rec emp%ROWTYPE;                                      →2
begin
    select * into v_emp_rec
      from emp
      where empNo=7369;
    DBMS_OUTPUT.put_line('Emp:'||v_emp_rec.empNo||
        ''||v_emp_rec.eName||'('||v_emp_rec.deptNo||')');
end;
```

→**2** In this case, you don't need your own datatype. You can reference the existing record type of the employee, emp%ROWTYPE.

Using this approach, you're always in sync with the database definitions. However, the downside is that you must bring in the whole record even though you might need only a couple columns. Therefore, you need to determine the best approach on a case-by-case basis.

Assigning values in a record

You have a number of ways to assign values to fields in a variable defined as a record. One way is to fetch data from the cursor. A second method is to use a RETURNING INTO clause as shown next. If you want to be able to see what you're updating in an UPDATE statement, you can use the following code to simultaneously update the record and see columns in the updated record:

```
declare
    type emp_ty is record (emp_tx VARCHAR2(256),
                        deptNo emp.deptno%TYPE);
    v_emp_rty emp_ty;
begin
    update emp
      set eName=eName||'*'
```

```
        where empNo=7369
    returning empNo||' '||eName, deptNo
    into v_emp_rty;
    DBMS_OUTPUT.put_line
    ('Updated: '||v_emp_rty.emp_tx||
            ' ('||v_emp_rty.deptNo||')');
end;
```

You can combine methods of assigning variable values in the same code section, as shown in Listing 11-8.

Listing 11-8:   Combining Ways of Assigning Variable Values

```
create or replace function f_generateNewEmp_rec
    (i_deptno number)
return emp%ROWTYPE
is
    v_emp1_rec emp%ROWTYPE;
begin
    select max(empNo)+1
        into v_emp1_rec.empNo                          →8
        from emp;                                      →9
    v_emp1_rec.deptNo:=i_deptNo;                       →10
    v_emp1_rec.eName:='Emp#'||v_emp1_rec.empNo;        →11
    return v_emp1_rec;
end;
/
declare
    v_emp_rec emp%ROWTYPE;
begin
    v_emp_rec:=f_generateNewEmp_rec(10);               →18
    DBMS_OUTPUT.put_line
    ('Generated:'||v_emp_rec.empNo||' '||v_emp_rec.eName);
end;
/
```

You can work directly with the fields of the record and not just with the record as a whole.

→**8–9** Fetches data from an implicit cursor directly to the field `v_emp1_rec.empno`.

→**10–11** Assigns values to the fields `v_emp1_rec.deptno` and `v_emp1_rec.ename` in the same way as if they were regular PL/SQL variables.

→**18** Retrieves a value for the record type variable from the function.

Variables can serve as input/output parameters.

The problem with using records as parameters is that they are just too big, and they require a lot of memory.

Chapter 3 introduced the concept of passing a parameter by using NOCOPY. This means that you are only passing a pointer to the variable rather than copying the values, increasing performance, and decreasing memory usage. NOCOPY is particularly useful when passing record variables (that may contain hundreds of columns). An example showing how you can pass variables without copying them is shown in Listing 11-9. This example passes in an employee record and modifies that record by giving it a new number (one higher than the highest number in the tables) and a fake name.

Listing 11-9: Passing Variables without Copying

```
create or replace procedure p_generateNewEmp
        (io_emp in out nocopy emp%ROWTYPE)          →2
is
begin
    select max(empNo)+1
      into io_emp.empNo
      from emp;
    io_emp.eName:='Emp#'||io_emp.empNo;
end;
/
declare
    v_emp_rec emp%ROWTYPE;                          →12
begin         →13
    v_emp_rec.deptNo:=10;
    p_generateNewEmp(v_emp_rec);                    →15
    DBMS_OUTPUT.put_line
        ('Generated:'||v_emp_rec.empNo||
                  ' '||v_emp_rec.eName);            →18
end;
```

Here are the details about Listing 11-9:

→2   Because you defined the parameter in the procedure as NOCOPY, no memory overhead existed because both variables were working with the same instance of the variable. For more explanation, see Chapter 3.

→12   Creates a variable in the main routine.

→13–18 Passes the variable to the procedure (line 13) and returns it.

Oracle sequences should generally be used for getting the next number for an identifying column, rather than the code shown here (lines 5 and 6).

With record variables, you can assign one record to another; doing so copies all columns in the original record to the target. This powerful feature was introduced in Oracle version 9. An example of copying an employee record is shown in Listing 11-10.

Listing 11-10:   Assigning Record Variables

```
declare
    v_emp_rec emp%ROWTYPE;
    v_empStart_rec emp%ROWTYPE;
begin
    v_emp_rec.deptNo:=10;
    p_generateNewEmp(v_emp_rec);
    v_empStart_rec:=v_emp_rec; -- store original data   →7
    DBMS_OUTPUT.put_line('Generated: '||
        v_empStart_rec.empNo||' '||v_empStart_rec.eName);
    p_processEmp(v_emp_rec); -- continue working
end;
```

→7   Copies newly generated record for future comparisons.

You can use direct assignment of records only in two cases:

- ✔ If both variables are identical user-defined record datatypes. (Having fields in the same order and of the same types is not sufficient.)

- ✔ If the source variable is defined by reference using %ROWTYPE and all the target variable fields are in the same order and of the same datatype.

Currently there is no easy way to compare two variables of type Record. To do this, you must perform a field-by-field comparison, as shown here:

```
function f_isDuplicate_yn
            (i_emp1_rec emp%ROWTYPE, i_emp2_rec emp%ROWTYPE)
return VARCHAR2
is
    v_out_tx VARCHAR2(1):='N';
begin
    if   i_emp1_rec.eName=i_emp2_rec.eName
    and i_emp1_rec.mgr=i_emp2_rec.mgr
    and i_emp1_rec.deptNo=i_emp2_rec.deptNo
    then
        v_out_tx:='Y';
    end if;
    return v_out_tx;
end;
```

Inserts and updates using record variables

You can use record datatypes to manipulate data inside PL/SQL routines. Using this approach means that you don't need to list all the fields, making the code significantly easier to read. For example, you might need to create a number of employees in a specified department of an organization. To do this, you can use Listing 11-11.

Listing 11-11:   DML Using Record Variables

```
procedure p_insertNewEmp(i_deptno number)
is
    v_emp_rec emp%ROWTYPE;                               →3
begin
    select max(empNo)+1                                  →5
      into v_emp_rec.empNo
      from emp;
    v_emp_rec.eName:='Emp#'||v_emp_rec.empNo;
    v_emp_rec.deptNo:=i_deptno;                          →9
--    v_emp_rec.sal := required code here
    insert into emp
      values v_emp_rec;                                  →12
end;
```

The following list provides more details about some of the lines in Listing 11-11:

→**3**   Declares a variable of exactly the same type as the record to be created.

→**5–10** Populates as many fields in the record as you need. If you need additional data for testing, you can just modify the routine to populate the required columns.

→**12**   INSERT statement is fired with no list of columns or variables. This method creates very clean code.

Taking the previous example one step farther, you might have a situation where, by mistake, when batch-loading new data into the system, the data associated with two employees was swapped. You cannot update primary keys, so you have to keep the existing records and replace all columns from record 1 with those from record 2. Because several columns exist, the code will be very messy. Using the record datatype provides a better solution, as shown in Listing 11-12.

Listing 11-12:   Using the Record Datatype

```
declare
    v_emp1_rec emp%ROWTYPE;
    v_emp2_rec emp%ROWTYPE;
begin
    select * into v_emp1_rec                             →5
      from emp
    where empNo=7369;--SMITH
    select * into v_emp2_rec
      from emp
    where empNo=7499;--ALLEN                             →10
```

```
      v_emp1_rec.empNo:=7499;                          →12
      v_emp2_rec.empNo:=7369;                          →13

   update emp
      set row = v_emp1_rec                             →16
   where empNo = 7499;--SMITH
   update emp
      set row = v_emp2_rec
   where empNo = 7369;--ALLEN                           →20
end;
```

The following list breaks down some of the lines from Listing 11-12:

> →**5–10** Collects all information about both employees into record
> variables.

> →**12–15** Swaps primary keys. (Nothing prevents you from doing it here,
> in memory.)

> →**16–20** The last step is the most interesting. The syntax set row allows
> you to update the whole row with your variable at once.

There are some restrictions on using records in INSERT and UPDATE
statements:

✔ The structure of the row and the variable must be exactly the same. This
is the reason why it is safer to create variables by reference rather than
explicitly.

✔ The right side of the set row must contain a variable. It cannot be a
subquery.

✔ If you use a record variable in an INSERT/UPDATE statement, you cannot
use any other variables in the statement. For example, update emp
set row=v_emp, ename='ABC' where empno=123 is illegal.

Object types

As mentioned earlier, records are PL/SQL datatypes. Although they provide
flexibility in your code, they also include many limitations. Using an object-
oriented (OO) programming approach removes many of those limitations.
The crux of this approach is the idea of *objects*. These objects can have *attributes* (something that helps to describe the object) and *methods* (things that
can happen to the object).

For example, the object EMPLOYEE has the following attributes: Name,
Salary, Commissions, and so on. Some activities that can happen with an
employee include a request to change name or to find total compensation.

Using a traditional approach, you would create a table named `EMP`, a procedure `p_changeName`, and a function `f_getIncome_nr`. You might place the code units in a package, but they still wouldn't be part of the `EMP` table. In an object-oriented environment, you can describe the whole thing as an object called `EMP`, as shown here:

```
create type emp_oty is object (
    empNo    NUMBER,
    eName    VARCHAR2(10),
    job      VARCHAR2(9),
    mgr      NUMBER,
    hireDate DATE,
    sal      NUMBER,
    comm     NUMBER,
    deptNo   NUMBER,
    member procedure p_changeName (i_newName_tx VARCHAR2),
    member function  f_getIncome_nr  return VARCHAR2
    );

create or replace type body emp_oty as
    member function f_getIncome_nr return VARCHAR2
    is
    begin
        return sal+comm;
    end f_getIncome_nr;
    member procedure p_changeName
        (i_newName_tx VARCHAR2)
    is
    begin
        eName:=i_newName_tx;
    end p_changeName;
end;
```

Because the object type includes methods, you need a place to store the code. Oracle provides the same structures that are available for packages, namely an *object type specification* (to declare methods) and an *object type body* (to provide the real code). Object elements are referenced by using *variable.attribute* and *variable.method* notation.

Logically speaking, the object `EMP` is still a datatype, so you can use the syntax `(type TypeName is object)`. However, that type can be stored in the database as an independent element, so you can prefix it with `CREATE` or `REPLACE` and execute it in the same way as procedures or functions. You can manipulate objects with the same standard DDL commands, as shown here:

```
drop type emp_oty; -- drop type
alter type emp_oty
   add attribute birthdate_dt DATE; -- add attribute
alter type emp_oty
   drop attribute birthdate_dt DATE; -- drop attribute
```

Listing 11-13 demonstrates the usage of object types in PL/SQL.

Listing 11-13: Object Type Code Example

```
declare
    v_emp_oty emp_oty;                                    →2
begin
    v_emp_oty:=emp_oty(100,                               →4
                    'TestEmp',
                    null,
                    null,
                    sysdate,
                    1000,
                    500,
                    10);                                  →11
    v_emp_oty.sal:=v_emp_oty.sal+500;                     →12
    DBMS_OUTPUT.put_line
        ('Employee:'||v_emp_oty.eName||
         ' has income '||v_emp_oty.f_getIncome_nr()); →15

end;
```

Here's what's happening in this bit of code:

→2   Declares the variable of the type EMP_OTY.

→4–11 Creates a new object of the specified type by using a *constructor*. It is a special built-in element of any type that creates a new instance of the object (real object made using a definition from the object type). By default, you're passing all the attributes declared in the defined type to the constructor.

→12   Reference and alter attribute SAL of the objects.

→15   Call method f_getIncome_nr of the object.

When you define a variable of object type, the object itself doesn't exist. Before you create it, there's no way to reference its element. You must create an *instance* of the object first. This is the difference between the object and record types: with object types, you cannot just start assigning values to attributes. For example, the following code is illegal:

```
declare
    v_emp_oty emp_oty;
begin
    v_emp_oty.sal:=500; -- ILLEGAL
end;
```

To make this legal, you would assign the values as follows:

```
declare
    v_emp_rec emp%ROWTYPE;
begin
    v_emp_rec.sal:=500; -- LEGAL
end;
```

You can use objects in SQL, too. You have two options. First, you can use object types as attributes in a traditional relational way, as shown here:

```
create table t_emp
   (employee emp_oty,
    remarks_tx VARCHAR2(2000));
```

Alternatively, you can create an *object table,* where each attribute becomes a column and each row contains a unique *object identifier* that will allow you to create references, as shown here:

```
create table t_emp of emp_oty;
```

You now have a persistent place to store objects more closely to the way you think about them rather than as pure data, as shown in Listing 11-14.

Listing 11-14:   Using SQL Objects

```
declare
    v_emp_oty emp_oty;
    v_out_tx VARCHAR2(2000);
begin
    v_emp_oty:=emp_oty
        (100,'TestEmp',null,null,sysdate,1000,500,10);
    insert into t_emp                                    →7
      values v_emp_oty;                                  →8

    update t_emp
      set sal=sal+500                                    →11
    where empno=100;

    select 'Income:'||t.f_getIncome_nr()
      into v_out_tx                                      →15
      from t_emp t
    where t.empno=100;                                   →17
end;
```

The following details are relevant to Listing 11-14:

→**7–8**   Inserts the object as a whole element (because in this case, the object is a record).

→**11–13** Updates table columns as if they were normal columns.

→**15–17** Calls object methods directly from SQL. To use this functionality, you need to create an alias to the table; otherwise, you won't have a way to access objects.

Now that you have an object in the database, you can retrieve it as a whole (not just one column at a time) by using the following code:

```
declare
    v_emp_oty emp_oty;
begin
    select value(t)
      into    v_emp_oty
      from t_emp t
    where empNo=100;

    DBMS_OUTPUT.put_line('Name: '||v_emp_oty.eName);
end;
```

The built-in function value returns an object that can be stored in the local variable. You also have to create an alias for the table because that is the only parameter that the function accepts.

There is also a special way of accessing the object table, namely by reference, as shown here:

```
declare
    v_emp_oref ref emp_oty;
begin
    select ref(t)
      into    v_emp_oref
      from t_emp t
    where empNo=100;

    update t_emp t
    set sal=sal+100
    where ref(t)=v_emp_oref;
end;
```

The built-in function ref returns a pointer to the object, so the variable you need to declare is not of type emp_oty, but ref emp_oty, which includes a reference to the object of specified type. Think of references as a unique primary key, which allows you to significantly speed up all of your update statements and to ensure that you're updating the object you need.

Object-oriented programming in PL/SQL is a very large topic and a complete discussion is beyond the scope of this book, but you can look at the "Application Developer's Guide - Object-Relational Features" on the Oracle Technology Network.

You can use objects in both SQL and PL/SQL.

Grouping Sets of Data into Collections

Although you can store almost everything in database tables, this isn't the most efficient way of processing data. Very often you need to create structures and process sets of data in memory. In the Oracle environment, these structures are called *collections*. A collection is an ordered group of elements, all of the same type, addressed by a unique subscript. Because all collections represent data, they are defined as datatypes. Several types of collections are discussed in this section.

Using VARRAYs

Variable-size arrays (*VARRAYs,* pronounced *vee-array*) are a well-known type of collection in many computer languages. Note that in the Oracle environment, array subscripts start from 1, and not from 0 (as in C and Java). VARRAYs are of fixed length. You specify the length of the array when you define it. Arrays of elements of the same type use sequential numbers as a subscript. VARRAYS can be used both in PL/SQL and SQL, as shown here:

```
declare
   type VarrayType is varray(size) of ElementType;
...

create or replace type VarrayType
          is varray(size) of ElementType;
```

The size of a VARRAY must be a positive integer and cannot be null. There are some restrictions on the datatypes you can use as the base element type:

✔ You cannot create an array of REF CURSORs (special datatype that allows you to specify logical pointers to datasets). There is more information about REF CURSORs in Chapter 13.

✔ In SQL, you cannot use BOOLEAN because it is a PL/SQL-only datatype.

Arrays always look like a list without any gaps in the subscripts, as in this example:

#1 – John

#2 – Ed

#3 – Marc

...

#<size of array> - Zena

In most cases, you should use VARRAYs when you know the size of your data set and that size is very stable. For example, the number of months is definitely stable, so using a VARRAY to generate a monthly report is appropriate, as shown in Listing 11-15.

Listing 11-15: A VARRAY Example

```
declare
    type month_va is varray(13) of VARCHAR2(20);          →2
    v_month_va month_va;
    v_count_nr number;                                     →4
begin
    v_month_va:=month_va('January','February',
                         'March','April','May',
                         'June','July','August',
                         'September','October','November',
                         'December');
    DBMS_OUTPUT.put_line('Length:'||v_month_va.count);
    v_month_va.extend;                                     →12
    v_month_va(v_month_va.last):='Null';                   →13
    -- v_month_va(13):='Null'; -- the same result

    DBMS_OUTPUT.put_line('Length:'||v_month_va.count); →16

    for i in v_month_va.first..v_month_va.last             →18
    loop
        select count(*)
          into v_count_nr
          from emp
        where nvl(replace(to_char(hiredate,'Month'),' '),
                  'Null')=v_month_va(i);

        DBMS_OUTPUT.put_line
           (v_month_va(i)||': '||v_count_nr);
    end loop;
end;
```

Here's what's happening in Listing 11-15:

→2   Creates a new datatype MONTH_VA that represents the array. For now, that array contains elements of simple VARCHAR2 type. The array size is 13 (12 months + null).

→6–10   Populates the array with real data. You can do this in a number of ways. This one uses a constructor of the appropriate type with a comma-separated 12-element list of strings inside the brackets. That will create 12 elements of the 13-element array. You can pass fewer elements than the maximum size of array, but never more than the defined size.

→4   The built-in method COUNT returns the number of initialized elements in the collection as shown by the output on line 11, which proves that there are indeed only 12 elements.

→12–13 The creation of the last element (for the NULL value) is a bit tricky. Even though the size of the array is declared, Oracle doesn't create all the elements of the array automatically. You need to create the new instance of the object by using the built-in method EXTEND. Only then can you assign the value.

You can do the last assignment in a number of ways: directly by using subscript 13 because you already had 12 elements or by using the built-in LAST method that will return the highest subscript of the array. The second method works better because if you created a new instance in the array one line earlier, you can be certain that you will specifically populate the last element.

→16   Checks to see whether you have all 13 objects so you can start working with the array.

→18   If a built-in LAST method exists, it seems logical that there should also be a built-in FIRST method that returns the lowest existing subscript in the array. In VARRAYs, subscripts are always consecutive, which allows you to create a FOR loop that can spin through the array.

Inside the loop, you're accessing array elements by their subscripts. This method works in both pure PL/SQL commands and SQL statements inside the PL/SQL.

Because arrays are always dense and have consecutive subscripts, you have no way of deleting an element inside the array. Even if you set it to NULL, it still exists. The only thing you can do is decrease the size of the array, as shown in Listing 11-16.

Listing 11-16: Decreasing the Size of an Array

```
declare
    type month_va is varray(13) of VARCHAR2(20);          →2
    v_month_va month_va:=month_va();
    v_count_nr number;
begin
    v_month_va.extend(3);                                 →6
    v_month_va(1):='January';
    v_month_va(2):='February';
    v_month_va(3):='March';                               →9

    v_month_va(2):=null;                                  →11
    if v_month_va.exists(2)                               →12
    then
        DBMS_OUTPUT.put_line('Object Exists');
    end if;

    v_month_va(3):=v_month_va(2);                         →17
    v_month_va.trim(1);                                   →18
```

```
      DBMS_OUTPUT.put_line('Count:'||v_month_va.count);
      DBMS_OUTPUT.put_line('Last:'||v_month_va.last);
end;
```

The following information explains Listing 11-16 in more detail:

→**2**   Declares a variable and assigns an empty constructor to it as a default variable. This raises the same issue as when dealing with objects. Not only do you need to declare the variable, but you also need to initialize it via the constructor.

→**6–9**   Initializes three elements in the array and populates them. You don't have to do this one at a time.

→**11**   Assigns NULL to the second element in the array.

→**12**   Uses the built-in method EXISTS to check whether the element with subscript 2 still exists.

→**17–18** Tries to remove the last element of the array by using the built-in method TRIM. Because you really need to delete the second element, this code copies the third one into the second and removes the last element of the array.

However, now the size of array decreased. Because the only way to decrease the size of the array is to trim it, there is a rule relating to VARRAYs. The subscript of the last element is always equal to the size of the array. This means that Listing 11-16 could use the following syntax:

```
for i in 1..v_month_va.count
...
```

Nesting variable data sets in tables

Although VARRAYs can be very useful, they have a fixed length. Oracle includes a different kind of collection called *nested tables.* Nested tables can hold an arbitrary number of elements and use sequential numbers as subscripts. You can define equivalent SQL types, allowing nested tables to be stored in database tables and manipulated through SQL, as shown here:

```
declare
  type <NestedTable> is table of <ElementType>;
...

create or replace type <NestedTable>
                    is table of <ElementType>;
```

Deleting internal elements from a collection

At first glance, nested tables look exactly like arrays without an upper limit. However, there is one major difference: Even at the creation point, nested tables have consecutive subscripts; it is possible to delete internal (not only the last) elements afterwards, as shown in Listing 11-17.

Listing 11-17: Creating Nested Tables

```
declare
    type month_nt is table of VARCHAR2(20);
    v_month_nt month_nt:=month_nt();
    i number;
begin
    v_month_nt.extend(3);
    v_month_nt(1):='January';
    v_month_nt(2):='February';
    v_month_nt(3):='March';

    v_month_nt.delete(2);                                    →11
    DBMS_OUTPUT.put_line('Count:'||v_month_nt.count);
    DBMS_OUTPUT.put_line('Last:'||v_month_nt.last);         →13

    i:=v_month_nt.first;
    loop
        DBMS_OUTPUT.put_line(v_month_nt(i));
        i:=v_month_nt.next(i);
        if i is null
        then
            exit;
        end if;
    end loop;
end;
```

Check out the details about Listing 11-17:

→11   Uses the built-in method DELETE to remove the second element from the table. That method allows you to delete an element from the table by its subscript or to clean up the whole table if you aren't passing any parameters into it.

         Some side effects are associated with deleting internal elements. For example, you cannot use FOR loops because you can't be sure that subscripts are contingent any more.

→12–13   The count of records became 2, although the highest subscript is still 3, so there is a gap.

There is a way to loop through this kind of collection by using the built-in NEXT method and its opposite built-in method, PRIOR. The NEXT built-in returns the subscript of the next existing element of the table and jumps over any gap. If there are no more elements, the built-in method will return NULL. This is the most efficient way to perform a safe loop through the nested table.

Returning a list based on parameters

Nested tables are more flexible than arrays and can be used in both SQL and PL/SQL. For example, if you need to get a list of employees that satisfies some number of parameters, you can get it by writing some advanced queries. However, very complex business rules can cause your SQL to be problematic. With nested tables, you can implement procedural logic to solve the problem.

The following code creates some appropriate types in SQL. In this case, creating them in a package specification is not an option because this is a PL/SQL-only datatype.

```
create type emp2_oty is object (empNo    NUMBER,
                                eName    VARCHAR2(10),
                                deptNo   NUMBER );
create type emp2_nt is table of emp2_oty;
```

Next, you can create a function to return a list of employees filtered by a number of rules (these rules are greatly simplified from those you might encounter in a working system):

- ✔ If the user passed a department number, return a list of all people in that department.

- ✔ If a department number is not passed and a hire date is passed, return a list of all people hired in the same month.

- ✔ If both parameters are null, return everybody.

The code to return the employee list is shown in Listing 11-18.

Listing 11-18:   A Nested Table Example to Return Employee List

```
create or replace function f_getEmps_nt
(i_deptNo number, i_hireDate DATE)
return emp2_nt
is
    v_emp2_nt emp2_nt:=emp2_nt();                        →5
    cursor c_emp is
      select *
        from emp;
begin
  for r_emp in c_emp
  loop
    if i_deptNo is null then
      if i_hireDate is null
      or to_char(i_hireDate,'mm')=
            to_char(r_emp.hireDate,'mm')
      then
        v_emp2_nt.extend;
        v_emp2_nt(v_emp2_nt.last):=
```

(continued)

Listing 11-18 *(continued)*

```
                emp2_oty(r_emp.empNo, r_emp.eName,
                    r_emp.deptno);
        end if;
    elsif i_deptNo=r_emp.deptNo then
        v_emp2_nt.extend;
        v_emp2_nt(v_emp2_nt.last):=
            emp2_oty(r_emp.empno, r_emp.ename,
                r_emp.deptno);
    end if;
  end loop;
  return v_emp2_nt;
end;
```

→5   Declares the variable of appropriate type. Because you don't know how many records could come back, use an empty constructor as the default value. Now the task is simple. Just loop through the cursor, check the rule procedurally, and populate the resulting collection. In this case, *object type* is used as a base element of the collection, and an appropriate constructor is needed for each new element.

The resulting code can now be used in PL/SQL or SQL:

```
declare
    v_temp_nt emp2_nt;
begin
    v_temp_nt:=f_getEmps_nt(20,null);
    DBMS_OUTPUT.put_line('Received:'||v_temp_nt.count);
    v_temp_nt:=f_getEmps_nt(null,sysdate);
    DBMS_OUTPUT.put_line('Received:'||v_temp_nt.count);
    v_temp_nt:=f_getEmps_nt(null,null);
    DBMS_OUTPUT.put_line('Received:'||v_temp_nt.count);
end;
```

Or

```
select F_GETEMPS_NT (10,null) from dual
```

You can "magically" transform a collection into a table so you can reference it in a SQL query just as if it were a regular database table. You do this by *casting* the collection to a table, as shown here:

```
select t.*
from table (
        cast (f_getEmps_nt (20,null) as emp2_nt)
        ) t
```

Two steps are needed to perform this magic. First, you need to indicate to the SQL compiler that the result of the function f_getEmps_nt is of a type understood by SQL. (That was the reason why you needed to create type

EMP2_NT as an element in the database, but not in the package.) You can do so by using a transformation function called *cast* that can change the datatypes of the passed objects. The second step is to use another function TABLE that converts the collection into a virtual table.

Now you can do whatever you want with this query. For example, if your front-end tool allows you to build a database query on the fly, you can create a very flexible filtering mechanism because the parameters of the function are user defined. If the business rules change, all you need to do is update the function with zero impact on the front end. If this doesn't work, you can create a few global variables and reference them in the view, as shown here:

```
create or replace package pkg_globals
is
    v_currentDeptno number:=10;
    function f_getCurrDeptNo return number;
    procedure p_setCurrDeptNo(i_nr number);

    v_currentHireDate date:=sysdate;
    function f_getCurrHireDate return date;
    procedure p_setCurrHireDate(i_dt date);
end;

create or replace package body pkg_globals
is
    function f_getCurrDeptNo return number is
    begin
        return v_currentDeptNo;
    end;
    procedure p_setCurrDeptNo(i_nr number) is
    begin
        v_currentDeptNo:=i_nr;
    end;
    function f_getCurrHireDate return date is
    begin
        return v_currentHireDate;
    end;
    procedure p_setCurrHireDate(i_dt date) is
    begin
        v_currentHireDate:=i_dt;
    end;
end;

create or replace view v_getEmps
as
select *
from table(
        cast (f_getEmps_nt (pkg_globals.f_getCurrDeptNo,
                            pkg_globals.f_getCurrHireDate)
                as emp2_nt)
            );
```

Associative arrays (index-by tables)

Both VARRAYs and nested tables have one major restriction: You can use consecutive integers only as subscripts. However, these subscripts very seldom have a separate meaning. For example, if you have a list of departments and you need to populate a column in that list with the list of employees, you might only know about the following way of resolving the problem:

```
declare
    type dept_rty is record
            (deptNo NUMBER, extra_tx VARCHAR2(2000));
    type dept_nt is table of dept_rty;
    v_dept_nt dept_nt:=dept_nt();
    cursor c_emp is
     select eName, deptNo
       from emp;
begin
  v_dept_nt.extend(3);
  v_dept_nt(1).deptNo:=10;
  v_dept_nt(2).deptNo:=20;
  v_dept_nt(3).deptNo:=30;
  for r_emp in c_emp loop
    for i in v_dept_nt.first..v_dept_nt.last loop
      if v_dept_nt(i).deptNo=r_emp.deptNo then
        v_dept_nt(i).extra_tx:=
          v_dept_nt(i).extra_tx||' '||r_emp.eName;
      end if;
    end loop;
  end loop;
end;
```

The problem is identifying the appropriate element of the array to update. There's a big difference between the actual key element of the collection and its subscript. In this case, it would be very convenient if DEPTNO could become the subscript of the collection. A third kind of collection can be useful in situations like this: *associative arrays.* An associative array is a collection of elements that use arbitrary numbers and strings for subscript values. Because of its amorphous structure, you cannot use an associative array in SQL. The only way to define these types is in the declaration portions of PL/SQL elements (packages, procedures, and so on), as shown here:

```
declare
  type AssocArray is table of ElementType
  index by binary_integer|pls_integer|VARCHAR2(size);
```

You can think of associative arrays as tables sitting in memory with the primary key (subscript). That primary key can be either Integer (BINARY_INTEGER and PLS_INTEGER enforce that) or String (VARCHAR2 or any of its subtypes). Because the primary key is unique, you cannot have two elements in the same collection with the same subscript. Listing 11-19 shows a modified version of the previous example.

Listing 11-19: Using Associative Arrays

```
declare
    type dept_rty is record
        (deptNo number, extra_tx VARCHAR2(2000));
    type dept_aa is table of dept_rty
        index by binary_integer;
    v_dept_aa dept_aa;                                      →6
    cursor c_emp is
      select eName, deptNo
        from emp;
begin
  v_dept_aa(10).deptNo:=10;                                →11
  v_dept_aa(20).deptNo:=20;
  v_dept_aa(30).deptNo:=30;                                →13
  for r_emp in c_emp loop
      v_dept_aa(r_emp.deptNo).extra_tx:=                   →15
          v_dept_aa(r_emp.deptNo).extra_tx||
            ' '||r_emp.eName;
  end loop;
end;
```

Here are the details for Listing 11-19:

→6   The first difference is in the declaration portion. You don't need any constructors for associative arrays. They exist from the moment of the declaration of the variable.

→11–13 Declares the elements of the collection. You don't need to extend a collection to add new elements. You can just assign any value to any attribute of the element with the appropriate subscript and that element with the specified subscript already exists. You should still use an assignment statement because you can't refer to an object that hasn't yet been created. Oracle creates the elements of the collection so that you can have subscript 20 immediately after 10.

→15–16 Because DEPTNO is used as the subscript of the collection, it is very easy to update the correct row in the array.

Indexing associative arrays by VARCHAR2 can add a new dimension to your code so that you don't need to create complex hash algorithms to implement the functionality of real hash tables. For example, if you need to generate a list of employees grouped by two parameters (department and quarter when they were hired) by using this strategy, your code will be significantly simplified, as shown in Listing 11-20.

Listing 11-20:   Indexing Associative Arrays

```
declare
    type list_aa is table of VARCHAR2(2000)
        index by VARCHAR2(256);
    v_list_aa list_aa;

    cursor c_dept is
      select deptNo
      from dept
      order by deptNo;
    cursor c_emp is
      select eName, deptNo,to_char(hireDate,'q') q_nr
      from emp;
    v_subscript_tx VARCHAR2(256);
begin
  for r_dept in c_dept loop                                    →15
    v_list_aa(r_dept.deptNo||'|1'):='Q1 Dept#'
          ||r_dept.deptno||':';
    v_list_aa(r_dept.deptNo||'|2'):='Q2 Dept#'
          ||r_dept.deptno||':';
    v_list_aa(r_dept.deptNo||'|3'):='Q3 Dept#'
          ||r_dept.deptno||':';
    v_list_aa(r_dept.deptNo||'|4'):='Q4 Dept#'
          ||r_dept.deptno||':';
  end loop;                                                    →20

  for r_emp in c_emp loop                                      →22
    v_list_aa(r_emp.deptNo||'|'||r_emp.q_nr):=
        v_list_aa(r_emp.deptNo||'|'||r_emp.q_nr)||
        ' '||r_emp.eName;
  end loop;                                                    →25

  v_subscript_tx:=v_list_aa.first;                             →27
  loop
    DBMS_OUTPUT.put_line(v_list_aa(v_subscript_tx));
    v_subscript_tx:=v_list_aa.next(v_subscript_tx);            →30
    exit when v_subscript_tx is null;
  end loop;
end;
```

The following are additional details about this code listing:

→15–20 Creates the result collection, where the key is department number concatenated with the quarter. When you're using concatenated values as hash functions, always use a separator that cannot be in any part of the key (which allows you to avoid mutating keys). The most convenient way to do this is to use pipe-delimited keys.

→22–25 This loop populates the destination collection with the real data. Because you know the hash function and have all the elements in hand (DEPTNO and quarter of the hiring), you can directly access and modify the appropriate records in the associative array.

→27–30 The last loop is the most complicated because of the inclusion of INDEX BY VARCHAR2. Because a FOR loop can work only with integers, you have to manually loop through the collection. You should do this in the same way as you did for nested tables. Because gaps exist between subscripts, you have to use the built-in FIRST method to start the loop and NEXT to detect the following element.

There is a way of using a FOR loop with the associative arrays INDEX BY BINARY_INTEGER, as shown in Listing 11-21, but this might not be very convenient.

Listing 11-21:   Using INDEX BY BINARY_INTEGER

```
declare
    type dept_rty is record
        (deptNo number, extra_tx VARCHAR2(2000));
    type dept_aa is table of dept_rty
        index by binary_integer;
    v_dept_aa dept_aa;
begin
  v_dept_aa(10).deptNo:=10;
  v_dept_aa(20).deptNo:=20;
  for i in v_dept_aa.first..v_dept_aa.last loop
    if v_dept_aa.exists(i) then                              →11
        DBMS_OUTPUT.put_line(v_dept_aa(i).deptno);
    end if;
  end loop;
end;
```

→11 You must check for the existence of the specified subscript in each turn of the loop. Otherwise, you'll try to reference a nonexistent element of the collection and raise an exception.

Speeding Up Data Collection with Bulk Operations

One programming concept that is very closely related to nested tables is called *bulk operations* between SQL and PL/SQL. With the introduction of collections, you're dealing with two sets of data: one sitting in tables and the other in memory. Of course, you can still perform operations one row at a time, but it is much more efficient to let Oracle perform all the repeating operations automatically.

Using the BULK COLLECT command

With the previously mentioned function `f_getEmps`, because of the specific business rules, you had to process one row at a time (see "Returning a list based on parameters" earlier in this chapter). But what if the task is much simpler and you need to create a function that returns a nested table with employees in a specified department? You can do this directly with the code shown here:

```
create or replace function f_getEmpDept_nt
    (i_deptNo number)
return emp2_nt
is
    v_emp2_nt emp2_nt:=emp2_nt();
    cursor c_emp is
      select *
        from emp
      where deptNo=i_deptNo;
begin
    for r_emp in c_emp loop
      v_emp2_nt.extend;
      v_emp2_nt(v_emp2_nt.last):=
          emp2_oty(r_emp.empNo, r_emp.eName,
          r_emp.deptNo);
    end loop;
    return v_emp2_nt;
end;
```

This code will fetch one row at a time. But because you're trying to transform one data set into another, you can use the BULK COLLECT command to perform this operation, as shown here:

```
create or replace function f_getEmpDept_nt
    (i_deptNo NUMBER)
return emp2_nt is
    v_emp2_nt emp2_nt:=emp2_nt();
begin
    select emp2_oty(empNo, eName, deptNo)
      bulk collect into v_emp2_nt
      from emp
    where deptNo=i_deptNo;
    return v_emp2_nt;
end;
```

To get the same result by using explicit cursors, use Listing 11-22.

Listing 11-22:   Using the BULK COLLECT Command

```
create or replace function f_getEmpDept_nt
    (i_deptNo NUMBER)
return emp2_nt is
    v_emp2_nt emp2_nt:=emp2_nt();
    cursor c_emp is
    select emp2_oty(empNo, eName, deptNo)                →5
    from emp
    where deptNo=i_deptNo;
begin
    open c_emp;
    fetch c_emp bulk collect into v_emp2_nt;             →10
    close c_emp;
    return v_emp2_nt;
end;
```

The relevant details of Listing 11-22 are shown here:

→5   Because the target collection has a base element of object type, use a constructor `emp2_oty`. The query was returning just one object for a row, rather than returning a set of database attributes.

→10   Fetches the whole result of the query into the collection via BULK COLLECT.

You must have the same datatypes in both the SELECT and INTO clauses. For example, the syntax shown in Listing 11-23 is valid because the base elements are of simple type.

Listing 11-23:   Bulk Query into Nested Tables

```
declare
    type text_nt is table of VARCHAR2(256);
    type number_nt is table of NUMBER;
    v_eName_nt text_nt;
    v_deptNo_nt number_nt;
begin
    select eName, deptNo
      bulk collect into v_eName_nt,v_deptNo_nt
      from emp
    where deptNo=40;
    DBMS_OUTPUT.put_line('Records:'||v_eName_nt.count());
            →11
    DBMS_OUTPUT.put_line('Fetched:'||sql%ROWCOUNT);      →12
end;
```

The following list includes more details about the code listing:

→11   Keep in mind that the implicit SELECT...INTO included with the BULK COLLECT command does not raise the NO_DATA_FOUND exception if the query returns no rows at all. Although this eliminates extra exception handling, you may end up with an unexpected empty collection.

→12   Checks the number of elements or cursor variables. SQL%ROWCOUNT works on bulk operations, too.

Adding a limit to BULK COLLECT

In addition to being able to fetch one row at a time or fetch the whole set of rows at once, with explicit cursors you can select a value somewhere in between. For example, you might need to print the list of employees in rows of two names. Using BULK COLLECT with a limit allows you to do this, as shown in Listing 11-24.

Listing 11-24:   Using BULK COLLECT with a Limit

```
declare
    type text_nt is table of VARCHAR2(256);
    v_ename_nt text_nt;
    cursor c_emp is
      select eName
      from emp
      where deptNo=20;
    procedure p_print_row is
    begin
        if v_eName_nt.count=2 then
           DBMS_OUTPUT.put_line
           (v_eName_nt(1)||' '||v_eName_nt(2));
        elsif v_eName_nt.count=1 then
           DBMS_OUTPUT.put_line(v_eName_nt(1));
        end if;
    end;
begin
    open c_emp;
    loop                                              →19
        fetch c_emp bulk collect into v_eName_nt limit 2;
        p_print_row;
        exit when c_emp%NOTFOUND;                     →22
    end loop;
    close c_emp;
end;
```

Here's what's going on in the code:

→**20** In this case, you're fetching two rows at a time into the collection by passing the clause LIMIT *NumberOfRows* to the FETCH statement.

→**22** The exit condition here is a bit tricky. If you're using BULK COLLECT with the limit, the flag %NOTFOUND becomes true if the number of fetched records is less than the specified limit. This means that in the last fetched set, you could have 0 or 1 record. This is the reason why you need to check the number of elements in the collection.

 The BULK COLLECT command works in one direction, from the database to memory, but what happens when you have a list of selected departments and you need to raise the salary of people working in these departments? You could use a FOR loop through the list and fire one update at a time, but a better option is available, as shown here:

```
declare
    type number_nt is table of NUMBER;
    v_deptNo_nt number_nt:=number_nt(10,20);
begin
    forall i in v_deptNo_nt.first()..v_deptNo_nt.last()
        update emp
            set sal=sal+10
        where deptNo=v_deptNo_nt(i);
end;
```

The FORALL command builds a set of SQL statements and executes all of them at once. The explanations of the restrictions and side effects related to using the FORALL command are beyond the scope of this book, but you should be aware of this option.

Part V
Taking PL/SQL to the Next Level

The 5th Wave   By Rich Tennant

"Yo—I think we've got a new kind of architecture problem."

In this part . . .

After you've mastered some of the more basic concepts and constructs of PL/SQL, this part includes a few more advanced topics to enhance your coding knowledge.

Chapter 12 discusses the important interactions with the database (commits, rollbacks, locks, and so on) and how to handle problems that may occur.

Chapter 13 shows you how to use SQL and PL/SQL dynamically to create very flexible applications where users can select the operations to be executed at runtime.

Chapter 14 explains many coding best practices and describes what to do to be a good PL/SQL programmer.

Chapter 12

Transaction Control

A *transaction* is a logical unit of work that comprises a series of SQL data manipulation statements. The COMMIT command permanently saves the changes that all the SQL DML commands (data manipulation — INSERT/ UPDATE/DELETE) made during the current transaction to the database. Conversely, a ROLLBACK command ends the transaction and undoes any changes made.

This ability to commit a set of database events is one of the cornerstones of a professional relational database. Many smaller, PC-based relational database products don't support this concept of a commit and are therefore unsuitable for real-world applications. Problems occur when something unexpected happens. The unexpected event could be the power going out, the network being interrupted, or even the application raising an unanticipated exception. When this unexpected event occurs, execution stops, and it is possible that only some of your database changes have been saved. How do you know what went into the database and what didn't? How do you get back to a stable point and continue processing? Without a COMMIT statement to make the changes made by a set of commands permanent, it is almost impossible to recover from unexpected events.

In addition to normal transaction processes, Oracle has a specialized type of transaction called an *autonomous transaction*. Autonomous transactions enable you to temporarily halt a transaction in progress, perform some SQL operations, either commit or roll back these transactions, and then return to the main transaction.

This chapter discusses how transactions are controlled in Oracle as well as how to leverage the power of autonomous transactions.

Using Transactions to Maintain Data Consistency

Transactions are logical units of work containing one or more SQL statements. The main purpose of transactions is to assist in keeping the environment logically consistent. For example, imagine that you want to do an electronic funds transfer (EFT) to swap the amounts in two bank accounts.

Performing this sample EFT involves three SQL DML statements: one to debit your account, one to credit the receiving account, and one to record the transaction for your monthly statement. What happens if the power goes out after the system has processed the debit to your account, but before the money is credited to the other account? Clearly, one of these actions cannot happen without the other, and without the bank ending up with very unhappy (or very happy) customers. The code to execute this transfer is shown in Listing 12-1.

Listing 12-1:   Performing an Electronic Funds Transfer

```
begin
   update account                                        →2
   set balance = balance - 100
   where acctno = 7902; -- Ford                          →4

   update account                                        →6
   set balance= balance + 100
   where acctno= 7499; -- Allen                          →8

   insert into txn_log                                   →10
        (acctno, txn_type, amt)
   values (7902, 'DEBIT', 100);                          →12
end;
```

Additional details for Listing 12-1 are shown here:

→**2–4**   These lines subtract the transaction amount from Ford's account.

→**6–8**   These lines add the transaction amount to Allen's account.

→**10–12** These lines log the transaction.

By introducing the concept of a transaction, Oracle tries to enforce that only one of two things can happen when changes are being made: either they're all permanently saved to the database and visible to other users (committed), or they're rolled back and the data is unchanged. Transactions always start with the first executable SQL statement and end when the application commits or rolls back the changes.

The time that the user spends in front of a Web application or ATM to do the fund transfer isn't part of the database transaction. The transaction starts after the payment has been specified and the user presses Submit to say, "Okay, do it."

When your code includes an UPDATE statement (as in Listing 12-1), Oracle starts a new transaction and tries to identify what records are being changed. Then it tries to lock the record so that no one else can do anything with it until you've finished your modification. If somebody else is working with the same record, Oracle either raises an exception or waits for a period of time until the resource is free (depending on your database settings).

For example, if you're trying to manipulate the record EMPNO=7902 (Ford), Oracle does three things at once:

- ✔ Copies the original version of the data you're trying modify in the buffers allocated for your session
- ✔ Makes changes in your copy of the data
- ✔ Creates a backup of changes in the REDO log buffers (In case Oracle needs to replicate changes in the database itself)

When you started the transaction, your changes hadn't yet been committed. Therefore, for anyone else looking at the system, Jones's account still has the $100 in it. This happens because everybody else is reading from the database, but you're reading from your buffer first (the place where changes from the previous step are located) and only after that do you read from the database. The same process will occur for the second update. At that point, there are two ways to proceed: You can save your changes (COMMIT) or discard them (ROLLBACK).

Committing or Rolling Back Changes to the Database

During a transaction, such as the one we describe in the preceding section, choosing to COMMIT or ROLLBACK obviously affects your transaction.

If you decide to commit changes, the following things happen:

- ✔ Changes are saved in the database and become visible to everyone.
- ✔ All locks held during the transaction are released.
- ✔ The transaction is marked as complete.

Rolling back means undoing any changes to data that have been made by SQL statements within an uncommitted transaction. Both commits and rollbacks come in two varieties: explicit and implicit. When you commit or rollback explicitly, you're in the driver's seat, telling Oracle what to do.

Implicit commits or rollbacks occur behind the scenes. A power failure or exception may trigger them. Although you don't necessarily have control over when these happen, it's nevertheless important to understand how they're connected to transaction control and keeping data consistent.

Firing explicit and implicit commits

Explicit commits are fired by using the COMMIT command, as shown in Listing 12-2.

Listing 12-2:   An Explicit Commit

```
begin
    update ...;                                         →2
    update ...;                                         →3
    insert ...                                          →4
    commit;                                             →5
end;
```

Here's what's going on in Listing 12-2:

→2–3   Changes made by both updates (lines 2 and 3) and the insert (line 5) will be posted to the database when the commit is executed.

→5   This line executes the commit.

Implicit commits fire automatically when you use any DDL commands that create, alter, or delete any database objects. It doesn't matter if the DDL command fails. For example, if you try to create a unique index that contains non-unique data, the command will fail but all prior activity is still committed. An implicit commit is also executed when you send a request to terminate a session in any one of a number of ways, such as using the EXIT command in SQL*Plus or closing your connection.

Rolling back changes

Explicit rollbacks occur when you use the command ROLLBACK. The rollback may be full or partial.

Assume that you wanted to discard all changes anywhere in your code where an error was logged in the T_LOGERROR table. A *full rollback* of the whole transaction, shown in Listing 12-3, discards all changes, releases all locks, and marks the transaction "closed."

Listing 12-3:   A Full, Explicit Rollback

```
declare
    v_errors_yn VARCHAR2(1) := 'N';
begin
    update emp
      set sal = sal * 1.1                                    →5
    where deptNo = 10;
    update emp
      set sal = sal * .9
    where deptNo = 20;                                       →9

  -- lots more code where bad things might happen

      select decode (count(*),
                  0,'N','Y')
    into v_errors_yn
    from t_logError;
    If v_errors_yn = 'Y' then                                →17
      rollback;
    end if;
end;
```

→17   If the T_LOGERROR table contains any records, changes made by both UPDATE statements (lines 5 and 9) will be discarded.

In a *partial rollback,* Oracle allows you to insert a marker in the transaction. This marker is called the *savepoint.* In this case, you may roll back the most recent changes in the transaction, as shown in Listing 12-4.

Listing 12-4:   Adding a Partial Rollback

```
declare
    v_errors_yn VARCHAR2(1) := 'N';
begin
    update emp
      set sal = sal * 1.1                                    →5
    where deptNo = 10;
    savepoint SaveDept10Update;
    update emp
      set sal = sal * .9
    where deptNo = 20;                                       →10

  -- lots more code where bad things might happen

      select decode (count(*),
```

(continued)

Listing 12-4 *(continued)*

```
                    0,'N','Y')
      into v_errors_yn
      from t_logError;
      if v_errors_yn = 'Y' then                        →18
        Rollback to SaveDept10Update;                  →19
      end if;
 end;
```

→18   If the condition is true, Oracle will discard changes and release all
      locks made by the second update (line 10). However, changes
      from the first update (line 5) will still be part of the current trans-
      action. They can be saved or discarded independently of the cur-
      rent rollback.

Names of savepoints follow the same naming rules and restrictions as variable names, as we describe in Chapter 3.

You may create multiple savepoints in the same transaction, but keep in mind
that you will lose any transactions made after the specified one, as shown in
Listing 12-5.

Listing 12-5:   Adding Savepoints

```
begin
   update ...;                                        →2
   Savepoint A;                                       →3
   update ...;                                        →4
   Savepoint B;                                       →5
   update ...;                                        →6
   if condition then                                  →7
     rollback to savepoint A;                         →8
   end if;
commit;
end;
```

If the condition in line 1 is true, the update in line 4 and line 6 will be discarded. The savepoint at line 5 is irrelevant in this routine. Only the update at
line 2 will be committed when the COMMIT statement is reached.

If you do use multiple savepoints in one transaction, give all savepoints
unique, descriptive names. Although Oracle allows you to reuse a savepoint
name, we recommend avoiding this. Reusing a savepoint name will make it
difficult to determine which savepoint was actually the most recent one
encountered.

Rolling back to a savepoint only discards changes to the database; it does not
undo any changes you made to local PL/SQL variables.

Knowing when to use implicit rollbacks

Oracle uses implicit rollbacks in special cases to maintain data consistency.

A *statement-level rollback* is fired if a SQL statement causes an error at any time during execution. This type of rollback causes the code to execute as if that statement had never been run. This means that all locks acquired for the failed statement are released.

Listing 12-6 attempts to place 11 characters into the column eName defined as VARCHAR2(10).

Listing 12-6:   Code Requiring a Rollback

```
begin
    update emp
       set eName=rpad (eName,10,'*')                              →3
    where empNo=7369;
    update emp
       set eName=rpad (eName,11,'*')                              →6
    where empNo=7499;
end;
```

→6   The second update will fail because eName is only ten characters long, but the critical thing to recognize is that there will be no locks in the record of employee 7499. Anyone else can edit employee 7499 and commit the changes while the routine is running. Employee 7369 is locked while the routine is running. No one will be able to modify that record until the routine terminates or releases its lock.

A transaction-level rollback is fired when a session is terminated abnormally. This can happen for many reasons:

✔ You mistakenly turn off your computer. For Web applications, this usually doesn't terminate the session until the application server times out your process.

✔ A DBA terminates your session.

✔ Your session terminates because of an unhandled exception (see Chapter 5 for a full discussion of exceptions).

✔ The Oracle database goes down.

✔ Your connection to the database is lost.

When any of these events occur, all uncommitted changes are lost.

A transaction-level rollback of all outstanding transactions is fired in the case of a database crash. In that case, powering down the server will cause any uncommitted data for all users connected at that moment to be discarded.

Resolving deadlocks

There is one more situation where a rollback might be necessary. A *deadlock* can occur when two or more users are waiting for a resource locked by each other. For example, suppose user 1 locks customer A and then tries to lock customer B and at the same time, and user 2 locks customer B and then tries to lock customer A. Then user 1 waits for user 2 to unlock customer B and user 2 waits for user 1 to unlock customer A. This is a deadlock. Oracle resolves it by raising a deadlock exception (`ORA-00060: deadlock detected while waiting for resource`) in user 1's session. This terminates the procedure and allows user 2's procedure to successfully complete.

Deadlocks are rare, and the Oracle DBMS is pretty good at detecting deadlocks. When a deadlock is encountered, instead of waiting forever for the situation to resolve itself, Oracle will terminate one of the sessions (causing a rollback) to resolve the deadlock.

It isn't very likely that you'll ever encounter this problem. But deadlocks do happen from time to time. If you use autonomous transactions a lot (as we describe in the next section), you'll have a higher chance of running into a deadlock situation.

Autonomous Transactions

Oracle has the ability to suspend the execution of a transaction and transfer execution control to an independent child transaction. This child transaction is called an *autonomous transaction*. An autonomous transaction is completely independent of the calling transaction, which means that it doesn't share resources, locks, or any commit dependencies with the main transaction.

Autonomous transactions can include just as much functionality as any other database transactions. They're very useful for creating software components that can be reused in numerous applications.

One advantage of using an autonomous transaction is that DML can be executed and committed, even if the main transaction is rolled back. For example, a row can be inserted in a transaction log, recording which data was accessed, even if the user doesn't update any of the data. This is a very useful feature for auditing and security.

Setting up the syntax for an autonomous transaction

Before we show you an example of autonomous transaction in context, it's helpful to know the syntax, which is outlined in Listing 12-7.

Listing 12-7:   Autonomous Transaction Syntax

```
declare
    pragma autonomous_transaction;                              →2
begin                                                          →3
    . . .
    number of statements
    . . .
  commit;(or rollback;) - End of transaction 1                 →7
    . . .
    number of statements
    . . .
  commit;(or rollback;) - End of transaction 2
end;
```

Here are more details about Listing 12-7:

→2   Begins an autonomous transaction. This command indicates that the autonomous transaction starts from the BEGIN statement of the block (line 3) in which the pragma statement is found. From this point until the end of the transaction, all PL/SQL blocks (functions, procedures, anonymous blocks, and triggers) belong to that new transaction.

The END statement doesn't close the autonomous transaction automatically. The transaction must be closed explicitly by issuing a COMMIT, ROLLBACK, or any command including an implicit commit. If one of these commands isn't executed and the block defined as an autonomous transaction ends, the Oracle RDBMS will roll back the entire transaction and raise an error with the following message: ORA-06519: active autonomous transaction detected and rolled back.

→7   If the transaction ended but the block defined as autonomous didn't finish, the new transaction also will be autonomous.

A *pragma autonomous transaction* (a PL/SQL compiler directive to define an autonomous transaction) can be used in the declaration part of the following:

✔ Top-level anonymous blocks

✔ Local, standalone, or packaged functions and procedures

✔ Database triggers

✔ Methods of object types

Handling auditing and security with autonomous transactions

Using the auditing and security example, when dealing with highly secure data such as the SAL (salary) column in the EMP table of an Employee database, you want to be aware of any modifications made to that column. There are several ways to try to do this. One obvious thing you can try that won't work is to create a trigger and a special procedure that would log the information into a special table, as shown in Listing 12-8.

Listing 12-8: Non-Working p_log_audit

```
create sequence audit_seq
/
Create table audit_emp (action_nr NUMBER,
      action_cd VARCHAR2(2000), descr_tx VARCHAR2(2000),
      user_cd VARCHAR2(10), date_dt DATE)
/
Create or replace procedure p_log_audit
          (what_tx VARCHAR2,              descr_tx VARCHAR2,
          who_tx VARCHAR2, when_dt DATE) is
begin
    insert into audit_emp
    values(audit_seq.nextval, what_tx, descr_tx,
          who_tx, when_dt);
    commit;                                                    →15
end;
/
create or replace trigger bu_emp
 before update of sal on emp
referencing new as new old as old for each row
begin
    p_log_audit ('update',
        'update of emp.salary', user, SYSDATE);
end;
/
```

→15 The COMMIT command in the procedure p_log_audit should post the inserted data to the permanent storage even if the update to the employee table fails.

If you try to increase the salary of employee 7900, you get an error, as shown in Listing 12-9.

Listing 12-9:   Error from COMMIT in a Trigger

```
SQL> update emp set sal=10000 where empNo=7900;
update emp set sal=10000 where empNo=7900
        *
ERROR at line 1:
ORA-04092: cannot COMMIT in a trigger
ORA-06512: at "SCOTT.P_LOG_AUDIT", line 9
ORA-06512: at "SCOTT.BU_EMP", line 2
ORA-04088: error during execution of trigger
           'SCOTT.BU_EMP'
```

From the error, you can see that you aren't allowed to perform a commit in the trigger. The current transaction wasn't completed, so it isn't possible to post changes and initialize the new transaction.

Because using this method can't solve the problem, you need to use another strategy to execute one set of commands independently from another. However, the commands should be in the same session and share the same session resources. This is a good place to use an autonomous transaction, as shown in Listing 12-10, which shows the corrected p_log_audit procedure that can be called in a trigger.

Listing 12-10:   p_log_audit as Autonomous Transaction

```
create or replace procedure p_log_audit
          (what_tx VARCHAR2,             descr_tx VARCHAR2,
          who_tx VARCHAR2, when_dt DATE)
is
    pragma autonomous_transaction;
begin
    insert into Audit_emp
    values(audit_seq.nextval, what_tx, descr_tx,
          who_tx, when_dt);
    commit;
end;
```

When you run this code, you get the following result:

```
SQL> update emp set sal=10000 where empno=7900;
1 row updated.
SQL> select action_nr, action_cd, user_cd, date_dt
  2  from audit_emp;
    ACTION_NR ACTION_CD USER_CD DATE_DT
--------------------------------------------------
            2 update    SCOTT   08-JUL-05
```

There are no errors, and the change was logged. But what happens if you roll back the update?

```
SQL> rollback;
Rollback complete.
SQL> select sal from emp where empno=7900;
      SAL
----------
      950
SQL> select action_nr, action_cd, user_cd, date_dt
  2  from audit_emp;
    ACTION_NR ACTION_CD USER_CD DATE_DT
-----------------------------------------------
            2 update      SCOTT    08-JUL-05
```

In this situation, the update of the salary was rolled back (it is still 950, not 10000), but the log wasn't changed, which means that you have a mechanism to track any transaction activity, regardless of the main activities.

To achieve the output shown above, the code works in five steps:

1. The UPDATE statement fires the trigger BU_EMP.

2. The trigger calls the function p_log_audit (still in the same transaction).

3. The declaration block of the procedure still belongs to the main transaction; however, the database found the line pragma autonomous_ transaction. This means that from the next BEGIN statement, it should start a new transaction in the current session.

4. Inside the autonomous transaction, a new record was inserted into the table AUDIT_EMP, and the change was committed. The commit only makes changes in this transaction permanent. It is completely independent from the parent transaction, and any data updated in the parent transaction still isn't committed.

5. When the autonomous transaction ends, because the insert has been committed, the database can properly return to the main transaction and the trigger from which the procedure was called.

Autonomous transaction features

To be able to properly describe an autonomous transaction, we compare it with nested transactions. *Nested transactions* occur when any function, procedure, method, or anonymous block is called within another block or trigger and the called procedure is not autonomous.

One of the really interesting things about nested transactions is that there is nothing interesting about them. If there is an INSERT, UPDATE, or DELETE command in a procedure, and then a second INSERT, UPDATE, or DELETE command in a function is called by that procedure, and then a third INSERT, UPDATE, or DELETE command in an anonymous PL/SQL block is in the called function, Oracle treats these transactions as though those three commands were right next to each other in your code. It is all one database transaction (even divided into a number of nested ones). What is going on behind the scenes is very complex, but you need not even be aware that this concept of a nested transaction exists. Everything is transparent to the developer. However, when you make a called function or procedure autonomous, it is a very different thing.

What are the differences between autonomous and nested transactions? One of the main differences is how autonomous and nested transactions treat scope. The concept of *scope* is defined as the ability to see values of various things within the database. These "things" could be variables, data changes, locks, settings, exceptions, and so on. It is important to understand how different Oracle constructs behave on different levels (session/transaction) and in different contexts (autonomous/nested transactions).

Data changes

The most critical aspect of any system functionality is what happens to your data. That question is bidirectional: What happens to changes in the main transaction? What happens to changes in the autonomous one?

As an example, Listing 12-11 is a small routine that will print out a number of records in the table AUDIT_EMP.

Listing 12-11:   Autonomous Transaction

```
create or replace procedure p_data_change_test is
    v_nr NUMBER;
    pragma autonomous_transaction;
begin
    select count(1) into v_nr from audit_emp;              →5
    DBMS_OUTPUT.put_line ('Count='||v_nr);                 →6
end;
/
delete from audit_emp                                      →8
/
commit                                                     →10
/
```

Here are the details about Listing 12-11:

→5–6   These lines fetch the records.

→8   To simplify the example, all records have been removed from the audit-emp table and the change committed (line 10).

The following routine inserts a record into AUDIT_EMP (line 2). After that, the p_data_change_test procedure will be called (line 3).

```
SQL> begin
  2      insert into audit_emp (action_nr) values (100);
  3      p_data_change_test;
  4  end;
  5  /
Count=0
PL/SQL procedure successfully completed.
SQL>
```

But there's a surprise. Inside the autonomous transaction, Oracle doesn't see a new record inserted from the parent transaction. Because of the data consistency, Oracle spawns an autonomous transaction as of the last stable moment. That moment is exactly the beginning point of the parent transaction. This is the reason why no uncommitted changes from the parent transaction are visible to the autonomous one.

What happens with data changes that are inside autonomous transactions? To answer this question, some additional definitions are needed:

✔ **Isolation level:** The degree to which the intermediate state of the data being modified by a transaction is visible to other concurrent transactions (usually from a different session); and, the data being modified by other transactions is visible to the current transaction.

✔ **Isolation level = Read committed:** A transaction rereads data that it has previously read and finds that another committed transaction has modified or deleted the data. This means that if somebody else changes the data after you connected to the database (starting the transaction), you'll see these changes.

✔ **Isolation level = Serializable:** The transaction can't see any changes in other transactions that have been processed after it started. In that case, until you start a new session/transaction, you'll see exactly what data existed in the database at the moment you connected.

Listing 12-12 includes another routine that still the clears table before each test.

Listing 12-12: Autonomous Transaction with Data Changes

```
create or replace procedure p_commit_test is
    pragma autonomous_transaction;
begin
    insert into audit_emp(action_nr) values(100);       →4
    commit;                                             →5
end;                                                    →6
/                                                       →7
```

```
delete from audit_emp
/
commit
/
```

Listing 12-12 works like so:

→**4**   The first test will be with the default Oracle setting (READ_
        COMMITTED). That routine calls p_commit_test (line 5).

→**5**   Inserts one record in the table AUDIT_EMP and checks the total
        number of records in the same table after the execution (lines 6–7).

The result of running Listing 12-12 is as follows:

```
SQL> declare
  2       V_nr NUMBER;
  3  begin
  4       set transaction isolation level read committed;
  5       p_commit_test;
  6       select count(*) into v_nr from audit_emp;
  7       DBMS_OUTPUT.put_line ('Count='||v_nr);
  8  end;
  9  /
Count=1
PL/SQL procedure successfully completed.
```

There are no surprises here. Oracle successfully detected the new record.
Now you can clean the table one more time and try another option, namely
the SERIALIZABLE (line 10) in the following code:

```
SQL> delete from audit_emp;
1 row deleted.
SQL> commit;
Commit complete.
SQL> Declare
  2       v_nr NUMBER;
  3  Begin
  4       set transaction isolation level serializable; →10
  5       p_commit_test;
  6       select count(*) into v_nr from audit_emp;
  7       DBMS_OUTPUT.put_line ('Count='||v_nr);
  8  End;
  9  /
Count=0
PL/SQL procedure successfully completed.
```

The result is indeed a surprise. For the Oracle, there is no difference between
an autonomous transaction and transactions from another session in the context of data visibility.

Locks

Autonomous transactions can be tricky. From the experience of working with isolation levels, it is clear that data changes can be troublesome. But what about locking (not updating) the record in the table? Some front-end tools might place a lock on the record that you just modified and keep that lock for some time. This can sometimes cause problems. For example, you might have a simple routine that gives a specified employee a 10 percent salary raise, which is defined as an autonomous transaction, as shown in Listing 12-13.

Listing 12-13:   A Locking Example

```
create or replace procedure p_raise (i_empNo number)
is
    pragma autonomous_transaction;
begin
    update emp
       set sal=sal*1.1
    where empNo=i_empNo;
    commit;
end;
```

Now you will try to lock the needed record for update (to be sure that nobody else touches it) and modify salary by using the newly created procedure p_raise:

```
SQL> declare
  2        v_emp_rec emp%ROWTYPE;
  3  begin
  4        select *
  5        into v_emp_rec
  6        from emp
  7        where empNo = 7900
  8        for update;                                    →8
  9        p_raise (7900);                                →9
 10  end;
 11  /
declare
*
ERROR at line 1:
ORA-00060: deadlock detected while waiting for resource
ORA-06512: at "SCOTT.P_RAISE", line 5
ORA-06512: at line 10
```

Here's what happens in the preceding code:

→8   Lock the whole record for update.

→9   Calls procedure p_raise.

The last action creates a deadlock within the same session. Because the record was locked for update in the parent transaction (started with anonymous block), the autonomous transaction (started in the procedure p_raise) was waiting for its turn. It needed to have its own row-level lock to perform an update. But the parent transaction couldn't release a lock because it was waiting for the autonomous one to finish. As a result, the deadlock is obvious.

When using any autonomous transaction routines, you need to understand locking because locks are transaction-level resources and not shared across transactions.

Exceptions

If changes in the autonomous transaction aren't committed or rolled back when the transaction ends, Oracle will raise an error and roll back the whole transaction. It is just a matter of habit to close all autonomous transactions appropriately. But it is possible that something in the autonomous transaction went wrong. What happens to uncommitted changes?

To answer that question, the procedure p_rollback_test, which contains two UPDATE statements, is shown in Listing 12-14.

Listing 12-14:   Handling Uncommitted Changes Using rollback_test

```
create or replace procedure p_rollback_test is
        pragma autonomous_transaction;
begin
    update emp
      set eName=rpad (ename,10,'*')                      →5
    where empNo=7369;
    update emp
      set eName=rpad (ename,11,'*')                      →8
    where empNo=7499
    commit;
end;
```

Here's what Listing 12-14 is doing:

→5   This statement is okay.

→8   Tries to place an 11-character string into the field ENAME defined as VARCHAR2(10).

In the parent transaction, an exception handler catches the raised exception and length of the column ENAME that should be modified by the first update. (Recall the example in Listing 12-6 with statement-level rollbacks.) The result of running the code in Listing 12-14 is as follows:

```
SQL> delete from audit_emp;
1 rows deleted.
SQL> commit;
Commit complete.
SQL> declare
  2       v_tx VARCHAR2(256);
  3  begin
  4       p_rollback_test;
  5  exception
  6  when others
  7  then
  8       select eName into v_tx from emp
  9       where empNo = 7369;
 10       DBMS_OUTPUT.put_line('Error:'||sqlerrm);
 11       DBMS_OUTPUT.put_line('eName='||v_tx);
 12  end;
 13  /
Error:ORA-01401: inserted value too large for column
Ename=SMITH
PL/SQL procedure successfully completed.
```

This produced another unexpected result; namely, eName remained the same. In most cases, it should become SMITH, but exceptions raised in an autonomous transaction caused a transaction-level rollback rather than a statement-level rollback. This means that all uncommitted changes in the autonomous transaction will be lost if the exception propagates to the parent level.

Applying autonomous transactions to other real-world situations

Autonomous transactions can be extremely powerful when used properly. The following are some real-world examples of when they can be used.

Activity audit

Listing 12-8, where you create a log of anyone modifying the SAL column, could be rewritten more simply with just a trigger. Triggers by themselves can be defined as autonomous transactions, as shown here:

```
create or replace trigger emp_bu
 before update of sal on emp
referencing new as new old as old for each row
declare
    pragma autonomous_transaction;
begin
    insert into audit_emp  values(audit_seq.nextval,
        'update', 'update of emp.salary',user, SYSDATE);
    commit;
end;
```

However, defining triggers as autonomous transactions might create dead-locks. If you want to add the business rule "If salary was decreased, commissions should be increased by half of the difference" to your code, the most straightforward solution would look like the following:

```
create or replace trigger emp_bu
 before update of sal on emp
referencing new as new old as old for each row
declare
    pragma autonomous_transaction;
begin
    insert into audit_emp
    values(audit_seq.nextval, 'update',
          'update of emp.salary', user, SYSDATE);
    if :new.sal < :old.sal then
        update emp
        set comm=(:new.sal-:old.sal)/2
        where empNo=:new.empNo;
    end if;
    commit;
end;
```

The problem is that the solution is wrong and produces this output:

```
SQL> update emp
  2   set sal = 400
  3   where empNo = 7369;
update emp
       *
ERROR at line 1:
ORA-00060: deadlock detected while waiting for resource
ORA-06512: at "SCOTT.BU_EMP", line 8
ORA-04088: error during execution of trigger
          'SCOTT.BU_EMP'
SQL>
```

The reason for the failure is very simple: Oracle already locked the record you're trying to update in the main transaction. When you spawned the autonomous one, you were trying to update exactly the same record. However, the main transaction waits for the trigger to complete before releasing the lock, thus resulting in a deadlock.

Query audit

Some situations require more than simple data modification. For example you may need to know who queries the SAL column from the table EMP. To retrieve this information, you can create a special function (f_log_nr), as shown in Listing 12-15.

Listing 12-15: **Query Audit Function**

```
create or replace function f_log_nr (v_value_nr NUMBER)
return number is
   pragma  autonomous_transaction;
begin
  insert into audit_emp (action_nr, user_cd, date_dt)
  values  (audit_seq.nextval, user, SYSDATE );          →6
  commit;                                                →7
  return v_value_nr;                                     →8
end;
/
```

Here's what goes on in Listing 12-15:

→**6–7**   Logs the activity into audit table.

→**8**   Returns exactly the same value it receives as a parameter.

You then need to create a special view (V_EMP) that looks exactly like the EMP table with one small difference. Instead of the column SAL, use the function f_log_nr with the SAL column passed into it. The code to create the view is shown here:

```
create or replace view v_emp as
select empNo, eName, deptNo, job, mgr, f_log_nr (sal) sal
from emp;
```

Because the function is defined as an autonomous transaction, you can use it in a SELECT statement, even though it has DML inside. Exception ORA-14551 will not be raised in that case, because the transactions are consistent. There are just two of them.

In SQL, you can use functions that do absolutely anything if they are defined as autonomous transactions. Just be very careful.

The function returns exactly the same value it received, so from the user's point of view, there is no change. But logs are generated each time the function is called, so a log is generated for each row retrieved from the database, which is exactly what you wanted.

Self-mutating transaction problems

To implement the business rule "An Employee's commissions cannot exceed the salary of his/her manager," check out the following direct solution:

```
create or replace trigger emp_bu
 before update of comm on emp
referencing new as new old as old for each row
declare
    v_sal_nr NUMBER;
```

```
begin
    select sal into v_sal_nr
    from emp
    where empNo=:new.mgr;
    if :new.comm > v_sal_nr then
        raise_application_error(-20999,
            'Commissions are too high!');
    end if;
end;
```

The problem is that you're trying to access the same table you're updating. In this case, Oracle has no way of ensuring that the data is consistent in the current transaction and just gives up, as shown here:

```
SQL> update emp
  2   set comm = 10000
  3   where empNo = 7369;
update emp
       *
ERROR at line 1:
ORA-04091: table SCOTT.EMP is mutating, trigger/function
           may not see it
ORA-06512: at "SCOTT.BU_EMP", line 4
ORA-04088: error during execution of trigger
           'SCOTT.BU_EMP'
SQL>
```

To allow Oracle to maintain consistency, use the code shown in Listing 12-16.

Listing 12-16:   Code Using an Autonomous Transaction

```
create or replace trigger emp_bu
 before update of comm on Emp
referencing new as new old as old for each row
declare
    pragma autonomous_transaction;                          →5
    v_sal_nr NUMBER;
begin
    select sal into v_sal_nr
    from emp where empNo=:new.mgr;
    if :new.comm > v_sal_nr then
        raise_application_error(-20999,
            'Commissions are too high!');
    end if;
end;
```

→5   Wraps the trigger in an autonomous transaction. No data modifications take place inside of the trigger so you aren't required to place COMMIT at the end.

Now you get the expected result:

```
SQL> update emp set comm = 10000 where empno = 7369;
update emp
       *
ERROR at line 1:
ORA-20999: Commissions are too high!
ORA-06512: at "SCOTT.BU_EMP", line 8
ORA-04088: error during execution of trigger
           'SCOTT.BU_EMP'
SQL>
```

When resolving self-mutation issues with autonomous transactions, don't use this approach if you want to query the same column you're updating. The business rule "The salary of the employee should not exceed the salary of his/her manager" must be implemented procedurally rather than in the trigger for the following reasons. Assume you're updating a set of records at one time by using this code:

```
update emp set sal=sal*1.1 where deptNo=10
```

Because you're updating salaries for the whole department, the salary of both the lower-level employee and his or her manager will be changed. But the autonomous transaction won't know about these changes, because it starts with the dataset that existed at the beginning of the main transaction (that is, before the update was fired). This means that you can compare the salary of the employee only with the original salary of the manager because the new one hasn't yet been posted. There is no simple solution for this problem.

Chapter 13

Dynamic SQL and PL/SQL

• •

• •

*W*hen writing code in most situations, you know what database information must be accessed and how the information might be manipulated. Using the simple Employee and Department example, you know what tables and columns are being used and/or changed, what criteria are used to select rows, and the column datatypes. However, in some cases, the clauses, commands, variable datatypes, number of variables, and database object references aren't known prior to compiling the code. In these cases, the code must be created at runtime and will change each time the program is executed. These code statements are *dynamic*.

Dynamic SQL and PL/SQL allow you to create very flexible applications, where users can select which operations, tables, columns, and so on are involved. This chapter shows how you can build queries, pieces of PL/SQL code, or even whole procedural routines on the fly.

Taking Advantage of Dynamic SQL

Having many (perhaps hundreds) of repetitive elements in your logic often causes problems. For example, you might have a huge table with 100 columns and a set of reports, each of which requires 2 or 3 columns, but not the whole set. Or each calendar quarter, you need to archive the data into a separate table. Or you need to build code to query archived information, but the table doesn't exist at the moment you're writing the code.

These situations would be extremely difficult to handle by using regular SQL or PL/SQL. For these cases, you can use the powerful feature *Native Dynamic SQL* (also called *dynamic SQL*). Native Dynamic SQL allows you to build SQL or PL/SQL statements dynamically by using text strings and some additional command syntax and by processing the statements at runtime.

The sections in this chapter discuss some of the ways in which Native Dynamic SQL can help you create more efficient code to handle specific problems, including the following:

- Querying SQL tables in many different ways and keeping the code efficient

- Building a generic data viewer so that you can enter parameters on the fly and see data in different ways, based on those parameters

- Creating DDL on the fly so you have a generic routine that works with any database object

A Simple EXECUTE IMMEDIATE

Eighty percent of all dynamic SQL is covered by some fairly simple commands that include EXECUTE IMMEDIATE. Here are a couple of examples:

```
begin
    execute immediate 'whatever_text_string_you_want';
end;
```

or

```
declare
   v_variable_tx VARCHAR2(32000);
begin
   v_variable_tx:='whatever_you_want';
      execute immediate v_variable_tx;
end;
```

From a syntax point of view, the following points are important:

- Only one command, EXECUTE IMMEDIATE, is used.

- The code to be executed can be passed as a variable or directly as a string in the command.

- The string cannot exceed 32K. The code can range from a single SQL command to a large block of PL/SQL. So, although 32K is generous, it might not be sufficient for all purposes. If you need to work with large strings, Oracle's DBMS_SQL package is available, but it is significantly less convenient than Native Dynamic SQL.

- All PL/SQL blocks passed as a string should have a semicolon at the end, as shown here:

```
execute immediate 'begin p_test; end;';
```

- All SQL statements passed as a string should not have a semicolon at the end, as shown here:

```
execute immediate 'select 1 from dual' into a;
```

A good illustration of the idea of Native Dynamic SQL is an enterprise with a few dozen departments. Each department has its own routine to build end-of-year summaries, as shown here:

```
create or replace procedure p_summary(i_deptNo NUMBER) is
begin
    if i_deptNo = 10
    then
        p_summary_10;
    elsif i_deptNo = 20
    then
        p_summary_20;
    ...
    and so on...
    ...
    end if;
end;
```

Each time a new department is opened or an existing department is closed, you would need to modify the routine. However, all these procedures have one common feature: The name looks like p_summary_*deptNo*. This is a perfect case for using dynamic SQL. The new routine needs only one line, as shown in Listing 13-1.

Listing 13-1:   A Dynamic SQL Example

```
create or replace procedure p_summary(i_deptNo NUMBER) is
begin
    execute immediate
        'begin p_summary_'||i_deptNo||'; end;';        →4
end;
```

> →4   The logic is simple. It creates the name of the procedure by concatenating the department number with the string 'p_summary_' and wrapping the procedure name in BEGIN...END to create an anonymous block. Using this approach, opening or closing a department doesn't matter. To review the code to be executed, you can use Listing 13-2.

Listing 13-2:   Reviewing Dynamic SQL

```
create or replace procedure p_summary(i_deptNo NUMBER)
is
    v_tx VARCHAR2(2000);
begin
    v_tx:= 'begin p_summary_'||i_deptNo||'; end;';     →5
    DBMS_OUTPUT.put_line(v_tx);                        →6
    execute immediate v_tx;
end;
```

→**5–6**   Places the string to be executed into the variable. Now you can
send it to the output before execution.

REMEMBER

The EXECUTE IMMEDIATE command must include a string. It can be a
VARCHAR2 variable, a literal quoted string, or any string expression. Using a
string variable gives you more flexibility. You can create the whole logical
flow at any level of complexity to build your code, print it out, save it, alter it,
and so on. But because you're building a string, it is just a string and not
source code, so there are no automatic syntax checks. Oracle checks the
syntax of your string only when you try to run it.

The following code does exactly the same thing as the code you would call
manually. It detects the appropriate procedure to execute and executes it.

```
SQL> set serveroutput on
SQL> exec p_summary(10);
begin p_summary_10; end;
PL/SQL procedure successfully completed.
```

Building SQL on the Fly

The preceding sections show how dynamic SQL works for PL/SQL, but what
about SQL? You can get the value of any column in the EMP table by knowing
the primary key and the name of the column, as shown in Listing 13-3.

Listing 13-3:   Using Dynamic SQL

```
create or replace function f_getEmp_tx
        (i_empNo NUMBER, i_column_tx VARCHAR2)
return VARCHAR2
is
    v_out_tx VARCHAR2(2000);
    v_sql_tx VARCHAR2(2000);                          →6
begin
    v_sql_tx :=                                       →8
        'select '||i_column_tx||                      →9
        ' from emp ' ||                               →10
        'where empNo='||i_empNo;                      →11

    execute immediate v_sql_tx                        →13
     into v_out_tx;                                   →14
    return v_out_tx;
exception
    when others then return null;
end;
```

The following are additional details about Listing 13-3:

→**8–11** Builds a SELECT statement. To make the SQL more readable, you can type it on separate lines, concatenated together, so the structure matches your standards for a SELECT statement.

→**13–14** You aren't just executing some code; you also need to access the data retrieved by the code. The logic here is comparable to that used when building a regular SELECT . . . INTO statement. At this point, you add INTO *variable_name* after the statement you want to execute (not inside the statement, after the SELECT command).

The restrictions are the same as for regular SELECT . . . INTO:

✔ The SELECT statement should return exactly one row (otherwise the exception TOO_MANY_ROWS or NO_DATA_FOUND will be raised).

✔ You must also ensure that the value to be returned is of the same type as the variable used in the INTO clause. In dynamic SQL, the Oracle database doesn't know anything about the code you're building before you try to run it.

Building dynamic SQL requires significantly more debugging efforts because you can't depend on the compiler to check for syntax errors.

Improve performance with bind variables

There is one problem with the way in which the dynamic query from Listing 13-3 was created. The execution of each statement is a multistep process: Oracle parses the statement, creates an execution plan, allocates memory, and so on.

But Oracle also tries to be smart and first checks to see whether a similar statement has recently been executed. If it has, the engine reuses the previously collected information about how the statement should be executed. Although this reuse might not represent a significant performance improvement in a single session or in a development environment with a limited number of users, in a production environment it can mean the difference between a working and a failing system. For example, Oracle keeps each of these statements in memory as independent entities:

```
select eName from emp where empNo=7896
select eName from emp where empNo=4564
...
select eName from emp where empNo=4546
```

Although these are the same statements with different parameters to be passed, you wouldn't code that way in production system SQL. The standard solution is to use variables — now Oracle would have to process the statement only once.

Native Dynamic SQL allows you to perform the same kind of code optimization by using *bind variables*. Bind variables have the following characteristics:

- ✔ They serve exactly the same purpose as regular variables, namely as placeholders for values that will be supplied only at runtime.

- ✔ They're part of the text string that forms the dynamic SQL.

- ✔ They start with a colon (:) and may contain any alphanumeric characters.

- ✔ Each bind variable should have a corresponding argument containing the real value at runtime. There is no way to automatically identify that all your bind variables have pairs when you're writing the code, so be careful.

In the sections that follow, we show you a few ways in which you can use bind variables to resolve this performance issue.

Comparing variables to bind variables

As we mention, variables are the typical solution to streamlining code, as shown in Listing 13-4.

Listing 13-4:   Using Variables in Static SQL

```
create or replace function f_getEname
        (i_empNo NUMBER)
return VARCHAR2
is
    v_out_tx VARCHAR2(2000);
begin
    select eName into v_out_tx
    from emp
    where empNo = i_empNo;                              →9
    return v_out_tx;
exception
    when others then return null;
end f_getEname;
```

→9   Uses a placeholder rather than the real value. Consequently, Oracle performs the whole preparation cycle only the first time this SQL statement is executed.

A more effective version of the previous dynamic procedure (Listing 13-4) is shown in Listing 13-5.

Listing 13-5:   Using Bind Variables in Dynamic SQL

```
create or replace function f_getEmp_tx
        (i_empNo NUMBER, i_column_tx VARCHAR2)
return VARCHAR2
is
    v_out_tx VARCHAR2(2000);
    v_sql_tx VARCHAR2(2000);
begin
    v_sql_tx :=
        'select '||i_column_tx||
        ' from emp ' ||
        'where empNo=:var01';                          →11
    execute immediate v_sql_tx
    into v_out_tx
    using i_empNo;                                     →13
    return v_out_tx;
exception
    when others then return null;
end;
```

Here are the details about certain important lines in Listing 13-5:

→11   Defines the bind variable ;var01. At runtime, it will be substituted
       with the value of i_empNo. That variable can be called the *bind
       argument*.

→13   Passes arguments with the USING clause.

Passing several bind variables

Bind variables can be considered as parameters. You're using them to pass
values into some special entities (for parameters, into stored procedures; for
bind variables, into dynamic SQL). You can have as many bind variables as
you want by using the following syntax:

```
execute immediate
  '...:var1,:var2,:var3...' (code with bind variables)
using
  v_A,v_B,'Y'...(comma-separated list of values/variables)
```

For example, if the task is to find the highest value of any column for any pair
of employees, you could use Listing 13-6.

Listing 13-6:   Using Multiple Bind Variables

```
create or replace function f_getMax
    (i_empNo1 NUMBER,i_empNo2 NUMBER,i_column_tx VARCHAR2)
return VARCHAR2
is
    v_out_tx VARCHAR2(2000);
```

(continued)

Listing 13-6 *(continued)*

```
    v_sql_tx VARCHAR2(2000);
begin
    v_sql_tx :=
        'select max('||i_column_tx||')'||          →9
        ' from emp ' ||
        'where empNo in (:var01, :var02)';          →11
    execute immediate v_sql_tx
    into v_out_tx
    using i_empNo1, i_empNo2;                        →14
    return v_out_tx;
exception
    when others then return null;
end f_getMax;
```

The following are details about Listing 13-6:

→11   Defines two bind variables in the script.

→14   Passes two bind variables into the dynamic script. Keep in mind
       that the order and number of real variables in the USING clause
       must exactly match the way in which the bind variables appear in
       the script.

You might wonder why concatenation is used (line 9) instead of passing the
column name as a parameter, too. Although `execute immediate 'select`
`max(:var0)...'` `using in_column_tx...` would look much cleaner, it
isn't valid syntax. Bind variables may not be used for columns in the SELECT
statement.

Bind variables can be used only to supply values to be passed to SQL code,
and not to define the structural elements of queries or PL/SQL blocks. Tables,
columns, functions, and operators are parts of the structure to be executed.
This is the reason why they must be completely prepared before parsing.
Otherwise, how could Oracle build an execution plan? Bind variables are
passed into the statement after parsing. This is the reason why everything
to do with structural elements must use string operators.

Understanding bind variable types

Bind variables are still just variables, which can be of type IN, OUT, or IN
OUT just like any other parameters.

By default, all parameters are of type IN, as shown in previous examples.
Listing 13-7 illustrates a typical situation for using bind variables.

Listing 13-7:   Using an OUT Parameter

```
SQL> declare
  2      a NUMBER;
  3      b NUMBER:=1;
```

```
  4      c NUMBER:=2;
  5      v_plsql_tx VARCHAR2(2000);
  6  begin
  7      v_plsql_tx =
  8      'begin ' ||
  9      '    :1:=:2+:3; ' ||                    →9
 10      'end;'';
 11      execute immediate v_plsql_tx           →11
 12      using out a, b, c;                     →12
 13      DBMS_OUTPUT.put_line('a='||a);
 14  end;
 15  /
a=3                                             →16
PL/SQL procedure successfully completed
```

Here are the details for Listing 13-7:

→9   Defines three bind variables :1, :2, :3.

→12   Passes three real variables a, b, and c. The first one is of type OUT, the second and third are the default type IN.

→11   Oracle adds the value of variable b to the value of variable c and returns it back into variable a as requested for the output.

Reusing bind variables

One interesting feature of bind variables from the previous example is that in PL/SQL you can reuse the same bind variable (in Listing 13-8; case :1, line 5) multiple times, but pass the real value only once (line 6).

Listing 13-8 passes and retrieves the same variable a.

Listing 13-8:   Reusing Bind Variables in Dynamic PL/SQL

```
SQL> declare
  2      a NUMBER:=2;
  3      b NUMBER:=3;
  4      v_plsql_tx VARCHAR2(2000);
  5  begin
  6      v_plsql_tx =
  7      'BEGIN ' ||
  8      '    :1 := :1*:2; ' ||
  9      'END;';
 10      execute immediate v_plsql_tx           →10
 11      using in out a, b;                     →11
 12      DBMS_OUTPUT.put_line('a='||a);
 13  end;
 14  /
a=6                                             →15
PL/SQL procedure successfully completed
```

Here's what Listing 13-8 is doing:

→**10–11** Oracle works exactly as requested by passing the default value of variable a (2) into the routine and multiplying it by the value of a (3).

→**15** Returns a=6. Two-way communication was allowed because the first bind argument was declared as IN OUT.

In dynamic PL/SQL blocks, Oracle counts only unique bind variables and associates them with arguments in the order of their appearance. In Listing 13-8, there are two unique variables (:1 and :2). That is why you need only two arguments (a and b).

The reusability of bind variables is not true for dynamic SQL statements, as shown in Listing 13-9.

Listing 13-9:   Reusing Bind Variables in Dynamic SQL

```
declare
    v_nr NUMBER:=100;
    v_where_tx VARCHAR2(2000):='deptNo=20';
    v_sql_tx VARCHAR2(2000);
begin
    v_sql_tx:=
        'update emp ' ||
        ' set sal=:1, comm=:1 ' ||                      →7
        'where '||v_where_tx;
    execute immediate v_sql_tx
            using v_nr, v_nr;                           →10
end;
```

Here's what's happening in Listing 13-9:

→**7** Although bind variable :1 is the same, Oracle associates bind variables by position, not by name.

→**10** You have to pass the same value twice.

Using a NULL bind variable

Although we indicated that you could use either variables or literals as bind parameters, there are some restrictions: You cannot explicitly pass any Oracle literals (NULL, TRUE, FALSE). Listing 13-10 shows how to pass a NULL value via the variable.

Listing 13-10:   Using a NULL Variable

```
declare
    v_null_nr NUMBER:=NULL;                             →2
    v_where_tx VARCHAR2(2000):='deptNo=20';
```

```
    v_sql_tx VARCHAR2(2000);
begin
    v_sql_tx:=
        'update emp ' ||
            ' set sal=:1, comm=:1 ' ||
            'where '||v_where_tx;
    execute immediate v_sql_tx
            using v_null_nr, v_null_nr;                    →11
end;
```

▌ →2, 11   The only way to pass NULL is by using the variable.

Getting a value with a RETURNING clause

Listing 13-11 shows that there are other ways besides using a SELECT statement to return a value.

Listing 13-11:   Using a RETURNING Clause (a)

```
create or replace function f_appendDept_tx
    (i_deptNo NUMBER, i_column_tx VARCHAR2,
     i_append_tx VARCHAR2)
    return VARCHAR2
is
    v_out_tx VARCHAR2(256);
    v_sql_tx VARCHAR2(2000);
begin
    v_sql_tx:='update dept set '||i_column_tx||'='||
            i_column_tx||'||:1 where deptNo=:2'||chr(10)||
            ' returning '||i_column_tx||' into :3';       →11
    DBMS_OUTPUT.put_line(v_sql_tx);
    execute immediate v_sql_tx
        using i_append_tx, i_deptNo, out v_out_tx;         →14
    return v_out_tx;
end f_appendDept_tx;
```

Here's what's going on with Listing 13-11:

▌ →11   Uses an UPDATE statement with a RETURNING clause to return a
            value.

▌ →14   Builds the statement by using the appropriate variable as an OUT
            parameter.

You can split the output line by using a special character CHR(10) (line 10 in
the preceding example). It is basically a "Carriage Return" command. The
Oracle parser ignores it, but it makes the generated code easier to read.

Listing 13-11 shows a function that could be used to append any string to any
column of the DEPT table and return a new value as a result of the update. This
trick is extremely useful because it allows you to get the new value without

extra querying. This means one less round trip to the database. An example of the function usage is shown in Listing 13-12.

Listing 13-12: Using a RETURNING Clause (b)

```
SQL>begin
  2    DBMS_OUTPUT.put_line
  3      (f_appendDept_tx(30,'dname','+'));              →3
  4 end;
  5 /
update dept set dname=dname||:1 where deptNo=:2
returning dname into :3
SALES+                                                  →8
PL/SQL procedure successfully completed.
```

> →3   Adds the symbol '+' to the end of the DNAME column of department 30 and sends new value to the output (line 8).

Return information using cursor variables

Dynamic SQL allows you to build whatever you want on the fly, but how is this code executed? For example, if you have a generic routine that deletes rows from any table, a logical question would be: Can I find out how many rows were deleted?

The answer is "Yes." Oracle opens an implicit cursor to execute the dynamic SQL you're building. By using "SQL" to refer to the implicit cursor, you can use any of the cursor variables discussed in Chapter 6, such as %ROWCOUNT. Listing 13-13 shows an example of how this works.

Listing 13-13: Dynamic SQL and Cursor Variables

```
create or replace function f_delete_nr (i_tab_tx VARCHAR2)
          return NUMBER
is
begin
    execute immediate 'delete from '||i_tab_tx;         →5
    return SQL%ROWCOUNT;                                →6
end;
```

> →5–6   Because the DELETE statement opens an implicit cursor, the results of the execution are retrieved.

You can prove this by using the following code:

```
SQL> begin
  2    DBMS_OUTPUT.put_line('Deleted:'||f_delete_nr('EMP'));
  3    end;
```

```
   4  /
Deleted: 14
PL/SQL procedure successfully completed.
```

Building DDL on the Fly

Listing 13-13 shows you how to use a generic routine to delete from any table. But what about a generic routine to drop any database object? As you already know, there is no way to place DDL statements (drop function, create table, and so on) into PL/SQL. But with dynamic SQL, this restriction is removed.

Dynamic SQL allows you to do whatever you want with database objects as long as the user has the appropriate privileges to execute the statement. For example, the following routine will drop any function from the schema:

```
create or replace procedure p_drop_function
          (i_function_tx VARCHAR2) is
begin
    execute immediate 'drop function '||i_function_tx;
end;
```

When building DDL on the fly, you can easily create deadlocks. For example, you could modify the preceding code to drop any procedure, as shown here:

```
create or replace procedure p_drop_procedure
          (in_proc_tx VARCHAR2) is
begin
    execute immediate 'drop procedure '||in_proc_tx;
end;
```

If you try to drop the procedure `p_drop_procedure` itself, the code creates a deadlock:

```
SQL> begin
  2      p_drop_procedure('p_drop_procedure');
  3  end;
  4  /
begin
*
ERROR at line 1:
ORA-04021: timeout occurred while waiting to lock object
          SCOTT.P_DROP_PROCEDURE
ORA-06512: at "SCOTT.P_DROP_PROCEDURE", line 4
ORA-06512: at line 2
```

There is another major caveat when using dynamic DDL. All DDL statements always fire implicit commits, as shown in Listing 13-14.

Listing 13-14:   Implicit COMMITS in DDL Statements (with Bug)

```
create or replace procedure p_removeDept
    (i_deptNo NUMBER) is
begin
    savepoint A;
    update emp                                              →5
    set deptNo=10 -- temporary department
    where deptNo=i_deptNo;

    p_drop_procedure ('p_summary_'||i_deptNo);              →9

    delete from dept                                        →11
    where deptNo=i_deptNo;
exception
    when others then
        rollback to savepoint A;                            →15
        raise;
end p_removeDept;
```

The following list gives you the details on Listing 13-14:

→5   Reassigns employees from the department to be deleted to the temporary one.

→9   Removes the summary procedure.

→11   Removes the department itself.

→15   If something goes wrong, a ROLLBACK is included in the exception handler to clean up any changes made in the current routine. This is the reason why you should use a partial (not full) rollback to the savepoint. Otherwise you could roll back changes made in other routines, too.

However, because the f_drop_procedure includes DDL, the rollback will be meaningless. After line 9, all changes to the EMP table are committed to the database (implicit COMMIT). If something does go wrong when deleting the department (for example, a lock from another application on the record you're trying to delete), these changes won't be canceled.

A better way to accomplish the same goal is shown in Listing 13-15.

Listing 13-15:   Implicit COMMITS in DDL Statements (Bug Fixed)

```
create or replace procedure p_removeDept
    (i_deptNo NUMBER) is
begin
    savepoint A;
    update emp
    set deptNo=10 -- temporary department
    where deptNo=i_deptNo;
```

```
    delete from dept
    where deptNo=i_deptNo;

    p_drop_procedure ('p_summary_'||i_deptNo);          →12
exception
    when others then
        rollback to savepoint A;
        raise;
end;
```

→12   Calls the procedure with DDL inside after all DML operations are complete. In this case, there will be no COMMIT until all the main activity is completed. This is a significantly safer way to code.

But there is an even better solution. Wrapping any code that dynamically generates DDL statements (or any other code that forces an implicit COMMIT) into autonomous transactions can prevent a number of problems, as shown here:

```
create or replace procedure p_drop_procedure
        (i_proc_tx VARCHAR2) is
    pragma autonomous_transaction;
begin
    execute immediate 'drop procedure '||i_proc_tx;
end;
```

Using this approach, you can place the call to that procedure anywhere in your code with no impact to the main routine at all.

In most cases, procedures and functions that generate DDL should be defined as autonomous transactions. This way you can be sure that they won't interfere with the logic of the core application. In addition, they can be used anywhere you want (triggers, SELECT statements, and so on).

Using Quoted Strings with Dynamic SQL

Using dynamic SQL can be a bit confusing when working with string literals. For example, in the generic routine to provide summaries for each department, each of the summary routines requires a parameter to be passed

```
procedure p_summary_10(i_upload_yn VARCHAR2) .
```

What if you wanted to hard-code "Yes" ('Y') for the i_upload_yn parameter? The code you're trying to execute might look like this:

```
begin p_summary_10('Y'); end;
```

The routine to generate this could be dynamically hard-coded, as shown here:

```
create or replace procedure p_summary (i_deptNo NUMBER)
begin
    execute immediate
      'begin p_summary_'||i_deptNo||'(''Y''); end;';
end;
```

The two single quotes around the Y are required: If you want to have a single quote in the string of the code, you must include two single quotes. The best way of dealing with this issue is to have an example of the code you're planning to build. This will significantly decrease the debugging time required.

Alternatively, you could use the following code to pass 'Y' with a bind variable:

```
create or replace procedure p_summary (i_deptNo NUMBER)
begin
    execute immediate
      'begin p_summary_'||i_deptNo||'(:1); end;'
        using 'Y';
end;
```

What happened? The quotes disappeared. Oracle understands that you're passing variable of type VARCHAR2 and builds the binding appropriately. But any time you're building the string manually, you should check the consistency of quotes carefully.

Working with Advanced Datatypes

The previous sections in this chapter discuss only the basic datatypes. But what about objects, records, and collections? Dynamic SQL works with them, too. For example, assume that you have an application, where you need to display any record from the database as a pair such as [ID; Display Value]. This could be very useful if you are building a generic data viewer.

Listing 13-16 shows how to create an object with the appropriate columns to be returned. The logic is fairly simple because you're passing all the parts you need into the routine.

Listing 13-16:   create type Illustrated

```
create type lov_oty is object
(id_nr NUMBER, display_tx VARCHAR2(256));

create or replace function f_getDisplay_oty
      (i_table_tx VARCHAR2,                              →5
       i_id_tx VARCHAR2, i_display_tx VARCHAR2,          →6
       i_pk_tx VARCHAR2, i_value_nr NUMBER)              →7
return lov_oty
```

```
is
    v_out_oty lov_oty;
    v_sql_tx VARCHAR2(2000);
begin
    v_sql_tx := 'select lov_oty('||                          →13
                i_id_tx||','||i_display_tx||
                ') from '||i_table_tx||
                ' where '||i_pk_tx||'=:1';

    execute immediate v_sql_tx into v_out_oty
        using i_value_nr ;

    return v_out_oty;
end f_getDisplay_oty;
```

Here's how Listing 13-16 works:

→5   `i_table_tx` allows you to identify a source of the data.

→6   `I_ID_TX` and `i_display_tx` define what columns/expressions
        should be used to display detected record.

→7   `I_PK_TX` and `i_value_nr` allow you to uniquely identify a record
        to be displayed.

→13   In the SELECT statement, two selected columns are wrapped into
        an object type. The returning value will be a single attribute of type
        Lov_ty rather than two columns from the table, as shown here:

```
SQL> select f_getDisplay_oty ('dept','deptNo',
  2           'deptNo||''-''||dname','deptNo',10)
dsp
  3   from dual
  4   /
DSP(ID_NR, DISPLAY_TX)
-----------------------------------------------------
LOV_OTY(10, '10-ACCOUNTING')
SQL>
```

This example builds a composite display value DEPTNO||'-'||DNAME and
passes 10 as a value for a primary key DEPTNO. As desired, the function
returned an object of type LOV_OTY.

Using BULK COLLECT with dynamic SQL

You can take this one step farther and work not just with objects, but object
collections. Assume, that you need to get the whole list of [ID; DisplayValue]
for the specified table. In that case, just an object isn't enough. You need the
whole object collection:

```
create type lov_nt as table of lov_oty;
```

Chapter 11 explains how you can fetch results of the whole SELECT statement into the collection by using BULK COLLECT. You can use that feature in dynamic SQL, too, as shown here:

```
create or replace function f_getLov_nt
        (i_table_tx VARCHAR2,
         i_id_tx VARCHAR2, i_display_tx VARCHAR2,
         i_order_tx VARCHAR2)
return lov_nt
is
    v_out_nt lov_nt := lov_nt();
begin
    execute immediate
    'select lov_oty('||i_id_tx||','||i_display_tx||')'||
          ' from '||i_table_tx||
          ' order by '||i_order_tx
    bulk collect into v_out_nt;

    return v_out_nt;
end;
```

The logic is exactly the same as in the previous example. You build the query on the fly, wrap the resulting columns as lov_oty type, and return the result. The only difference is that you're returning all the rows at once.

Dynamic OPEN...FOR

The preceding section shows you how to build SQL statements and PL/SQL blocks dynamically. But it is also very useful to be able to build cursors at runtime.

Imagine a set of requirements where you need to print a list of employees, but you don't know what the filter (WHERE clause) should be. The basic implementation logic is as follows:

1. The cursor spins through table EMP.

2. The DBMS_OUTPUT.put_line procedure prints all needed information.

But there's a major roadblock. How can you build a cursor if you don't know about the filter? (That is, what if you don't know which columns and conditions are needed in the WHERE clause in the SELECT statement?) Dynamic SQL allows you to answer this question in conjunction with an Oracle construct called REF CURSOR.

Chapter 6 discusses cursors that allow you to specify sets of data to be processed. You can use this approach to create pointers to whole datasets. But to define an Oracle cursor, you need to specify the query to use. REF

CURSOR constructs are just logical pointers that don't require you to specify any query at the moment of declaration.

Creating a REF CURSOR datatype

To use REF CURSOR variables, you need to use a REF CURSOR datatype. The REF CURSOR datatype cannot be used outside a PL/SQL environment.

There are two kinds of REF CURSOR types: weak and strong. A *weak* REF CURSOR can point to any data set, as shown here:

```
declare
  type weak_rcty is ref cursor;
  c_weak rcty weak_rcty;
```

For small projects with limited scope, creating your own user-defined type might be a viable strategy. However, in complex or multiple environment situations, it is a better idea to use built-in standard weak REF CURSOR datatype to avoid confusion between developers, as shown here:

```
declare
  c_weak sys_refcursor;
```

A *strong* REF CURSOR explicitly declares the type of data that can be referenced. In the following example, only queries that return rows exactly as in the EMP table are allowed:

```
declare
  type strong_rcty is ref cursor return emp%ROWTYPE;
  c_strong_rcty strong_rcty;
```

Defining your query with OPEN...FOR

Working with REF CURSOR variables is similar to working with explicit cursors. (Cursor variables are also applicable to REF CURSORs.) You can define your query directly in the special OPEN...FOR construct, instead of defining the query when declaring the cursor, as shown here:

```
declare
    type strong_rcty is ref cursor return
         table%ROWTYPE;
    c_strong_rcty strong_rcty;
    v_table_rec table%ROWTYPE;
begin
    open c_strong_rcty for select * from table;
    loop
        fetch c_strong_rcty into v_table_rec;
        exit when c_strong_rcty%NOTFOUND;
        ...
    end loop;
    close c_strong_rcty;
end;
```

A complete discussion of how to use strong REF CURSORs is beyond the scope of this book, but you can find information about them in Oracle's "PL/SQL User's Guide and Reference," available on OTN.

You can work with a cursor without declaring the full SELECT statement in the declaration part of the code. Taking this one step farther, you can open a cursor against a STRING representing the SELECT statement, as shown here (in this case you have to use weak REF CURSORs):

```
declare
    c_weak_ref SYS_REFCURSOR;
begin
    open c_weak_ref for 'any_select_statement_you_want';
        ...
end;
```

Or

```
declare
    v_string_tx VARCHAR2(32000);
    c_weak_ref sys_refcursor;
begin
    v_string_tx:= 'any_select_statement_you_want'
    open c_weak_ref for v_string_tx;
        ...
end;
```

Using this code structure provides part of the required code, as shown in Listing 13-17.

Listing 13-17:   Using a Weak REF CURSOR

```
create or replace procedure p_report
    (i_where_tx VARCHAR2)
is
    c_emp_ref sys_refcursor;                                    →4
begin
    DBMS_OUTPUT.put_line('------------------------');
    open c_emp_ref for                                          →7
     'select * from emp where'|| i_where_tx;                    →8
    loop
        fetch c_emp_ref into ???;
        exit when c_emp_ref%NOTFOUND;
        DBMS_OUTPUT.put_line(???);
    end loop;
    DBMS_OUTPUT.put_line('------------------------');
end;
```

See the following details about the code in Listing 13-17:

→4   Builds a cursor variable. As we mention earlier, it is better to use the Oracle predefined datatype SYS_REFCURSOR for weak REF CURSORs instead of defining one of your own.

→7–8   Opens the cursor variable for the whole SELECT statement to be built on the fly.

Telling Oracle what to data to return

There is one missing part of the code in Listing 13-17 . . . namely, where to fetch? That question is a bit trickier to answer than you might think. Because you're building the SELECT statement dynamically, Oracle has no way to check the kind, number, or type of columns you're planning to return. Because you're planning to return all columns, you have three alternatives:

✔ Explicitly declare variables for each column with the appropriate datatype. If the number of columns is more than a few, it could make future maintenance very difficult.

✔ Declare a variable of type RECORD with all variables in it. This solution is viable, but it still raises the issue of maintenance.

✔ Declare a variable of EMP%ROWTYPE. This is the best choice because you're getting datatypes directly from EMP and don't care about any possible changes.

An example of how to use EMP%ROWTYPE is shown in Listing 13-18.

Listing 13-18:   Using %ROWTYPE

```
create or replace procedure p_report
        (i_where_tx VARCHAR2)
is
    c_emp_ref sys_refcursor;
    v_emp_rec emp%ROWTYPE;                                  →5
begin
    DBMS_OUTPUT.put_line('----------------------');
    open c_emp_ref for
        'select * from emp where ' ||i_where_tx;
    loop
        fetch c_emp_ref into v_emp_rec;                    →11
        exit when c_emp_ref%notfound;
        DBMS_OUTPUT.put_line(v_emp_rec.empNo||' '          →13
        || v_emp_rec.eName||' - '|| v_emp_rec.job);
    end loop;
    DBMS_OUTPUT.put_line('----------------------');
end p_report;
```

Here are the details relevant to Listing 13-18:

→**5**   Creates a new variable `v_emp_rec`.

→**11**   Fetches the cursor variable into it.

→**13**   All information about the employee is available so you can print anything required.

Use the following code to verify the functionality:

```
SQL> begin
  2      p_report('deptNo=10');
  3  end;
  4  /
-----------------------
7782 CLARK - MANAGER
7839 KING - PRESIDENT
7934 MILLER - CLERK
-----------------------
PL/SQL procedure successfully completed.
```

The result is exactly what you wanted. It lists all the employees in department 10.

Chapter 14

PL/SQL Best Practices

Many people believe that being a good PL/SQL programmer means knowing all about the latest features, obscure syntax for commands in the packages, VARRAYs, object collections, and so on. Knowing all these things means that you're knowledgeable about the PL/SQL language, but it doesn't make you a good PL/SQL programmer.

Well-written code executes within a reasonable period of time, provides good performance, and is bug-free whenever possible. But even more important, the code is structured in such a way that you can be assured that it does what it is supposed to do, and when modifications are necessary, you can easily see where they are needed. To help you create code that meets these goals, this chapter discusses some important best practices to keep in mind when programming in PL/SQL. These best practices are taken from our experiences in building real systems.

Why Are Best Practices Important?

If you aren't an experienced programmer, the idea of general "best practices" might not make much sense. The following are some examples from actual systems where failure to follow these best practices caused companies to lose hundreds of millions of dollars. In each case, the mistakes were not made by students or people unfamiliar with PL/SQL, but by consultants from well-known consulting firms doing work for very large companies on highly visible projects. Each one resulted in catastrophic software failures for different reasons:

- ✔ The code ran so slowly that it made the system unusable. It would have taken 26.5 years for a month-end routine to run.

- ✔ The code was so difficult to modify that it took three and a half months to change the code in order to add a single attribute to one table.

- ✔ The system included so many complex rules that, even after years of development, it never worked.

These failures were all due to the way in which the software and its underlying code were designed and constructed — not because the programmer didn't know how to use a particular command.

Laying the Groundwork for Good Coding

Coding is 90 percent thinking and 10 percent actual writing of the code. In the sections that follow, we explain how to think through a program before you write it. It is unlikely that you will ever undertake a PL/SQL project all on your own, so you also have to be an effective member of the development team. So this section also discusses ways that PL/SQL programmers can be good system development team players.

Understanding the big picture

As a PL/SQL programmer, you might not have any control over the larger system architecture, but you do need to understand that architecture in order to create the appropriate code and integrate it into the rest of the system. By *system architecture,* we mean the overall design and structure of the system as a whole, including the following:

- ✔ The database design
- ✔ How and where the business rules will be enforced
- ✔ What programming languages are used
- ✔ How the programming algorithms will work

It is a very common mistake for programmers and developers to say something like "I don't need to understand the whole system; just tell me what you want the code to do." But being that shortsighted is one of the reasons that systems fail. To program well, you should:

- ✔ **Know what the business function is for your code.** You should also be able to accurately describe what your code does in terms that users can understand. The more clearly you can express what the code is intended to do, the more likely it is that the system will actually satisfy the user

requirements. For example, when asking for help in debugging an algorithm, the first question that a good programmer should ask is, "What is
the code supposed to do from a business perspective?" Until you understand the answer to that question, you won't be able to successfully
debug the code.

✔ **Keep a copy of the system data model showing the relevant portion of
the database handy at all times.** If there is no data model, you can draw
your own on a piece of paper. Having and understanding the data model
is important because you need to understand where the code you're
writing fits into the bigger system. By keeping a copy of the entire
system data model handy, you can continually check to make sure you
understand what your piece of code is supposed to do and what other
portions of the system might be impacted by it. If you don't understand
data modeling, see *Database Development For Dummies,* by Allen G.
Taylor (Wiley Publishing, Inc.).

Communicating effectively

As a developer, you probably spend no more than 30 percent of your time sitting alone, in front of a terminal, writing code. Most of the time, you are working with a second developer (or pair programming, as we discuss later in this
chapter), talking to someone about getting the system requirements, or figuring out how to write the code.

In all three project failures that we mention earlier in this chapter, one
common mistake made was that people who were aware that the system
failures were likely to occur either neglected to call this to the attention of
the system architects or were ignored when trying to point out problems
with the system architecture. As the rules of the system are captured and
coded, you might discover that the architecture is inadequate to support the
system requirements. PL/SQL programmers should recognize possible problems in the system architecture and point these out to the database designers and system architects so that the necessary changes can be made.

Creating a code specification

Before you ever start writing code, you need written specifications. Writing
good code specifications encourages developers to think about what the
code does and puts this information on paper. Having this document makes
talking to others about the code much easier and allows better sharing of
information. In modern development environments, it isn't uncommon to
have Java and .NET developers on the same team as PL/SQL developers.
However, all these developers might be unable to read each others' code.
A specification written in English or pseudo-code allows the document to
be readable by all members of the team.

A good code specification describes what the software or program modification entails at a reasonable level of detail. The specification document should describe the function of the code as well as outline key design decisions. For example, the document should address the following questions:

- Why is this code or modification being written (in business terms)?
- What procedures will be created?
- How will these procedures be named?
- What modifications to the database (new tables, columns, and so on) are required?
- What are the detailed design constraints, if any? (For example, "This is a rarely called routine from the user interface. As long as it executes in less than half a second, it is okay." or "This is a critical batch routine that must execute in under an hour.")

The specification should also include any special factors that people need to take into account when developing or testing. An example might be "This routine will be executed by many simultaneous users."

By including all this information in the code specification, you significantly increase the probability that the team will understand the requirements and write good code. However, keep in mind that the goal is to create functioning code, and not to create a large pile of documentation that few will read. Also, don't think that the code specification will be complete, accurate, or not undergo changes as the project moves forward. As more code is written and changes are needed, you might need to talk to users for additional clarification about some undiscovered requirement or subtle area of the program. Having the specification handy provides a starting point for discussion.

Writing Code with Best Practices in Mind

When you're trying to decide how to proceed with coding a new project or even making changes to an existing software project, how do you determine the appropriate code structure? This section describes some of the things you can do to write effective PL/SQL code that is maintainable over time, as well as avoid some of the pitfalls common to many PL/SQL projects.

Stub out your code

Don't just sit down and start writing code right from the beginning. First, figure out how you want your code to be structured and create the necessary procedure and function headers with no code in them. This gives you an idea of what information will be needed at each point in your routine and what each routine needs to return. These little stubs of code will help you see the overall routine. If the project is a large one, you can then easily pass parts of the code to someone else to write by using this "code outline." By following this stubbing method, your code will naturally be well structured and easier to debug if something goes wrong.

Check the architecture as you go

Be sure that the underlying system architecture is sound before spending days, weeks, or even months writing code. For example, one large batch routine we encountered was architected to make so many round trips to the database that, even if all the complex logic that the program needed to perform executed in zero time, the program would never execute within an acceptable time frame. It had to be almost entirely rewritten in order to perform adequately. In another situation, we designed a program to take precise code statements and translate them into business language statements. The first attempt to create the program was not able to logically manage the required elements. Although this early version worked in limited circumstances, the code had to be completely rewritten before it was usable in the larger system.

You can use the following tricks to ensure that the system architecture is sound:

- ✔ **Periodically take a step back and evaluate.** Does the approach being used make sense? Draw the algorithm on a white board and discuss it with a colleague. Sometimes, the exercise of simply describing the algorithm to someone else can help clarify your thinking and prevent serious coding errors from occurring.

- ✔ **Have someone review your code with you and make sure that it works.** Don't be afraid to take the time to run some tests on your code.

- ✔ **Check the performance time of your code and its memory requirements.** Just because a particular architecture works well with a few sample data points and a single user, the same code won't necessarily work on a production system with 100 million records and 200 simultaneous users. We discuss evaluating performance in more detail later in this chapter.

- ✔ **Don't be afraid to discard code and start over.** Despite the planning and discussions, you might create a bunch of code and still feel that something isn't working right. Often, the pressure to keep everyone running along and covering ground is so great that no one bothers to notice that the project is headed for failure. Stop periodically and ask these questions: Is the team moving in the right direction? Will the team's current direction ultimately result in a working system?

You might face an almost irresistible temptation to forge ahead because so much time and effort has been invested. Unfortunately, in many cases, if your intuition is telling you that you're going down a blind alley and the code will never work correctly, it is probably right. You're better off discarding all the old code and starting over rather than trying to fix badly architected code.

"You can't see the forest for the trees" is an important phrase to remember when writing PL/SQL code. Don't get so lost in endless routines that you lose sight of the big picture. Every two weeks, you should climb to the top of the tallest tree around (figuratively speaking, of course) to see where you are, make sure you're still going in the right direction, and look out for any nasty obstacles between you and your goal. Then climb back down the tree, have a group meeting, and have the project manager clearly point in the direction where everyone should be heading. As silly as this sounds, you can't imagine the number of huge project failures that could have been prevented by using this strategy.

Prove code works with test cases

The first time you use a feature that you haven't used before, make sure you understand how it works by writing a separate, small, example program to demonstrate its functionality. Similarly, when you're embedding a complex expression such as a combination of INSTR and SUBSTR or regular expressions, isolate the piece of code in a simple SQL expression to prove that the code is correct. This can save you hours of debugging time later. The way you can prove that your code works is by setting up small test cases by using DBMS_OUTPUT statements to print out interim results. Do this frequently for each section of code written.

Use code libraries

Although it's easy to think you're the only person who will ever need to use the code that you write, this usually isn't the case. If you look at any large system, you will find that the same code has been written dozens of times (frequently by the same developer). If that code had been placed in a code library and referenced each time it was used, there would not only be less code, but the remaining code would be less prone to errors. Every time a piece of logic is rewritten, there is the chance that the code will be written slightly differently. This can cause code errors that are very difficult to find.

Code that you write needs to be well documented and placed where it can be reused easily. Code that is used only once in a large system is the exception rather than the rule. You probably will have hundreds of reusable components in a large system, so you need to divide them into logical packages to avoid losing track of them.

Keep the code maintainable

The technology to support the myriad of information systems being used to work with databases seems to evolve faster and faster with each passing year. Designing and coding a system that can be used and easily maintained over time requires some thought and skill. Make sure that someone else down the road will be able to read and understand your code and find potential problem areas. You can find additional information about writing maintainable code in Chapter 9.

Don't forget about performance

In addition to understanding what the program you're creating needs to do, you need to have some sense about how fast the code needs to execute and return the desired information. If you're creating a month-end routine that must interact with other batch routines and execute within a 4-hour time window, your portion of the program might need to execute in 10–20 minutes. Understanding what constitutes acceptable performance in a given situation is very important.

You also need to know how often a given programming routine will be run. PL/SQL is capable of supporting a range of capabilities, some of which are used only once, such as data migration routines or low-level translations for changing system time into local time around the world that might be accessed millions of times a day. If a routine will be run only once, performance and maintainability of the code are not critical issues. See "Testing Your Code" later in this chapter for more details about evaluating performance.

Be careful before deciding that a routine will never be used again and discarding the code. Very often, you will find that you need to run the same or a very similar routine to one you wrote a few months ago.

Compile as you go

We mention earlier in this chapter that you don't want to just start writing code. Here, we expand on that point by reminding you that you don't want to write code without compiling it as you go, either.

Many inexperienced programmers create an entire first draft of a program (possibly hundreds of lines of code) without ever compiling it. When they do compile the code for the first time, hours of debugging are usually required. Writing more than a few lines of code without at least one mistake is very unusual, even for experienced programmers. Sometimes errors are nothing more than simple misspellings or typos, but errors are always there.

Compile your code every few minutes from the very beginning of the process. For example, when writing a new function or procedure, create the function name with one line of code (which might even be NULL;) and save it before doing anything further. Every few lines, compile the code again to see whether there are any errors.

Never write more than about ten lines of code without compiling it.

Debug the timesaving way

If your code doesn't work, how can you fix it? It might not compile or it might compile and not do what you expect it to do. The process of identifying and fixing errors in code is called *debugging*. (Legend has it that the term originates from an early computer that malfunctioned because a moth got into the circuitry and caused a short circuit.)

The most important thing to remember when debugging is to always start with a piece of code that works. This means that the first step to take when the code won't compile or behave as expected is not to look through the code to try to find the problem. Instead, comment out portions of the code until the code runs successfully. The point is to find out precisely where the problem is occurring. Programs can be made up of thousands of lines of code. The problem might not be located in an obvious place.

When a developer asked one of the authors for assistance in debugging a very complex routine where the developer had spent many hours looking for the problem, the authors immediately tried to determine whether the identified routine was indeed causing the problem. The author commented out the entire routine and re-executed the program. Within five minutes, it was clear that there was nothing wrong with the routine. The mistake was in the code calling the routine.

Commenting

For the reasons stated in the preceding section, the main debugging technique to use is *commenting out* parts of your code. This allows you to remove selected portions of the code to help isolate problems quickly and efficiently. This same technique can be used for both compilation and logic errors.

The SQL compiler isn't perfect. Sometimes it will indicate that an error exists in a place that is far from the actual mistake. Unfortunately, this often occurs in some of the most common types of errors, namely forgetting a semicolon, missing a comma in a SELECT statement, and missing an END statement. (We discuss these errors in more detail in Chapter 3.)

With a compilation error, the error message might not be very helpful. The best strategy is to not let your routines get too large in the first place. If you limit your routines to no more than a few hundred lines, even a problem that results in a misleading compilation error might not be too difficult to find.

When your routine is in a package, it is common for packages to contain hundreds, if not thousands, of lines of code, and finding an error will be more difficult without using the commenting technique to sequentially add portions of the routine until the error is found. In complex routines, it is helpful to comment out individual lines to narrow down where the compilation error is occurring.

The technique of commenting and un-commenting portions of a routine to help isolate a problem is very easy to use. A programmer should always have an idea about where to find the problem area in the code. It is acceptable not to know how to fix the problem, but even beginning programmers should be able to locate the precise trouble spot in the code.

Finding out what the program is doing at various points

If you're using a PL/SQL Integrated Development Environment (IDE), it might include some sophisticated debugging functionality that allows you to set *watches* (where you can see the values of variables) and *breakpoints* (places where you pause the program) in your code. Know how to use these because they will greatly assist you in finding errors. Each IDE will have its own debugging features. Consult the appropriate documentation for more details.

You might also want to use DBMS_OUTPUT or autonomous transactions to log information to a database table (like the p_log_audit procedure we describe in Chapter 12).

Testing Your Code

Often, the most reviled people on a software development project are the members of the Quality Assurance (QA) team who test the code. They are the evil nitpickers who get in the way of pushing things out the door. Inexperienced developers will do anything they can to avoid the QA process. Experienced developers recognize that no code is perfect. Having another set of eyes looking at your code greatly reduces the chance that errors will be missed.

If the QA team does nothing more than making sure you've filled out the proper paperwork and put a comment block at the top of your code, your QA process isn't sufficient. The QA process helps to make sure that code is well written and that standards have been followed.

It isn't enough to deliver a program after running it once without noticing any errors or problems. You must be much more thorough. You must make sure that your code does what it was intended to do.

Proving that the code you have written works in the way you expect is just as important as writing it correctly in the first place. In recent years, software testing has become a much more disciplined practice.

Testing code well is an extensive topic that goes far beyond the scope of this book. There are many excellent books on software testing. Your organization might have a dedicated testing group devoted to setting standards for writing and testing code. This section briefly discusses how to write tests for your code, how to manage the tests, and how these tests fit into the software development cycle. Before you dig into the details, understanding the following basics of testing is helpful:

✔ **The essence of testing is the idea of an *assertion*.** You assert that the software will do X when Y happens. Each test can be translated formally into such an assertion.

✔ **Tests come in different types.** Some tests are a manual set of steps that need to be performed by a human tester. (College interns are great resources for this kind of task.) However, whenever possible, tests should be written as code scripts that can be easily run every time someone modifies the code.

✔ **Although creating and executing good tests is a huge expense, the cost of delivering bad software is much more expensive than testing.** If you don't test your code well, you might think it works, and then later someone will discover that the system has a problem. The problem might require many hours (or weeks) to be tracked down and isolated. Then many more hours (or weeks) will be spent figuring out how to fix the code. As a result of the problem, the database might have incorrect data in it that will require time to fix. Testing software is expensive, but not testing software is much more expensive.

✔ **Even thorough testing doesn't guarantee perfect code.** It isn't possible to test everything. The most you can do is ensure core functionality. Anyone can easily miss subtle problems. Usually, the best approach is to test all the main functions and deal with the bugs when they are found.

If your software has to be perfect, you have a very difficult job. Ensuring perfection in software means that you will spend many times the development cost of the software in testing that software. If you're building software where bugs can result in serious consequences, count on spending lots of time testing. Software that controls medical devices, some military systems, and systems that control financial institutions all need to be tested differently from most business systems. Even then, it is very hard to find every problem. In such cases, the errors can have catastrophic effects on the organization. In one well-publicized software error, a simple coding error caused a multi-billion dollar loss to AT&T and an outage of phone service along most of the eastern seaboard.

What are you testing?

The first step in effective testing is knowing what the code is supposed to do. Without written specifications (as we discuss earlier in this chapter), testing is impossible because you don't have anything to test the code against. The essence of testing is to start with a functional specification. This is what you use to see whether the code meets the requirements of the specification.

In addition to the basic functions of the code outlined in the code specification, you have many other things to test, too, including the following:

✔ **The operation of specific portions of your routine:** You need to test the exception conditions and verify that appropriate error messages are issued in each context.

✔ **Software performance:** The code must continue to operate quickly in the actual production environment. Code can perform very differently when hundreds of users are on the system or when millions of rows are in the tables.

✔ **Naming and coding standards:** Simply having standards is no guarantee that those standards are actually being followed. Someone should check to see that the code is written according to those standards.

In the following sections, we offer more details about testing performance. We offer details on identifying exceptions in Chapter 5 and explain tips for creating naming standards in Chapter 8.

Creating a testing architecture

The actual testing of your code involves making sure that the code does the right task. The tests themselves should be written, saved, and rerun every time there is a modification. To manage the testing code, you can either use a package like Quest Software's utPLSQL or create your own testing environment. Don't just write tests in PL/SQL in a script without any testing architecture. Otherwise, each developer on a team will come up with his or her own ideas about how to test (assuming they write any tests at all).

Performance and load testing

Ensuring that your code is going to run well in a production environment is the hardest test to do. It requires effectively simulating the actual production environment. If you're working on a large system, this can be very expensive.

The easiest way to make sure that your code will work well in production is to have an exact copy of the production environment (including processes) to simulate the normal production load on the system. If you're working in a multi-million dollar computer environment, this means setting up two copies of the entire environment: one for production and one for testing. Because this might not be economically feasible (for large systems), typically, the best you can do is to create a smaller system that represents some fraction of the production environment. In such cases, making the test environment as close as possible to the production environment is essential.

It is absolutely essential that the test and production environments use the same version of the Oracle DBMS, down to the exact patch release. With each release, Oracle changes the way that both SQL and PL/SQL are executed. There is no guarantee that code that works well in one release will perform the same way in a different release.

It is also essential for the test system to have exactly the same database objects as the production release. Differences in indexes, hints in SQL, and even database statistics can have a profound effect on performance.

You must use the same application server software and front-end software for testing (if applicable).

If the system will have hundreds (or thousands) of users or large batch jobs might be running while the software is executing, you will need to simulate the entire load on the real production system.

Tuning performance

After you have written a routine and verified that it does what it is supposed to do, you need to consider the time required by the routine to execute its task. If it doesn't perform quickly enough, here are steps you can follow to find and fix the problem:

1. **Isolate the performance problem.**

   If a database procedure requires 10 seconds to execute, it might consist of thousands of lines of code, probably combining both SQL and PL/SQL. To identify the source of the problem, you need to scatter many timing messages throughout the code to find the slow part(s).

   Performance bottlenecks are typically found within a single SQL statement. A cursor might be taking a long time to execute.

2. **Extract the SELECT statement from the cursor and run it alone in SQL Navigator, Toad, SQL*Plus, or whatever tool you're using.**

If this query takes 9.9 of the total 10 seconds to execute, you can be fairly certain that you've found the problem code, and spending time working on other portions of the code is a waste of time.

3. Tune the problematic part of the code and test the code as a whole again.

Many developers spend hours reviewing slowly running code to try and improve it because they don't fully understand how to tune the code efficiently. A full discussion of SQL performance tuning is beyond the scope of this book. There are many helpful books and articles to consult about this topic.

4. After tuning the problematic SQL statement, your code might still not be running quickly enough. At this point, you need to *refactor* (redesign) the algorithm in the code.

There is no general solution to this type of problem. Sometimes, you can't do anything to speed up the code processing. However, in some cases, you can improve performance of PL/SQL by using various techniques:

- Tune the SQL (beyond the scope of this book).

- Minimize the number of database operations.

If you find that you do need to minimize operations, here are a few common problems, where these operations can often be pared back:

- **Repeatedly accessing the same object:** This is a relatively common mistake that can impact performance. For example, when retrieving a record from the database, you should retrieve the entire record at once. You shouldn't individually retrieve each attribute. Conversely, when processing an object where each operation updates an attribute, instead of executing an UPDATE statement for each operation, make all the modifications to the object in memory and execute a single UPDATE statement.

  As obvious as this might sound, many programmers make this mistake. Object-oriented programmers tend to think in terms of getters (retrieve information) and setters (update information) and view the database as the means of storing persistent copies of classes. If a table contains 100 columns, this means the code will execute 100 separate SQL statements to retrieve an object and 100 statements to update the object. (This is one of the techniques that caused the month-end routine mentioned at the beginning of this chapter to require 26 years to complete.) Few experienced programmers make the mistake of using the getter/setter method to interact with the database. However, it is common to see programs where the same object is inserted and later updated within the same routine or updated multiple times.

- **Retrieving information with too many cursors:** Frequently, when information must be retrieved from multiple tables, instead of writing a single SQL statement that will return information from all the tables simultaneously, developers might write individual cursors that are executed hundreds of times to retrieve the same information. You can refactor a routine with nested CURSOR FOR loops to require a single (although somewhat more complex) query that needs to be executed only once.

Another place where multiple cursors might be hiding is in SQL where one of the columns in the SELECT statement is a function that itself invokes a cursor. For every row in that SELECT statement, the cursor will be executed. Depending upon how the query is written, the cursor might execute millions of times even though the query returns only a few rows.

✔ **Not using bulk operations:** You can use SQL bulk operations to replace or modify whole areas of PL/SQL code. When you need to update millions of rows in the database by using PL/SQL, traditional PL/SQL coding techniques usually won't suffice. You must adopt a different programming style to support high-performance PL/SQL coding. This usually requires using one or more of the bulk SQL operations used in conjunction with PL/SQL collections. A full discussion of this topic is beyond the scope of this book. See Chapter 11 for some additional information about bulk operations.

Minimizing calls to SYSDATE that involve a query to the database behind the scenes can significantly impact performance. For example, looping through a million records to compare a date to the SYSDATE, you should calculate SYSDATE once in the header and reference it in the loop.

Note that the performance-tuning tips listed here don't mention anything about the way in which the PL/SQL code is written directly. Instead, most involve database interaction and how the SQL is written. This is because tuning problems are almost always due to the SQL or something that can be fixed by using SQL. Very rarely is the problem with the raw PL/SQL code.

There is one exception. PL/SQL itself does not execute as quickly as code written in a language like C. For example, if you need to perform millions of complex mathematical operations and performance is an important issue, you might want to consider moving the data to an external C routine that can be called from PL/SQL. The only time you might encounter this type of requirement is when trying to use PL/SQL to perform complex bulk mathematical operations for a statistical, financial, scientific, or linear program.

"Good enough is best"

The expression "good enough is best" comes from the world of engineering. It means that when an engineer is building something, there is a set of specifications that must be complied with. When these are met, the task is complete. Spending additional time, money, and resources to meet a higher level of specifications is considered wasteful and inappropriate. For example, if a particular bearing must be manufactured to within +/- 0.1mm tolerance, spending additional manufacturing resources to achieve 0.001mm tolerance would be considered a waste of resources and might even result in a reprimand for over-engineering the process.

This same principle is true for software engineering. If the system requirement is that a routine provide subsecond response and tests show that the routine executes in 0.5 seconds, the developer should stop work and recognize that making the routine execute in 0.05 seconds isn't a worthwhile task. There are always other tasks to be accomplished.

Judgment must be used to temper this philosophy. If the requirement for a user interface element is subsecond response but 10,000 users will, on average, execute the relevant operation 1,000 times per day, taking this operation from 1 second to 0.9 seconds would save the organization many hours each day. On the other hand, a routine that is only called once in a monthly batch routine that executes in 10 seconds is not worth spending 3 hours to reduce to 9 seconds because the organization will save only 12 seconds per year. You need to think about the trade-offs between time and resources spent to improve something and the purpose of the code being modified.

Low-level routines that might be executed millions of times in a single day should be tuned as carefully as possible. For example, a routine that takes the current system date and transforms it into local time might be called millions of times in a day and should be written as efficiently as possible from a performance standpoint.

Coding the Agile Way

The Agile movement evolved in the mid-1990s as an alternative to the traditional, more structured waterfall development method. The Agile approach to system development includes some very useful best practices for PL/SQL developers.

Working together in Agile teams

Agile development teams aren't so different from any other teams. However, users have a greater role; more small meetings are held; and the core idea is that, ultimately, it is the users' system. Delivery cycles average 2 to 4 weeks using a rapid response/adaptive process. Team members participate in planning, performance, and acceptance of work. The goal is to match the right people with the right tasks as well as to take into account workloads, task allocations, and resources. Team members work in close physical proximity. Memos and other documents are replaced with more face-to-face communications. Team members have access to key users.

Agile teams are self-organized. They can be reconfigured multiple times for best results. Decisions are made as part of a collaborative process with all team members. The entire team is accountable for deliverables, which helps to spread the responsibility. To make this work, skilled team members are essential. They must be autonomous. Agile teams include "generalizing specialists." The goal is to have these team members be experts in one or more technical specialties. They try to master new skills in a number of areas. This makes them better workers as part of a team with a better sense of the overall project.

Agile teams have several advantages over traditional software development teams: Information moves more quickly and directly among team members, decision-making time is reduced, feedback is rapid to encourage iterative process, morale is improved, team members focus on individual areas of competence, and the collaboration is organized.

Because of the rapidity of the process, productivity is also improved. Small teams are easier to manage. More user involvement helps ensure that users' requirements are being met. Focus is placed on tasks rather than roles. Each IT person on the team is process focused, and communication is plentiful.

Programming in pairs

Another useful idea taken from the Agile approach is *pair programming*. Pair programming is carried out by having two developers sit side by side to create the same code. Logistically, pair programming can take place with one developer coding while the other might be preparing documentation, reviewing the code, tracking down answers to system requirement issues, testing the code, or writing test scripts. Pair programming provides automatic quality assurance on all code. Because pairings are frequently changed, a unified coding standard can be enforced with less deviation from printed standards. By having two people working on code, productivity is improved because more attention is devoted to the task at hand, and code or design errors might be caught early.

Delivering code quickly

In a pure Agile environment, very rapid delivery of a new version of the software (deployment) every few weeks is important. However, for database systems, a 2–4 week deployment is lunacy. Training and data migration can't be adequately accomplished that quickly. Although deployment can't be done so quickly, a 2–4 week delivery from the developers to the testing team is essential for project success. In this way, developers and users stay "hot" and there is no danger of "analysis paralysis." User acceptance testing works against deliveries. Deployment is a business decision, but delivery is what makes the process work.

Agile development still requires a project plan including the following documents:

- ✔ A high-level plan describing the detailed steps for the first three months including Task/Feature lists prioritized by users.

- ✔ A Strategy Document that describes the goals, objectives, and high-level plan for the project.

- ✔ Possibly some system architecture white papers that describe, in detail, the key technical aspects of the project.

In addition, weekly status reports should be prepared by the development team summarizing the progress to date, listing any outstanding issues and proposing tasks for the following two weeks.

Test first

Test first means writing tests to validate your software before you even write the software. It is one of the most important concepts in Extreme Programming (XP) and other Agile techniques. Every project would benefit from this technique, although it is most popular with Agile teams.

There Is a strong philosophical foundation to test first. The idea is that you're always writing software to fulfill an established need. Test first formalizes that need. The software needs to pass all its tests. If the tests formalize the requirements of the software and the software passes all those tests, there is a good chance that the software will meet the system requirements.

No code is accepted until it passes tests. In practice, tests are written and modified as the code is written. No code is considered complete until tests are written and passed. Test first not only drastically reduces the number of bugs, but also makes versioning easier.

According to studies such as "A Structured Experiment of Test-Driven Development" (Boby George and Laurie Williams, *Information and Software Technology* 46 (2004), 337–342) moving to a test-first approach resulted in a number of significant reductions in the following:

- ✔ Software bugs

- ✔ Delivery time for version 1 of software

- ✔ Cost of system version 1

- ✔ Cost of subsequent system versions

Keeping Up-to-Date with Oracle

SQL and PL/SQL are constantly evolving. With every release of Oracle, new features are added and older features get better. The best practices of this year will be outdated coding next year. Features that have been added in version 9*i* and 10*g* of Oracle are used only by a minority of developers. So, how do you stay up-to-date? In this section, we offer some helpful tips as well as some useful resources for keeping current with the new releases.

Conventional wisdom isn't always right

Your mother always told you that "just because everyone else does something, that doesn't mean you have to do it." This applies to coding, too. Just because conventional wisdom says to do something a certain way, that doesn't mean it is necessarily the best way.

Every time Oracle releases a new version, things change. New features are added, and the performance characteristics of older features might change drastically. CPUs and other hardware also change rapidly. Disk storage and performance have gotten larger and faster by orders of magnitude in just a few years. The cost of main memory has plummeted so that larger program units are no longer a problem. There are a number of classic examples where the prevailing conventional wisdom has changed radically in the last few years.

- ✔ Explicit cursors (see Chapters 6 and 15) used to always be faster than implicit cursors when doing a single row fetch. Several years ago, Oracle fixed this problem, and now implicit cursors are marginally faster. The new wisdom is that both implicit and explicit cursor calls both execute so rapidly that the performance cost of using one or the other is, in almost every case, negligible.

- ✔ Oracle's management of tables with large numbers of columns used to be problematic, so designers would routinely try to limit tables to a handful of columns whenever possible. Database designers who have kept up with Oracle's improvements now recognize that tables with hundreds of columns can be used without degrading performance.

- ✔ Oracle recently introduced bulk operations into SQL. The conventional wisdom was that bulk operations were always faster than processing records one at a time. Although it is true that, in most cases, bulk operations will significantly outperform single record operations, in many cases, there is now no performance improvement at all.

When someone tells you to do X instead of Y, make sure he or she can demonstrate the reasons. Create a test to quickly find out whether the new conventional wisdom is accurate. After you've proven that a tidbit of conventional wisdom is true or not, recognize that, as soon as any relevant variable changes (new release of the database, operating system, or data characteristics), you will need to reassess and retest the conventional wisdom.

You might be overwhelmed at the thought of trying to keep up with all the possible changes that occur. But remember, you also don't need to find the absolute best solution to every problem. As we mention earlier in this chapter, you don't need to come up with perfect code, just code that meets the requirements. You'll have an easier time keeping up with the changes If you check out the resources we discuss in the following sections.

Buy books

This book is designed to help you get started programming in PL/SQL. It is not a complete reference. There are too many important features in PL/SQL to discuss in any one book. Fortunately, plenty of good PL/SQL books are available on the market. Most of them have been written by Steven Feuerstein (published by O'Reilly), arguably the best author of PL/SQL references in the industry. As your first purchase, you should buy his recent books. You should also look at Scott Urman's excellent PL/SQL book, *Oracle Database 10g PL/SQL Programming,* from Oracle Press. After you've been coding for a while, you will easily be able to read a PL/SQL complete reference book cover to cover. No matter how much coding you've done, you'll be amazed at how many things you didn't know.

Go to conferences

One of the best-kept secrets in the industry is that you can see the same content at almost any large Oracle conference. The same speakers tend to go to most of the national and regional conferences, and many frequent local Oracle user group meetings, too. You'll see more vendors and presentations from Oracle employees at a large conference, but also pay more to attend. For developers, the two best conferences are the Oracle Development Tools User Group (ODTUG, www.odtug.com) and the Independent Oracle Users Group (IOUG, www.ioug.org) annual conferences. Both are technically focused events. ODTUG is geared for developers. If you're also interested in DBA topics, go to the IOUG conference. Oracle OpenWorld in San Francisco (Oracle's annual conference) usually has more Oracle marketing presentations and fewer user papers, but the most attendees and biggest vendor hall. To find out the latest Oracle has to offer and hear it directly from Oracle, this is the best conference to attend.

At a regional conference, you can almost as much technical content as the national conferences, with less travel and for less money. The Rocky Mountain Oracle User Group (RMOUG), the New York Oracle Users Group (NYOUG), the Northern California Oracle User Group (NOCOUG), the Mid-Atlantic Oracle Users Group (MAOP-AOTC), and others all host annual conferences that have multiple tracks and provide excellent content.

Join your local Oracle user group

Join your local Oracle user group and get to know people. It's helpful to know someone you can call when you have a question. You should also become an ODTUG and/or IOUG member. You'll receive discounts for the conferences, access to conference papers and presentations online, and well-written journals with technical articles about a variety of Oracle-related topics. Also, many large companies have internal user groups where you can exchange tips. Smaller companies might host brown bag lunches where you can present useful tips. Be sure to take advantage of these resources, as well.

Use online resources

Surfing the Web is one of the best ways to find out about PL/SQL features. Most conference papers are posted on one or more Web sites. You can also post questions to various Internet list-serves and get your questions answered (usually within a day). Probably the best list for PL/SQL questions is ODTUG's ODTUG-SQLPLUS-L list. You can sign up for this free list (you don't even have to be a member of ODTUG) at www.odtug.com.

Part VI
The Part of Tens

The 5th Wave — By Rich Tennant

"Before we hire you as our newest PL/SQL developer, we need to see how you work under pressure."

In this part . . .

The Part of Tens summarizes some of the best and worst that we've encountered when writing PL/SQL code.

In Chapter 15, we have assembled useful tips gleaned from our years of experience building database systems, both large and small.

Chapter 16 describes some of the worst mistakes that both beginner and experienced programmers often make in their PL/SQL coding. By reading this chapter carefully, hopefully you can take our advice and avoid making these errors in your own code.

Chapter 15

Ten PL/SQL Tips

*E*xperienced PL/SQL developers can give you hundreds of tips based on their programming experience. The list in this chapter represents ten of the most useful ones we encountered in our work building real-world systems.

Use SELECT INTO Correctly

Each time you use SELECT INTO, remember that your query might return more than one row or no rows at all. Therefore, you need to include exception handlers to take care of these situations if there is any possibility of them occurring.

The reason this is so important is that your code might execute correctly for many months before some unusual condition shows up that causes it to fail. Then you can spend days trying to figure out what went wrong.

For example, if you want to write a function in which you take EMPNO as an input parameter and return the EMPNO and ENAME of the person with highest salary in the department, you would use something like the following:

```
function f_getTopEmp_tx (i_deptNo NUMBER) return VARCHAR2
         is
    v_max_sal_nr NUMBER;
    v_out_tx VARCHAR2(2000);
begin
    select max(sal) into v_max_sal_nr
     from emp
     where deptNo=i_deptNo;
    select empNo||' '||eName into v_out_tx
     from emp
     where sal=v_max_sal_nr and deptNo=i_deptNo;
    return v_out_tx;
end;
```

At the first glance, the code looks fine, so you can run the following:

```
SQL> declare
  2      cursor c_dept is
  3        select deptNo, dName
  4          from dept
  5        order by deptNo;
  6  begin
  7      for r_dept in c_dept loop
  8          DBMS_OUTPUT.put_line('Dept: '||r_dept.dName
  9              ||'-'||f_getTopEmp_tx(r_dept.deptNo));
 10      end loop;
 11  end;
 12  /
Dept: ACCOUNTING-7839 KING
declare
*
ERROR at line 1:
ORA-01422: exact fetch returns more than requested number
         of rows
ORA-06512: at "SCOTT.F_GETTOPEMP_TX", line 8
ORA-06512: at line 8
```

However, the result isn't exactly what you wanted. Looking more closely at the data in the EMP table, department 20 has more than one person with the highest salary in the department. This is what caused the problem. In this case, fortunately the problem was encountered right away. But what if you wanted to find out which salesperson had the most sales in a given year? In that case, the probability of more than one person having the exact same sales amount is very low, so you might go a long time without ever noticing the problem.

To fix the procedure, you might use something like Listing 15-1.

Listing 15-1:   SELECT INTO with the Wrong Result

```
function f_getTopEmp_tx (i_deptNo NUMBER) return VARCHAR2
         is
    v_max_sal_nr NUMBER;
    v_out_tx VARCHAR2(2000);
begin
    select max(sal) into v_max_sal_nr                         →5
      from emp
      where deptNo=i_deptNo;                                  →7
    select empNo||' '||eName into v_out_tx                    →8
      from emp
      where sal=v_max_sal_nr and deptNo=i_deptNo;             →10
    return v_out_tx;
exception
    when too_many_rows then
         return '<Multiple hits>';
end;
```

Running the loop one more time produces a different (but not much better) result.

```
SQL> /
Dept: ACCOUNTING-7839 KING
Dept: RESEARCH-<Multiple hits>
Dept: SALES-7698 BLAKE
declare
*
ERROR at line 1:
ORA-01403: no data found
ORA-06512: at "SCOTT.F_GETTOPEMP_TX", line 8
ORA-06512: at line 8
```

Here's what you see going on in Listing 15-1:

→**5–7** Department 40 doesn't have any employees at all. As a result, the first query returns NULL. (Queries with grouping functions never fail with NO_DATA_FOUND.)

→**8–10** The second query fails because there is nobody in the department.

To solve this problem, use Listing 15-2.

Listing 15-2:   SELECT INTO with the Correct Result

```
function f_getTopEmp_tx (i_deptNo NUMBER) return VARCHAR2
         is
    v_max_sal_nr NUMBER;
    v_out_tx VARCHAR2(2000);
begin
    select max(sal) into v_max_sal_nr
```

(continued)

Listing 15-2 (continued)

```
      from emp
      where deptNo=i_deptNo;
    select empNo||' '||eName into v_out_tx
      from emp
      where sal=v_max_sal_nr and deptNo=i_deptNo;
    return v_out_tx;
exception
    when too_many_rows then
          return '<Multiple hits>';
    when no_data_found then
          return '<Nobody found>';
end;
```

Now your SELECT INTO function is ready to use:

```
SQL> /
Dept: ACCOUNTING-7839 KING
Dept: RESEARCH-<Multiple hits>
Dept: SALES-7698 BLAKE
Dept: OPERATIONS-<Nobody found>
PL/SQL procedure successfully completed.
```

If you're working with the BULK COLLECT clause, you need to check for the number of fetched records because the exception NO_DATA_FOUND is never raised, even when no rows were fetched. See Chapter 11 (in the section about the BULK COLLECT command) for an example.

Don't Assume Column Order in DML Statements

When you have a DML statement in your code, you should explicitly list the columns you're referencing. Never assume that the number and order of the columns in a table or view are constant. Columns that are added to a table later will break your code. Rebuilding your database might result in the default column order being changed.

Using an INSERT statement as an example, assume you need a procedure to create new departments and validate the data entered previously. You could use code like the block shown in Listing 15-3.

Listing 15-3: An Improper INSERT Statement

```
procedure p_createDept
    (i_deptNo NUMBER, i_dName VARCHAR2, i_loc VARCHAR2) is
begin
    if length(i_dName)>10 then
        raise_application_error
        (-20999,'Department name is too long');
    end if;
    insert into dept                                    →8
            values (i_deptNo, i_dName, i_loc);          →9
end;
```

→8–9   The code works, but it hides a major potential problem because you didn't explicitly list the columns in the DEPT table when you created your INSERT statement.

If someone needs an extra column in the DEPT table such as Remarks (which contains no critical data), you may assume that adding this column by using the following code is safe:

```
alter table dept add remarks_tx VARCHAR2(2000)
```

Now your routine will stop working because there are more columns in the DEPT table than values being passed in the INSERT statement. The same problem will occur even without adding new columns. The DBA might rebuild the DEPT table and switch the order of columns in the CREATE TABLE.

Protect the code by using something like Listing 15-4.

Listing 15-4: A Safe INSERT Statement

```
procedure p_createDept
    (i_deptNo NUMBER, i_dName VARCHAR2, i_loc VARCHAR2) is
begin
    if length(i_dName)>10 then
        raise_application_error
        (-20999,'Department name is too long');
    end if;
    insert into dept (deptNo, dName, loc)
        values (i_deptNo, i_dName, i_loc);
end;
```

If you're working with a large number of columns, using variables of type RECORD is a better approach (see Chapter 11 for more details about the RECORD datatype). The previous example worked fine for a table with just three columns. However, if you need to initialize a very complex row, the list of columns can make your code incredibly messy and unmaintainable. To avoid this problem, use Listing 15-5.

Listing 15-5:   Insert by Using RECORD Type Variable

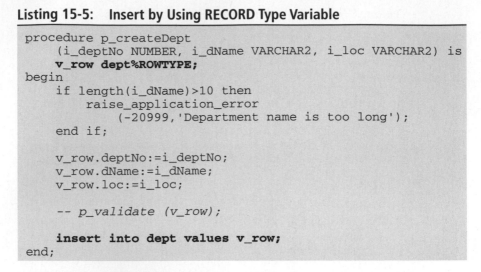

```
procedure p_createDept
    (i_deptNo NUMBER, i_dName VARCHAR2, i_loc VARCHAR2) is
    v_row dept%ROWTYPE;
begin
    if length(i_dName)>10 then
        raise_application_error
            (-20999,'Department name is too long');
    end if;

    v_row.deptNo:=i_deptNo;
    v_row.dName:=i_dName;
    v_row.loc:=i_loc;

    -- p_validate (v_row);

    insert into dept values v_row;
end;
```

Using this approach, you don't have to list anything in the INSERT statement, because you're inserting a variable into the DEPT table that is defined as a row from the same table. Now there is no chance for inconsistency.

Here's another good reason for having a variable of type RECORD: It's a much easier way of passing data to different routines. For example, you might have a procedure (such as the p_validate procedure in this example) that will perform validation for the data you entered. You would need to pass only one variable and not a whole list of columns.

Use the NOCOPY Command

Use NOCOPY when passing an IN/OUT parameter to avoid passing by value. This is mainly a performance rather than a logic issue.

Normally when you pass an IN/OUT parameter, Oracle makes a copy of the parameter in memory and uses that copy in the called program unit. When the program unit is executed, it copies the values back to the original variable. Performing this operation once doesn't take a lot of time, but in a procedure that's called thousands of times, the time can add up.

The previous section shows how to perform validation on a row from the DEPT table by passing a record parameter, rather than a list of columns:

```
    p_validate (v_row);
```

The p_validate procedure might look like Listing 15-6.

Listing 15-6: Validating Rows

```
procedure p_validate(io_dept_rec in out dept%ROWTYPE) is
    v_count_nr NUMBER;
begin
    if io_dept_rec.dName!=
            f_checkString_tx(io_dept_rec.dName)
    then
        io_dept_rec.remarks_tx:=io_dept_rec.remarks_tx
        ||chr(10)||'Error: DNAME contains invalid chars!';
    end if;
    if io_dept_rec.loc is null then
        io_dept_rec.loc := 'UNKNOWN LOC';
        io_dept_rec.remarks_tx:=io_dept_rec.remarks_tx
            ||chr(10)||'Warning: LOC not specified!';
    end if;
end;
```

The idea is simple. Take the record as an input/output parameter and run a number of tests. The tests may simply detect problems or attempt to correct minor issues by modifying the original data. Place a report on the results in the remarks_tx column and return the (potentially updated) record.

What you're actually doing is passing the same record in and out of the procedure. But each time the procedure is called, the database has to create a local copy of the input/output variable. In the case of simple parameters such as numbers or dates, it isn't much of an issue, but it can be with memory-consuming items such as records, objects, and collections. To decrease the performance overhead, give Oracle the hint NOCOPY (which we also discuss in Chapters 3 and 11), as shown here:

```
procedure p_validate(io_dept_rec in out NOCOPY
        dept%ROWTYPE) is ...
```

Now the validation routine won't take a value from the original record and make a local copy. Instead, it will take a pointer to the original record and update the original record appropriately.

NOCOPY is just a hint, not a directive. This means that Oracle may ignore it. Also, depending upon the version of Oracle used, there are a number of restrictions on using NOCOPY. But if you violate one of those restrictions, there will be no raised error. Oracle will ignore your hint without notifying you.

Another thing to be aware of when using a NOCOPY hint is exception handling. If you're passing a variable by value to a subroutine and that routine fails, the original value of the variable doesn't change. But if you're passing the variable by reference, the failed subroutine might have changed the original variable's value (before it failed), unless you have an exception-handling block in that subroutine.

Be Careful of Function Calls That Impact Performance

If you have a loop and need to calculate some values, ask yourself whether you can perform the calculations before the loop, or reduce the number of times the calculations are performed within the loop. Otherwise, you might be running the same function many more times than needed.

For example, you might have a function that takes EMPNO as a parameter and returns a string that could be used as a display value for the employee (Chapter 6 offers such an example), as shown here:

```
function f_emp_dsp (i_empNo NUMBER)
                    return VARCHAR2 is
    v_out_tx VARCHAR2 (256);
begin
    select initcap(eName)||': '||initcap(job)
      into v_out_tx
      from emp
      where empNo = i_empNo;
    return v_out_tx;
exception
    when no_data_found
         then return null;
end;
```

Now you decide to create a loop that prints a list of all employees and their managers, as shown here:

```
declare
    cursor c_emp  is
    select empNo, mgr
    from emp
    order by mgr;
begin
    for r_emp in c_emp loop
        DBMS_OUTPUT.put_line(f_emp_dsp(r_emp.mgr)
            ||'>'||f_emp_dsp(r_emp.empNo));
    end loop;
end;
```

The function f_emp_dsp will be fired exactly 28 times (14 employees × 2). But if you look at the output, a large number of values repeat. For example, BLAKE is the manager for five people and is also managed by KING. This means that the code will run exactly the same query six times. With a small amount of data, running the query six times isn't a big problem. But with thousands of records, even though each execution takes a millisecond, the time can add up quickly.

You can decrease that overhead in a number of ways. The idea is to cache the calculated data in the local variables, as shown in Listing 15-7.

Listing 15-7:   Caching Calculated Data

```
declare
   cursor c_emp is
     select empNo, mgr
       from emp
     order by mgr;
   type list_aa is table of VARCHAR(2000)
     index by binary_integer;
   v_emp_aa list_aa;
begin
  for r_emp in c_emp loop
    if not v_emp_aa.exists(r_emp.empNo) then
      v_emp_aa(r_emp.empNo):=f_emp_dsp(r_emp.empNo);   →12
    end if;
    if not v_emp_aa.exists(nvl(r_emp.mgr,-1)) then
      v_emp_aa(nvl(r_emp.mgr,-1)):=f_emp_dsp(r_emp.mgr);
                                                          →15
    end if;

    DBMS_OUTPUT.put_line
      (v_emp_aa(nvl(r_emp.mgr,- 1)) ||'>'
          ||v_emp_aa(r_emp.empNo));
    end loop;
end;
```

Here's more information about Listing 15-7:

> →12   In this case, you can use an associative array indexed by BINARY_ INTEGER. Because you have a uniquely identified EMPNO, you can first check the array for appropriate records and call the procedure only if an entry for that employee does not yet exist in the array.

> →15   The NVL (checking whether the value is null) on MGR is needed because KING has no managers and an associative array can't have NULL as an index. As a result, the total number of executions of the function f_empDsp dropped from 28 to 15 (14 records plus NULL).

The same logic of reducing the number of executions is true not only for user-defined functions and procedures, but for built-in ones. Even executing SYSDATE several hundred thousand times could cause some problems. If you need to move a few million records from a production table to an archive, use the following logic:

```
declare
    v_sysdate DATE;
begin
    v_sysdate := sysdate;
    insert into back_emp (empNo, eName, ..., archive_dt)
    select empNo, eName, ..., v_sysdate
      from prod_emp;
end;
```

A function in an SQL statement will execute at least once for every row returned. However, sometimes in SQL queries that join multiple tables, the function might execute so many times that the query never returns. You have to look closely at the execution plan of the query to see how many times the function will execute.

Beware of Implicit Commits

As we discuss in Chapter 12, any DDL command causes an implicit commit. This isn't a major issue because you won't usually have DDL commands in your code. But every experienced developer has encountered situations similar to the following when building a system: Imagine that you insert or delete a bunch of data, and then you recompile your procedure and your changes are instantly committed. The problem is that you might not need to commit (for example, you just discovered a bug in your code). Always think about any uncommitted changes whenever performing DDL operations.

The TRUCNATE TABLE command is also DDL and forces an explicit commit, as well.

Each time you work with the data and the code simultaneously, try to do only one thing at a time. Make a habit of always using an explicit commit or rollback before you start modifying your code.

The same problem of unintentional commits could happen if you're using Dynamic SQL to build DDL statements on the fly, as shown here in a routine that creates a backup of the EMP table:

```
create or replace procedure p_backupEmp is
    v_name_tx VARCHAR2(30);
begin
    v_name_tx:='emp'||TO_CHAR(sysdate,'YYYYMMDDHH24MISS');
    execute immediate  'create table '||v_name_tx||
        ' as select * from emp';
end;
```

Now you want to include that procedure in the backup routine, assuming that the EMP table has a column to store the date of the last backup. The code to do this is shown in Listing 15-8.

Listing 15-8: Backup Routine Procedure

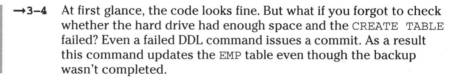

```
procedure p_backupMain is
begin
    update emp                                          →3
        set backup_dt = sysdate;                        →4
    p_backupEmp;
exception
  when others then
    rollback;
    raise_application_error
        (-20999,'Backup Failed with error: '||sqlerrm);
end p_backupMain;
```

→3–4   At first glance, the code looks fine. But what if you forgot to check whether the hard drive had enough space and the CREATE TABLE failed? Even a failed DDL command issues a commit. As a result this command updates the EMP table even though the backup wasn't completed.

This problem has a number of solutions. The simplest is to modify the code so that, at the moment of DDL execution, there is no uncommitted data that would be rolled back in case of a fatal error. In Listing 15-8, simply swapping the order of the UPDATE and p_backupEmp commands would work.

How can you guarantee that the procedure p_backupEmp won't be called from another routine that might involve some data changes? In large systems, you might have a tough time searching through ten levels of function calls to figure out what caused an implicit commit.

An alternative and more efficient solution involves using autonomous transactions, as shown in Listing 15-9.

Listing 15-9: Using Autonomous Transactions with DDL Commits

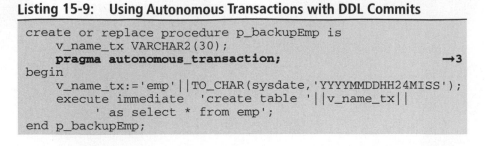

```
create or replace procedure p_backupEmp is
    v_name_tx VARCHAR2(30);
    pragma autonomous_transaction;                          →3
begin
    v_name_tx:='emp'||TO_CHAR(sysdate,'YYYYMMDDHH24MISS');
    execute immediate  'create table '||v_name_tx||
            ' as select * from emp';
end p_backupEmp;
```

┃ **→3**   Declares that the procedure p_backupEmp should be executed in
a different transaction from the parent one.

Now the implicit commit caused by the CREATE TABLE command doesn't
have any impact on the uncommitted data changes in the parent routine.
As a result, it is safe to call p_backupEmp in any part of the code.

Autonomous transactions don't see uncommitted parent changes (see
Chapter 12 for more details). In Listing 15-9, the backup will use the old
values of backup_dt. In this particular case, that limited visibility is irrelevant because you have a precise timestamp in the name of the table.
However, in some cases, this issue may be critical.

There is another "cheat" with using autonomous transactions that can help
resolve restrictions on what functions you can use in SQL. Using the Chapter
6 example of giving employees a raise, you could write the following code:

```
function f_giveRaise_tx (i_empNo NUMBER, i_pcnt NUMBER)
                    return VARCHAR2 is
begin
    update emp
      set sal=sal*(i_pcnt/100)+sal
      where empNo = i_empNo;
    return 'OK';
exception
    when others then
        return 'Error:'||substr(sqlerrm,1,256);
end f_giveRaise_tx;
```

Calling the function in SQL (select f_giveRaise_tx from dual) raised
an ORA-14551 error, but you can define the function as an autonomous
transaction, as shown here:

```
function f_giveRaise_tx (i_empNo NUMBER, i_pcnt NUMBER)
                    return VARCHAR2 is
    pragma autonomous_transaction;
begin
    update emp
      set sal=sal*(i_pcnt/100)+sal
```

```
        where empNo = i_empNo;
    commit;
    return 'OK';
exception
    when others then
        rollback;
        return 'Error:'||substr(sqlerrm,1,256);
end f_giveRaise_tx;
```

Now you can use that function whenever you want.

You have to either commit or roll back your changes before the return (whether the return is successful or not) from the function or procedure declared as an autonomous transaction to ensure that your function can be used appropriately.

Use Only One RETURN Statement per Function

Keeping function returns to a minimum is important. One very useful technique is to use a single OUT point in the routine. This means that

✔ Functions have only one RETURN statement.

✔ The RETURN statement should be the last line before the exception block.

By sticking to both of these rules, you can clearly see when a function expects to return a value. As an example, you might write the function f_empDsp to include multiple display types, as shown in Listing 15-10.

Listing 15-10: **Limiting Function Returns**

```
function f_emp_dsp (i_empNo NUMBER,
        i_type_tx VARCHAR2:='DEFAULT',
        i_limit30char_yn VARCHAR2:='N')
return VARCHAR2 is
    v_out_tx VARCHAR2 (256);
begin
    if i_empNo is null then
        v_out_tx:=null;
    elsif i_type_tx='NO_ID' then
        select eName into v_out_tx
        from emp
        where empNo = i_empNo;
```

(continued)

Listing 15-10 *(continued)*

```
    elsif i_type_tx = 'JOB' then
        select eName||': '||job into v_out_tx
        from emp
        where empNo = i_empNo;
    else
        select empNo||' '||eName into v_out_tx
        from emp
        where empNo = i_empNo;
    end if;
    if i_limit30char_yn = 'Y' then
        v_out_tx:=substr(v_out_tx,1,29)||'>';
    end if;
    return v_out_tx;                              →25
exception
    when no_data_found then
        v_out_tx:= '<Error>';
        return v_out_tx;                          →29
end;
```

| →**25–29** | The idea is that you have only one variable to monitor (V_OUT_TX) and that variable will be returned to the calling routine in only one place in the body of the function and one place in the exception handler.

Save Debugging Time with WHEN OTHERS

Most programmers know better than to use WHEN OTHERS THEN NULL in their code because it hides errors and makes the code harder to debug. However, using the exception WHEN OTHERS can save you a lot of debugging time because it captures unpredictable events.

Many things can go wrong in your code, but explicitly placing exception handlers to cover all situations is impossible. On the other hand, debugging an exception raised somewhere deep in a chain of function calls is also difficult.

The exception WHEN OTHERS allows you to intercept these unspecified exceptions. But the question is: what do you do with them? One option is to return an error message (as shown in the function f_giveRaise_tx example in Listing 15-11). Although developers need to know what is going on in the system, it isn't possible to return an error to the end user in all cases.

There is a good debugging method involving a custom routine `p_log` (for more information, see Chapter 14), as shown here:

```
create sequence log_seq
/
create table log_info (id_nr NUMBER,
        message_tx VARCHAR2(4000),
        timestamp_ts TIMESTAMP)
/
create or replace procedure p_log (i_message_tx VARCHAR2)
is
  pragma autonomous_transaction;
begin
  insert into log_info
    (id_nr, message_tx, timestamp_ts)
  values
    (log_seq.nextval, i_message_tx, current_timestamp);
    commit;
end p_log;
/
```

The procedure `p_log` is declared as an autonomous transaction and saves any message that you want to pass to the database without interrupting any other transactions.

Using this procedure, you can store an exception message, as shown in Listing 15-11.

Listing 15-11:   Storing an Exception Message

```
function f_giveRaise_tx (i_empNo NUMBER, i_pcnt NUMBER)
                    return VARCHAR2 is
    pragma autonomous_transaction;
begin
    update emp
      set sal=sal*(i_pcnt/100)+sal
      where empNo = i_empNo;
    commit;
    return 'OK';
exception
    when others then
        rollback;
        p_log('f_giveRaise_tx-ERROR:'||sqlerrm);
        return '<Contact help desk>';
end f_giveRaise_tx;
```

Now the end user sees a much friendlier error message, and you have real information about the problem in the database.

If you don't want to intercept the error, you can always re-raise an exception in the exception block, as shown here:

```
exception
    when others then
        rollback;
        p_log('f_giveRaise-ERROR:'||sqlerrm);
        raise;
end f_giveRaise_tx;
```

Using this approach, the routine raises the same error that it would raise without exception handling, but now you have a log record indicating the existence of an error. This log can be very useful in debugging.

Know When to Pass Parameters or Use Global Variables

In a stateless, Web-based environment, cursors, functions, and procedures sometimes are unable to reference values outside of themselves. Instead, they should pass parameters.

Although global variables might appear very convenient, there is a good reason for passing parameters into the routines instead of keeping global values. In an environment with stateless Web applications, you can't be sure of getting the same session each time you request the data.

The following code shows an example of code formatted for a client/server environment, where packaged variables can be used as session-level global variables. (You can read more about using packages and packaged variables in Chapter 7.)

```
create or replace package pkg_emp  is
    v_current_empNo NUMBER;
    procedure p_setEmpno (i_empNo NUMBER);
    function f_getEmpno return NUMBER;
    -----------------------------------------
    procedure p_giveRaise (i_pcnt NUMBER);
END;
/
create or replace package body pkg_emp IS
    gv_current_empNo NUMBER;

    procedure p_setEmpno (i_empNo NUMBER) is
    begin
        gv_current_empNo:=i_empNo;
```

```
      end p_setEmpno;

      function  f_getEmpNo return NUMBER is
      begin
          return gv_current_empNo;
      end f_getEmpNo;

      procedure p_giveRaise (i_pcnt NUMBER) is
      begin
          update emp
          set sal=sal*(i_pcnt/100)+sal
          where empNo = f_getEmpNo;
      end p_giveRaise;
end;
/
```

This code works perfectly in client/server mode with special APIs to set/
get the value of the employee you're working with. These APIs can be referenced whenever you need them (in this case, to give a raise to the selected
employee).

But in a Web-based environment, you can't always guarantee that your
second request will go to the same session. This means that, instead of
keeping global variables in the session, the global variables become properties of the client. (Some Web developers store them as cookies in browsers.)
Therefore, you need to pass all parameters explicitly, as shown here:

```
procedure p_giveRaise (i_pcnt NUMBER, i_empNo NUMBER) is
begin
    update emp
    set sal=sal*(i_pcnt/100)+sal
    where empNo = i_empNo;
end p_giveRaise;
```

Before writing any APIs to support front-end developers, you need to understand the environment in which they're working. If you can't guarantee that
subsequent calls will be in the same session, you need to make sure that all
necessary variable values are passed on each call to the program unit.

Use Implicit Cursors When Appropriate

Implicit cursors are marginally faster than explicit cursors for single record
fetches. But, the main reason to use them is that they make code easier to
read. Instead of having a cursor in the declaration section of your code that is
referenced in the body of the code (as with an explicit cursor), the cursor is
defined right where it is executed.

Because there is now no good reason to use explicit cursors whenever you need to get a single record, use implicit cursors instead. The difference between the two is shown in Listing 15-12.

Listing 15-12:   The Difference between Explicit and Implicit Cursors

```
-- Explicit cursor
function f_empExp_dsp (i_empNo NUMBER)
return VARCHAR2 is
    v_out_tx VARCHAR2(2000);
    cursor c_emp (ci_empNo NUMBER) is
       select empNo||' '||eName||' ('||job||')' emp_dsp
        from emp
        where empNo=ci_empNo;

    v_emp_rec   c_emp%ROWTYPE;
begin
    open c_emp(i_empNo);
    fetch c_emp into v_emp_rec;
    close c_emp;
    return v_emp_rec.emp_dsp;
exception
    when others then
        if c_emp%ISOPEN then
            close c_emp;
        end if;
        return null;
end f_empExp_dsp;

-- Implicit cursor
function f_empImp_dsp(i_empNo NUMBER)
return VARCHAR2 is
    v_out_tx VARCHAR2(2000);
begin
    select empNo||' '||eName||' ('||job||')' into v_out_tx
     from emp
     where empNo=in_empNo;
    return v_out_tx;
exception
    when no_data_found then
        return null;
    when too_many_rows then
        return '<Error>';
end f_empImp_dsp;
```

The implicit code is cleaner, but keep the following issues in mind:

✔ You can't simply replace explicit cursors with implicit ones. Explicit cursors don't raise the exceptions NO_DATA_FOUND (only the first fetch is null) and TOO_MANY_ROWS. (If developers didn't bother to fetch a second row in the cursor, this doesn't mean that there is no second row.

> ✔ To store a fetched value, you can reference an explicit cursor with
> %ROWTYPE, but with an implicit one you have to think about the appro-
> priate variables into which to fetch the data.

Remember That Dates Are Numbers

Internally in Oracle, dates are really numbers, so you can perform numeric
operations against dates.

Oracle 9*i* and 10*g* have new datatypes to store dates: TIMESTAMP and INTER-
VAL (for more details, see Chapter 10). But good old dates are still very useful
when you don't need to know the time zone or granularity below the time
unit of a second. Internally, dates are stored as numbers, so you can do whatever you want with them. A common set of date tasks can be resolved if you
think about dates as numbers.

For example, to find the difference between two dates down to the second,
use Listing 15-13.

Listing 15-13:   Finding the Difference between Dates

```
function f_secBetween_nr (i_date1_dt DATE,i_date2_dt DATE)
return NUMBER is
    v_ret_nr NUMBER;
begin
    v_ret_nr:=i_date1_dt-i_date2_dt;                        →5
    return v_ret_nr*(24*60*60);                             →6
end f_secBetween_nr;
```

Here's what Listing 15-13 does:

> →**5**   The default level of date rounding is a day, so this line finds the
> difference in days.
>
> →**6**   This line converts days into seconds. (24 hours in a day, 60 min-
> utes in an hour, 60 seconds in a minute)

Now you have the difference in seconds, but you want to have something
more understandable to end users, so use the code shown here:

```
function f_getTime_tx (i_diff_nr NUMBER)return VARCHAR2 is
    v_out_tx VARCHAR2(2000);

    v_hr_nr NUMBER;
    v_min_nr NUMBER;
    v_sec_nr NUMBER;
```

```
begin
    v_hr_nr:=trunc(i_diff_nr/(60*60));
    v_min_nr:= trunc((i_diff_nr-v_hr_nr*60*60)/60);
    v_sec_nr:=mod(i_diff_nr,60);

    v_out_tx:=v_hr_nr||' hours '||
                v_min_nr||' min '||v_sec_nr||' sec';
    return v_out_tx;
end f_getTime_tx;
```

It isn't difficult to get hours, minutes, and seconds from the difference.

Another common task is returning a point just before a specific midnight, as shown here:

```
function f_getMidnight_dt (i_date_dt DATE) return date is
begin
    return trunc(i_date_dt)+1-1/(24*60*60);
end;
```

In this case, you first truncate a passed date, add one full day, and subtract one second.

Chapter 16

Ten Common Mistakes to Avoid in PL/SQL

. . . .

In This Chapter

▶ Recognizing bad exception handling

▶ Controlling conditions, cursors, and loops

▶ Reusing code effectively

▶ Writing code that's easy to read and maintain

. . . .

*N*o matter how hard programmers try to make their code error free, they're still human, and every system includes code that contains mistakes. In addition to simple mistakes in coding, some global mistakes are common among inexperienced programmers. To help you recognize these problems and get up to speed with PL/SQL more easily, this chapter describes ten of the most important mistakes to avoid when writing PL/SQL.

Catching an Exception with WHEN OTHERS THEN NULL

Never catch an unidentified exception without logging information about it. Chapter 15 mentions that the exception handler WHEN OTHERS is extremely useful, but it can also be the source of the most dangerous line of code that can exist in PL/SQL, as shown here:

```
begin
    ...
exception
    when others then
        null;
end;
```

Unless you're in the debugging or development mode, never use an exception handler like this, especially in production instances of a system.

All exception handlers that have WHEN OTHERS without additional activity (you might need to have that exception) should look like this:

```
function f_assignManager_tx (i_empNo NUMBER, i_mgr NUMBER)
return VARCHAR2
is
    v_job_tx VARCHAR2(10);
begin
 -- Update employee
    update emp
    set mgr=i_mgr
    where empNo=i_empNo
    returning job into v_job_tx;
-- If person is managing analysis - there will be no
-- commissions. Give 5% raise per person to the manager
    if v_job_tx = 'ANALYST' then
        update emp
        set sal=sal*1.05
        where empNo=i_mgr;
    end if;
    return 'OK';
exception
    when others then
        p_log('f_assignManager_tx('||i_empNo||','||i_mgr||
                        ') ERROR:'||sqlerrm);
        return 'ERROR';
end;
```

Here, you aren't raising an exception if something goes wrong, but instead, returning ERROR rather than OK and logging a real error (see the P_LOG procedure in Chapter 15). You can use this logic if, because of front-end restrictions, you can't throw Oracle exceptions (for example, in a Web-based environment). This technique is a cleaner way of notifying the front end that something has gone wrong without destroying performance, and it also provides useful debugging information.

This exception handler includes a call to the logging routine, to which you are passing the current function name, its parameters, and the SQL error message. This is the minimum information that should be logged, but you could add the current user, the client's IP address, global parameter settings, and other data.

Don't hesitate to add a lot of information to debugging messages. When you're trying to identify and solve a problem, you never know what data you might need. These debugging statements shouldn't be executed at all, but even if they are executed, the performance impact is negligible.

Forgetting to Handle NULL Values

Operating on variables or columns that might contain NULL values without explicitly handling these NULL values can cause problems and produce strange results. That's because NULL is handled differently from other values. As mentioned in Chapter 3, you should keep the following rules in mind:

1. All logical operations (including NOT) that involve NULL values always return FALSE.

2. All operations (built-in functions, arithmetic) with NULL return NULL, with the following exceptions:

   - Concatenations of strings ignore NULL.

   - DECODE can compare values with NULL.

   - REPLACE can take NULL as a third parameter.

As an example, if you need to create a trigger to enforce a number of rules related to the salaries and commissions of employees, you might write:

```
create or replace trigger emp_biu
  before insert or update on emp
referencing new as new old as old
  for each row
begin
    if :new.sal+:new.comm >= 10000 then
        raise_application_error (-20999,'Salary with
            commissions should be less than 10000');
    end if;
end;
```

Now when you try to run a basic update, you get the following result:

```
SQL> update emp
  2   set sal=15000
  3   where eName='KING';
1 row updated.
SQL>
```

The trigger didn't work, and it might take you hours to debug. The real problem is that this trigger is correct only when neither SAL nor COMM have NULL values. Because the commission value is NULL for KING and SAL+COMM is NULL (Rule #2 from earlier), you're trying to compare NULL with 10000. But any comparison of NULL always returns NULL (Rule #1). Therefore, the IF statements don't catch the problem.

The trigger should look like this:

```
create or replace trigger emp_biu
 before insert or update on emp
referencing new as new old as old
 for each row
begin
    if nvl(:new.sal,0)+nvl(:new.comm,0) >= 10000 then
        raise_application_error (-20999,'Salary with
            commissions should be less than 10000');
    end if;
end;
```

Using this code, all cases are covered. By applying NVL to the columns, you can be certain that an operation won't result in a NULL value.

In grouping functions (SUM, AVG, COUNT), you also need to watch out for NULL values. The rule is that these functions process only not-NULL values; but if all values are NULL, the result is also NULL, as shown here:

```
SQL> select deptNo, sum(comm), sum(sal),
            sum(comm)+sum(sal)
  2  from emp
  3  group by deptNo;

    DEPTNO   SUM(COMM)    SUM(SAL) SUM(COMM)+SUM(SAL)
---------- ---------- ---------- --------------------
        10              12750
        20              10875
        30       2200    9400             11600
SQL>
```

Even employees from department 30 have some NULL values in the COMM column, SUM(COMM), because department 30 is not NULL (Oracle adds up all not-NULL values). But in departments 10 and 20, there are no employees with not-NULL commissions. That's why SUM(COMM) is NULL for these departments, and consequently, SUM(COMM)+SUM(SAL) is also NULL.

Creating Unintended Boolean Expressions

Be careful when building complex logical conditions. You need to group logical conditions appropriately so that others can maintain your code in the future. Using the trigger from the previous example, add more complex rules:

Salary + commissions may not be greater than $10,000 if you work in department 20, or if you are a clerk.

With complex conditions like this, you need to define each element:

1. Is the total of salary + commissions > $10,000?

2. Does the employee work in department 20?

3. Is the employee's job title CLERK?

Now you need to group the rules. In this case, you have two groups for the error condition: check salary (Rule #1 should be true) and check extra conditions (either Rule #2 or Rule #3 should be true).

The last step is to convert a group into logical operations. Inside the second group, you have an OR condition. Between groups, you have AND conditions, as shown in Listing 16-1.

Listing 16-1: Grouping Conditions

```
create or replace trigger emp_biu
 before insert or update on emp
 referencing old as old new as new
 for each row
begin
    if nvl(:new.sal,0)+nvl(:new.comm,0) >= 10000
    and (:new.deptNo=20                              →7
        or :new.job='CLERK')                         →8
    then
        raise_application_error (-20999,'Salary with
            commissions should be less than 10000');
    end if;
end;
```

→7–8 Note the parentheses around the two conditions connected with OR. Because the first group contains only one condition, no extra parentheses are necessary. This is the only correct way of coding. Each group of conditions should be enclosed in parentheses.

But if you forgot the parentheses and wrote the code like this:

```
...
if nvl(:new.sal,0)+nvl(:new.comm,0) >= 10000
and :new.deptNo=20
        or :new.job='CLERK'
...
```

you will have an error each time you try to update the salary or commissions of any employee with the job CLERK because the logical operator AND has a higher precedence than OR (like multiplying rather than adding). As a result, the last condition can be translated as: "The update will fail if salary + commissions for a person working in department 20 are more than $10,000. The update will also fail if the job title is 'CLERK'." This is definitely not what you wanted.

You should use the same syntax rule of enclosing condition groups in parentheses, not only in PL/SQL but in SQL, too. Remembering this could save you hours of debugging afterward. The following is an example of good syntax for a situation when you need to retrieve all records from the EMP table with a number of different rules:

```
select *
from emp
where (
        (deptNo=30
         and sal>1500)
      or
        (deptNo=20
         and sal>1000)
      )
and job!='ANALYST'
```

Note how we applied parentheses to group each condition so that Oracle knows exactly how those conditions should be interpreted.

Forgetting to Close an Explicit Cursor

Each time you use an explicit cursor, don't forget to close it.

Using explicit cursors (which we introduce in Chapter 6) is good coding practice. Remember that the database parameter OPEN_CURSORS defines the maximum number of cursors that can be open at the same time. The value of the variable might change from one environment to another, but the point is that the number of cursors is limited. Forgotten cursors that are left open can bring a system to a halt. Listing 16-2 shows a correctly written routine.

Listing 16-2:   Correctly Written Explicit Cursors

```
create or replace function f_getList_tx
    (i_source_tx VARCHAR2,
     i_column_tx VARCHAR2,
     i_filter_tx VARCHAR2,
     i_separator_tx VARCHAR2)
return VARCHAR2
is
    v_string_tx VARCHAR2(4000);
    v_temp_tx    VARCHAR2(4000);
    v_out_tx     VARCHAR2(4000);
    v_weak_ref sys_refcursor;
begin
    v_string_tx:='select '||i_column_tx||
                 ' from '||i_source_tx||
                 ' where '||i_filter_tx;
```

```
    open v_weak_ref for v_string_tx;
    loop
        fetch v_weak_ref into v_temp_tx;
        exit when v_weak_ref%NOTFOUND;

        if v_out_tx is null then
            v_out_tx:=v_temp_tx;
        else
            v_out_tx:=v_out_tx||i_separator_tx||v_temp_tx;
        end if;
    end loop;

    close v_weak_ref;
    return v_out_tx;
exception
    when others then
        if  v_weak_ref%isOpen then
            close v_weak_ref;
            raise;
        end if;
end;
```

The problem was to generate a list of any columns from any table with a specified condition and separator. As we discuss in Chapter 13, if you have an undefined data source, you can always use dynamic SQL. But with dynamic SQL, you have to use explicit cursors. If you stick to the following rules, you should be able to use explicit cursors successfully:

✔ When you start typing a routine, immediately include both the OPEN and CLOSE cursor statements.

✔ Never add a RETURN clause before closing the cursor.

✔ In the exception-handling block, always check to see whether explicit cursors are open, and if so, close them.

If you're using recursive calls to the same routine, be very careful about using explicit cursors. In a structure with 20 levels of hierarchy, at some point, you're likely to have 20 cursors open simultaneously. If you have a large number of users, this could cause your system to reach or exceed the maximum number of cursors.

Oracle is fairly smart about closing cursors if you forget to do so. When a program unit terminates, all cursors that it opened are automatically closed. But relying on this capability is dangerous and can ultimately result in having too many cursors open at once, so remember to close your cursors explicitly.

Starting Endless Loops

Endless loops can cause endless problems. Common among those problems is freezing your system. So each time you create a loop, you must think about how the code will exit from the loop.

Listing 16-3 illustrates how easy it is to create loop-related problems, if you're not careful. This code creates a function that checks whether, in a given department, the number of employees with an income less than the defined amount is in fact limited to the number specified.

Listing 16-3:   Endless Loop Example

```
function f_limit_yn(i_deptNo NUMBER,
        i_limit_nr NUMBER, i_income_nr NUMBER)
return VARCHAR2
is
    cursor c_emp is
    select nvl(sal,0)+nvl(comm,0) income_nr
    from emp
    where deptNo=i_deptNo;

    v_income_nr   NUMBER;
    v_counter_nr NUMBER:=0;
    v_error_yn    VARCHAR2(1):='N';
begin
    open c_emp;
    loop
        fetch c_emp into v_income_nr;
        if v_income_nr < i_income_nr then
            v_counter_nr:=v_counter_nr+1;
        end if;
        if v_counter_nr=i_limit_nr  then
            v_error_yn:='Y';
            exit;
        end if;
    end loop;
    close c_emp;
    return v_error_yn;
end;
```

You could write this function, test it a few times, and deploy it to production. But if you select department 40 in the user interface, you'll be stuck in a dead loop. This is because you can exit from the loop only if the major condition is satisfied. But what about the case when it isn't satisfied, as is the case with department 40, which has no employees? Listing 16-4 shows the correct way.

Listing 16-4:   Correct Code to Exit a Loop

```
function f_limit_yn(i_deptNo NUMBER,
            i_limit_nr NUMBER, i_income_nr NUMBER)
return VARCHAR2
is
    cursor c_emp is
    select nvl(sal,0)+nvl(comm,0) income_nr
    from emp
    where deptNo=i_deptNo;

    v_income_nr  NUMBER;
    v_counter_nr NUMBER:=0;
    v_error_yn   VARCHAR2(1):='N';
begin
    open c_emp;
    loop
        fetch c_emp into v_income_nr;
        exit when c_emp%NOTFOUND;                           →17
        if v_income_nr < i_income_nr then
            v_counter_nr:=v_counter_nr+1;
        end if;
        if v_counter_nr=i_limit_nr  then
            v_error_yn:='Y';
            exit;                                           →23
        end if;
    end loop;
    close c_emp;
    return v_error_yn;
end;
```

  →17   Provides the exit from the loop if the department has no
            employees.

Usually, developers focus on the major condition and forget that other
scenarios could cause problems.

The best way to avoid endless loops is to use CURSOR FOR loops or FOR
loops whenever possible. If you don't need to interrupt processing, always
use a FOR loop. It's much safer.

In some cases, you can replace regular loops with SQL. Listing 16-4 could be
rewritten, as shown in Listing 16-5.

Listing 16-5:   A SQL Replacement for Regular Loops

```
function f_checkDeptLimit_yn (i_deptNo NUMBER,
        i_limit_nr NUMBER, i_income_nr NUMBER)
return VARCHAR2
```

(continued)

Listing 16-5 *(continued)*

```
is
    v_counter_nr NUMBER:=0;                           →5
    v_error_yn    VARCHAR2(1):='N';
begin
    select count(*)
    into v_counter_nr
    from emp
    where deptNo = i_deptNo
    and nvl(sal,0)+nvl(comm,0)<i_income_nr
    and rownum < i_limit_nr+1 ;

    if v_counter_nr=i_limit_nr then                   →15
        v_error_yn:='Y';
    end if;
    return v_error_yn;
end;
```

▌ →**5, 15**   Limits number of counted rows with the passed limit.

As a result, the value of v_counter_nr could be less than or equal to the limit. This solution, although elegant, is significantly less clear. Even though you're getting rid of loops, you're increasing the complexity of the code. You need to use your judgment about whether the added complexity is warranted.

Reinventing the Wheel

Don't try to create code structures that have already been developed for you by Oracle.

Before you start coding, it is a good idea to review an Oracle manual with the list of built-in functions. This tip is especially true when working with strings.

For example, if you need to create a routine to check Social Security numbers, the specifications would be:

▌ ✔ A correct string is 11-characters long.

▌ ✔ A string should contain 9 numbers and 2 dashes.

Your first reaction might be to just start coding. You could write something like Listing 16-6 in 20 minutes.

Listing 16-6:   A Routine to Check Social Security Numbers

```
function f_validSSN_yn (i_ssn_tx VARCHAR2)
   return VARCHAR2
is
   v_ctr_nr    NUMBER := 0;
   v_ssnNr_tx VARCHAR2(256);
   v_out_yn    VARCHAR2(1);
   v_error_yn VARCHAR2(1);
begin
   if i_ssn_tx is null then
       v_out_yn:='Y';
   else
       v_ssnNr_tx:=replace(i_ssn_tx,'-','');
       if length(v_ssnNr_tx)!=9 then
           v_error_yn:='Y';
       else
          v_ctr_nr:=1;
          loop
              if instr ('0123456789',
                   substr (v_ssnNr_tx, v_ctr_nr, 1))= 0
              then
                  v error yn:='Y';
              end if;
              exit when v_ctr_nr=9 or v_error_yn='Y';
              v_ctr_nr:=v_ctr_nr+1;
          end loop;
       end if;
   end if;

   if v_error_yn='Y' then
       v_out_yn:='N';
   else
       v_out_yn:='Y';
   end if;

   return v_out_yn;
end;
```

Listing 16-6 works exactly as you specified. But is it the best way to code? Definitely not. You could code exactly the same functionality in a different way, as shown in Listing 16-7.

Listing 16-7:   A Better Routine to Check Social Security Numbers

```
function f_validSSN_yn (i_ssn_tx VARCHAR2) return VARCHAR2
is
   v_out_tx            VARCHAR2(1);
```

(continued)

Listing 16-7 *(continued)*

```
        v_temp_string_tx VARCHAR2(256);

begin
    if i_ssn_tx is null then
        v_out_tx:='Y';
    elsif length(i_ssn_tx)!=11 then
        v_out_tx:='N';
    else
        v_temp_string_tx:=
            translate(i_ssn_tx,'?-0123456789','?');          →13
        if v_temp_string_tx is not null
        then
            v_out_tx:='N';
        else
            if length(replace(i_ssn_tx,'-'))=9 then
                v_out_tx:='Y';
            else
                v_out_tx:='N';
            end if;
        end if;
    end if;

    return v_out_tx;
end;
```

→13 Instead of manually looping through the string character by character, this code uses the TRANSLATE function to extract from the passed string all characters that are not in the valid list.

Note that you need to add a character before the list because you cannot pass NULL in TRANSLATE as a third parameter. Now the code is significantly simpler and more understandable. Also, because you don't have a loop, as in Listing 16-6, you avoid the danger of creating an infinite loop.

There is one more reason to use built-in functions. Oracle has tuned them to improve performance speed. Using the Social Security number example, the length of the possible input parameter is fairly small, so there isn't much difference in performance. But if you need to parse very large strings or even CLOBs, built-in functions can significantly improve performance.

Converting Datatypes Implicitly

Although Oracle sometimes *can* implicitly convert one datatype to another, that doesn't mean you should trust implicit conversions of datatypes — especially dates. In fact, this isn't a good idea at all.

As an example, if you need to build a function that converts a past year, month, and day into a DATE value, you could write code as in Listing 16-8.

Listing 16-8: Cross Datatype (Unstable Example)

```
function f_getDate_dt
   (i_day_nr NUMBER, i_month_tx VARCHAR2, i_year_nr NUMBER)
return date is
    v_out_dt DATE;
begin
    v_out_dt:= i_day_nr||'-'||i_month_tx||'-'||i_year_nr;
    return v_out_dt;
exception
    when others then
       return null;
end;
```

You can use this code only because you know that the default date format is DD-MON-YYYY, so you have one less TO_DATE call. But the potential side effect is worse, because changing the default date format or moving the code to a different database will destroy the function. Because your code shouldn't be that fragile, you should use something like Listing 16-9.

Listing 16-9: Cross Datatype (Stable Example)

```
function f_getDate_dt
(i_day_nr NUMBER, i_month_tx VARCHAR2, i_year_nr NUMBER)
return date is
    v_out_dt DATE;
begin
    v_out_dt:=
       to_date(i_day_nr||'-'||i_month_tx||'-'||i_year_nr,
              'DD-MON-YYYY');                                →8
    return v_out_dt;
exception
    when others then
       return null;
end;
```

→8   This line means that the code is not dependent on any database parameters to run correctly.

Another common problem with implicit conversion occurs when working with numeric values that aren't exactly numeric. As an example, Listing 16-10 formats an address.

Listing 16-10:   Incorrect Code to Format an Address

```
function f_formatAddress_tx
(i_street_tx VARCHAR2, i_city_tx VARCHAR2,
 i_state_tx VARCHAR2,  i_zip_nr NUMBER)                    →3
return VARCHAR2 is
    v_out_tx VARCHAR2(2000);
begin
    v_out_tx:=i_street_tx||chr(10)||i_city_tx||
        ', '||i_state_tx||' '||i_zip_nr;
    return v_out_tx;
end;

SQL> select f_formatAddress_tx('701 Amboy Ave.',
  2  'Woodbridge', 'NJ', '07095') Address  from dual;
Address
-----------------------------------------------------------
701 Amboy Ave.
Woodbridge, NJ 7095
SQL>
```

→3   If you run this code, the ZIP code loses the first digit, because you declared the input variable I_ZIP_NR as NUMBER. Even though you passed the ZIP code in quotes, it was dynamically converted into a number, which automatically dropped the leading zero.

These errors are detected only at runtime and only under certain circumstances (ZIP codes that start with zero), which is what makes them so dangerous. Although Oracle allows you to be a bit sloppy, finding these types of problems later on could take you hours. The correct code is shown in Listing 16-11.

Listing 16-11:   Correct Code to Format an Address

```
function f_formatAddress_tx
(i_street_tx VARCHAR2, i_city_tx VARCHAR2,
 i_state_tx VARCHAR2,  i_zip_tx VARCHAR2)                  →3
return VARCHAR2 is
    v_out_tx VARCHAR2(2000);
begin
    v_out_tx:=i_street_tx||chr(10)||i_city_tx||
        ', '||i_state_tx||' '||i_zip_tx;
    return v_out_tx;
end;
```

→3   The ZIP code is passed as text. Under these conditions, you can be sure that there won't be any more surprises.

Not everything that looks like a numeric value is a numeric value. Oracle cannot differentiate these cases. You must define the appropriate datatypes.

Cutting and Pasting Code

Sooner or later, all developers are tempted to copy and paste an existing piece of code, modify it a bit, and be done with it. But a quick shortcut during development can cost more time and effort than you might think down the road. For example, you might have a function that prints a list of employees for a specified department, as shown here:

```
procedure p_printEmp (i_deptNo NUMBER) is
    cursor c_emp (ci_deptNo NUMBER) is
    select empNo, eName, sal
    from emp
    where deptNo=ci_deptNo
    order by empNo;
begin
    for r_emp in c_emp (i_deptNo) loop
       DBMS_OUTPUT.put_line(r_emp.empNo||
          ' '||r_emp.eName||' - '||r_emp.sal);
    end loop;
end;
```

Now you need to write a routine that will produce the same printout for any two departments. Your first inclination might be to write something like this:

```
procedure p_printEmp (i_deptNo1 NUMBER, i_deptNo2 NUMBER)
is
    cursor c_emp (ci_deptNo NUMBER) is
    select empNo, eName, sal
    from emp
    where deptNo=ci_deptNo
    order by empNo;
begin
    for r_emp in c_emp (i_deptNo1) loop
       DBMS_OUTPUT.put_line(r_emp.empNo||
          ' '||r_emp.eName||' - '||r_emp.sal);
    end loop;

    for r_emp in c_emp (i_deptNo2) loop
       DBMS_OUTPUT.put_line(r_emp.empNo||
          ' '||r_emp.eName||' - '||r_emp.sal);
    end loop;
end;
```

Using this structure, how many places will you have to check if you need to modify the way in which the data is displayed? There will definitely be more than one. Can you guarantee that you'll find all these places? The code shown in Listing 16-12 has no repeated sections and is much better in this situation.

Listing 16-12:   Code with No Repeated Sections

```
procedure p_printEmp (i_deptNo1 NUMBER, i_deptNo2 NUMBER)
is
    cursor c_emp (ci_deptNo NUMBER) is
    select empNo, sal
    from emp
    where deptNo=ci_deptNo
    order by empNo;

    procedure p_intPrint (pi_deptNo NUMBER) is
    begin
        for r_emp in c_emp (pi_deptNo) loop
        DBMS_OUTPUT.put_line(f_emp_dsp(r_emp.empNo)||  →12
            ' - '|| r_emp.sal);
        end loop;
    end;
begin
    p_intPrint (i_deptNo1);
    p_intPrint (i_deptNo2);
end;
```

→**12**   Uses f_emp_dsp to display the employee. Each display value is a
        query to the EMP table, but because it is directly accessed by the
        primary key, the performance impact should be minor.

Copying and pasting code does have some advantages:

✔ You aren't touching the existing code, just adding code.

✔ The code has already been checked and therefore doesn't contain
  syntax errors.

✔ You don't need to retest the code that is dependent on the original code.

The drawbacks of cutting and pasting are:

✔ The same modification has to be replicated everywhere.

✔ The code becomes less readable and more spaghetti-like.

Ironically, the advantages are relevant only for developers, and the disadvantages are relevant for those who maintain the system. Although time spent by
developers to create the code can be very expensive, the cost of ongoing
errors when maintaining the code is hundreds of times higher.

Although there is technically nothing wrong with cutting and pasting code, a
few development hours saved can mean hours of downtime for an entire
organization, so cut and paste at your own risk.

Ignoring Code Readability

You don't want the next person who looks at your code to have to guess about your naming conventions or program structure. Ongoing maintenance can consume large portions of the total cost of building an information system. That's why your goal as a developer should be to think about the long-term maintenance of the system when you're writing code.

Listing 16-13 is an example of badly written code.

Listing 16-13:   Badly Written Code

```
function f1 (i VARCHAR2) return VARCHAR2 is
a VARCHAR2(1); b VARCHAR2(256);
begin
if i is null  then a:='Y';
elsif length(i)!=11 then a:='N';
else b:=translate(i,'?-0123456789','?');
if b is not null then a:='N';
else
if length(replace(i,'-'))=9 then a:='Y';
else a:='N';
end if;end if;end if;
return a;
end;
```

Although you can piece together the meaning in Listing 16-13, the code is very badly structured and difficult to read. It requires some effort to figure out where the procedure begins, not to mention trying to understand what the three END IF statements are doing at the end. Listing 16-14 accomplishes the same result. (See Chapter 9 for coding standard suggestions.)

Listing 16-14:   Somewhat Improved Code

```
function f1 (i VARCHAR2) return VARCHAR2
is
    a VARCHAR2(1);
    b VARCHAR2(256);
begin
    if i is null
    then
        a:='Y';
    elsif length(i)!=11
    then
        a:='N';
    else
        b:=
```

(continued)

Listing 16-14 *(continued)*

```
            translate(i,'?-0123456789','?');
        if b is not null
        then
            a:='N';
        else
            if length(replace(i,'-'))=9
            then
                a:='Y';
            else
                a:='N';
            end if;
        end if;
    end if;

    return a;
end;
```

Listing 16-14 is a big improvement. Using appropriate indentation and line separation makes it much easier to understand the logical structure of the code. But the question of what each function does remains. Names like a, b, i, and f1 don't tell you anything at all.

It makes sense to call a function that is used for displaying records from the EMP table so that you don't have to look inside the function to figure out what it's doing. In this case, the name F_EMP_DSP is perfect. If a variable is used to store a numeric counter, why not name it V_COUNTER_NR? To find out more about naming objects and variables, see Chapter 8.

Listing 16-15 applies these naming standards to the code from Listing 16-14.

Listing 16-15:   Well-Written Code

```
function f_validSSN_yn (i_ssn_tx VARCHAR2) return VARCHAR2
is
    v_out_tx VARCHAR2(1);
    v_temp_string_tx VARCHAR2(256);
begin
    if i_ssn_tx is null
    then
        v_out_tx:='Y';
    elsif length(i_ssn_tx)!=11
    then
        v_out_tx:='N';
    else
        v_temp_string_tx:=
            translate(i_ssn_tx,'?-0123456789','?');
        if v_temp_string_tx is not null
        then
            v_out_tx:='N';
```

```
        else
            if length(replace(i_ssn_tx,'-'))=9
            then
                v_out_tx:='Y';
            else
                v_out_tx:='N';
            end if;
        end if;
    end if;
    return v_out_tx;
end;
```

This code accomplishes the same thing as Listing 16-7. Although both examples work exactly the same way and both have correct syntax, this one is much easier to read and maintain.

Assuming Code Doesn't Need Comments

There is no such thing as self-documenting code. The mistake of thinking that working code is perfectly self-documenting has caused thousands of lost hours in organizations all over the world. Even with the best naming and coding conventions, you must still explicitly note many details. And you do that by adding comments.

In the many systems that require complex code, the trick to adding useful comments is to make sure that you (or someone else) will be able to understand the code a few months (or even years) later. Writing code that enables a system to be efficiently maintained is a critical part of building successful information systems. Using the example of finding the number of employees in a department with incomes less than a certain amount, Listing 16-16 demonstrates best practices for commenting.

Listing 16-16:   Correctly Commented Code

```
function f_checkDeptLimit_yn
  (i_deptNo NUMBER, i_limit_nr NUMBER, i_income_nr NUMBER)
return VARCHAR2
is
-- Owner: MRosenblum
-- Purpose: check whether in department I_DEPTNO
--          there are more than I_LIMIT_NR employees
--          with an income less than I_INCOME_NR
-- Comments:
-- *COMM or SAL could be NULL - NVL is used
-- *ROWNUM is applied after WHERE clause - counter is
```

(continued)

Listing 16-16 *(continued)*

```
--    always less than or equal to limit. If there is more
--    valid records than limit it will still return a limit
----WHO--------WHEN----------WHAT----------------
-- MRosenblum  11-30-05  created original version

    v_counter_nr NUMBER:=0;
    v_error_yn   VARCHAR2(1):='N';
begin
    -- Get number of employees that satisfy condition
    select count(*)
    into v_counter_nr
    from emp
    where deptNo = i_deptNo
    and nvl(sal,0)+nvl(comm,0)<i_income_nr
    and rownum < i_limit_nr+1 ;  -- limit fetch

    -- Check for error
    if v_counter_nr=i_limit_nr
    then
        v_error_yn:='Y';
    end if;
    return v_error_yn;
end;
```

Anyone can read this code, because you included a number of special elements:

- ✔ A header that includes the following:

  - Basic information (ownership and functionality)

  - Functional comments that explain the implemented solution and possible issues with the code

  - A change log to keep track of all changes to the routine

- ✔ Inline comments, which separate different parts of the code and explain specific code lines

Don't over comment your code — a comment on every line isn't necessary. Use your judgment and plan an external code review to determine how much commenting your routines require. See Chapter 9 for more specifics on adding comments.

Index

• E •

• *W* •

• *Y* •

NESS, CAREERS & PERSONAL FINANCE

0-7645-5307-0

0-7645-5331-3 *†

Also available:
- Accounting For Dummies †
  0-7645-5314-3
- Business Plans Kit For Dummies †
  0-7645-5365-8
- Cover Letters For Dummies
  0-7645-5224-4
- Frugal Living For Dummies
  0-7645-5403-4
- Leadership For Dummies
  0-7645-5176-0
- Managing For Dummies
  0-7645-1771-6

- Marketing For Dummies
  0-7645-5600-2
- Personal Finance For Dummies *
  0-7645-2590-5
- Project Management For Dummies
  0-7645-5283-X
- Resumes For Dummies †
  0-7645-5471-9
- Selling For Dummies
  0-7645-5363-1
- Small Business Kit For Dummies *†
  0-7645-5093-4

ME & BUSINESS COMPUTER BASICS

0-7645-4074-2

0-7645-3758-X

Also available:
- ACT! 6 For Dummies
  0 7645-2645-6
- iLife '04 All-in-One Desk Reference
  For Dummies
  0-7645-7347-0
- iPAQ For Dummies
  0-7645-6769-1
- Mac OS X Panther Timesaving
  Techniques For Dummies
  0-7645-5812-9
- Macs For Dummies
  0-7645-5656-8

- Microsoft Money 2004 For Dummies
  0-7645-4195-1
- Office 2003 All-in-One Desk Reference
  For Dummies
  0-7645-3883-7
- Outlook 2003 For Dummies
  0-7645-3759-8
- PCs For Dummies
  0-7645-4074-2
- TiVo For Dummies
  0-7645-6923-6
- Upgrading and Fixing PCs For Dummies
  0-7645-1665-5
- Windows XP Timesaving Techniques
  For Dummies
  0-7645-3748-2

OD, HOME, GARDEN, HOBBIES, MUSIC & PETS

0-7645-5295-3

0-7645-5232-5

Also available:
- Bass Guitar For Dummies
  0-7645-2487-9
- Diabetes Cookbook For Dummies
  0-7645-5230-9
- Gardening For Dummies *
  0-7645-5130-2
- Guitar For Dummies
  0-7645-5106-X
- Holiday Decorating For Dummies
  0-7645-2570-0
- Home Improvement All-in-One
  For Dummies
  0-7645-5680-0

- Knitting For Dummies
  0-7645-5395-X
- Piano For Dummies
  0-7645-5105-1
- Puppies For Dummies
  0-7645-5255-4
- Scrapbooking For Dummies
  0-7645-7208-3
- Senior Dogs For Dummies
  0-7645-5818-8
- Singing For Dummies
  0-7645-2475-5
- 30-Minute Meals For Dummies
  0-7645-2589-1

TERNET & DIGITAL MEDIA

0-7645-1664-7

0-7645-6924-4

Also available:
- 2005 Online Shopping Directory
  For Dummies
  0-7645-7495-7
- CD & DVD Recording For Dummies
  0-7645-5956-7
- eBay For Dummies
  0-7645-5654-1
- Fighting Spam For Dummies
  0-7645-5965-6
- Genealogy Online For Dummies
  0-7645-5964-8
- Google For Dummies
  0-7645-4420-9

- Home Recording For Musicians
  For Dummies
  0-7645-1634-5
- The Internet For Dummies
  0-7645-4173-0
- iPod & iTunes For Dummies
  0-7645-7772-7
- Preventing Identity Theft For Dummies
  0-7645-7336-5
- Pro Tools All-in-One Desk Reference
  For Dummies
  0-7645-5714-9
- Roxio Easy Media Creator For Dummies
  0-7645-7131-1

* parate Canadian edition also available
* parate U.K. edition also available

lable wherever books are sold. For more information or to order direct: U.S. customers visit www.dummies.com or call 1-877-762-2974.
customers visit www.wileyeurope.com or call 0800 243407. Canadian customers visit www.wiley.ca or call 1-800-567-4797.

RTS, FITNESS, PARENTING, RELIGION & SPIRITUALITY

0-7645-5146-9   0-7645-5418-2

Also available:
- Adoption For Dummies
  0-7645-5488-3
- Basketball For Dummies
  0-7645-5248-1
- The Bible For Dummies
  0-7645-5296-1
- Buddhism For Dummies
  0-7645-5359-3
- Catholicism For Dummies
  0-7645-5391-7
- Hockey For Dummies
  0-7645-5228-7

- Judaism For Dummies
  0-7645-5299-6
- Martial Arts For Dummies
  0-7645-5358-5
- Pilates For Dummies
  0-7645-5397-6
- Religion For Dummies
  0-7645-5264-3
- Teaching Kids to Read For Dumm
  0-7645-4043-2
- Weight Training For Dummies
  0-7645-5168-X
- Yoga For Dummies
  0-7645-5117-5

TRAVEL

0-7645-5438-7   0-7645-5453-0

Also available:
- Alaska For Dummies
  0-7645-1761-9
- Arizona For Dummies
  0-7645-6938-4
- Cancún and the Yucatán For Dummies
  0-7645-2437-2
- Cruise Vacations For Dummies
  0-7645-6941-4
- Europe For Dummies
  0-7645-5456-5
- Ireland For Dummies
  0-7645-5455-7

- Las Vegas For Dummies
  0-7645-5448-4
- London For Dummies
  0-7645-4277-X
- New York City For Dummies
  0-7645-6945-7
- Paris For Dummies
  0-7645-5494-8
- RV Vacations For Dummies
  0-7645-5443-3
- Walt Disney World & Orlando For Dumm
  0-7645-6943-0

GRAPHICS, DESIGN & WEB DEVELOPMENT

0-7645-4345-8   0-7645-5589-8

Also available:
- Adobe Acrobat 6 PDF For Dummies
  0-7645-3760-1
- Building a Web Site For Dummies
  0-7645-7144-3
- Dreamweaver MX 2004 For Dummies
  0-7645-4342-3
- FrontPage 2003 For Dummies
  0-7645-3882-9
- HTML 4 For Dummies
  0-7645-1995-6
- Illustrator CS For Dummies
  0-7645-4084-X

- Macromedia Flash MX 2004 For Dumm
  0-7645-4358-X
- Photoshop 7 All-in-One Desk
  Reference For Dummies
  0-7645-1667-1
- Photoshop CS Timesaving Techniqu
  For Dummies
  0-7645-6782-9
- PHP 5 For Dummies
  0-7645-4166-8
- PowerPoint 2003 For Dummies
  0-7645-3908-6
- QuarkXPress 6 For Dummies
  0-7645-2593-X

NETWORKING, SECURITY, PROGRAMMING & DATABASES

0-7645-6852-3   0-7645-5784-X

Also available:
- A+ Certification For Dummies
  0-7645-4187-0
- Access 2003 All-in-One Desk
  Reference For Dummies
  0-7645-3988-4
- Beginning Programming For Dummies
  0-7645-4997-9
- C For Dummies
  0-7645-7068-4
- Firewalls For Dummies
  0-7645-4048-3
- Home Networking For Dummies
  0-7645-42796

- Network Security For Dummies
  0-7645-1679-5
- Networking For Dummies
  0-7645-1677-9
- TCP/IP For Dummies
  0-7645-1760-0
- VBA For Dummies
  0-7645-3989-2
- Wireless All In-One Desk Reference
  For Dummies
  0-7645-7496-5
- Wireless Home Networking For Dumm
  0-7645-3910-8